First World War
and Army of Occupation
War Diary
France, Belgium and Germany

58 DIVISION
173 Infantry Brigade
Headquarters
3 October 1915 - 31 December 1917

WO95/2999

The Naval & Military Press Ltd
www.nmarchive.com
Published in association with The National Archives

Published by

The Naval & Military Press Ltd

Unit 10 Ridgewood Industrial Park,

Uckfield, East Sussex,

TN22 5QE England

Tel: +44 (0) 1825 749494

www.naval-military-press.com

www.nmarchive.com

This diary has been reprinted in facsimile from the original. Any imperfections are inevitably reproduced and the quality may fall short of modern type and cartographic standards.

© **Crown Copyright**
Images reproduced by permission of The National Archives, London, England, 2015.

Contents

Document type	Place/Title	Date From	Date To
Heading	58th Division 173rd Infy Bde Bde Headquarters Jan-Dec 1917		
Heading	58 Division H.Q. 173 Bde 1915 Sep-1916 Feb		
Miscellaneous	War Diary Statement		
War Diary	Ipswich	03/10/1915	29/02/1916
Heading			
War Diary	Southampton	23/01/1917	23/01/1917
War Diary	Le. Havre	24/01/1917	25/01/1917
War Diary	Frevent	27/01/1917	27/01/1917
War Diary	Bonnieres	29/01/1917	29/01/1917
War Diary	Ivergny	30/01/1917	31/01/1917
War Diary	Sutton Veny	23/01/1917	23/01/1917
War Diary	Southampton	23/01/1917	23/01/1917
War Diary	Havre	24/01/1917	25/01/1917
War Diary	Frevent	26/01/1917	26/01/1917
War Diary	Beauvais	29/01/1917	29/01/1917
War Diary	Ivergny	29/01/1917	29/01/1917
Heading	War Diary Of H.Q 173 Inf Bde		
War Diary	Ivergny	01/02/1917	20/02/1917
War Diary	Souastre	22/02/1917	25/02/1917
War Diary	Basseux	25/02/1917	27/02/1917
Operation(al) Order(s)	173rd Infantry Brigade Order No. 2	19/02/1917	19/02/1917
Operation(al) Order(s)	173rd Infantry Brigade Order No. 1	17/02/1917	17/02/1917
Miscellaneous	March Table Issued With 173rd Infantry Bde Order No. 1		
Operation(al) Order(s)	173rd Infantry Brigade Order No. 3	19/02/1917	19/02/1917
Operation(al) Order(s)	173rd Infantry Brigade Operations Order No. 4	22/02/1917	22/02/1917
Miscellaneous	March Table Issued With 173rd Infantry Brigade Order No. 4		
Miscellaneous	173rd Infantry Brigade Daily Summary Of Intelligence Period 24 hours ending 5 pm. 21/3/17	21/03/1917	21/03/1917
Miscellaneous	Amendment To March Table Accompanying 173rd Infantry Brigade Order No. 4	23/02/1917	23/02/1917
Miscellaneous	173rd Infantry Brigade Operations	22/03/1917	22/03/1917
Miscellaneous	173rd Infantry Brigade Daily Summary Of Intelligence period 48 hours ending 5 p.m. 24th March 1917	24/03/1917	24/03/1917
Map	Map		
Miscellaneous	173rd Infantry Brigade Operations	25/03/1917	25/03/1917
War Diary	Basseux	27/02/1917	06/03/1917
War Diary	Pommier	07/03/1917	19/03/1917
War Diary	Ransart	20/03/1917	20/03/1917
War Diary	Boiry Ste Rictrude	21/03/1917	25/03/1917
War Diary	Pommier	25/03/1917	26/03/1917
Miscellaneous	173rd Infantry Brigade Relief Table	02/03/1917	02/03/1917
Operation(al) Order(s)	173rd Infantry Brigade Order No. 5	01/03/1917	01/03/1917
Operation(al) Order(s)	173rd Infantry Brigade Order No. 6		
Miscellaneous	March Table Issued With 173rd Infantry Brigade Order No. 6		
Miscellaneous	March Table Issued With 173rd Infantry Brigade Order No. 8		

Type	Description	Date	Date
Operation(al) Order(s)	173rd Infantry Brigade Order No. 7	06/03/1917	06/03/1917
Miscellaneous	March Table Issued With 173rd Infantry Brigade Order No. 7		
Operation(al) Order(s)	173rd Infantry Brigade Order No. 8	10/03/1917	10/03/1917
Operation(al) Order(s)	173rd Infantry Brigade Order No. 9	16/03/1917	16/03/1917
Miscellaneous	March Table Issued With 173rd Infantry Brigade Order No. 9		
Miscellaneous	173rd Infantry Brigade Instructions No.1	13/03/1917	13/03/1917
Miscellaneous	Amendment To March Table Accompanying 173rd Infantry Brigade Order No. 8	11/03/1917	11/03/1917
Operation(al) Order(s)	173rd Infantry Brigade Order No. 10	19/03/1917	19/03/1917
Miscellaneous	173rd Infantry Brigade Order No. 9	17/03/1917	17/03/1917
Miscellaneous	Amendments And Additions To Table Accompanying 173rd Infantry Brigade Operation Order No. 11	23/03/1917	23/03/1917
Heading	War Diary Of H.Q 173rd Inf Bde. From 27/2/17 To 26/3/17		
Miscellaneous	Relief Table Accompanying 173rd Infantry Brigade Operation Order No. 11		
Operation(al) Order(s)	173rd Infantry Brigade Operation Order No. 11	23/03/1917	23/03/1917
Miscellaneous	173rd Infantry Brigade Daily Summary Of Intelligence 5 p.m. March 17th to 5 p.m. March 20th 1917	20/03/1917	20/03/1917
War Diary	Pommier	27/03/1917	28/03/1917
War Diary	Pommera	28/03/1917	01/04/1917
War Diary	Bonnieres	01/04/1917	02/04/1917
War Diary	Vaulx	02/04/1917	03/04/1917
War Diary	Souastre	03/04/1917	13/04/1917
War Diary	Bus Les Artois	13/04/1917	15/04/1917
War Diary	Achiet Le Grand Under Canvas Tent And Shelters	15/04/1917	17/04/1917
War Diary	Camp	18/04/1917	26/04/1917
Operation(al) Order(s)	173rd Infantry Brigade Operation Order No. 12	25/03/1917	25/03/1917
Miscellaneous	March Table 173rd Infantry Brigade Issued With Operation Order No. 12		
Miscellaneous	Amendments And Additions To Table Accompanying 173rd Infantry Brigade Operation Order No. 12	25/03/1917	25/03/1917
Operation(al) Order(s)	173rd Infantry Brigade Operation Order No. 13	31/03/1917	31/03/1917
Miscellaneous	March Table Accompanying 173rd Infantry Brigade Order No. 13	31/03/1917	31/03/1917
Operation(al) Order(s)	173rd Inf. Bde. Order No. 14	01/04/1917	01/04/1917
Miscellaneous	March Table Accompanying 173rd Inf. Bde. Order No. 14	01/04/1917	01/04/1917
Operation(al) Order(s)	173rd Inf. Bde Order No. 15	12/04/1917	12/04/1917
Miscellaneous	March Table Accompanying 173rd Inf. Bde Order No. 15	12/04/1917	12/04/1917
Operation(al) Order(s)	173rd Inf. Bde Order No. 16	14/04/1917	14/04/1917
Operation(al) Order(s)	173rd Inf. Bde Order No. 17	14/04/1917	14/04/1917
Miscellaneous	March Table Accompanying 173rd Inf. Bde Order No. 17	14/04/1917	14/04/1917
Heading	War Diary Of H.Q. 173rd Inf Bde From 27/4/17 To 27/5/17		
Heading	H.Q. 173 Infy Bde Vol 3 March 1917		
War Diary		16/03/1917	22/03/1917
War Diary	Achite Le Petit	27/03/1917	15/04/1917
Miscellaneous	Operation Report 14th To 15th 5/17 173rd Infantry Brigade	15/05/1917	15/05/1917
Miscellaneous	173rd Infantry Brigade Daily Intelligence Summary Period 24 hours 9. am. 15th to 9. am. 16th May.	16/05/1917	16/05/1917

Type	Description	Date From	Date To
Miscellaneous	173rd Infantry Brigade Daily Summary Of Intelligence period 24 hours 9 a.m. 16th to 9 a.m. 20/5/17	17/05/1917	17/05/1917
Operation(al) Order(s)	173rd Infantry Brigade Operation Order No. 19	19/05/1917	19/05/1917
Miscellaneous	March Table Appendix A		
Miscellaneous	Appendix B		
Miscellaneous	173rd Infantry Brigade Daily Summary Of Intelligence period 24 hours ending 9 am 19/5/17	19/05/1917	19/05/1917
Miscellaneous	173rd Infantry Brigade Daily Summary Of Intelligence period 24 hours ending 9 am 20/5/17	20/05/1917	20/05/1917
Miscellaneous	173rd Infantry Brigade Daily Summary Of Intelligence Period 15 hours ending 12 midnight-20/21st 5/17	21/05/1917	21/05/1917
Heading	Minor Operations Raid On Plush Trench By 173rd Inf. Bde. 58th Division		
Miscellaneous	58th Div. No. G.S.844/25	01/08/1917	01/08/1917
Miscellaneous	IV Corps	30/07/1917	30/07/1917
Operation(al) Order(s)	173rd Infantry Brigade Order No. 18	11/05/1917	11/05/1917
Miscellaneous	March Table Accompanying 173rd Infantry Bde Order No. 18	11/05/1917	11/05/1917
Heading	Officer i/c War Diaries A.Gs Office Base		
Miscellaneous	Original Administrative Instructions Issued With Operation Order No. 25 Stands	14/06/1917	14/06/1917
Miscellaneous	Reference Para 17 173rd Brigade Order No. 30	14/06/1917	14/06/1917
Map	Map		
Operation(al) Order(s)	173rd Infantry Brigade Operation Order No. 30	14/06/1917	14/06/1917
Operation(al) Order(s)	173rd Infantry Brigade Operation Order No. 25	08/06/1917	08/06/1917
Miscellaneous	173rd Artillery Barrage Time Table-Attached Operation Order No 25.		
Operation(al) Order(s)	173rd Infantry Brigade Operation Order No. 32	19/06/1917	19/06/1917
Miscellaneous	The word "Retire" Does Not Exist Any Man making use Of This word In action will Be Treated as an enemy and Shot		
Miscellaneous	173rd Infantry Brigade Administrative Instruction No. 6	01/06/1917	01/06/1917
Miscellaneous	173rd Infantry Brigade Administrative Instruction No.5	27/05/1917	27/05/1917
Miscellaneous	173rd Infantry Brigade Ammunition Dumps		
Miscellaneous	Amendments To 173rd Infantry Brigade Operation Order No. 25	10/06/1917	10/06/1917
Miscellaneous	173rd Brigade Amended Barrage Time Table Attached To Operation Order No. 25		
Operation(al) Order(s)	173rd Infantry Brigade Order No. 29	13/06/1917	13/06/1917
Operation(al) Order(s)	173rd Infantry Brigade Order No. 28	11/06/1917	11/06/1917
Operation(al) Order(s)	173rd Infantry Brigade Order No. 27	10/06/1917	10/06/1917
Operation(al) Order(s)	173rd Infantry Brigade Order No. 26	09/06/1917	09/06/1917
Operation(al) Order(s)	173rd Infantry Brigade Order No. 22		
Operation(al) Order(s)	173rd Infantry Brigade Order No. 24	06/06/1917	06/06/1917
Operation(al) Order(s)	173rd Infantry Brigade Order No. 23	04/06/1917	04/06/1917
Operation(al) Order(s)	173rd Infantry Brigade Order No. 21	02/06/1917	02/06/1917
Miscellaneous	March Table		
Operation(al) Order(s)	173rd Infantry Brigade Operation Order No. 20	27/05/1917	27/05/1917
Miscellaneous	March Table Appendix A		
Miscellaneous	Amendments To 173rd Infantry Brigade Administrative Instruction No.5	27/05/1917	27/05/1917
War Diary	Bihucourt	28/05/1917	29/05/1917
War Diary	L' Homme Mort	29/05/1917	20/06/1917
War Diary	Ablainzeville	20/06/1917	30/06/1917
Miscellaneous	173rd Infantry Brigade Intelligence Summary for Period of 24 hours ending 9 a.m. 29/5/17	29/05/1917	29/05/1917

Miscellaneous	173rd Infantry Brigade Summary of Intelligence for Period of 24 hours ending 9 a.m. 30/5/17	30/05/1917	30/05/1917
Miscellaneous	173rd Infantry Brigade Summary of Intelligence for 24 hours ending 9 a.m. 31/5/17	31/05/1917	31/05/1917
Miscellaneous	173rd Infantry Brigade Summary Of Intelligence for 24 hours ending 9 a.m. 1/6/17	01/06/1917	01/06/1917
Miscellaneous	173rd Infantry Brigade Summary Of Intelligence for the Period of 24 hours ending 9 a.m. 2/6/17	02/06/1917	02/06/1917
Miscellaneous	173rd Infantry Brigade Summary Of Intelligence for 24 hrs ending 9 a.m. 3rd June 1917	03/06/1917	03/06/1917
Miscellaneous	173rd Infantry Brigade Summary Of Intelligence for 24 hours ending 9 a.m. 4/6/17	04/06/1917	04/06/1917
Miscellaneous	173rd Infantry Brigade Summary Of Intelligence for Period of 24 Hours Ending 9 A.M. 5/6/17	05/06/1917	05/06/1917
Miscellaneous	173rd Infantry Brigade Summary Of Intelligence for 24 hours ending 9 a.m. 6th June 1917	06/06/1917	06/06/1917
Miscellaneous	173rd Infantry Brigade Summary Of Intelligence Period 24 hours ending 9 a.m. June 7th 1917	07/06/1917	07/06/1917
Miscellaneous	173rd Infantry Brigade Summary Of Intelligence for 24 hours ending 9 a.m. 8/6/17	08/06/1917	08/06/1917
Miscellaneous	173rd Infantry Brigade Summary Of Intelligence for 24 hrs ending 9 a.m. 9.6.17	09/06/1917	09/06/1917
Miscellaneous	173rd Infantry Brigade Summary Of Intelligence for period of 24 hours 9 a.m. 10/6/17	10/06/1917	10/06/1917
Miscellaneous	173rd Infantry Brigade Summary Of Intelligence for the Period of 24 hours ending 9 a.m. 11/6/17	11/06/1917	11/06/1917
Miscellaneous	173rd Infantry Brigade Summary Of Intelligence for Period 24 hours ending 9 a.m. June 12th 1917	18/06/1917	18/06/1917
Miscellaneous	173rd Infantry Brigade Summary Of Intelligence for Period of 24 hours ending 9 a.m. 13/6/17	13/06/1917	13/06/1917
Miscellaneous	173rd Infantry Brigade Summary Of Intelligence for Period of 24 hours ending 9 a.m. 14/6/17	14/06/1917	14/06/1917
Operation(al) Order(s)	173rd Infantry Brigade Operation Order No. 31	15/06/1917	15/06/1917
Heading	War Diary Of H.Q. 173 Inf. Bde. From 28/5/17 To 30/6/17		
War Diary	Ablainzeville Logeast Wood	01/07/1917	07/07/1917
War Diary	Bancourt	08/07/1917	09/07/1917
War Diary	Neuville	10/07/1917	10/07/1917
War Diary	Boorsonval	10/07/1917	10/07/1917
War Diary	Ytres Area	11/07/1917	15/07/1917
War Diary	(H.Q Gouzerocourt Wood)	16/07/1917	16/07/1917
War Diary	Beaucamp Section	16/07/1917	29/07/1917
War Diary	Neuville Bourjonval	30/07/1917	30/07/1917
War Diary	Manin	31/07/1917	31/07/1917
Heading	H.Q 173 Inf. Bde (58 Div) Vol 6 June 1917		
Operation(al) Order(s)	173rd Infantry Brigade Operation Order No. 33	06/07/1917	06/07/1917
Miscellaneous	March Table Issued With 173rd Infantry Brigade Operation Order No. 33		
Miscellaneous	173rd Infantry Brigade Administrative Instructions No. 7	06/07/1917	06/07/1917
Miscellaneous	To All Recipients Of 173rd Inf. Bde Operation Order No. 53	07/07/1917	07/07/1917
Operation(al) Order(s)	173rd Infantry Brigade Operation Order No. 34	14/07/1917	14/07/1917
Miscellaneous	173rd Infantry Brigade Administrative Instruction No. 7	15/07/1917	15/07/1917
Miscellaneous	S.A.A Grenades Etc. To Be Maintained By Battalion In Front System	15/07/1917	15/07/1917

Miscellaneous	To All Recipients Of 173rd Infantry Brigade Operation Order Number 34	14/07/1917	14/07/1917
Miscellaneous	Relief Table		
Miscellaneous	173rd Infantry Brigade Summary Of Intelligence for Period 9 a.m. 16/7/17 to 9 a.m. 17/7/17	17/07/1917	17/07/1917
Miscellaneous	173rd Infantry Brigade Summary Of Intelligence Period from 9 a.m. 18th July 1917 to 9 a.m. 19th July 1917	19/07/1917	19/07/1917
Miscellaneous	173rd Infantry Brigade Summary Of Intelligence Period from 9 a.m. 19th July 1917 to 9 a.m. 20th July	20/07/1917	20/07/1917
Miscellaneous	173rd Infantry Brigade Summary Of Intelligence Period from 9 a.m. 20th July 1917 to 9 a.m. 21st July	21/07/1917	21/07/1917
Operation(al) Order(s)	173rd Infantry Brigade Operation Order No. 35	22/07/1917	22/07/1917
Miscellaneous	173rd Infantry Bde Relief Table		
Miscellaneous	173rd Infantry Brigade Administrative Instructions No. 8	22/07/1917	22/07/1917
Miscellaneous	173rd Infantry Brigade Summary Of Intelligence Period from 9 a.m. 21st July 1917 to 9 a.m. 22nd July	22/07/1917	22/07/1917
Miscellaneous	173rd Infantry Brigade Summary Of Intelligence for Period 6 a.m. 22/7/17 to 6 a.m. 23/7/17	22/07/1917	22/07/1917
Miscellaneous	173rd Infantry Brigade Summary Of Intelligence Period from 9 a.m. 23rd July 1917 to 9 a.m. 24th July 1917	24/07/1917	24/07/1917
Miscellaneous	Intelligence Summary Period 6. am to 6 am. 25.7.17	25/07/1917	25/07/1917
Miscellaneous	173rd Infantry Brigade Summary Of Intelligence for Period of 24 hours from 6 a.m. 25th to 6 a.m. 26th July 1917	26/07/1917	26/07/1917
Miscellaneous	173rd Infantry Brigade Summary Of Intelligence Period 9 a.m. 26th July to 9 a.m. 27th July 1917	27/07/1917	27/07/1917
Miscellaneous	Intelligence Summary Period 6 AM-6 AM. 28-7-17	28/07/1917	28/07/1917
Miscellaneous	Report On Raid Carried Out On Plush Trench	29/07/1917	29/07/1917
Map	Map		
Miscellaneous	173rd Infantry Brigade Summary Of Intelligence period 24 hours ending 9 a.m. 29th July 1917	29/07/1917	29/07/1917
Miscellaneous	To All Recipients Of 173rd Infantry Brigade Operation Order Number 36	25/07/1917	25/07/1917
Operation(al) Order(s)	173rd Infantry Brigade Operation Order Number 36	25/07/1917	25/07/1917
Miscellaneous	Minor Enterprises Report Of Raids By 58th Division		
Miscellaneous	Third Army No.G.12/73	27/07/1917	27/07/1917
Miscellaneous	IV Corps	25/07/1917	25/07/1917
Miscellaneous	Relief Table (A) Issued With 173rd Inf. Bde. Operation Order No. 36		
Miscellaneous	Move Table "B" Issued With 173rd Inf. Bde. Operation Order No. 36		
Miscellaneous	173rd Infantry Brigade Administrative Instruction No. 9	25/07/1917	25/07/1917
Miscellaneous	Instructions Part I-General		
Miscellaneous	Medical Arrangements		
Miscellaneous	Notes		
Miscellaneous	Time Table Shewing Move Of Units From Line To Staging Area By Light Railway		
Miscellaneous	Table Shewing Moves From Staging Area To Bapaume Station By Light Ry. or Bus	31/07/1917	31/07/1917
Miscellaneous	The undermentioned Personnel Transport and animals will proceed By Omnibus Trains from Bapaume Stn. To Saulty at The Times Stated		
Miscellaneous	Table D Departure Of Tactical Trains From Bapaume	31/07/1917	31/07/1917
Heading	Defence Scheme No.3		
Map	Map		

Type	Description	From	To
Diagram etc	Diagram		
Miscellaneous	173rd Infantry Brigade Defence Scheme Number 3		
Miscellaneous	173rd Infantry Brigade Defence Scheme Contents	25/07/1917	25/07/1917
Miscellaneous	173rd Inf. Bde. Defence Scheme		
Miscellaneous	173rd Inf. Bde. Defence Scheme Section B		
Miscellaneous	173rd Inf. Bde. Defence Scheme Section C		
Miscellaneous	173rd Inf. Bde. Defence Scheme Section D		
Miscellaneous	173rd Inf. Bde. Defence Scheme Section E		
Miscellaneous	Precautions Against Hostile Gas Attack		
Miscellaneous	Establishment Of S.A.A & Grenades Appendix B		
Map	Map		
Miscellaneous	No.10 War Diary		
War Diary	Manin	01/08/1917	24/08/1917
War Diary	Sheet 28 ASO Central	25/08/1917	30/08/1917
War Diary	Sheet 28 B 27 8	31/08/1917	31/08/1917
War Diary	Manin	23/08/1917	24/08/1917
War Diary	Sheet 28 A30 Central	25/08/1917	30/08/1917
War Diary	Sheet 28 B 278	31/08/1917	31/08/1917
Operation(al) Order(s)	173rd Infantry Brigade Order Number 37	22/08/1917	22/08/1917
Miscellaneous	173rd Infantry Brigade Administrative Instructions No.10		
Miscellaneous	Administrative Instruction No. 10	22/08/1917	22/08/1917
Miscellaneous	Move Of 173rd Infantry Brigade From Aubigny To Hopoutre		
Miscellaneous	Addenda To 173rd Infantry Brigade Order No. 37	22/08/1917	22/08/1917
Operation(al) Order(s)	173rd Infantry Brigade Order Number 38	28/08/1917	28/08/1917
Miscellaneous	March Table Issued With 173rd Inf. Bde Order No. 38		
Miscellaneous	To All Recipients Of 173rd Infantry Brigade Order No. 38	28/08/1917	28/08/1917
Heading	War Diary Appendix A 173rd Infantry Brigade		
Miscellaneous	173rd Infantry Brigade Programme Of Sports	18/08/1917	18/08/1917
Miscellaneous	Notes		
War Diary	28.B27c65 Camp Dambre	01/09/1917	12/09/1917
War Diary	Yser Canal Bank C 25 d 2090	13/09/1917	18/09/1917
War Diary	Cheddar Villa	18/09/1917	21/09/1917
War Diary	Dambre Camp	22/09/1917	27/09/1917
War Diary	Brake Camp	27/09/1917	30/09/1917
War Diary	Nordausques	30/09/1917	30/09/1917
Operation(al) Order(s)	173rd Infantry Brigade Order Number 39	08/09/1917	08/09/1917
Miscellaneous			
Miscellaneous	173rd Infantry Brigade Administrative Instruction No. 12	09/09/1917	09/09/1917
Miscellaneous	173rd Infantry Brigade Summary Of Intelligence Period 24 hours ended 7 a.m. 14/9/17	14/09/1917	14/09/1917
Miscellaneous	173rd Infantry Brigade Patrol Report		
Miscellaneous	173rd Infantry Brigade Summary Of Intelligence Period 24 hours ended 9 a.m. 15/9/17	15/09/1917	15/09/1917
Miscellaneous	173rd Infantry Brigade Patrol Report		
Miscellaneous	173rd Infantry Brigade Summary Of Intelligence For Period of 24 hours ending 7 a.m. 16th Sept	16/09/1917	16/09/1917
Miscellaneous	173rd Infantry Brigade Patrol Report		
Operation(al) Order(s)	173rd Infantry Brigade Order No. 40	17/09/1917	17/09/1917
Operation(al) Order(s)	173rd Infantry Brigade Order No. 41	17/09/1917	17/09/1917
Miscellaneous			
Miscellaneous	To All Recipients Of 173rd Infantry Brigade Order No. 41	18/09/1917	18/09/1917

Type	Description	Date From	Date To
Miscellaneous	173rd Infantry Brigade Operation Instructions No.4	18/09/1917	18/09/1917
Miscellaneous	Tank Action Table		
Miscellaneous	173rd Infantry Brigade Operation Report	24/09/1917	24/09/1917
Map	Map		
Diagram etc	Diagram Of Communications		
Miscellaneous	173rd Infantry Brigade Operation Instructions No. 3	18/09/1917	18/09/1917
Miscellaneous	173rd Infantry Brigade Operation Instructions No. 2	18/09/1917	18/09/1917
Miscellaneous	173rd Infantry Brigade Operation Instructions No. 1		
Miscellaneous	173rd Infantry Brigade Summary Of Intelligence For Period of 24 hours ending 7 a.m. 17/9/17	17/09/1917	17/09/1917
Miscellaneous	173rd Infantry Brigade Summary Of Intelligence Period of 24 hours ending 7 a.m. 19/9/17	19/09/1917	19/09/1917
Miscellaneous	173rd Infantry Brigade Patrol Report		
Miscellaneous	173rd Infantry Brigade Summary Of Intelligence Period of 24 hours ended 7.30 a.m. 18/9/17	18/09/1917	18/09/1917
Miscellaneous	173rd Infantry Brigade Patrol Report		
Miscellaneous	173rd Infantry Brigade Addendum To Brigade Order No. 40	18/09/1917	18/09/1917
Map	Map		
Operation(al) Order(s)	173rd Infantry Brigade Order Number 42	26/09/1917	26/09/1917
Miscellaneous	Move Table "A"		
Miscellaneous	Move Table "B"		
Miscellaneous	Amendments To 173rd Infantry Brigade Order Number 42	26/09/1917	26/09/1917
Miscellaneous	173rd Infantry Brigade Administrative Instruction No. 14	26/09/1917	26/09/1917
Miscellaneous	Table "A"		
War Diary	Nordausques	01/10/1917	22/10/1917
War Diary	Canal Bank	23/10/1917	24/10/1917
War Diary	Varna Farm	25/10/1917	28/10/1917
War Diary	Siege Camp	29/10/1917	30/10/1917
War Diary	Road Camp	31/10/1917	31/10/1917
Miscellaneous	173rd Infantry Brigade Administrative Instructions No. 16	22/10/1917	22/10/1917
Miscellaneous	The Undermentioned personnel Transport and animals will proceed By Omnibus Train from Audruicq Station at The Times Stated		
Operation(al) Order(s)	173rd Infantry Brigade Order No. 43	24/10/1917	24/10/1917
Heading	H.Q 173rd Infy. Brigade Vol 11 Operation Report		
Map	Map		
Operation(al) Order(s)	173rd Infantry Brigade Order Number 44	24/10/1917	24/10/1917
Miscellaneous	Appendix "A" (Issued with 173rd Bde.Order No. 44.)	24/10/1917	24/10/1917
Miscellaneous	Move Table Attached Appendix "A"		
Miscellaneous	Appendix "B" (Issued in connection with 173rd Inf. Bde. Order No.44)	25/10/1917	25/10/1917
Miscellaneous	Appendix "C" (Issued in connection with 173rd Inf. Bde. Order No.44)		
Miscellaneous	173rd Infantry Brigade Administrative Instructions No. 17	24/10/1917	24/10/1917
Miscellaneous	Table "A"		
Miscellaneous	Summary Of Messages. Sent After Zero	26/10/1917	26/10/1917
Miscellaneous	Summary Of Messages	26/10/1917	26/10/1917
Miscellaneous	Appendix "A" (Issued with 173rd Inf. Bde. Order No.44)	24/10/1917	24/10/1917
Map	Map D		
Map	Map C		

Map	Map		
Map	Map B		
Miscellaneous	Message Form		
Map	Map A		
Map	Map		
Miscellaneous	Appendix B. Communications.		
Miscellaneous	Move Table Attached Appendix "A"		
Miscellaneous	173rd Infantry Brigade Administrative Instructions No. 17	24/10/1917	24/10/1917
Miscellaneous	Table A		
Miscellaneous	Appendix "C" Issued In connection with 173rd Infantry Brigade Order no.44	28/10/1917	28/10/1917
Diagram etc	Diagram		
Map	Sketch Map referred To In Notes para 4		
Miscellaneous	173rd Infantry Brigade Operation Report	03/11/1917	03/11/1917
War Diary	St. Janster Biezen	01/11/1917	06/11/1917
War Diary	Brake Camp	07/11/1917	15/11/1917
War Diary	Penge Camp	16/11/1917	25/11/1917
War Diary	Lumbres A	26/11/1917	26/11/1917
War Diary	Alincthun	27/11/1917	30/11/1917
Operation(al) Order(s)	173rd Infantry Brigade Order Number 45.	29/10/1917	29/10/1917
Operation(al) Order(s)	173rd Infantry Brigade Order Number 46	05/11/1917	05/11/1917
Operation(al) Order(s)	173rd Infantry Brigade Order No. 47	13/11/1917	13/11/1917
Miscellaneous	Reference 173rd Infantry Brigade Order No. 47	13/11/1917	13/11/1917
Miscellaneous	173rd Infantry Brigade March Table Issued With Order No. 47		
Map	Map		
Operation(al) Order(s)	173rd Infantry Brigade Order Number 48	24/11/1917	24/11/1917
Miscellaneous	Move Table Issued With 173rd Infantry Brigade Order No. 48		
Miscellaneous	Table "B" Issued With 173rd Infantry Brigade Order Number 48		
Miscellaneous	173rd Infantry Brigade Administrative Instructions No. 19	24/11/1917	24/11/1917
Miscellaneous	Time Table Of Trains		
Heading	D.A.G 3rd Echelon		
War Diary	Alincthun	01/12/1917	07/12/1917
War Diary	Samette	08/12/1917	08/12/1917
War Diary	White Mill Camp	09/12/1917	15/12/1917
War Diary	Line	16/12/1917	31/12/1917
Operation(al) Order(s)	173rd Infantry Brigade Order Number 48	05/12/1917	05/12/1917
Miscellaneous	Move Table Issued With 173rd Infantry Bde. Order No. 49		
Miscellaneous	Details Of Trains For Move		
Miscellaneous	173rd Infantry Brigade Warning Order No. 1	03/12/1917	03/12/1917
Miscellaneous	Amendment To 173rd Inf. Bde. O.O.no.49	07/12/1917	07/12/1917
Miscellaneous	173rd Infantry Brigade Administrative Instruction No. 20	05/12/1917	05/12/1917
Miscellaneous	Part II Marching portion Of Transport	05/12/1917	05/12/1917
Miscellaneous	To All Recipients Of 173rd Inf. Bde Warning Order No. 2	10/02/1917	10/02/1917
Operation(al) Order(s)	173rd Infantry Brigade Warning Order No. 2	10/12/1917	10/12/1917
Miscellaneous	173rd Infantry Brigade Order Number 50	15/12/1917	15/12/1917
Miscellaneous	Move Table To Accompany 173rd Inf. Bde Order Number 50	15/12/1917	15/12/1917

Type	Description	Date	Date
Miscellaneous	173rd Infantry Brigade Administrative Instruction No. 21		
Map	Map "A"		
Map	Map		
Miscellaneous	173rd Infantry Brigade Provisional Defence Scheme		
Miscellaneous	173rd Infantry Brigade Defence Scheme	15/12/1917	15/12/1917
Diagram etc	Diagram		
Miscellaneous	Appendix "A" To 173rd Inf. Bde. Provisional Defence Scheme		
Operation(al) Order(s)	173rd Infantry Brigade Order Number 58	22/12/1917	22/12/1917
Miscellaneous	173rd Infantry Brigade Administrative Instruction No. 23	22/12/1917	22/12/1917
Miscellaneous	173rd Infantry Brigade Further to 173rd Inf. Bde. Intelligence Summary for Period 24 hours ended 8 a.m. 17/12/17	17/12/1917	17/12/1917
Miscellaneous	173rd Infantry Brigade Summary of Intelligence Period 24 hours ending 8 a.m. 17/12/17	17/12/1917	17/12/1917
Miscellaneous	173rd Infantry Brigade Summary of Intelligence Period 8 a.m. 17th December to 8 a.m. 18th December 1917	18/12/1917	18/12/1917
Miscellaneous	173rd Infantry Patrol Reports	18/12/1917	18/12/1917
Miscellaneous	173rd Infantry Brigade Summary Of Intelligence Period 8 a.m. 18th Dec to 8 a.m. 19th Dec 1917	19/12/1917	19/12/1917
Miscellaneous	173rd Infantry Brigade Patrol Report		
Miscellaneous	173rd Infantry Brigade Summary Of Intelligence Period 8 a.m. 19/12/17 to 8 a.m. 20/12/17	20/12/1917	20/12/1917
Miscellaneous	173rd Infantry Brigade Patrol Report		
Miscellaneous	173rd Infantry Brigade Summary Of Intelligence Period 8 a.m. 20th Dec to 8 a.m. 21st Dec 1917	21/12/1917	21/12/1917
Miscellaneous	173rd Infantry Brigade Patrol Report		
Miscellaneous	173rd Infantry Brigade Intelligence Summary Period 24 hours ending 8 a.m. 22nd December 1917	22/12/1917	22/12/1917
Miscellaneous	173rd Infantry Brigade Patrol Report		
Miscellaneous	173rd Infantry Brigade Intelligence Summary Period 24 hours ending 8 a.m. 22nd December 1917	22/12/1917	22/12/1917
Miscellaneous	173rd Infantry Brigade Patrol Report		
Miscellaneous	173rd Infantry Brigade Intelligence Summary Period 24 hours ending 8 a.m. Dec. 23rd 1917		
Miscellaneous	173rd Infantry Brigade Patrol Report		
Miscellaneous	To All Recipients Of 173rd Inf. Bde. Intelligence Summary of 23rd Dec. 1917	23/12/1917	23/12/1917
Miscellaneous	173rd Infantry Brigade Patrol Report		
Miscellaneous	173rd Infantry Brigade Intelligence Summary Period 24 hours ending 8 a.m. 24th Dec. 1917	24/12/1917	24/12/1917
Miscellaneous	173rd Infantry Brigade 2/2nd London Regiment. Patrol Report		
Operation(al) Order(s)	173rd Infantry Brigade Order Number 51	19/12/1917	19/12/1917
Miscellaneous	Instructions As To Use Of Light-Railway For Delivery Of Stores & Rations	29/12/1917	29/12/1917
Operation(al) Order(s)	173rd Infantry Brigade Order Number 53	29/12/1917	29/12/1917
Miscellaneous	Move Table (Issued With 173rd Bde. Order No. 50)		
Miscellaneous	To All Recipients Of Administrative Instructions No.24	30/12/1917	30/12/1917
Miscellaneous	173rd Infantry Brigade Administrative No. 24	29/12/1917	29/12/1917
Heading	H.Q 173 Infy Bde Vol 12		

58TH DIVISION
173RD INFY BDE

BDE HEADQUARTERS
JAN - DEC 1917

58TH DIVISION
173RD INFY BDE

58 DIVISION

H.Q. 173 BDE

1915 SEP — 1916 FEB

58th (London) Division. (T.F.)

WAR DIARY STATEMENT.

UNIT:- 173rd Infantry Brigade.

DIVISION:- 58th (London) Division T.F.

MOBILIZATION
CENTRE:-

TEMPORARY WAR
STATION:- Ipswich from 12th. August.

STATIONS OCCUPIED   Tadworth Near Epsom, May 1915-June 1st '15
SUBSEQUENT TO   Bury St Edmunds, June 1st-August 12th '15
CONCENTRATION:-   Ipswich, August 12th to date.

N Walmandley
                    Colonel,
Commanding, 173rd Infantry Brigade.

Army Form C. 2118

WAR DIARY
or
~~INTELLIGENCE SUMMARY~~
(Erase heading not required.)

HEADQUARTERS,
173rd **INFANTRY BRIGADE**.

58th LONDON DIV.
GENERAL STAFF
3 - OCT. 1915
No. ....

Instructions regarding War Diaries and Intelligence Summaries are contained in F.S. Regs., Part II. and the Staff Manual respectively. Title Pages will be prepared in manuscript.

Place	Date	Hour	Summary of Events and Information	Remarks and references to Appendices
Ipswich.			NIL	

Ipswich.
1.10.15

[signature], Colonel,
Commanding, 173rd Infantry Brigade.

1875 Wt. W593/826 1,000,000 4/15 J.B.C. & A. A.D.S.S./Forms/C. 2118.

Army Form C. 2118

WAR DIARY

or ~~INTELLIGENCE SUMMARY~~

(Erase heading not required.)

HEADQUARTERS,
173RD INFANTRY BRIGADE,

Instructions regarding War Diaries and Intelligence Summaries are contained in F. S. Regs., Part II. and the Staff Manual respectively. Title Pages will be prepared in manuscript.

Place	Date	Hour	Summary of Events and Information	Remarks and references to Appendices
Ipswich.	November 2nd 1915.		N I L.	

[Stamp: 58th (LONDON) DIVISION · GENERAL STAFF · 3 – NOV 1915]

[signature] Colonel,
Commanding, 173rd Infantry Brigade.

1875 Wt. W 593/826 1,000,000 4/15 J.B.C. & A. A.D.S.S./Forms/C. 2118.

Army Form C. 2118

WAR DIARY
or
INTELLIGENCE SUMMARY

(Erase heading not required.)

Instructions regarding War Diaries and Intelligence Summaries are contained in F.S. Regs., Part II. and the Staff Manual respectively. Title Pages will be prepared in manuscript.

Place	Date	Hour	Summary of Events and Information	Remarks and references to Appendices
Ipswich.	1.12.15		NIL.	

[signature] Colonel,
Commanding, 173rd Infantry Brigade, Ipswich.

Army Form C. 2118

WAR DIARY

~~INTELLIGENCE SUMMARY~~

(Erase heading not required.)

Instructions regarding War Diaries and Intelligence Summaries are contained in F. S. Regs., Part II. and the Staff Manual respectively. Title Pages will be prepared in manuscript.

Place	Date	Hour	Summary of Events and Information	Remarks and references to Appendices
IPSWICH	17/12/15		Lieut. H. R. B. Watkins gazetted Brigade Machine Gun Officer.	

Ipswich,
1/1/16.

[signature] Colonel,
Commanding, 173rd Infantry Brigade.

[Stamp: 58th (LONDON) DIVISION GENERAL STAFF 2 - JAN 1916]

1875 Wt. W593/826 1,000,000 4/15 J.B.C. & A. A.D.S.S./Forms/C. 2118.

WAR DIARY of 173rd Infantry Brigade

Army Form C. 2118.

WAR DIARY
INTELLIGENCE SUMMARY.

(Erase heading not required.)

Instructions regarding War Diaries and Intelligence Summaries are contained in F.S. Regs., Part II. and the Staff Manual respectively. Title pages will be prepared in manuscript.

Hour, Date, Place	Summary of Events and Information	Remarks and references to Appendices
1st Jan 1916 IPSWICH	Major G.P.S. HUNT 1st Royal Berks Regt reported to take over command of 173 Inf. Bde	A.F.
9 Jan 1916 IPSWICH	Col. H. CHOLMONDELEY C.B. handed over command of the Brigade to Major G.P.S. HUNT	A.F.
	Major H.N. ROWLATT Brigade Major left to take up duty as Brigade Major 2nd Provisional Inf. Bde NEWCASTLE-ON-TYNE.	A.F.
	Captain H.A.H. STEWARD 2/8th Bn London Regt took up duty as Acting Brigade Major 173 Inf. Bde	A.F.
18 Jan 1916 IPSWICH	Major A.G. FOORD Manchester Regt reported to take up duty as Brigade Major 173 Inf. Bde	A.F.
28 Jan 1916 IPSWICH	9.20 p.m. message from Div. H.Q. "Turn out piquets" 10.5 p.m. All road piquets & firing parties from this Bde had left billeting areas for respective stations 10.15 p.m. Guards for Zeppelin wreck fell in at alarm Post to midnight dismissed & instructions from Div. H.Q.; reports NIL. Night was dark, much mist.	A.F.

Army Form C. 2118.

WAR DIARY
or
INTELLIGENCE SUMMARY.
(Erase heading not required.)

Instructions regarding War Diaries and Intelligence Summaries are contained in F.S. Regs., Part II and the Staff Manual respectively. Title pages will be prepared in manuscript.

Hour, Date, Place	Summary of Events and Information	Remarks and references to Appendices
31 Jan. 1916 IPSWICH.	5:59 p.m. Message Borough Police that 3 supposed ZEPPELINS were being fired at at MUNDESLEY in NORFOLK at 5:10 p.m. 6.5 p.m. Message from Units - Aircraft Station that their gun craft were out - two at RUSHMERE and one at the CHAPEL ST MARY. A.S.T. 6.10 p.m. Units of the Brigade were warned re above but were not ordered to turn out - No message from this H.Q. having been received. Night dark, some rain & mist.	A.S.T. A.S.T. A.S.T.

E. Monk.
Bg. Gen.
Commanding 173rd Infantry Brigade.

Army Form C. 2118.

WAR DIARY
INTELLIGENCE SUMMARY.

(Erase heading not required.)

Headquarters,
173rd Infantry Brigade.

Instructions regarding War Diaries and Intelligence Summaries are contained in F. S. Regs., Part II. and the Staff Manual respectively. Title pages will be prepared in manuscript.

Place	Date	Hour	Summary of Events and Information	Remarks and references to Appendices
IPSWICH	FEBY 29th 1916		N I L.	

[Stamp: 58th (LONDON) DIVISION — 2 MAR 1916 — GENERAL STAFF]

Brigadier-General,
Commanding, 173rd Infantry Brigade.

On His Majesty's Service.

WAR DIARY - Headquarters, 173rd Infantry Bde.

INTELLIGENCE SUMMARY

(Erase heading not required.)

Army Form C. 2118.

Vol I.

Place	Date 1917	Hour	Summary of Events and Information	Remarks and references to Appendices
	Jan.			
SOUTHAMPTON	23	6.30pm	Embarked on board S.S. "Huntscraft". Strength 4 Offrs 29 O.R.	A.S.F.
LE HAVRE	24	1.30pm	Disembarked.	A.S.F.
	25	5.30pm	Moved out to No 2 Rest Camp.	A.S.F.
	25	11.0 a.m	Entrained for point of concentration.	A.S.F.
FRÉVENT	27	10.30am	Detrained and marched to BONNIÈRES. Staff Captain reported. No 2 Signal Section Strength 1 Offr + 26 O.R.	A.S.F.
BONNIÈRES	29	10.45am	Moved to IVERGNY. Concentration complete.	A.S.F.
IVERGNY	30			A.S.F.
IVERGNY	31			A.S.F.

E. W. S. ?
Brig. Gen.
Commanding 173 Infantry Brigade

Army Form C. 2118.

WAR DIARY
or
INTELLIGENCE SUMMARY.

173rd Light Trench Mortar Battery

(Erase heading not required.)

Instructions regarding War Diaries and Intelligence Summaries are contained in F. S. Regs., Part II. and the Staff Manual respectively. Title pages will be prepared in manuscript.

Place	Date	Hour	Summary of Events and Information	Remarks and references to Appendices
	1917			
Sutton Veny	23 Jany 3.30		Left for Southampton	
Southampton	23 Jany 4 pm		Embarked for France	
Havre	24 Jany 1 pm		Landed at Havre	
"	25 Jany 11 am		Entrained	
Prevent	26 Jany 2 pm		Detrained + marched to Beauvoir	
Beauvoir	29 Jany 10 am		Marched to Ivergny	
Ivergny	29 Jany 10 pm		Arrived at Ivergny	

J.H. Howden Capt.

Vol # 2

WAR DIARY
OF
HQ 13 INF. BDE.

WAR DIARY

Army Form C. 2118.

INTELLIGENCE SUMMARY of Headquarters, 173rd Infantry Brigade

(Erase heading not required.)

Place	Date	Hour	Summary of Events and Information	Remarks and references to Appendices
IVERGNY	1.2.17 to 7.2.17		nil	A.S.7.
	8.2.17		Major A.G. Food, Brigade Major, visited Headquarters, 138th Infantry Brigade	A.S.7.
	9.2.17 to 12.2.17		nil	A.S.7.
	13.2.17		Major A.G. Food, Brigade Major, returned from visit to Headquarters, 138th Infantry Brigade	A.S.7.
	13.2.17		Rev. W.T. Heuston proceeded to Course of Instruction, ST OMER	A.S.7.
	14.2.17		nil	A.S.7.
	15.2.17		2/Lieut C.J. Graham, 2/4th Bn. London Regt., attached for instruction	A.S.7.
	16.2.17		Brig-Gen. G.P. Hunt, Commanding and Capt. J.H. Garraway, Staff Captain, visited Headquarters, 138th Infantry Brigade, BIENVILLERS.	A.S.7.
	18.2.17		Brig. Gen. G.P. Hunt, Commanding, and Capt. J.H. Garraway, Staff Captain, returned from visit to Headquarters, 138th Infantry Brigade, BIENVILLERS	A.S.7.
	16.2.17		1 Riding Horse of Signal Section shot under orders O.C., Mobile Vet. Section	A.S.7. Appendices 1 & 2.
	20.2.17		Left IVERGNY. Strength 7 Officers, 78 Other Ranks & 27 Horses (1 L.D. Horse left behind – lame) arrived SOUASTRE 4 p.m. Steady rain during march.	A.S.7.
SOUASTRE	22.2.17		2/Lieut J.S.W. Stone, O.C., Signal Section & 2/Lieut C.J. Graham proceeded to Headquarters, 148th Infantry Brigade to take over Signal Equipment and Bomb Stores respectively	A.S.7.

WAR DIARY of Headquarters 173rd Infantry Brigade

INTELLIGENCE SUMMARY

Army Form C. 2118.

Place	Date	Hour	Summary of Events and Information	Remarks and references to Appendices
SOUASTRE	22.2.17		Capt. F.H. Garraway, Staff Captain visited Headquarters, 148th Infantry Brigade.	A.S.7.
	23.2.17		Brig. Gen. G.P. Hunt, Commanding and Major A.G. Foord, Brigade Major, visited Headquarters 148th Infantry Brigade.	A.S.7.
	24.2.17		Major A.G. Foord, Brigade Major, visited Headquarters, 148th Infantry Brigade.	A.S.7.
	24.2.17		Capt. F.H. Garraway, Staff Captain proceeded to Headquarters, 148th Infantry Brigade with reference to pending relief.	appendix 3. A.S.7.
	25.2.17		Left SOUASTRE. Strength 3 Officers, 74 Other Ranks + 24 Horses (4 M.M.P. with horses left behind on instruction from A.P.M.)	
BASSEUX	25.2.17		Command of D Sector passed from G.O.C., 148th Infantry Brigade to G.O.C. 173rd Infantry Brigade.	A.S.7.
	26.2.17		nil	A.S.7.
	27.2.17		nil	A.S.7.
			WEATHER from 1st – 19th. Very cold with hard frost. Thaw set in on 19th, when weather became warmer.	A.S.7.
			ROADS Condition of roads from 1st – 19th good for motor vehicles but difficult for horse transport owing to slippery surface.	

Army Form C. 2118.

WAR DIARY
~~INTELLIGENCE~~ SUMMARY.
(Erase heading not required.)

of Headquarters, 173rd Infantry Brigade

Place	Date	Hour	Summary of Events and Information	Remarks and references to Appendices
			ROADS (Contd) After the thaw set in condition of roads became bad, but in this particular area they are fair. The trenches owing to thaw very muddy, but condition improving daily. There have been fine days since taking over, which helped matters greatly.	A57

E.J. Hunt.
Brigadier-General,
Commanding 173rd Infantry Brigade.

SECRET.   Copy No. 8
                                                        OO/2.
                        173rd Infantry Brigade
                        Order No. 2.
            (Reference Map - Sheet LENS 11:1/100,000.)   19/2/17.

                  1. The following amendment to 173rd Infantry
                     Brigade Order No. 1. is issued:-

                     H.Qrs. 173rd Inf. Bde. will move on the
                     20th from IVERGNY to SOUASTRE. Hour of
                     start 10 a.m. Route LUCHEUX - L'ESPERANCE -
                     MONDICOURT - PAS.

                                                    A. G. Foord
                                                              Major,
                                                         Brigade Major,
Issued at 1145a   173rd Infantry Brigade.

1. 2/1st Bn. London Regt.
2. 2/2nd Bn. London Regt.
3. 2/3rd Bn. London Regt.
4. 2/4th Bn. London Regt.
5. 2/1st Home Counties Field Ambulance.
6. 510th H.T. Coy. A.S.C.
7. 504th Field Company R.E.
8.) War Diary.
9.)

SECRET.   Copy No. 8

                    173rd Infantry Brigade
                    Order No. - 1 -

Reference Map - Sheet
LENS #,1:100,000.   17/2/17.

_____

        1. 173rd Inf. Bde. will relieve the 146th Inf. Bde.,
            with Headquarters at BASSEUX by 8 a.m. February,
            20th.

        2. In connection with the above reliefs, the moves
            for the 19th; 20th; 21st and 22nd will be as
            shewn on the attached March Table.

                                    J. E. Foord
                                            Major,
                                        Brigade Major,
                                    173rd Infantry Brigade.

Issued to Signals at   7.30 p.m.

1. 2/1st Bn. London Regt.
2. 2/2nd Bn. London Regt.
3. 2/3rd Bn. London Regt.
4. 2/4th Bn. London Regt.
5. 2/1st Home Counties Field Ambulance.
6. 510th M.T. Coy. A.S.C.
7. 504th Field Coy. R.E.
8.) War Diary.
9.)

MARCH TABLE ISSUED WITH 173RD INFANTRY BDE. ORDER NO. 1.
(Reference Map –LENS– Sheet 11, 1/100,000 & Sheet 57 D.1/40,000 ....).

UNIT.	DATE.	FROM.	TO.	HOUR OF START.	ROUTE.	REMARKS.
2/1st H.Q.Field Ambce.	19th.	SUS–ST.LEGER.	D.26 Central.	As arranged by A.D.M.S.		
H.Qrs.173rd Inf.Bde. and Sig.Sect.	20th.	IVERGNY.	SOUASTRE POMMERA.			
2/3rd Bn. London Regt. 510 Co. A.S.C.	" "	"	POMMERA WARLINCOURT.	10 a.m.	LUCHEUX–L'ESPERANCE.	Further Orders will be issued later.
2/1st Bn. London Regt.	"	SUS–ST.LEGER.	ST AMAND.			
2/4th Bn. London Regt. 504 Field Coy. R.E.	" "	" "	GAUDIEMPRE. HENU.	9.30 a.m.	LUCHEUX–MONDICOURT–PAS.	Further Orders will be issued later.
2/2nd Bn. London Regt.	"	IVERGNY.	LE SOUICH.	Further Orders will be issued later.		To be clear of IVERGNY by 11 a.m.
2/3rd Bn. London Regt.	21st.	POMMERA.	SOUASTRE.	11 a.m.	MONDICOURT–PAS–HENU.	
2/2nd Bn. London Regt.	"	LE SOUICH.	POMMERA.	10 a.m.	LUCHEUX–L'ESPERANCE.	
H.Qrs.173rd Inf.Bde. and Sig. Sect.	22nd	POMMERA.	SOUASTRE.	As convenient.		
2/2nd Bn. London Regt.	"	POMMERA.	SOUASTRE.	10 a.m.	MONDICOURT–PAS–HENU.	

SECRET.   Copy No. ..12

173RD INFANTRY BRIGADE ORDER NO. 5.

(Reference: Map Sheet 51c and 57d. : 1/40000

                                                          19/2/17

	1.	In connection with the moves for the 20th, 21st, and 22nd February, 1917, the following more detailed instructions are issued:-
Headquarters, 173rd Infantry Bde. Signal Section, and 2/3rd Bn. London Rgt.	2.	(a) Starting Point - Cross roads at A 27.a 7.9. (b) Headquarters 173rd Infantry Brigade will pass the Starting Point at 10.15 a.m. 2/3rd Bn. London Regt. will pass the Starting Point at 10.16 a.m.
2/4th Bn.Lon.Regt. 2/1st Bn.Lon.Regt. 504 Coy. R.E.	3.	Starting Point - Road junction at N 30.a.5.1. 2/4th Bn. London Regt. will pass the Starting Point at 9.35 a.m. 2/1st Bn. London Regt. will pass the Starting Point at 9.40 a.m. 504 Coy. Royal Engineers will pass the Starting Point at 9.45 a.m.
2/2nd Bn.Lon.Regt.	4.	The 2/2nd Bn. London Regt. will march under orders issued by O.C., 2/2nd London Regt., to be clear of IVERGNY by 11a.m. 20th February, 1917, but will not pass the cross roads at A 27.a.7.9 before 10.25 a.m.
510 Coy., A.S.C.	5.	The 510 Coy. A.S.C. will march under orders of the O.C., 510 Coy. A.S.C., but will not pass the road junction at N.30 a.5.1 before 9.45 a.m.
	6.	Units are forbidden to use any roads EAST of a line drawn from N.W. to S.E. through the first S in SUS-ST.LEGER - H in HUMBERCOURT - W in WARLINCOURT (Reference: Map Sheet LENS 11 : 1/100000).
	7.	Brigade Headquarters will close at IVERGNY at 9.30 a.m., 20th February, 1917, and will open at SOUASTRE at 3 p.m. same date.
2/2nd Bn.Lon.Regt.	8.	(a) The O.C, 2/2nd Bn. London Regt., will issue the necessary orders for the subsequent moves of his Battalion on the 21st and 22nd February, 1917.
2/3rd Bn. Lon.Regt.		(b) The O.C., 2/3rd Bn. London Regt. will issue the necessary orders for the move of his Battalion on the 21st February, 1917.

                                        A G Foord
                                            Major,
                                            Brigade Major.
                                            173rd Infantry Brigade

Issued to Signals at

                                                          (OVER

SECRET   2.   Copy No. 12

173RD INFANTRY BRIGADE ORDER NO. 3 (Contd).

(Reference: Map Sheet 51c and 57d ; 1/40000)

19/2/17.

Issued to Signals at ...6.45 pm

   (1) O.C., 2/1st Bn. London Regt.
   (2) O.C., 2/2nd Bn. London Regt.
   (3) O.C., 2/3rd Bn. London Regt.
   (4) O.C., 2/4th Bn. London Regt.
   (5) O.C., 504 Coy. R.E.
   (6) O.C., 510 Coy. A.S.C.
   (7) O.C., Signal Section.
   (8) G.O.C., 58th Division.   )
   (9) O. C., Light Trench Mortar Battery) For information.
(10) File.
(11) & (12) War Diary.

SECRET   Copy No. 22

173RD INFANTRY BRIGADE OPERATION ORDER NO. 4.

(Reference Maps - Sheet LENS.11 : 1/100,000 and Sheet 51c S.E.
Edition 3.A.)

22/2/17

---

1. The 173rd Infantry Brigade is to relieve the 148th Infantry Brigade in the line commencing on the 23rd February, 1917.

2. The relief will be carried out in accordance with the attached March Table.

3. All movement East or North of LA CAUCHIE will be by platoons at 200 yards interval, and 50 yards interval will be maintained between each pair of vehicles.

4. Battalions going into the line will take over Brigade Observation Posts from the 148th Infantry Brigade. The Intelligence Officer, 148th Infantry Brigade will make the necessary arrangements for handing them over.

5. Lists of trench stores will be compiled in triplicate by battalions of the 148th Infantry Brigade in the line, and of billet stores by battalions of the 148th Infantry Brigade in support and Divisional Reserve. All three copies will be signed by representative officers of ingoing and outgoing units, one copy will be retained by the relieving unit.

6. Completion of all moves will be reported by orderly to this office as soon as practicable.

7. Units on arrival in BASSEUX area will come under the command of the G.O.C., 148th Infantry Brigade until 2 p.m., 25th February, 1917.

8. The Command of "D" Sector will pass to G.O.C., 173rd Infantry Brigade from G.O.C., 148th Infantry Brigade at 2 p.m., 25th February, 1917.

9. Brigade Headquarters will close at SOUASTRE at 7 a.m. on the 25th February, 1917, and will re-open at BASSEUX at 10 a.m.

10. Acknowledge.

[signature]
Major,
Brigade Major.
173rd Infantry Brigade.

Issued to Signals at ....

Copy No.		Copy No.		
1	2/1st Bn. London Regt.	12	S.S.O.	)
2	2/2nd Bn. London Regt.	13	A.P.M.	)
3	2/3rd Bn. London Regt.	14	C.R.E.	) For
4	2/4th Bn. London Regt.	15	A.D.M.S.	) Inform-
5	Machine Gun Coy.	16	A.D.V.S.	) ation.
6	173rd Light Trench Mortar Bty.	17	148th Inf.Bde.	)
7	Staff Captain, 173rd Inf. Bde.	18	58th Division "Q"	)
8	510 Coy., A.S.C.	19	58th Division "A"	)
9	No.2 Sig. Section	20	File	
10	504 Coy. R.E.	21	) War	
11	2/1st Field Amb. (For information	22	) Diary	

SECRET

MARCH TABLE ISSUED WITH 173RD INFANTRY BRIGADE ORDER NO. 4.

(Reference maps Sheet LENS.11: 1/100,000 and Sheet 51c S.E. Edition 3.A:)

No.	Unit	Date Feb.	From	To	Route	Relief of	Guides	Remarks
1.	2/4th Bn. Lon.Regt.	23rd	GAUDIEMPRE	BELLACOURT & Post in Divl. Line	LA CAUCHIE - BAILLEULMONT - BASSEUX.	5th K.O.Y.L.I.	of 5th K.O.Y.L.I. 1 per Bn.Hd.Qtrs. & 1 per Platoon will be at cross roads BELLACOURT (R.31.a.40.55) at 8.00 a.m.	3 leading Platoons of 2/4th London Regt. will relieve 3 Platoons of 5th K.O.Y.L.I. in posts in Divisional Line. Transport may move at any convenient time after daybreak. Cookers may be taken with Bns. if desired.
2.	2/4th Bn. Lon. Regt.	24th	BELLACOURT	Trenches D.1 sub-sector.		4th K.O.Y.L.I.	of 4th K.O.Y.L.I. as above at end of CHURCH St ((R.32.b.20.10) at 8.00 a.m.	Relief to be complete by 12 noon. 3 Platoons of 2/4th London Regt. will not vacate posts in Divl.Line until relieved by 2/1st Lon. Regt.
3.	2/1st Bn. Lon.Regt.	24th	ST.AMAND	BELLACOURT & Posts in Divl.Line.	POMMIER - LA CAUCHIE - BAILLEULMONT - BASSEUX.		of 2/4th Lon.Rgt. as above at cross roads BELLACOURT (R.31.a.40.55) at 8.00 a.m.	3 leading Platoons 2/1st Lon.Rgt. will relieve 3 Platoons of 2/4th Lon.Regt. in posts in Divl.Line Transport may move at any convenient time after daybreak. Cookers may be taken with Bns. if desired.

4. 24 Other Ranks and 12 Machine Guns of 173rd M.G. Coy.	24th	SOUASTRE		173th M.G.Coy.	POMMIER - LA CAUCHIE - BAILLEULMONT	To be arranged by C.O's concerned.	To take up as little equipment as possible.
5. 2/1st Br. Lon.Regt.	25th	BELLACOURT	Trenches D.2 sub-sector		5th York & Lancs.	of 5th York & Lancs. as above at cross roads at ERETENCOURT (R.26.d.80.50) 8 a.m.	Relief to be complete by 12 noon. 3 leading Platoons 2/1st Lon.Regt. will not vacate posts in Divl.Line until relieved by 2/3rd Lon.Regt.
6. 2/3rd Bn. Lon.Regt.	25th	SOUASTRE	BELLACOURT & Posts in Divl. Line			of 2/1st Lon.Regt. as above at cross roads BELLACOURT (R.31.a.40.55) at 8 a.m.	3 leading Platoons of 2/3rd Lon.Regt. will relieve 3 Platoons of 2/1st Lon.Regt. in posts in Divl.Line. Transport may move at any convenient time after daybreak. Cookers may be taken with Bns. if desired.
7. Hd.Qtrs. 173rd Inf. Bde. and Sig.Section	25th	SOUASTRE	BASSEUX		Hd.Qrs. 148th Inf. Bde. and Sig.Section.	ST.AMAND - POMMIER - LA CAUCHIE - BAILLEULMONT.	
8. 173rd M.G. Coy.	25th	SOUASTRE	Trenches		148th M.G. Coy.		In completion of relief arranged for 24th February 1917.

9.	173rd T.M. Batty. Reserve	25th Batty.		Reserve T.M. Batty. personnel of Bns. in the Line to take over emplacements, ammunition & stores pending arrival of 173rd T.M. Batty.
10.	2/2nd Bn. Lon.Regt.	26th SOUASTRE	Hd.Qtrs. & 2 Coys. BAILLEULVAL. 2 Coys. BASSEUX.	ST.AMAND - POMMIER - LA CAUCHIE	148th T.M. Batty.	Take over billots vacated by 5th York. & Lancs. at BASSEUX by 8 a.m., at BAILLEULVAL by 8.30 a.m.

N.B.:- Particular attention is directed to the provision of guides to be provided by the 2/4th Bn. for the 2/1st Bn. and the 2/3rd Bn. London Regt.

173rd INFANTRY BRIGADE.

DAILY SUMMARY OF INTELLIGENCE - Period 24 hours ending 5 pm. 21/3/17.

OPERATIONS.

1. On the Right of the Brigade Front the 2/4th London Regt. with headquarters at T.25.a.25 are holding from T.27.a.2040 along the railway line to T.13.c.40&50. with groups on the road ST. LEGER MILL to T.14.b.05. They are in close touch with the 8th Devons on their right at JUDAS FARM and with the 2/2nd London Regt. on their left.

The 2/2nd London Regt. relieved the 1st London Regt on the morning of the 21st and are holding a line running from T.13.c.30.20 round the Eastern outskirts of BOYELLES to the cutting in T.13.a., thence round East of BOIRY BECQUERELLES to the COJEUL RIVER, where they are in close touch with the 19th Kings Liverpool Regt. Their headquarters are at BOISLEUX ST. MARC.

With both the right and left Battalions is one section of the 197 M.G.Coy. and the 197 M.G.Coy. less these two sections is holding a supporting line in the road running from S.16 central through HAMELINCOURT.

The 2/1st London Regt. with its headquarters at BOISLEUX AU MONT, ready to take up a supporting position and hold the line of road running South towards HAMELINCOURT.

2. Hostile activity has consisted of a certain amount of shelling of BOYELLES and BOIRY BECQUERELLES and a few shots on neighbouring villages. He has been registering on the valley between the two villages, and any attempt to move forward from BOYELLES in strength is met with heavy shrapnel fire from batteries which appear to be firing from direction of CROISILLES and WANCOURT. Machine Gun fire from both HENIN and CROISILLES is always directed on our cavalry when they attempt to enter these villages. Fires are reported in both villages which have apparently been systematically destroyed, and it was reported to-day that the enemy shelled HENIN this afternoon. Uhlan patrols have come in contact with our patrols at several points and have always retired at a gallop when fired on. An enemy outpost is reported at T.23.a.1070.

S E C R E T.   Copy No...........

Amendment to MARCH TABLE accompanying 173rd Infantry
Brigade Order No. 4.
----

4.   Column 2.   for "24 Other Ranks" and 12 Machine Guns of
                 173rd M.G. Coy." substitute "9th Machine Gun
                 Coy. attached 173rd Infantry Brigade."

     Column 7.   for "174th M.G.Coy." substitute "148th M.G.Co."

                                               A.G. Ford
                                                          Major,
                                                   Brigade Major,
                                                173rd Infantry Brigade.
23/2/17.

173RD INFANTRY BRIGADE

Period 24 hours ending 5 p.m., 22nd March, 1917

OPERATIONS

The dispositions of our troops on the Brigade Front are unchanged, with the exception of the 2/4th Bn. London Regt., which has been relieved by the 2/3rd London Regt. The enemy's artillery have shewn considerable activity, our front line having been subjected to intermittent shelling from field guns, a battery of which is suspected at N.35.d. and another battery fires from direction of CROISILLES. The Railway embankment near BOISLEUX ST.MARC was heavily shelled this afternoon with field guns and guns of heavier calibre and about 20 shells were fired at the high ground just north of BOIRY ST.RICTRUDE about 5 p.m. The enemy is apparently holding the HENIN - CROISILLES Road which is sunken, in some strength. Large numbers of the enemy exposing themselves on this road all day. CROISILLES and HENIN are still occupied by the enemy but an explosion occurred at HENIN at 2.25 p.m. and large fires were observed there all day. NEUVILLE VITASSE - ST.MARTIN-SUR-COJEUL and CROISILLES have also been smoking and burning. Villages in rear of ARRAS were also reported to be burning but MONCHY-LE-PREUX is apparently undamaged. The houses appear to be uninjured and the trees are still standing.

173RD INFANTRY BRIGADE

DAILY SUMMARY OF INTELLIGENCE

Period - 48 hours ending 5 p.m., 24th March, 1917

A. OPERATIONS

1. The Brigade Line is held as follows:-
RIGHT BATTALION
Front Line - Right Company. No. 1 Post - T.27.a.18 to T.21.c.00.
No. 2 Post - T.21.c.00 to T.20.d.92. No. 3 Post - T.20.d.92 to T.20.d.83. No. 4 Post - T.20.d.83 to T.20.d.75.
   Left Company. No. 1 Post - T.20.d.75 to T.20.a.93. No. 2 Post - T.20.a.93 to T.19.b.15. No. 3 Post - T.19.b.15 to T.19.a.98. No. 4 Post - T.19.a.98 to T.19.a.49.
Advanced Posts:- T.19.b.09 and T.20.a.98. By night a Post is maintained at T.21.a.40.90, and patrols proceed to cross roads T.21.d.58, where unit on our right maintains a Post.
   Support Company from T.25.c.89 along the road through T.19.c. and a. with Battalion Headquarters at T.25.a.72, and a Company in reserve at HAMELINCOURT.
LEFT BATTALION.
The Left Battalion, 2/2nd London Regt. has been relieved by the 2/5th London Regt., and moved to BOISLEUX AU MONT. The dispositions of 2/2nd London Regt. were :-
Front Line:- One platoon in T.13.c., one in S.18.d. and b., one platoon in S.18.b. north of the forked roads, and one in T.13.a. with two posts on COJEUL RIVER South.
Left Company:- A post at the QUARRY in T.7.d.80.60. Two platoons in T.7.b., the left one extending to COJEUL RIVER. One platoon in T.7.a. and one in S.12.b.
   Company in Support:- S.18.a. and one Company in Reserve at S.11.d.09.99. Battalion Headquarters at S.11.d.20.40.
BATTALION IN SUPPORT:- At BOISLEUX AU MONT, and BATTALION IN RESERVE. BRIGADE HEADQUARTERS at BOIRY ST. RICTRUDE.

2. Enemy artillery has again been fairly active, both with field guns and 105 mm H.E. howitzers. T.25.c., T.20.a. and d. and c., T.21.c. BOIRY BECQUERELLES, BOYELLES and BOISLEUX ST. MARC, all being shelled, the latter place less than the others. Hostile M.G's have not been particularly active.
   At 8.20 a.m. on the morning of the 23rd our post at T.7.d.80.60 consisting of 8 men, was raided by the enemy, who came down HENIN - ST.LEGER road and entered the trenches at T.8.c. Opening fire on post, they shot the sentries and picked off the rest of the section. The post was withdrawn, as all the men were wounded, one man was killed endeavouring, when wounded, to save his Lewis Gun. The withdrawal was covered by Lieut. Newton, a Sergeant, and 5 men of the post all wounded, got safely back into our lines, one being brought in by Lieut. Newton. On the night of the 23rd the post was reoccupied, and the body of one man, Lewis Gun, and one wounded man, were brought in. The post has since been wired.
   The enemy apparently advances snipers and sometimes a M.G. from HENIN SUR COJEUL towards T.1.d. or b., at night, and fires down our line and at the Unit on our left. This unit, 16th Manchesters, proposed to establish themselves last night (23rd) on a line east of BOIRY COPSE. This was not, however, carried out. They report that they were raided, and that the raiders were beaten off. The Unit on our right pushed posts out to the outskirts of CROISILLES with which our Right Battalion got into touch. Patrols report no sign of the enemy on the right, and that the practice trenches in T.8.c. were not occupied by the enemy at 9.15 p.m. on the night of the 22nd.

P.T.O.

B. INTELLIGENCE

Enemy Aircraft has been particularly active on the 23rd and 24th: one of them on the 23rd dropping a number of bombs and signalling by dropping in one case one red light, and in the other one red followed by two green. A shell came over so quickly after this second signal that it is doubtful whether there was any connection between the two. On the 24th our M.G's fired 1,500 rounds at an enemy machine at 8.30 am and drove it back over the enemy line. The strong wind and height at which aeroplane was flying made accurate firing difficult. At 10 a.m. on the 24th two of our machines engaged a hostile aeroplane which retired over its own lines. At 3.29 p.m. one of our machines, a B.2c. was brought down at W.24.a.50.90, both airmen being killed. Machine was only slightly damaged. Enemy artillery promptly shelled the ground around the fallen plane.

Material. In an embankment at S.11.d.20.20, in a dug-out, a large number of rifle grenades, hand grenades, detonators, and fuses, were found and a number of stick grenades and egg bombs (in a dug-out now used as a Company Headquarters.

A working party of 35 - 40 men, apparently unarmed, was observed below the ridge at T.10.d. at 5.15 a.m., disappearing over the ridge 15 minutes later. Small parties were frequently observed on this ridge.

Two explosions occurred at HENIN SUR COJEUL at 8.20 a.m., and smoke was rising from the same village all day.

Communications:- Have much improved, the strong wind having hardened the roads, which have been made practicable by the Engineers for lorries as far as ADINFER and horse transport up to our present front.

Water. No further sources of water supply have been discovered other than those already reported. The pond at ADINFER is a large one and sufficient for the needs of at least a Brigade for a considerable time, but the water is not so good as in the COJEUL RIVER just West of BOISLEUX ST. MARC where there is a practically unlimited supply of good running water, which however requires boiling before use.

General. Visibility has been extremely good all day. Weather has been cold and clear and a strong easterly wind.

C. J. Graham 2/Lt.
Intelligence Officer
173rd Infantry Brigade

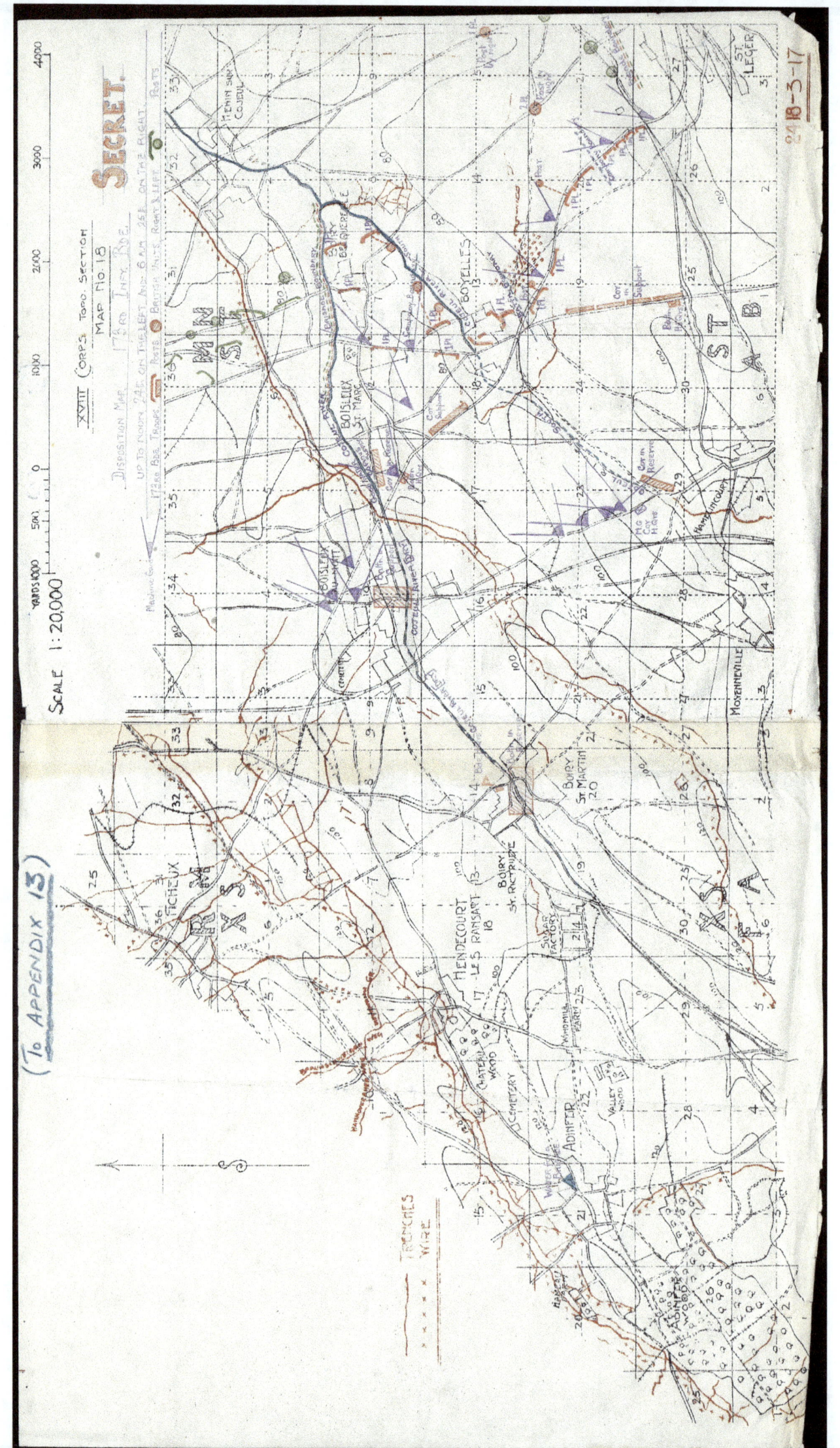

173RD INFANTRY BRIGADE

Period 24 hours ending 5 p.m. March 25th 1917
....

OPERATIONS

Hostile Artillery shewed considerable activity during the night, firing on our front line, and also firing a fairly large number of shells on BOISLEUX AU MONT.
Patrols of 2/3rd Bn. London Regt. having again established close touch with the unit on our right, 2 platoons were pushed out to re-establish the post at T.21.a.35.90, which is withdrawn by day. Traces of occupation by unit on our right were found at T.15.c.20.15, but nothing else. Another platoon established a post at T.15.d.90.80 where traces of occupation by the unit on our right were also found. Close touch was maintained with the post at T.22.a.20.70 established by unit on our right. A patrol of 1 Officer and 3 other ranks proceeded from T.15.d.90.80 along the road running N.N.W. from this point to the forked roads at T.9.a.45.50. They met with no signs of the enemy whatever.
173rd Infantry Brigade Headquarters moved from BOIRY ST. RICTRUDE to POMMIER, being relieved by the 174th Infantry Brigade at noon. The 2/3rd London Regt. moved from the Right sub-sector, front line to BOIRY ST.RICTRUDE being relieved by the 2/6th Bn. London Regt. 197th Machine Gun Company moved from A area to POMMIER on completion of relief.

Army Form C. 2118.

WAR DIARY of HEADQUARTERS.
INTELLIGENCE SUMMARY. 173rd 2/1 Brigade.
(Erase heading not required.)

Instructions regarding War Diaries and Intelligence Summaries are contained in F. S. Regs., Part II. and the Staff Manual respectively. Title pages will be prepared in manuscript.

Place	Date	Hour	Summary of Events and Information	Remarks and references to Appendices
BASSEUX	27/2/17		Nil.	A.S.I.
	28/2/17			A.S.I.
	1/3/17			A.S.I.
	2/3/17			A.S.I.
	3rd		173rd Trench Mortar Battery returned from course of instruction at LIGNY-ST-FLOCHEL	A.S.I.
	4th		Nil.	A.S.I.
	5th		Bde.Hd.Qtrs at Basseux shelled about 12 noon, 10.5 c.m. no casualties.	A.S.I.
	6th	"	" 1.7-1.37 p.m. 20, 10.5 c.m. Sgt Metcalfe (Trench Mortar Attd) wounded (Slight)	A.S.I.
	7th	2 p.m.	Command of Z1 Sector passed from O.C. 137th Infty Brigade to O.C. 173rd Infty Brigade	Appendix 3
			173rd Infty Bgde Headquarters moved to POMMIER	
POMMIER	7th	7- 8.30 p.m	POMMIER shelled — 25 Shells falling round Bde Hd Qtrs	A.S.I.
	8th		2nd Lieut Bennet (Signalling Officer of 2/2nd London Regt) attached for instruction	A.S.I.
		5 p.m.	1/9th Lr.R.Coy relieved 9th R. Coy in Z.1 + Z.2 Sub-Sector	
	9th	10.15 p.m	POMMIER shelled 7 Shells falling round Bde Hd Qtrs	A.S.I.
		1.30 p	" " 6 " "	
		2.30 p	" " 6 " "	
		2.45	" " 10 " "	
		3.10	" " 18 " "	
		3.30	" " 12 " "	
		3.45	" " " "	
	10th	4.0 pm	Nil.	
		10.15 pm		
	11	10.30 p	" 10th No.2 Signal Section - wounded (3th)	

Army Form C. 2118.

WAR DIARY (Cont'd)
INTELLIGENCE SUMMARY.

(Erase heading not required.)

of Headquarters 173rd Inf Bde.

Place	Date	Hour	Summary of Events and Information	Remarks and references to Appendices
(Cont'd)				
POMMIER	12th	10 am	POMMIER shelled. 10 Shells falling around Bde Hd Qtrs	O.S.T.
		10.30am	" " " " " (1 OR 2/4th) A.H. wounded (Bessy)	O.S.T.
		1pm	" " " " "	O.S.T.
		1.45pm	" " " " "	O.S.T.
	13th		Nil-	
	14th		The two sections of 197th Fd. S. Coy attached 174th Infantry Bde in Z 2 Sector relieved by 192nd	O.S.T.
			Fd. S. Coy. The two sections then moved into billets in POMMIER. From completion	
			of relief the whole of 197th Fd. S. Coy came under the orders of O.C. 173rd Infy Bde	O.S.T.
	15th		Nil-	O.S.T.
	16th		-	O.S.T. See
	17th		-	O.S.T. Appendix
	18th		Situation at dusk 18th (See appendix 7.)	O.S.T. 9
POMMIER	19th	10 am	Left POMMIER.	O.S.T. 10
RANSART		2.30pm	Arrived RANSART	O.S.T. 11
	20th	9 am	Left RANSART.	O.S.T. 12
BOIRY STE RICTRUDE	21 to 24	3pm	Arrived BOIRY STE RICTRUDE	O.S.T. 13
	25th		Left BOIRY STE RICTRUDE on command of front ponim from G.O.C. 173rd Infantry Bde to G.O.C. 174th Infty	O.S.T. + App
POMMIER	25th	5pm	Bde - Arrived POMMIER	O.S.T. accompanying App 13.

WAR DIARY (Part 2) or **INTELLIGENCE SUMMARY**

Headquarters 173rd Infantry Bde.

Army Form C. 2118.

(Erase heading not required.)

Place	Date	Hour	Summary of Events and Information	Remarks and references to Appendices
POMMIER	25"		2/4th Lon R. Coy came under orders of O.C. 173rd Infantry Bde.	452
	26"		187th Fd. Coy left for ETRUN.	a.57

A.Y. Ford Major

173RD INFANTRY BRIGADE.
RELIEF TABLE.
2nd March 1917.

Date March.	Unit.	From.	To.	Route.	Relieved by.	Guides.	REMARKS.
1. 1st.	2/1st. Lon. Regt.	Trenches. D2.	BELLACOURT, & Posts in Divl.Reserve	QUARRY ST and ENGINEER ST. Regt.	2/3rd. Lon. Regt.	of 2/1st Lon. Regt. 1 per Bn.Hd.Qrs. & 1 per platoon at cross roads BELLACOURT (R.31.a.40.55) at 8.00 a.m.	(a) To take over billets vacated by 2/3rd London Regt. (b) ENGINEER ST will NOT be available between 10 and 11 a.m. (c) Three platoons to take over posts in Divl. Reserve at time to be arranged mutually with 2/3rd Lor. Regt.
2. 2nd.	2/4th Lon. Regt.	Trenches. Hd.Qrs.& 2 Coys. BAILLEULVAL. 2 Cos. BASSEUX. D 1.	CHURCH ST. BURNT FARM ST. and ENGINEER ST.		2/2nd of 2/4th Lon. Regt. as above at end of CHURCH ST. (R.26.b.20.10). at 8.00 a.m.		(a) To take over billets vacated by 2/2nd London Regt. (b) ENGINEER ST will be available for one hour ONLY i.e. between 10 and 11 a.m.
3. 2nd.	2/3rd Lon. Regt. Reserve.	BELLACOURT & Posts in Divl. Reserve.	Trenches D2.	QUARRY ST and ENGINEER ST. Regt.	2/1st Lon. Lon. Regt.		(a) 3 platoons of 2/3rd Lon. Regt. will not vacate posts in Divl. line until relieved by 2/1st Lon. Regt. Time to be arranged mutually with 2/1st Lon. Regt. (b) ENGINEER ST will NOT be available between 10 and 11 a.m.
4. 2nd.	2/2nd Lon. Regt.	Hd.Qrs.& 2 Cos. Trenches BAILLEULVAL. D1. 2 Cos. BASSEUX.		CHURCH ST & ENGINEER ST.	2/4th Lon. Regt.		ENGINEER ST will be available for one hour ONLY i.e. between 10 and 11 a.m.

All reliefs to be completed by 12 noon.

SECRET   Copy No. 22

173rd INFANTRY BRIGADE ORDER NO. 5.

(Reference Map Sheet 51c.)

1/3/17

	1.	2/2nd London Regt. will relieve 2/4th London Regt. in D.1 Subsector and 2/3rd London Regt. will relieve 2/1st London Regt. in D.2 Subsector on the morning of 2nd March.
ROUTES	2.	2/3rd London Regt., except the garrison of STARFISH POST will be East of the cross roads at R.26.c.2/1 by 9 a.m. QUARRY ST will be available for 2/3rd and 2/1st London Regts. and ENGINEER ST except between 10 and 11 a.m.
		The leading Platoon of 2/2nd London Regt. will not pass the bend of the road at R.26.c.1/3 before 9 a.m. CHURCH ST and BURNT FARM ST, and ENGINEER ST between 10 and 11 a.m. will be available for 2/2nd and 2/4th London Regts.
POSTS	3.	The three posts occupied by the support battalion will not be vacated until relieved.
DETAILS	4.	Battalions will arrange details of their reliefs mutually.
PRECAUTIONS	5.	(a) No party larger than a platoon will march together. Parties will maintain 200 yards intervals. (b) 100 yard intervals will be maintained between pairs of vehicles. (c) The usual precautions will be taken against observation by hostile aircraft such as marching in file on the sides of roads, etc. (d) Officers will be responsible that there is no congestion or crowding and that when parties are halted they are behind cover.
TRENCH STORES	6.	Lists of all trench stores handed over to incoming units will be made out and handed to them.
REPORTS	7.	The completion of the relief will be reported in code (B.A.B.).

Major,
Brigade Major.
173rd Infantry Brigade.

Issued to Signals at 7.30 a.m.

Copy No.
1. 2/1st Bn. London Regt.
2. 2/2nd Bn. London Regt.
3. 2/3rd Bn. London Regt.
4. 2/4th Bn. London Regt.
5. 9th Machine Gun Coy.
6. 173rd Light Trench Mortar Bty.
7. Staff Captain, 173rd Inf.Bde.
8. 510 Coy. A.S.C.
9. No. 2 Signal Section) For
10. 504 Coy. R.E.   ) inform-
11. 2/1st Field Ambulance) ation

Copy No.
12. S.S.O.
13. A.P.M.   )
14. C.R.E.   ) For
15. A.D.V.S.   ) inform-
16. A.D.M.S.   ) ation
17. 174th Inf.Bde.)
18. 175th Inf.Bde.)
19. 58th Division "G")
20. 58th Division "A"
21. File.
22.) War
23.) Diary

SECRET  Copy No. 24

173RD INFANTRY BRIGADE ORDER NO. 6.

(Reference Map Sheet LENS 11: 1/100,000 & Trench Maps)

---

1. Moves and reliefs as notified in Bm/S/R.1 of to-day's date having been changed, moves and reliefs will now take place in accordance with March Table attached.

2. The 9th Machine Gun Company and 173rd Trench Mortar Battery will be withdrawn from D.Sector on the 6th March, 1917.
   Two Sections 9th Machine Gun Coy. and one Section 173rd Trench Mortar Battery will relieve Sections of 137th Infantry Brigade in Z.2 sector.

3. Acknowledge.

A.G. Ford
Major,
Brigade Major,
173rd Infantry Brigade.

Issued to Signals at 11.31pm

Copy No.
1. 2/1st Bn. London Regt.
2. 2/2nd Bn. London Regt.
3. 2/3rd Bn. London Regt.
4. 2/4th Bn. London Regt.
5. 9th Machine Gun Coy.
6. 173rd Light Trench Mortar Battery
7. Staff Captain, 173rd Infantry Brigade.
8. 510 Coy. A.S.C.
9. No. 2 Signal Section.
10. 504 Coy. R.E.
11. 2/1st Field Ambulance
12. S.S.O.
13. A.P.M.
14. C.R.E.
15. G.R.A.
16. A.D.V.S.
17. A.D.M.S.
18. 137th Infantry Brigade.
19. 174th Infantry Brigade.
20. 175th Infantry Brigade.
21. "G", 58th Division
22. "A", 58th Division
23. File
24. (War
25. (Diary.

For information.

SECRET

MARCH TABLE ISSUED WITH 173RD INFANTRY BRIGADE ORDER NO. 6

(Reference Map Sheet LENS 11: 1/100,000 & Trench Maps)

No.	Date March	Unit	From	To	Route	Relieved by	Guides	Remarks
1.	5th	2/1st Lon. Regt.	BELLACOURT & POSTS in Divisional Line.	BAILLEULVAL	BASSEUX	2/11th Lon. Regt.	Of 2/1st Lon. Rgt. for ORCHARD & BURNT FARM POSTS. 1 per Platoon at cross roads BELLACOURT (R.31.a.40.55) at 12 noon.	2/1st London Regt. loss 2 platoons to leave BELLACOURT at 10.30 a.m. 2 platoons 2/1st London Regt. will not vacate posts in Div. Line until relieved.
2.	6th	2 Sections 9th Machine Gun Coy.	D Sector	Z.2 sector	BAILLEULMONT - BERLES.	137th Machine Gun Coy.		As arranged by O.Cs. 9th. 175th & 137th Machine Gun Coys. Remaining 2 sections in billets at GROSVILLE.
3.	6th	Sections 137th Machine Gun Coy.	Z.2 Sector	POMMIER		2 Sections 9th Machine Gun Coy.		As arranged by O.Cs. 9th, and 137th Machine Gun Companies.
4.	6th	1 Section 173rd T.M Battery	D.Sector	Z.2 Sector	BAILLEULMONT - BERLES	175th T.M. Battery.		As arranged by O.Cs. 173rd, 175th & 137th T.M.Batteries. Remaining 1 Section in billets at GROSVILLE.

MARCH TABLE ISSUED WITH 173RD INFANTRY BRIGADE ORDER NO. 16. (Cont'd)

No.	Date March	Unit	From	To	Route	Relieved by	Guides	Remarks
5	6th	137th T.M. Battery	Z.2 Sector	POMMIER		1 Section 173rd T.M. Battery		As arranged by O.Cs. 173rd and 137th T.I. Batteries.
6.	6th	2/9th Lon. Regt.	RIVIERE	D.2 Sector				As arranged by O.Cs. 2/3rd and 2/9th London Regt.
7.	6th	2/3rd Lon. Regt.	D.2 Sector	RIVIERE		2/9th Bn. Lon. Regt.	Of 2/3rd Lon. Regt.	To take over billets vacated 2/9th Lon. Regt.
8.	7th	2/11th Lon. Regt.	BELLACOURT	D.1 Sector			Of 2/2nd Lon. Regt.	As arranged by O.Cs. 2/2nd & 2/11th London Regt.
9.	7th	2/2nd Lon. Regt.	D.1 Sector	Orders will be issued later		2/11th London Regt.		
10.	6th	2/4th Lon. Regt.	Hd.Qtrs. & 2 Cos. BAILLEULVAL & 2 Cos. BASSEUX	HUMBERCAMP		Battalion of 174th Inf. Bde.		To billets. Billeting parties to proceed in advance. 2 Cos. at BASSEUX to move off at 8.30 a.m.
11.	6th	2 Cos. 2/1st Lon. Regt.	BAILLEULVAL	LA CAUCHIE				To billets. For Working Parties commencing 7/3/17.
12.		173rd Brigade Headquarters will remain at BASSEUX.						

MARCH TABLE ISSUED WITH 173RD INFANTRY BRIGADE ORDER NO.8.

No.	Date March	Unit.	From.	To.	Relief of.	Guides.	Remarks.
1.	11th.	Hd.Qrs. & 2/1st Bn. (less 2 Cos)	HUMBERCAMP	POMMIER	-	-	As arranged by C.O's. concerned. Relief to be complete by 10 a.m. Billeting Parties in advance.
2.	11th.	Hd.Qrs. & 2/3rd Bn. (less 2 Cos)	POMMIER	HUMBERCAMP.	-	-	ditto. ditto.
3.	11th	1 Co. 2/1st Bn.	GAUDIEMPRE & GOMBREMETZ.	POMMIER.	-	-	) Special Working Parties.
4.	11th	1 Co. 2/1st Bn.	LA CAUCHIE.	POMMIER. GAUDIEMPRE & GOMBRE ETZ.	-	-	) Relief to take place after
5.	11th	1 Co. 2/3rd Bn.	POMMIER.	-	1 Co. 2/1st Bn.	-	)
6.	11th	1 Co. 2/3rd Bn.	POMMIER	LA CAUCHIE.	1 Co. 2/1st Bn.	-	) work in the afternoon.
7.	12th	2/1st Bn.	POMMIER.	Z.I. SECTOR.	2/4th Bn.	Guides of 2/4th Bn. 1 for Hd.Qrs. and each platoon.	As arranged by C.O's. concerned. Relief to be completed by 12 noon.
8.	~~15~~ 12	2/4th Bn.	Z.I.SECTOR.	POMMIER. to billets vacated by 2/3rd. Bn.	-	-	As arranged by C.Os. concerned. Relief to be completed by 12 noon. Billeting parties in advance.

SECRET  Copy No. 24

173RD INFANTRY BRIGADE ORDER NO. 7.

(Reference Map Sheet LENS 11, 1/100,000 & Trench Map)

6/3/17

1. The 173rd Inf. Bde. will take over Z.1 Sector from the 137th Inf. Bde. to-morrow.
   For this purpose Z.1 Sector will be from the HANNESCAMP - MONCHY Road (inclusive) at E.11.a.9055 to W.28.d.8538 (91 St. exclusive).

2. Moves and reliefs will take place in accordance with March Table attached.

3. The Command of Z.1 Sector will pass from the G.O.C., 137th Infantry Brigade to G.O.C., 173rd Infantry Brigade at 2 p.m. to-morrow, 7th March, 1917.

4. (a) Quartermaster's Stores and Transport Lines of 2/1st, 2/2nd, & 2/3rd Battalions, will remain at BAILLEULMONT.

   (b) Transport Lines of 9th Machine Gun Coy. will remain at BAILLEULMONT.

   (c) Quartermaster's Stores and Transport Lines of 2/4th Battalion will remain at HUMBERCAMP.

5. Acknowledge.

A.G. Ford
Major,
Brigade Major,
173rd Infantry Brigade.

Issued to Signals at 11.30 p.m.

Copy No.
1   2/1st Bn. London Regt.
2   2/2nd Bn. London Regt.
3   2/3rd Bn. London Regt.
4   2/4th Bn. London Regt.
5   9th Machine Gun Coy.
6   173rd Light Trench Mortar Battery.
7   Staff Captain, 173rd Inf. Bde.
8   510 Coy. A.S.C.
9   No. 2 Signal Section
10 504 Coy. R.E.
11 2/1st Field Ambulance)
12 S.S.O.   )
13 A.P.M.   )
14 C.R.E.   )
15 C.R.A.   )
16 A.D.V.S.   ) For information.
17 A.D.M.S.   )
18 137th Infantry Brigade)
19 174th Infantry Brigade)
20 175th Infantry Brigade)
21 "G" 58th Division   )
22 "A" 58th Division   )
23 File
24 (War
25 (Diary

MARCH TABLE ISSUED WITH 173RD INFANTRY BRIGADE ORDER NO. 7

(Reference Map Sheet LENS 11. 1/100,000 and Trench Maps)

No.	Date March	Unit	From	To	Route	Remarks
1.	7th	2/4th Lon. Rgt.	HUMBERCAMP	Z.1 Sector	POMMIER	As arranged by C.Os. concerned.
2.	7th	9th Machine Gun Coy. (less 2 Sections).	GROSVILLE	Z.1 Sector	BASSEUX - BAILLEULVAL Q.31.d.2.7 - V.5.b.20.25 - LA CAUCHIE - POMMIER.	To arrive POMMIER by 12 noon. Billeting parties in advance.
3.	7th	173rd Trench Mortar Battery (less 1 Section)	GROSVILLE	Z.1 Sector	BASSEUX - BAILLEUL-VAL - Q.31.d.2.7 - V.5.b.20.25 - LA CAUCHIE - POMMIER.	To arrive POMMIER by 12 noon. Billeting parties in advance.
4.	7th	Hd. Qtrs. & 2/1st. Lon. Regt. (less 2 Cos.)	BAILLEULVAL	HUMBERCAMP	LA HERLIERE - LA BAZEQUE M	Leave BAILLEULVAL at 10 a.m.
5.	7th	Hd. Qtrs. 173rd Inf. Bde. & No. 2 Sig. Section.	BASSEUX	POMMIER	BAILLEULVAL - Q.31.d.2.7 - V.5.b.20.25 - LA CAUCHIE.	Leave BASSEUX at 10 a.m.

SECRET

MARCH TABLE ISSUED WITH 173RD INFANTRY BRIGADE ORDER NO. 7 (Contd)

No.	Date March	Unit	From	To	Route	Remarks
6.	7th	2/2nd Lon. Regt.	D.1 Sector	BAILLEULVAL	BASSEUX	As arranged by O.Cs. 2/2nd and 2/11th London Regt.
7.	7th	2 Sections 504 Coy. R.E.	----	POMMIER		Under orders 58th Division.
8.	8th	2/3rd. Lon.Regt.	RIVIERE	POMMIER	BASSEUX - BAILLEULVAL - Q.31.d.2.7 - V.5.b.20.25 - LA CAUCHIE.	Time of arrival POMMIER will be notified later.

SECRET.   Copy No. 23

173RD INFANTRY BRIGADE ORDER NO. 8.

(Reference Map Sheet LENS - 11 - 1/100,000)   10/3/17.

1.	Moves and reliefs will take place in accordance with March Table attached.
2.	Quartermaster's Stores and Transport Lines will remain where they are at present.
3.	Acknowledge.

A G Ford
Major,
Brigade Major,
173rd Infantry Brigade.

Issued to Signals at 9/am

Copy No. 1. 2/1st Bn. London Regt.
      2. 2/2nd Bn. London Regt.
      3. 2/3rd Bn. London Regt.
      4. 2/4th Bn. London Regt.
      5. 197th Machine Gun Coy.
      6. 173rd Light Trench Mortar Battery.
      7. Staff Captain, 173rd Inf. Bde.
      8. 510th Coy. A.S.C.
      9. No.2 Signal Section.
   10. 504 Coy. R.E.
   11. 2/1st Field Ambulance.   )
   12. S.S.O.   )
   13. A.P.M.   )
   14. C.R.E.   )
   15. C.R.A.   )   For information.
   16. A.D.V.S.   )
   17. A.D.M.S.   )
   18. 138th Infantry Bde.   )
   19. 174th Infantry Bde.   )
   20. "G" 58th Division.   )
   21. "A" 58th Division.   )
   22. File.
   23. (War
   24. (Diary.
   25. Intelligence Officer.

R.E.	6.	The R.E. and Pioneers will work under instructions issued by 504th Company R.E.
Dress	7.	Marching Order, but that the contents of the Pack (Greatcoats and Hosetins excepted) will be stored under regimental arrangements in sand bags to be drawn for the purpose. Water bottles are to be full of good drinking water, which should not be used without permission from an Officer.
S.A.A.	8. (a)	O.C. will make arrangements for carrying forward ammunition from the present front system of trenches. Os.C. Machine Gun Company and 173rd Trench Mortar Battery will form their own carrying parties for ammunition
Grenades	(b)	2/4th and 2/3rd London Regt. will carry two grenades or rifle grenades in separate pockets of their jackets. These will be collected into dumps on reaching the objective.
Rockets	(c)	Rockets for S.O.S. Signal will be taken forward under Battalion arrangements.
Rations	9.	Rations for 48 hours and an iron ration will be carried on the man.
Periscopes.	10.	Officers if in possession of collapsible periscopes should carry them, and a proportion of box periscopes for each platoon should be taken.
Aid Post. Evacuation of Sick and Wounded.	11.	Arrangements for evacuation of sick or wounded by a Field Ambulance will be notified later.
	12.	Brigade Headquarters will remain at POMMIER
	13.	ACKNOWLEDGE.

A G Ford
Major,
Brigade Major,
173rd Infantry Brigade.

Issued to Signals at 11.30 AM

Copy No.
1. 2/1st Bn. London Regt.
2. 2/2nd Bn. London Regt.
3. 2/3rd Bn. London Regt.
4. 2/4th Bn. London Regt.
5. 173rd Trench Mortar Battery.
6. 197th Machine Gun Company
7. Staff Captain, 173rd Inf. Bde.
8. Intelligence Officer, 173rd Inf. Bde.
9. 510 Company A.S.C.
10. No. 2 Signal Section.
11. 504 Coy. R.E.
12. 2/1st Field Ambulance)
13. S.S.O.)
14. A.P.)
15. C.R.A.)
16. C.R.E.)
17. A.D.M.S.) For information
18. A.D.V.S.)
19. 174th Inf. Bde.)
20. 139th Inf. Bde.)
21. "A", 58th Division)
22. "G", 58th Division)
23. O.C., Right Group, R.A.)
24. Brigade Bombing Officer)
25. Brigade Transport ")
26. File
27. War
28. (Diary

SECRET  Copy No. 24

173RD INFANTRY BRIGADE ORDER NO. 9

(Reference Map Sheet 51c S.E. - 1/20,000)

16/3/17

1. Moves and relief will take place in accordance with March Table attached.

2. Quartermasters' Stores and Transport Lines of Battalions will remain at HUTBERCAMP.

3. ACKNOWLEDGE.

cancelled

A. G. Foord
Major,
Brigade Major,
173rd Infantry Brigade.

Issued to Signals at 1.15 p.m.

Copy No.
1. 2/1st Bn. London Regt.
2. 2/2nd Bn. London Regt.
3. 2/3rd Bn. London Regt.
4. 2/4th Bn. London Regt.
5. 173rd Trench Mortar Battery
6. 197th Machine Gun Company
7. Staff Captain, 173rd Inf. Bde.
8. Intelligence Officer
9. No. 2 Signal Section
10. 510th Coy. A.S.C.
11. 504 Coy. R.E.
12. 2/1st Field Ambulance)
13. S.S.O.)
14. A.P.M.)
15. C.R.E.)
16. C.R.A.)
17. A.D.V.S.) For information.
18. A.D.M.S.)
19. ~~fifth Infantry Brigade~~)
20. 174th Infantry Brigade)
21. "Q" Division)
22. "A" Division)
23. File
24. (War
25. (Diary

MARCH TABLE ISSUED WITH 173RD INFANTRY BRIGADE ORDER NO. 9.

No.	Date March	Unit	From	To	Relief of	Guides	Remarks
1.	18th	2/2nd Lon.Regt.	BAILLEULVAL	BIENVILLERS			To billets. As arranged by O.C., 2/2nd London Regt. Billeting parties in advance.
2.	18th	Hd.Qtrs. & 2/3rd London Regt. (less 2 Cos.)	HUMBERCAMP	LA CAUCHIE			To billets. As arranged by O.C., 2/3rd London Regt. Billeting parties in advance.
3.	18th	2/2nd Lon.Regt.	BIENVILLERS	Trenches Z.1 Sector	2/1st Lon. Regt.	Of 2/1st Bn 1 for Hd. Qtrs.& 1 for each platoon	As arranged by C.O's concerned.
4.	18th	2/1st Lon.Regt.	Trenches Z.1 Sector	HUMBERCAMP			As arranged by C.O's concerned. To billets. Billeting parties in advance.

SECRET (6) Copy No. 28

173RD INFANTRY BRIGADE INSTRUCTIONS NO. 1

(Reference Map Sheets 51c 1/10,000 and 57d 1/20,000)

13/3/17

1. Reference 58th Divisional Instructions No. 1, dated 11th March, 1917, forwarded under this office No. BM/S/27 dated 12th March, 1917:-

    (i) Para. 3 (a) will be carried out by the 2/1st London Regt.

    (ii) Para. 3 (b) and (c) will be carried out by the 2/4th London Regt. After securing the high ground S of LOUCHY by occupying the position named, the Battalion Headquarters 2/4th London Regt. will move to HAMELSCAMPS.

    (iii) As soon as patrols of 2/4th London Regt. have advanced through LOUCHY on the left, 2/3rd London Regt. will relieve the 2/4th London Regt. on the left. Battalion Headquarters 2/3rd London Regt. will move to SHELL STREET at E.10.b.30.84. The Dividing Line between 2/4th and 2/3rd Battalions will be as follows :- E.10.a.0.0. - LOUCHY HILL SOUTH - road to E.5.b.11.30 - TOWER HOUSE - W. side of the road through Point 137 - RUSSART.

2. When the 2/4th London Regt. has occupied the line mentioned in para. 3 (b) (i) the 2/1st London Regt. will be relieved by the 2/4th London Regt. in the right half of Z.1 Sector.

3. When the 2/3rd London Regt. has taken up their portion of the line on the EAST side of LOUCHY, the 2/1st London Regt. will be withdrawn to billets in POMMIER.

4. (a) The O.C., 197th Machine Gun Company will attach One Section (less one gun) to each of the advanced Battalions to move forward with them.

    (b) O.C., 173rd Trench Mortar Battery will likewise attach two Stokes Mortars to each of the advanced Battalions.

    (c) O.C., 197th Machine Gun Company will also carry out the instructions contained in para. 3 (f) of Divisional Instructions No. 1.

Communications.

5. (a) Communications will be arranged according to the Chart which will be issued to all concerned. Two trained Signallers per Battalion will be attached to Brigade Headquarters and for these operations and will report to O.C., No. 2 Signal Section by 8 p.m., 14th March, 1917.

Liaison

    (b) The O.C., 2/4th London Regt. will detail an officer as Liaison Officer to the Brigade on the Right, and the O.C., 2/3rd London Regt. will detail an Officer to the Brigade on the Left. Each to be accompanied by his servant as an Orderly. They will report at 173rd Brigade Headquarters to-morrow, 14th March, 1917, on receipt of these instructions.

    The Os.C., 2/4th and 2/3rd London Regt. will likewise send Liaison Officers or N.C.O's to Battalions on either flank.

SECRET

AMENDMENT TO MARCH TABLE ACCOMPANYING
173RD INFANTRY BRIGADE ORDER NO. 8,
DATED 10/3/17

1. Move 8, Column 2, substitute the "12th" for "13th" as regards the date of relief of 2/4th London Regt.

A.G. Ford

Major,
Brigade Major,
173rd Infantry Brigade.

11/3/17

SECRET   Copy No. ....

173RD INFANTRY BRIGADE ORDER NO. 10

(Reference Map 1/20,000 Sheets 51c, S.E., 57d N.E. & 51b S.W.)

19/3/17

1. The situation at dusk on 18th March, was roughly as follows:-

    175th Infantry Brigade Outpost Line joins 30th Division of VIIth Corps at MADELEINE REDOUBT at N.23.d. and extends as far as cross roads at X.10.b.8.2.

    The Outpost Line of the 2/2nd London Regt. extends Southward from this point East of HENDECOURT to the SUGAR FACTORY at S.24.a., where they join the 138th Infantry Brigade. The Line then runs E.S.E. to MOYENNEVILLE where the VIIth Division carry it on.

2. (a) The 2/1st London Regt. will move off from POMMIER and pass through the outposts of the 2/2nd London Regt. in time to be EAST of the railway running N. and S. through S.3., by 8.30 a.m., 19th March. In this advance care will be taken to maintain touch with the 175th Infantry Brigade on the left and the 138th Infantry Brigade on the right.

    (b) The advance will be continued as far as the Eastern outskirts of BOYELLES and BOIRY BECQUERELLE where an outpost line will be taken up. The point of junction with 175th Infantry Brigade being T.7.a.9.8. Patrols will be pushed forward to the HINDENBURG LINE beyond road CROISILLES - HENIN SUR COJEUL

3. (a) The 2/2nd London Regt. will act in support of the 2/1st London Regt. and will concentrate on HENDECOURT LEZ RANSART when the outpost line in para. 2_b has been taken up.

    (b) The 2/4th London Regt. will remain at RANSART, in Bde. reserve.
    (c) The 2/3rd London Regt. at HUMBERCAMP will be attached to the R.E. for road construction.

    (d) 173rd Infantry Brigade Headquarters will be at RANSART.

    (e) Advanced Dressing Station at RANSART.

4. Reports to POMMIER up to 8 a.m., after that hour to RANSART

5. ACKNOWLEDGE.

A. G. Foord
Major,
Brigade Major,
173rd Infantry Brigade.

Issued to Signals at 1.15 am

Copy No.		Copy No.		
1	2/1st London Regt.	14	A.P.M.	)
2	2/2nd London Regt.	15	C.R.A.	)
3	2/3rd London Regt.	16	C.R.E.	)
4	2/4th London Regt.	17	A.D.V.S.	)
5	173rd Trench Mortar Bty.	18	A.D.M.S.	) For
6	197th Machine Gun Coy.	19	138th Inf.Bde.	) inform-
7	Staff Captain, 173rd Inf.Bde.	20	174th Inf.Bde.	) ation
8	Intelligence Officer	21	175th Inf.Bde.	)
9	No.2 Signal Section	22	B.290 Bde.R.F.A.	)
10	510 Coy. A.S.C.	23	2/3rd H.C.F.A.	)
11	504 Field Coy. R.E.	24	"G" Division	)
12	2/1st Field Ambulance	25	"A" Division	)
13	S.S.O	26	File	

~~March Table issued with~~ 173rd Infantry Brigade Order No.9, d/16/3/17 is cancelled.

17/3/17.

A G Ford
Major,
Brigade Major,
173rd Infantry Brigade.

S E C R E T.

AMENDMENTS AND ADDITIONS TO TABLE ACCOMPANYING 173RD INFANTRY BRIGADE OPERATION ORDER No.11 23/3/17.

No.	Date. MARCH	Unit.	From.	To.	Guides.	Remarks.
7	to read 25th	2/3rd Lon. Regt.	Right Sub-sector in the Line.	BOIRY STE RICTRUDE.		
	Add new Nos. 11 and 12 *g'belete*					
11.	25th	2/3rd Lon.Regt.	BOIRY STE RICTRUDE.	POMMIER		When relieved by 12th Northumberland Fusiliers.
12.	26th	2/2nd Lon.Regt.	BOISLEUX AU MONT.	BIENVILLERS		When relieved by 13th Northumberland Fusiliers.

The 197th Machine Gun Company on relief will proceed to LA BAZIQUE FM on the 25th March and not to POMMIER.

On His Majesty's Service.

Confidential

WAR DIARY

of

HQ 173rd Bde

June — July 1917

Time Table accompanying 173rd Infantry Brigade Operation Order No. 11.

No.	Date March	Unit	From	To	Guides	Remarks
1.	23rd	2/1st London Regt	BOISLEUX AU MONT	POMMIER	—	To billets vacated by 2/5th London Regt. Billeting parties in advance.
2.	23rd	2/5th London Regt	POMMIER	BOISLEUX AU MONT	Of 2/1st London Regt. 1 for Bn. Hd. Qrs. and 1 per Coy. at SUGAR FACTORY S.19.a.12.40.	
3.	24th	2/5th London Regt	BOISLEUX AU MONT	Left sub-sector in the line.	Of 2/2nd London Regt.	Arrangements for this relief to be made between C.Os. concerned.
4.	24th	2/2nd London Regt	Left sub-sector in the line.	BOISLEUX AU MONT		
5.	24th	2/4th London Regt	BOIRY STE RICTRUDE	BIENVILLERS		To billets vacated by 2/6th London Regt. Billeting parties in advance.
6.	24th	2/6th London Regt	BIENVILLERS	BOIRY STE RICTRUDE		
7.	25th	2/3rd London Regt	Right sub-sector in the line.	HUMBERCAMP		To billets vacated by 2/7th London Regt. Billeting parties in advance.
8.	25th	2/6th London Regt	BOIRY STE RICTRUDE	Right sub-sector in the line.	Of 2/3rd London Regt.	Arrangements for this relief to be made between C.Os. concerned.
9.	25th	2/2nd London Regt	BOISLEUX AU MONT	BIENVILLERS		To billets vacated by 2/8th London Regt. Billeting parties in advance.
10.	25th	Hd. Qrs 173rd Inf. Bde + No 2 Sig. Sec.	BOIRY STE RICTRUDE	POMMIER		To billets vacated by Headquarters 174th Inf. Bde + No. 3 Sig. Sect. Billeting party in advance.

197th Machine Gun Coy. will be relieved by 198th Machine Gun Coy. in the arrangements to be made by the C.Os. concerned. On completion the 197th Machine Gun Coy. will move into billets at POMMIER.

SECRET (8) Copy No. 29

173rd Infantry Brigade Operation Order No. 11
(Reference Map 1/20,000 Sheets 51c 3E. and 51 b SW)

23.3.17

1. The 174th Infantry Brigade will relieve the 173rd Infantry Brigade in the line.
   Relief will commence to-day, 23rd March and will be completed by 6 p.m. 25th March.

2. The Command of the front will pass from the G.O.C. 173rd Infantry Brigade to G.O.C. 174th Infantry Brigade at 12 noon 25th March.

3. Moves and reliefs will take place according to attached table.

4. (a) All full boxes of S.A.A. and all Bombs and Rifle Grenades will be handed over to relieving Units.
   (b) All picks and shovels will be handed over to relieving Units.

5. Completion of reliefs will be reported to this Office.

6. 173rd Infantry Brigade, Headquarters, will open at POMMIER, at noon 25th March.

7. ACKNOWLEDGE.

A. G. Ford, Major
173rd Infantry Bde, Brigade Major

Handed to Signals at ... 11.45 p.m.

Copy No.
1. 2/1st London Regt
2. 2/2 "
3. 2/3 "
4. 2/4 "
5. 173rd T.M.B.
6. 197th M.G. Coy.
7. Staff Capt. 173rd I/Bde
8. Intelligence Officer.
9. No. 2 Signal Sect.
10. 510 Coy A.S.C.
11. 504 Coy R.E.
12. 2/1st Fd. Amb. } for
13. S.S.O.   } information
14. A.P.M.
15. C.R.A.
16. C.R.E.
17. A.D.V.S.
18. A.D.M.S.
19. 20th Inf Bde ⎫
20. 70th "   ⎪
21. 174th "   ⎪
22. 175   ⎪ for
23. 290th Bde R.F.A.⎬ information
24. 2/3rd Fd. Amb. ⎪
25. "Q" Divn   ⎪
26. "A" Divn   ⎭
27. File
28. } War Diary
29. }

173RD INFANTRY BRIGADE

DAILY SUMMARY OF INTELLIGENCE

5 p.m., March 17th to 5 p.m., March 20th, 1917

A. OPERATIONS

During the evening of the 16th and up to 3.30 a.m. on the 17th Very Lights were discharged at frequent intervals, and rifle fire was at about its usual volume. Patrols returning to our lines at 3.45 a.m. report no activity in the enemy lines other than rifle fire, and heavy transport was heard continuously in MONCHY from 9.45 to 10.15 p.m. by another patrol.

On the morning of the 17th no activity whatever was observed in the enemy lines, and our patrols found the enemy trenches to be unoccupied in the afternoon of that day. Platoons of the 2/1st London Regt. occupied the enemy's front line and the high ground South of MONCHY by the evening of the 17th, and the 2/4th Battalion were in possession of the trench running from F.1.a.90.40 to E.6.a. 40.70 (Sheet 57D N.E.) in the early hours of the morning of the 18th, being in touch with the 3th South Staffs on their right, and the 2/2nd London Regt. on their left. The latter were holding from E.6.a.40.70 to W.29.d.50.90 (Sheet 51C S.E.) their left being in touch with 175th Brigade. On the morning of the 18th the 2/1st London Regt. was withdrawn to billets in POMMIER.

By 5 p.m. on the 18th the 2/4th London Regt. were holding a line from RABBIT WOOD to X.19.d.05 (Sheet 51C S.E.) where they were in touch with 46th Division on right and 175th Brigade on left.

At 8 p.m. on the 18th the 2/2nd London Regt. moved through the 2/4th Bn. to take up a line from HAMEAU FARM via the right, and at 4 a.m. on the 19th had swung their left round to X.10.b.80.20, where they were in touch with the 175th Brigade, the 1/4th Lincolns having pushed on through ADINFER and HENDECOURT.

At 12 midnight 18/19th the 2/4th London Regt. arrived in RANSART.

At 4.30 a.m. on the 19th the 2/1st London Regt. moved from POMMIER to take up a line from BOIRY BECQUERELLES along the road running thence to ST.LEGER MILL.

At 7.30 a.m. the Headquarters, 173rd Infantry Brigade moved to RANSART.

By 10 a.m. on the 19th the 2/2nd London Regt. had two Companies in ADINFER and two in HENDECOURT, the troops on the right of our Brigade having pushed on, and the 2/1st London Regt. having passed on its way to take up the position allotted to it.

By noon on the 19th the 2/1st London Regt. had taken up a line running from BOIRY BECQUERELLES to BOYELLES, but every attempt to advance from the latter place towards the ST LEGER MILL road, was met by heavy shrapnel fire. In advancing on BOIRY BECQUERELLES they came in contact with the enemy, and came under fire, Machine Gun, at S.12.d.78 One platoon moved across the open and another endeavoured to work round the flank and capture the gun, but the latter was withdrawn.

At 5.30 p.m. on the 19th the 2/1st London Regt. was in touch with the unit on our right at HAMELINCOURT and had its Headquarters at BOISLEUX ST MARC.

At 3.15 p.m. on the 19th the 2/4th London Regt. moved up to the line BOYELLES - ST.LEGER along the railway embankment and cutting, with Headquarters at T.25.a.60.40., being in touch with the 20th Manchesters on the right, and 2/1st Battalion on the left.

On the 20th the Headquarters of the 173rd Infantry Brigade moved from RANSART to BOIRY ST.RICTRUDE, and the 2/2nd London Regt. moved to BOISLEUX AU MONT.

approached BOISLEUX ST. MARC on the 19th. A land-mine at RANSART on the 19th was exploded by a trooper of the South Irish Horse, who was killed by the explosion. Various traps and mines were found unexploded, and with the exception of the one instance recorded above no casualties resulted from any of them. Thorough as was the destruction of everything likely to be of use to us, a number of excellent dug-outs remain untouched, and a quantity of corrugated iron sections for elephant dug-outs were left at the Pioneer Dump near BOYELLES.

C. J. Graham 2/Lt.
INTELLIGENCE OFFICER,
173RD INFANTRY BRIGADE

WAR DIARY of HEADQUARTERS 173rd INFANTRY BRIGADE

INTELLIGENCE SUMMARY.

(Erase heading not required.)

Army Form C. 2118.

Vol 4

Place	Date	Hour	Summary of Events and Information	Remarks and references to Appendices
POMMIER	27/3/17		Nil	A.F. Appendix
	28/-	10am	Left POMMIER	A.F. 1.
		2pm	Arrived POMMERA	A.F.
POMMERA	29/-		Nil	A.F.
	30/-		Nil	A.F.
	31/-		Nil	A.F.
	1/4/17	8am	Left POMMERA	A.F. Appendix 2
BONNIERES		12.15pm	Arrived BONNIERES - Roads in bad state - Occasional snow.	A.F.
	2/4/17	10.20am	Left BONNIERES	A.F. Appendix 3
VAULX		2pm	Arrived VAULX - Frost overnight and at commencement of march - occasional snow during day.	A.F.
	3/4/17	8am	Left VAULX for AUXI LE CHATEAU and were embused at 9.30am for SOUASTRE	A.F.
SOUASTRE		7pm	Arrived SOUASTRE - Roads between AUXI LE CHATEAU and DOULLENS in very bad state - occasional snow	A.F.
		6	Transport left VAULX at 9.30am for OCCOUCHES	
	4/4/17		Transport left OCCOUCHES 5.30am and arrived SOUASTRE 7pm	A.F.
	5/-		Nil	A.F.
	6/-		Nil	A.F.

Army Form C. 2118.

WAR DIARY
INTELLIGENCE SUMMARY.
(Erase heading not required.)

HEADQUARTERS 173rd INFANTRY BDE.

Place	Date	Hour	Summary of Events and Information	Remarks and references to Appendices
SOUASTRE	7/4/17		Nil. Little rain.	A.S.T.
	8/4/17		Boche aeroplane overhead – fired on by our Anti-aircraft guns. – Sunshine – Roads drying rapidly.	A.S.T.
	9/-		Nil. Heavy rain during night turning to snow during day.	A.S.T.
	10/-		Nil.	A.S.T.
	11/-		Nil. Heavy snow. 6" deep.	A.S.T.
	12/-		Nil.	A.S.T.
	13/-	10.0am	Left SOUASTRE	A.S.T. Appendix 4
BUS LES ARTOIS		1.15pm	Arrived BUS LES ARTOIS – Roads in fairly good condition.	A.S.T. Appendix 5
	14/-		Advance party proceeded to ACHIET LE GRAND to lay out Camp.	A.S.T. Appendix 6
	15/-	8.30am	Left BUS LES ARTOIS	A.S.T.
ACHIET LE GRAND Under Canvas. Tent and SHELTERS.		3.40pm	Arrived in Camp. Map Reference Sheet 57d. G.4.a.15.60. – Rain throughout march – Roads in fairly good condition. Transport left BUS LES ARTOIS 9.30pm arrived in Camp 6.30pm	
	16/-		Nil – Rain.	A.S.T.
	17/-		Nil – Rain.	A.S.T.

Army Form C. 2118.

WAR DIARY
—or—
INTELLIGENCE SUMMARY.

HEADQUARTERS 173rd INFANTRY BRIGADE

(Erase heading not required.)

Instructions regarding War Diaries and Intelligence Summaries are contained in F. S. Regs., Part II. and the Staff Manual respectively. Title pages will be prepared in manuscript.

Place	Date	Hour	Summary of Events and Information	Remarks and references to Appendices
CAMP.	18/4/17		Nil – Rain.	A.F.F.
	19/-		2nd Lieut BEAZLEY. SG from GENERAL LIST relieved Lieut. STONE. J.S.W. No.2 Signal Section	A.F.F.
	20/-	8am	Brig. Signal Hunt. GPS. OMG. Left for ENGLAND	A.F.F.
			Lieut-Col BERESFORD. P.W. 2/3rd LONDON REGT assumed temporary command of Brigade.	A.F.F.
	21/-		Brig-Genl. B.C. FREYBERG. V.C. DSO. ROYAL WEST SURREY REGT assumed command of Brigade.	A.F.F.
			Lieut J.S.W. STONE No.2 Signal Section left to join 8th DIV.	
	22/-		weather – fine	A.F.F.
	23/-		weather – fine	A.F.F.
	24/-		weather – fine	A.F.F.
	25/-		weather – fine	A.F.F.
	26/-		weather – fine	A.F.F.

A.G. Ford Major
Bde. Major
for Brig. Genl. Comdg 173rd Inf. Bde.

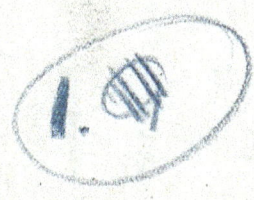

SECRET.   Copy No. 24

173RD INFANTRY BRIGADE OPERATION ORDER NO. 12.

(Reference Map 1/100,000 Sheet LENS 11.)

25/3/17.

1. The Division (less Artillery) will be relieved by the 21st Division on the front ST.LEDGER (exclusive) to COJEUL RIVER (inclusive) N. of BOIRY BECQUERELLE.

2. The Division (less Artillery) on relief will be concentrated in the LUCHEUX area.

3. The relief of the 173rd Infantry Brigade will be completed the 28th March 1917, and will take place according to the attached table.

4. The 2/1st Bn. London Regt. is detailed for work on tramway construction at DAINVILLE; This Battalion will move to DAINVILLE on 28th instant vide attached table.

5. 173rd Infantry Brigade Headquarters will close at POMMIER at 10 a.m. and open at the same time at POMMERA on 28th March.

6. ACKNOWLEDGE.

A. G. Ford
Major,
Brigade Major,
173rd Infantry Brigade.

Issued to Signals at ...11.30 p.m.

Copy No.
1. 2/1st London Regt.   13. S.S.O.
2. 2/2nd London Regt.   14. A.P.M.
3. 2/3rd London Regt.   15. C.R.A.
4. 2/4th London Regt.   16. C.R.E.
5. 173rd Trench Mortar Battery.   17. A.D.V.S.   ) For information
6. Bde. Machine Gun Company.   18. A.D.M.S.
7. Staff Captain, 173rd Inf.Bde.   19. Divl. Train.
8. Intelligence Officer.   20. 174th Inf.Bde.
9. No.2. Signal Section.   21. "G" Division.
10. 510th Coy.A.S.C.   22. "A" Division.
11. 504th Field Coy. R.E.   23. File.
12. 2/1st Field Ambulance.   24.)
    (for information)   25.) War Diary.

SECRET.

MARCH TABLE   173RD INFANTRY BRIGADE.   -   ISSUED WITH OPERATION ORDER NO. 12.

No.	Date. MARCH.	Unit.	From.	To.	Remarks.
1.	25th	2/1st Lon.Regt.	POMMIER	LAHERLIERE	To start at 12 noon.
2.	25th	2/4th Lon.Regt.	BIENVILLERS	LA CAUCHIE	
3.	25th	2/2nd Lon.Regt.	BOISLEUX AU MONT	BIENVILLERS	Via ADINFER AND MONCHY after relief by 13th and 12th NORTHUMBERLAND FUSILIERS respectively.
4.	26th	2/3rd Lon.Regt.	BOIRY STE RICTRUDE	POMMIER	
5.	27th	2/2nd Lon.Regt.	BIENVILLERS	POMMERA	Via HUMBERCAMP - GAUDIEMPRE - MONDICOURT to clear present billets by 11 a.m.
6.	27th	2/3rd Lon.Regt.	POMMIER	POMMERA	
7.	28th	2/1st Lon.Regt.	LAHERLIERE	DAINVILLE	Via main ARRAS Road. To relieve 1 Battn. 64th Inf.Bde. on tramway construction under VII Corps. To clear LAHERLIERE by 10 a.m.
8.	28th	2/4th Lon.Regt.	LA CAUCHIE	GRENAS	Via LAHERLIERE and main ARRAS - ALBERT road. To start at 10 a.m.
9.	28th	173rd Inf.Bde. H.Qrs. Bde.M.G Coy. & 173rd T.M.Battery.	POMMIER	POMMERA	

S E C R E T.   AMENDMENTS AND ADDITIONS TO TABLE ACCOMPANYING 173RD INFANTRY BRIGADE OPERATION ORDER NO. 12 25/3/17

No.	Date. MARCH.	Unit.	From.	To.	Remarks.
3.	To read 26th	2/2rd Lon.Regt.	BOISLEUX AU MONT	BERLES	
5.	To read 27th	H.Qrs. & 2/2nd Lon.Regt. less 2 Coys.	BERLES	POMMERA	Via HUMBERCAMP – GAUDIEMPRE – MONDICOURT to clear present billots by 11 am.
5a.	Insert 27th	2 Coys 2/2nd Lon.Regt.	BERLES	MONDICOURT	
9.	Should not include Brigade Machine Gun Company.				
10.	Add 28th	Bde.M.G.Coy.	POMMIER	GRENAS	

SECRET Copy No. 26.

173RD INFANTRY BRIGADE OPERATION ORDER NO. 13

(Reference Maps 57D and 51C - 1/40,000)

31/3/17

1. The Division, less Artillery and detached troops, will come under the orders of the XIXth Corps at midnight, March 31st/April 1st, 1917, and will move to the BOUQUEMAISON AREA on the 1st April and to the FROHEN LE GRAND area on the 2nd April.

2. The Brigade will move:-

   (a) On 1st April to Area B (BONNIERES - BEAUVOIR - BOUQUEMAISON), in accordance with March Table attached.

   (b) On 2nd April to Area E (BOUFFLERS - SELLANDRE - VAULX - LA NEUVILLE - VITZ VILLEROY) in accordance with orders which will be issued later. Head of column to cross line N and S through T in FORTEL at 10.30 a.m.

   (c) The 2½ Battalions of the Brigade now employed under VIIth Corps will not move.

   (d) First Line Transport will march in rear of their respective Units.

3. 500 yards distance will be maintained in rear of each Battalion.

4. Starting Point to-morrow, 1st April, will be cross roads at B.12.a.60.90 POMMERA.

5. 2/1st Fd. Amb. will detail one Ambulance Wagon to march in rear of each of the 2/3rd and 2/4th Battalions.

6. Billeting parties from all units except 504 Coy. R.E. and 2/1st Field Ambulance will meet the Staff Captain at the MAIRIE, BONNIERES, at 10.30 a.m.

7. ACKNOWLEDGE.

A.G. Foord
Major,
Brigade Major,
173rd Infantry Brigade

Issued to Signals at 1.30pm

Copy No.		Copy No.		
1	2/1st London Regt.	15	A.P.M.	)
2	2/2nd London Regt.	16	C.R.A.	)
3	O i/c Details, 2/2nd London Rgt.	17	C.R.E.	)
		18	A.D.V.S.	)
4	2/3rd London Regt.	19	A.D.M.S.	)
5	2/4th London Regt.	20	Divisional Train	)
6	173rd Trench Mortar Batty.	21	174th Inf. Bde.	) For information
7	214th Machine Gun Coy.	22	175th Inf. Bde.	)
8	Staff Captain, 173rd Inf.Bde.	23	"G" Division	)
9	Intelligence Officer	24	"A" Division	)
10	No. 2 Signal Section	25	File	
11	510 Coy. A.S.C.	26	(War	
12	504 Field Coy. R.E.	27	(Diary	
13	2/1st Field Amb. (For information			
14	S.S.O.			

"For information" applies to copies 1, 2, 3.

MARCH TABLE ACCOMPANYING 173RD INFANTRY BRIGADE ORDER NO. 13 of 31/3/17

No.	Unit	From	To	Time of Passing Starting Point	Route	Remarks
1.	Bde.Hd.Qtrs.	POMMERA	BONNIERES	8. 0 a.m.		Head of the column to pass BOUQUEMAISON Church at 10.45 a.m.
2.	214th M.G. Coy.	Do.	Do.	8. 1 a.m.		
3.	173rd T.M. Batty.	Do.	Do.	8. 3 a.m.		
4.	2/3rd Bn.	Do.	Do.	8. 4 a.m.	L'ESPERANCE - LUCHEUX - BOUQUEMAISON - MON. LEBLOND.	
5.	2/4th Bn. (less 2 Coys.)	GRENAS	BONNIERES	8.14 a.m.		(Details 2/2nd Bn. will march
6.	Details 2/2nd Bn.	MONDICOURT	BONNIERES			(under orders of O.C., 2/4th Bn.
7.	2/1st Fd.Amb.	MONDICOURT	BEAUVOIR	8.27 a.m.		
8.	510 Coy. A.S.C.	GRENAS	BONNIERES	As convenient		
9.	504 Field Coy. R.E.	LUCHEUX	BOUQUEMAISON	At road junction T.22.a.00.05 9.20 a.m.		Will join the column and march 500 yards in rear of 2/4th Bn.

SECRET ③ Copy No. 26

173RD INF. BDE. ORDER NO. 14

(Reference Map LENS 11 - 1/100,000)

1/4/17

1. The Brigade, less the 2½ Battalions now employed under VIIth Corps, will move to-morrow, 2nd April, to the FROHEN LE GRAND Area in accordance with March Table attached.

2. 500 yards distance will be maintained in rear of each Battalion.

3. Starting Point will be road junction ½ mile due S. of the B in BONNIERES.

4. O.C., 2/1st Fd. Amb. will detail one Ambulance Wagon to march in rear of each of the 2/3rd and 2/4th Battalions.

5. ACKNOWLEDGE.

A. G. Foord
Major,
Brigade Major,
173rd Infantry Brigade

Issued to Signals at 8 p.m.

Copy No.
1. 2/1st London Regt. (For information)
2. 2/2nd London Regt. (" ")
3. O i/c Details, 2/2nd London Regt.
4. 2/3rd London Regt.
5. 2/4th London Regt.
6. 173rd Trench Mortar Batty.
7. 214th Machine Gun Co.
8. Staff Captain, 173rd Inf.Bde.
9. Intelligence Officer
10. No. 2 Signal Section.
11. 510 Co. A.S.C.
12. 504 Co. R.E.
13. 2/1st Fd. Amb.
14. S.S.O.   )
15. A.P.M.   )
16. C.R.A.   )
17. C.R.E.   )
18. A.D.V.S.   )
19. A.D.M.S.   ) For information
20. Divisional Train)
21. 174th Inf. Bde.)
22. 175th Inf. Bde.)
23. "G" Division)
24. "A" Division)
25. File
26. (War
27. (Diary

MARCH TABLE ACCOMPANYING 173RD INF.BDE. ORDER NO. 14 of 1/4/17

No.	Unit	From	To	Time of Passing Starting Point	Route	Remarks
1.	Edn. Hd. Qtrs.	BONNIERES	VAULX	10.20 a.m.		(Billeting parties to meet
2.	214 M.G.Co.	Do.	Do.	10.21 a.m.		(Staff Captain at VAULX
3.	173rd T.M.Batty.	Do.	Do.	10.23 a.m.		(Church at 12 noon.
4.	2/3rd Bn.	Do.	GENNE-IVERGNY	10.24 a.m.	VILLERS-L'HÔPITAL - WAVANS - AUXI-LE-CHATEAU	
5.	2/4th Bn. (less 2 Cos.)	Do.	(LE PONCHEL - (VITZ VILLEROY (VILLEROY SUR (AUTHIE	10.34 a.m.		Details 2/2nd Bn. will march under orders of O.C., 2/4th Bn. Billeting party to meet Staff Captain at road junction 400 yards W. of first L in LE PONCHEL at 10.30 a.m.
6.	Details 2/2nd Bn.	Do.	WILLENCOURT			
7.	2/1st Fd.Amb.	BEAUVOIR	VAULX	10.47 a.m.		Billeting party to meet Staff Captain at VAULX Church at 12 noon
8.	510 Co.A.S.C.	BONNIERES	LE PONCHEL La Neuville — 2nd	10.51 a.m.		Billeting party as for No. 5.
9.	504 Fd.Co.R.E.	BOUQUEMAISON	BOUFFLERS — 3rd	---	NEUVILLETTE - BARLY - MEZEROLLES	Head of the Co. to pass the N.E. exit of MEZEROLLES at 10.30 a.m.

SECRET   Copy No. 24

173RD INF. BDE. ORDER NO. 15

(Reference Map Sheet 57D - 1/40,000)

12/4/17

1. (a) The Brigade will be transferred from the Third Army (VIIth Corps) to the Fifth Army (Vth Corps), and will concentrate in the BUS LES ARTOIS – BERTRANCOURT area on the 13th April.

   (b) The Location of Units on the night of 12/13th April being as follows :-

Brigade Headquarters	SOUASTRE
2/1st Bn.	ST AMAND
2/2nd Bn. (less 2 Cos)	BUS LES ARTOIS
2 Cos. 2/2nd Bn.	BIENVILLERS
2/3rd Bn.	SOUASTRE
2/4th Bn.	POMMIER
173rd T.M. Battery	BIENVILLERS
504th Fd. Co. R.E.	MONCHY AU BOIS
510th Co. A.S.C.	GAUDIEMPRE

2. Units will move to-morrow, 13th April, in accordance with March Table attached.

3. Care will be taken that wagons are not overloaded, the roads being in a very bad condition in many places.

4. ACKNOWLEDGE.

A. G. Ford
Major,
Brigade Major,
173rd Infantry Brigade.

Issued to Signals at 11.55 pm

Copy No.
1. 2/1st London Regt.
2. 2/2nd London Regt.
3. O.C. Detachment, 2/2nd London Regt.
4. 2/3rd London Regt.
5. 2/4th London Regt.
6. 173rd Trench Mortar Battery
7. Staff Captain, 173rd Inf. Bde.
8. Intelligence Officer
9. No. 2 Signal Section
10. 510 Co. A.S.C.
11. 504 Co. R.E.
12. 58th Div. Salvage Co.
13. S.S.O.   )
14. A.P.M.   )
15. C.R.E.   )
16. A.D.V.S.   )
17. A.D.M.S.   )
18. Divisional Train) For information
19. 174th Inf. Bde.)
20. 175th Inf. Bde.)
21. "G" Division   )
22. "A" & "Q" Division)
23. File
24. (War
25. (Diary.

MARCH TABLE ACCOMPANYING 173RD INF. BDE. ORDER NO. 15 of 12/4/17

No.	Unit	From	To	Route	Remarks
1.	Hd.Qtrs	SOUASTRE	BUS LES ARTOIS	COUIN - ST LEGER LES AUTHIE - road junction at I.16.b.90.60	To march at 10.0 a.m.
2.	2/1st Bn.	ST AMAND	Do.	SOUASTRE and as in No. 1	To march at 10 a.m.
3.	2 Cos 2/2nd Bn.	BIENVILLERS	Do.	As in No. 2.	To march at 11 a.m.
4.	2/3rd Bn.	SOUASTRE	BERTRANCOURT	As in No. 1	To march at 10 a.m.
5.	2/4th Bn.	POMMIER	BERTRANCOURT	ST AMAND - SOUASTRE and as in No. 1.	Do. do.
6.	58th Div. Salvage Co.	Do.	BUS LES ARTOIS	As in No. 5.	To march under orders of O.C., 2/4th Bn.
7.	504th Fd.Co. R.E.	MONCHY	Do.	BIENVILLERS - SOUASTRE and as in No. 1.	To be clear of BIENVILLERS by 9 a.m.
8.	173rd T.M. Battery	BIENVILLERS	Do.	As in No. 2.	To march at 10 a.m.
9.	510th Co. A.S.C.	GAUDIEMPRE	Do.	As arranged by O.C.	

SECRET.   Copy No......

173rd Inf. Bde. Order No. 16.

Reference Map Sheet 57c 1/40,000.   14/4/17.

---

1. Advance Parties as detailed below under command of Major J.A. MILLER, 2/2nd Bn. London Regt. will proceed to ACHIET LE GRAND to-day 14/4/17 for the purpose of pitching the Brigade Group Camp at G 4 a :-

   Brigade Headquarters. -10 Other Ranks and one G.S. Wagon.
   504th Fd. Co. R.E.   - (Party to be detailed by O.C.
                          (and one vehicle.
   2/1st Bn.   - (Two Platoons and a Party of Pioneers.
                          (3 G.S. Limbered Wagons including one for
                          (tools and one Water Cart.
   2/2nd Bn.   -)Same as for 2/1st Bn.
   2/3rd Bn.   - (Two Platoons and a party of Pioneers.
                          (3 G.S. Limbered Wagons including one for tools.
   2/4th Bn.   -)Same as for 2/3rd Bn.
   510 Co. A.S.C.   - Party to be detailed by O.C. and one
                          vehicle.
   173rd T.M. Battery   - 1 Officer and 25 Other Ranks.

   Parties from each unit will take Cookers or Cooking Utensils as desired.

2. Route. BERTRANCOURT - MAILLY - MAILLET - BEAUCOURT SUR ANCRE - ACHIET LE PETIT - ACHIET LE GRAND.

3. Rations for to-days consumption will be carried. Officer i/c Supplies 173rd Inf. Bde. will arrange to deliver rations for 15th April at the Camp.

4. Tents and Bivouac Shelters will be drawn from Ordance Officer Corps Troops, ACHIET LE GRAND under arrangements to be made by a Staff Officer of the Brigade.

5. Acknowledge.

A.G. Ford
Major,
Brigade Major,
173rd Infantry Brigade.

Issued to Signals at 4.45 AM.

Copy No.
1. Major J.A. Miller, 2/2nd Bn. Lon. Regt.
2.)
3.) 504 Co. R.E.
4. (Copy No.
5.) 173rd T.M.Battery.   17. Staff Captain, 173rd Inf. Bde.
6.)   18. A.D.M.S.
7.) 2/1st London Regt.   19. "G" 58th Division.
8.)   20. "A" & "Q" 58th Division.
9.) 2/2nd London Regt.   21. File.
10.   22. (
11.) 2/3rd London Regt.   23. (War Diary.
12.
13. (2/4th London Regt.
14.)
15.) 510 Coy. A.S.C.
16. (O. i/c Supplies,
     173rd Inf. Bde.

SECRET Copy No. 23.

173RD INF. BDE. ORDER NO. 17.

(Reference Maps Sheets 57D and 57C - 1/40,000)

14/4/17

1. The Brigade with 504th Field Company R.E. and affiliated Train Company, will move to-morrow, 15th April, to camp in G.4.a. near ACHIET-LE-GRAND in accordance with March Table attached.

2. Starting Point will be cross-road BERTRANCOURT J.33.d.15.40.

3. After passing the Starting Point troops will march in file with a distance of 200 yards between each Company and also between the transport of each unit.

4. (a) Transport will be massed in rear of the Brigade and will march in the following order :-

   Brigade Headquarters
   504th Co. R.E.
   2/3rd Bn.
   2/4th Bn.
   2/2nd Bn.
   2/1st Bn.

   (b) One water bucket and one hay net (filled) will be carried on each vehicle. One food in nosebag will be carried on each animal.

5. O.C., 2/1st Bn. will detach one platoon to march in rear of the column to collect stragglers, etc.

6. ACKNOWLEDGE.

L. G. Ford
Major,
Brigade Major.
173rd Infantry Brigade.

Issued to Signals at 4.30 pm.

Copy No.
1. 2/1st London Regt.
2. 2/2nd London Regt.
3. 2/3rd London Regt.
4. 2/4th London Regt.
5. 173rd Trench Mortar Battery
6. Staff Captain, 173rd Inf. Bde.
7. Intelligence Officer
8. No. 2 Signal Section
9. 510 Co. A.S.C.
10. 504 Co. R.E.
11. S.S.O.   )
12. A.P.M.   )
13. C.R.E.   )
14. A.D.V.S.   )
15. A.D.M.S.   )
16. Divisional Train) For information
17. 174th Inf. Bde.)
18. 175th Inf. Bde.)
19. "G" 58th Division)
20. "A" & "Q" 58th Divn.)
21. Bde. Transport Offr.)
22. File
23. (War
24. (Diary

MARCH TABLE ACCOMPANYING 173RD INF. BDE. ORDER NO. 17 of 14/4/17

No.	Unit	From	To	Time of Passing Starting Point.	Route
1.	Bde. Hd. Qtrs.	BUS LES ARTOIS	Camp G.4.a. near ACHIET-LE-GRAND	9. 0 a.m.	MAILLY-MAILLET - AUCHONVILLERS - BEAUCOURT - ACHIET-LE-PETIT.
2.	173rd Trench Mortar Battery	Do.		9. 2 a.m.	
3.	2/3rd En.	BERTRANCOURT		9. 4 a.m.	
4.	2/4th En.	Do.		9.16 a.m.	
5.	2/2nd En.	BUS LES ARTOIS		9.28 a.m.	
6.	2/1st En.	Do.		9.40 a.m.	
7.	504th Fd. Co.	Do.		9.52 a.m.	
8.	510th Co. A.S.C.	Do.		Will march independently under orders of O.C.	

CONFIDENTIAL
****
W A R   D I A R Y
OF
HQ 73rd Inf Bde
From 27/4/17
To 27/5/17

HQ 173 Infy Batt
Vol 3
March 1917

WAR DIARY or INTELLIGENCE SUMMARY

Army Form C. 2118.

Place	Date	Hour	Summary of Events and Information	Remarks and references to Appendices
	16th		Relief of 2/4 by 2/1st 13th in left subsector completed by 2.a.m. At 6 p.m. 3 platoons of 2/1st 13th Captured Bovis Trench E. of U.22 C.44 and consolidated under arrangements made by Maj THOMSON Cmdg.	C app
	17th		Relief of 2/3rd Bn by 2/2 Bn in right subsector completed during night 16/17th.	D app
	18th		Portion of BOVIS TR captured on 16th handed over to a Bn of 174th Inf. Bde	C app
	19th		Quiet day. Enemy Shelly rather less active. Relief by 175 Inf. Bde began	E ① app
	20th		Enemy put down considerable Barrage on our front system in reply to attack on unkapDeved posn of Bovis TR by 174 & 175 Inf Bdes.	F
			Relief by our Troops of N. of BULLECOURT	C app
	21st		174th Bde on our left made unsuccessful attack on unkaptured portion of BOVIS TR. Enemy's retaliatory barrage considerably interfered with relief of our front system by 175th Inf Bde which was eventually	C app
	22/23		Completed by 6.30 a.m. after which Bde Arrangements at BULLECOURT Coy and Shoulder Training and Inspection Kall carried by Coy. Bdes.	C app C app

Signed Brigade Major
173rd Infantry Brigade.

Army Form C. 2118.

Headquarters
173rd Inf. Bde.

WAR DIARY
or
INTELLIGENCE SUMMARY.
(Erase heading not required.)

Instructions regarding War Diaries and Intelligence Summaries are contained in F.S. Regs., Part II. and the Staff Manual respectively. Title pages will be prepared in manuscript.

Place	Date	Hour	Summary of Events and Information	Remarks and references to Appendices
ACHIET LE PETIT	27/4 to 12/4		In Camp at G.4.a (57cNW) Bat. engaged in Training and working parties	(1) AAA
	12/13		Took over Sector F of BULLECOURT from 15th Manch Bat. Relief carried out without casualties. Captd (SO) Bedford Road. Bat. C.F.G. Sheahman M.C. joined Bat. as Bat. Surgeon	(2)
	13th		Enemy shelling very active. Enemy in Victoria.	(2)
	14th		Enemy Artillery very active. Enemy in Trenches about S.P. 10 at which our snipers were observed to be busy. On artillery informed and after an hour	(2) Operation Orders A (2)
	15th		Enemy Artillery very active. At snipper 14/15th and stay conducted after was launched at 3.40am. Attack severely repulsed by heavy gun & MG fire. Enemy effected to punish in about 10 of front trench but home opened by unconquer counter attack. Report B [2/3rd under Lt/Lt BETTESTON] gave valuable assistance in every respect from lodgement he had obtained in front line of 14 Austr. Bat on Report. 7 Bat. Sect.	(3)

OPERATION REPORT 14th to 15th 5/17.

173rd Infantry Brigade

Appendix "A"

Very heavy shelling of front and support lines with H.E. on the night of the 13th was followed by heavy bombardment of our front lines and incessant searching with shrapnel and H.E. of the area S. of Railway in C.4. and 5 throughout the whole day of the 14th.

All Signal communications were broken off by a direct hit on the signal dug-out which killed the personnel and destroyed all instruments.

After a short time the power buzzer also gave out and all communications were made by runner.

At 3.pm on the 14th enemy were reported by 2/4th London Regt. to be massing for attack in U.10.central and U.22.b. at the FACTORY. Our Artillery was put on to them on receipt of the message, with good results. Enemy then increased the heavy shelling of our lines to an intense bombardment. Later an attack appeared to be in progress between 10.30. and 11.30.pm. in BULLECOURT. At about 4.am. 15th Lt. Col. Dann, Comdg., 2/4th Bn. London Regt. reports that enemy was seen advancing from the FACTORY in direction of his right company. S.O.S. was put up and our Artillery at once put up a barrage and the enemy turned and fled affording good enfilade target for Lewis Guns of his left company. The enemy who were assembling in the valley in front of the FACTORY in U.22.b. were kept under heavy shell fire. At about 4.40.am. the enemy were seen advancing at the double towards BULLECOURT which appeared to be the real object of his attack.

Parties of the enemy who advanced against the left Company, 2/4th London Regt. were repulsed. Our barrage was reported as very effective. Lt.Col.BERESFORD, Comdg., 2/3rd London Regt. (right Battalion) reported at 5.15.am. that the situation on his Battalion front line was satisfactory. By Liaison with 54th Australians on his right he learned that the enemy got into about 20 yards of trench but were likely to be ejected as at this time there were 50 men in support line of our right Battalion.

Lt.Col. DANN reports 5.55.am. that the enemy was seen retiring at the double from before BULLECOURT.

At 6.36.am. Major MILLER, 2/2nd Bn. London Regt., Battalion in support, reports from the front line right Battalion that the Germans are massing for attack on the right of the Australian Battalion on our right and requested that Artillery should be put on to them, which was done. Major MILLER reports that they have been asked for assistance, that he was sending 50 men from his support line to the Bn. on his right.

We have lost about 12 of our Lewis Guns, buried and destroyed, also almost all the reserve S.A.A. and bombs in the front line system have been buried or blown to pieces.

The cartage of rations, water, S.A.A. etc., is impossible to keep pace with. I have to send a Battalion into the line with three days rations.

Casualties are approximately 300 but it is impossible to form an estimate with any degree of accuracy.

Sd. C.E.SHEARMAN, Captain,
Brigade Major,
173rd Infantry Brigade.

15-5-17.

173rd Infantry Brigade

DAILY INTELLIGENCE SUMMARY

Period 24 hours 9.am. 15th to 9.am. 16th May.

In continuation of the attacks carried out by the enemy on the night of the 14th and early morning of the 15th the enemy were seen by our right Battalion to be advancing over the ridge at about U.23.a.5.8. at 3.15.am. 15th.

Our Artillery barrage cut them up but a number of them succeeded in passing it and attempted to rush the trench. Only two men succeeded in effecting an entrance into our lines and these started bombing and put a Lewis Gun out of action. They were however quickly disposed of. The enemy casualties were severe.

The Unit on our right was attacked at the same time and the enemy succeeded in effecting a lodgement in some 39 yards of their front line, but were ejected by a counter attack. Our right Battalion was able to render assistance in beating off the attack on the left of the Unit on our right, by counterattacking the enemy across the open, and our left Battalion who were not attacked raked the enemy with flanking fire from Lewis Guns.

The chief feature of the two counter attacks was the extreme intensity of the enemy barrage which lasted from 2.pm. 14th till 3.45.am. the 15th and reduced the trench to a string of shell holes in which it is almost impossible to distinguish the original line in any point.

After the failure of the second attack the enemy's barrage died down and was succeeded by a quiet morning.

B. INTELLIGENCE - MOVEMENT. Small parties of men move continually between HENDECOURT and HENDECOURT CHATEAU also between HENDECOURT and FACTORY in U.28.b. Four horsed wagons are also seen moving along road from U.12.c.0.6. to U.12.a.9.0. usually in the afternoon. The activity of our Snipers prevents the enemy from showing himself freely within range. Lewis Gun of 2/4th however dispersed a party of about 20. at U.22.b. causing some casualties.
IDENTIFICATIONS. On the morning of the 14th the 2/4th Bn. Killed 9 and captured 3 men of the 9th Grenadier Regt., 3rd Guard Division, who were endeavouring to re-establish post at U.22.d.1.3. These men were subsequently killed by their own shell fire when they were being brought down. A wounded prisoner of the LEHR Regt. was taken by our right Battalion in the attack of the 15th and our patrols on the morning of the 16th took prisoners, 1 Officer and 6 Other Ranks of the 9th Grenadier and the LEHR Regiment.
SIGNALS. Flags were taken to-day intended apparently for use to indicate position of troops in event of gaining a footing in our lines. A large number of red rockets which burst into two floating stars are sent up if our fire is in any way increased.
AERIAL ACTIVITY. Our Planes have been seen flying low over BULLECOURT, but the enemy planes are seldom seen over our lines.
GENERAL. Five Machine Guns have so far (17-5-17), been captured by 173rd Infantry Brigade.

Sd. C.J.GRAHAM. 2/Lieut.
I.O., 173rd Infantry Brigade.
for Brigade Major.

173rd Infantry Brigade.

DAILY SUMMARY OF INTELLIGENCE.

Period 24 hours 9 a.m. 16th to 9 a.m. 17th May.

A. OPERATIONS. Following the unsuccessful attacks on the 15th the enemy was inactive throughout the day of the 16th. Until midday their Artillery fire was practically nil. It revived slightly in the afternoon and a few rounds of shrapnel were put over the railway embankment (Support Bn.) and few H.E. on to our reserve battalion whose dugouts were damaged.

At 6 a.m. our Artillery barrage round the factory in preparation of our attack on BOVIS TRENCH caught the enemy who were reported massing for attack and dispersed them. Three platoons of the 2/1st Bn. took possession of BOVIS TRENCH from U.22.d.0.4. to U.22.c.40.45. by an attack in two waves. The attack met with opposition but we suffered only 5 casualties wounded and took a few prisoners and a machine gun.

Enemy snipers were very active all day but M.G. fire was nil except during our attack on BOVIS TRENCH. Two of his snipers were hit near the factory by our men and a third was hit by us to our right flank.

The portion of BOVIS TRENCH captured was consolidated and is strongly held and we are in touch with the 2/8th London Regt. on our left.

The enemy attitude on the night 15/16 led us to think a retirement probable and patrols were pushed out on the night and morning of the 15/16th who found the trench S. of RIENCOURT held in some strength and also the FACTORY in U.22.B. with snipers and M.Gs. covering the front. An enemy dug-out visited near the front of our left company on the night of the 15th was found to contain some 25 dead and 4 or 5 wounded Germans who had been there for some days. They belonged to the 9th Grenadier and LEHR Regiment.

A patrol of our left battalion brought in one wounded prisoner of the 9th Grenadier Regt. and another patrol brought in a German Officer and 3 privates of the LEHR Regt. wounded in the attack of the 15th. A patrol of our right battalion brought in 2 unwounded and 4 wounded prisoners of the FUSILIER REGT., 3rd GUARD DIV. and 2 men of this regiment were challenged by a sentry of our support battalion infront of the railway embankment. No answer was returned and one man was shot and the other surrendered and was brought in. They had apparently been hiding in shell holes since the attack of the 15th and thought they were approaching their own lines.

The enemy put down a barrage on our support lines from 6.30 to 8.30 p.m. and the sunken road (Reserve Bn.) in C.9.d. was heavily shelled with gas shells for about 15 minutes which did no damage owing to the heavy rain.

After the lift of our barrage during our attack on BOVIS TRENCH the enemy were seen to leave trench in U.17.b.1.5. and bolt for HENDICOURT.

When BOVIS TRENCH had been consolidated patrols investigated sunken road in U.22.d. and found it occupied by the enemy. The light railway at U.23.a.20.30. was also found to be occupied and snipers opened fire on patrols from both points. The enemy appeared extremely nervous and his shooting was bad. The Brigade on our left reported the complete capture and mopping up of BULLECOURT.

SECRET   Copy No. ....

173RD INFANTRY BRIGADE OPERATION ORDER NO. 19

(Reference Map Sheet 57C N.W. 1/20,000)

19/5/17

1. The Brigade will be relieved in the line by 175th Infantry Brigade and will move to the rear area in accordance with attached March Table (Appendix A).

2. The relief will start at 10 p.m., 19th May and will be completed by 5 a.m., 21st May, being divided into two phases as follows :-

   (a) Relief of 2/4th and 2/3rd Bns. in Reserve and Support respectively on night of 19/20th May by two Battalions of 175th Infantry Brigade.

   (b) Relief of 2/1st and 2/2nd Bns. in front system on night of 20/21st May by the Battalion of 175th Infantry Brigade which relieved 2/4th Bn. as in (a) and the substitution in reserve of another battalion of 175th Infantry Brigade.

   The remaining battalion of 175th Infantry Brigade will eventually be accommodated near VRAUCOURT.

3. The relief of 206th Machine Gun Coy. by 214 Machine Gun Coy. and of 173rd Light Trench Mortar Battery by 175th Light Trench Mortar Battery will be carried out by arrangements made direct between the O.C. Companies and Batteries respectively.
   One man per Gun and one Officer per Company and Battery will remain in position for 24 hours after the remainder of their units have been relieved.

4. Guides will report in accordance with attached table (Appendix B).

5. All trench stores, including petrol tins, as many as possible of which will be full, will be handed over on relief and a receipt obtained. These receipts will be forwarded to Brigade Headquarters by noon, May 23rd. Empty petrol tins will be collected under arrangements to be made by Brigade Bombing Officer and dumped at Advanced Brigade Headquarters in Sunken Road.

6. Command of the section will pass to G.O.C., 175th Infantry Brigade when relief is complete.

7. ACKNOWLEDGE.

                                               C.G.SHEARMAN, Captain,
                                                    Brigade Major,
                                                173rd Infantry Brigade.

Copy No.

Copy No.
1. 2/1st Lon. Regt.
2. 2/2nd Lon. Regt.
3. 2/3rd Lon. Regt.
4. 2/4th Lon. Regt.
5. 173rd T.M. Battery
6. 206th M.G.Co.
7. "G", 58th Division
8. "A" & "Q" 58th Division
9. 510 H.T.Co., A.S.C.
10. G.O.C.
11. Staff Captain
12. Brigade Signalling Officer
13. War Diary
14. Do.
15. File
16. 504 Field Co. R.E.
17. 2/1st Field Ambulance
18. C.R.A.
19. C.R.E.
20. A.D.M.S.
21. 14th Australian Infantry Brigade
22. 174th Infantry Brigade
23. 175th Infantry Brigade

MARCH TABLE - APPENDIX A

Date	Unit	Time of Starting	From	To	Route	Remarks
Night 19/20th May	2/4th Bn.	On completion of Coy. reliefs	Reserve Line	Bivouac at H.12.central	C.14.central - cross roads B.24.d. - G.12.central	Guides (1 per Coy. and 1 per Bn. Hd.Qtrs.) for Bivouac will meet Coys. at cross roads H.3.c.3.1
Do.	2/3rd Bn.	Do.	Support Line	Do.	Do.	Do.
Night 20/21st May	2/1st Bn.	Do.	Front system	Do.	Do.	Do.
Do.	2/2nd Bn.	Do.	Do.	Do.	Do.	Do.
20th May	2/4th Bn.	Battalion arrangements but not later than 3 p.m.	Bivouac	Camp at G..12.c.& d.	Track B.29.central - SAPIGNIES	Usual intervals will be kept between Companies and Battalions - 2/3rd Bn. will lead.
20th May	2/3rd Bn.	Do.	Do.	Do.	Do.	
21st May	2/1st Bn.	Do.	Do.	Do.	Do.	Usual intervals will be kept between Companies and Battalions - 2/1st Bn. will lead.
21st Bn.	2/2nd Bn.	Do.	Do.	Do.	Do.	

Instructions for move of transport of 173rd L.T.M.Battery and 203th Machine Gun Co. will be issued separately.
Brigade Headquarters will move direct to Camp at G..12.c.& d. on completion of relief.
Battalion 1st Line transport will accompany units on the march.

APPENDIX B

Battalion	No. of Guides	To report at	Time	Remarks
2/3rd	1 per platoon, and 2 per Bn. Hd.Qtrs.	Advanced Bde.Hd.Qtrs Sunken road C.9.d.	9.45 p.m.	
2/4th	Do. do.	Do.	10.45 p.m.	
2/1st	2 per Coy. and 2 per Bn. Hd.Qtrs.	Do.	9.45 p.m.	
2/2nd	Do. do.	Do.	10.45 p.m.	

173rd Infantry Brigade.

Daily Summary of Intelligence.   Period 24 hours ending 9 am 19/5/17.

A.   Operations.- There has been no change in the situation except that an enemy relief has, so far as indications show, taken place opposite our Brigade Sector as appears in attached Map and Report.   Intermittent but fairly heavy shelling of our Support Lines takes place and the active Batteries appear to be located in the RIENCOURT GROUP chiefly.   An aeroplane shoot resulted in some very good shooting on the part of the enemy who secured direct hits on two guns.   Aeroplane activity has revived generally after two days during which no planes were seen, 7 enemy machines flew over our trenches and fired on our men who engaged them with L.G and M.G fire.   They arrived at 7-45 pm and remained over our lines for ¾ of an hour, flying low.

173rd Infantry Brigade.

Daily Summary of Intelligence. Period 24 hours ending 9 am
20/5/17.

A. Operations.- The situation is unchanged. The enemy's artillery shelled on our front and support lines heavily yesterday morning from the direction of QUEANT. On our artillery retaliating the enemy ceased to fire. During the afternoon the enemy artillery was quiet but was again active on our front line system from 9 pm onwards. At 5-25 am the enemy put down a barrage on our Sector chiefly on our front line of left Sub-Sector and on the whole of the Support Line. The barrage lasted till 6-30 am when it died down. During the barrage the following bearings were taken from U.22.d.85.05 at 3 Batteries firing "Whizzbangs" and two Batteries firing heavy.

"Whizzbangs"	Firing from bearing of.	On
"	40°	Front line our Sector.
"	47°	Guns.
"	51°	Front line our Sector.
Heavies.	94°	Guns.
"	65°	Guns.

Our artillery during the morning retaliated on enemy's lines and Villages, and effectively shelled the sniping posts located in the Sunken Road U.22.a & c., and Trees on S & E edge of RIENCOURT. During the afternoon they fired on the important Dug-outs located at U.17.d.40.50 and U.12.c.40.20 and two direct

173rd Infantry Brigade.

Daily Summary of Intelligence.   Period 15 hours ending 12 midnight - 20/21st 5/17.

A.	Operations.- The situation remains unchanged. Occasional light shelling of our trenches from the RIENCOURT GROUP and considerable aeroplane activity. Enemy snipers activity revived, but our men have the ascendancy and claim several hits. Consequently the enemy is careful of exposing himself but sufficient movement has been observed to make it certain he is holding his line as usual and no signs of withdrawal have so far been observed from our O.Ps. The enemy is not however holding his front lines in any great strength as far as can be judged, and the men holding the positions under close observation from our O.Ps would naturally be the last to go.

At about 7-30 pm a moderate barrage of our front line system and railway embankment was met by N.F. on the RIENCOURT GROUP and immediately abated.

FILE No. G.12.

Sub-Nos. 82.-

SUBJECT. Minor Operations.

Sub-head. Raid on Plush Trench

by 173rd Inf. Bde. - 58th Division.

night July 28/29, 1917.

XVII Corps.

Referred to	Date.	Referred to	Date.

58th Div. No.G.S.844/25.   IV Corps No.G.S.17/1.

GENERAL STAFF
THIRD ARMY

No. G/12/82
Date 2-8-17

Third Army.
~~III Corps.~~

    Herewith a report on raid carried out by 173rd Infantry Brigade on the night of July 28th/29th on PLUSH Trench.

    The trench had been subjected to a fairly heavy bombardment by 6" Howitzers for two or three days in order to cut the wire

    Up to that time it had been continuously occupied.

    A copy of the report is being sent to III Corps.

H.Q., IV Corps,　　　　　　　　　　Lieutenant General,
1st August, 1917.　　　　　　　　　Commanding IV Corps.
======================　　　　　　 ======================
PH.

IV Corps.

Reference Third Army No. G.14/134 dated 14th June, 1917, herewith reports on raid carried out by this Division on night of 28/29th July, 1917.

Reference Map. Sheet 57 C. S.E. 1/20,000.

(a) Name of Commander ..... Capt. S.G.LIPSCOMB,
     O.C. A Coy. 2/3rd London Rgt.

(b) Troops employed .... 2 Officers 38 O.R.

(c) Objective............... PLUSH TRENCH R.1.d.6.1. -
     R.1.d.1.3.

(d) Short narrative of events :-

The Raiders took up their position in the line at R.7.b.1.6. They crossed "No Man's Land" in two parties, a right and a left party under a machine-gun and Artillery barrage. No difficulty was met with until the Hun wire was reached. There was no enemy artillery nor M.G.fire nor at any time during the raid were lights sent up by the enemy from PLUSH TRENCH. At right and left points of entry, the wire had not been completely cut, at both points the crossing proved a difficult task, and blankets had to be used. On the right several coils of wire were found as if a working party had been repairing the wire.
     Owing to the delay in crossing the wire, the right party had not sufficient time to enter the Trench. 2/Lieut. L.F.C.Arnold got to the parapet with an N.C.O. and 3 men but by this time the return signal had been sent up and in view of the returning barrage, he did not deem it advisable to make an entry. The left party reached and entered the trench. A reconnoitring party under Cpl. H.V.Wayt, proceeded along it for 250 yards to the right. The trench was found to be unoccupied. The return to our line was effected without incident.
     At 1.10 a.m. after the raiders had safely returned, the enemy retaliated on our support line and ASHE ALLEY and swept "No Man's Land" with M.G. fire and heavy minenwerfer.
     By 1.45 a.m. situation was again normal.

(e) Result........ The following information about the enemy trench was obtained :-

Trench is of an average depth of 6 feet, of uneven floor and unrevetted. A M.G. emplacement was found at R.1.d.30.15. midway between two island traverses shewn in Aeroplane Map 3L275. At R.1.d.15.20. approx. there is an emplacement about 8' x 5'6" x 5'6" deep, with a well bottom.

             CROSS SECTION.   PLAN.

     Nothing was found inside it to indicate the use to which it is put. No dug-outs were found.

- 2 -

(f) Prisoners and war material captured ..... Nil.

(g) Approximate casualties......... 2 slightly wounded.

(h) General Remarks .... From the information gained by the raid, the position of a M.G. which had been firing from about that locality has been confirmed.

(i) Lessons drawn from the operation for future guidance.
The use of tapes to serve as guides to the parties for their return journey proved very valuable, especially so in getting back the two casualties.

[signature] Lt Col.

for Major-General,
Commanding 58th (London) Division.

30th July, 1917.

SECRET.

173rd Infantry Brigade Order No. 18.
Reference Maps 1/20,000
Sheets 51B.S.W., 57C. N.W.

Copy No. 13.

11.5.17.

1. The Brigade will take over the front from U.23.c.8.0 to U.28.a.8.8., at present held by the 15th Australian Infantry Brigade, 5th Australian Division, on the night 12/13th May.
Relief to be complete by 5 a.m. 13th May.

2. On completion of the relief, the Brigade will come under the orders of the 5th Australian Division until 7 a.m. 13th May, at which hour the command of the front mentioned in para 1 will be transferred to V Corps, and the Brigade will come under the orders of the 7th Division.

3. The Brigade will move in accordance with the attached March Table.

4. Starting Point will be Brigade Headquarters G.4.a.15.60.

5. The Section of front to be taken over is sub divided into two by a line running through U.23.c.05.35. - U.22.d.9.0. - U.28.d.3.8.

   The Right Sub-section to be known as No.1 will be taken over by 2/3rd Bn.
   The Left sub-section to be known as No.2 will be taken over by 2/4th Bn.
   The Support sub-section to be known as No.3 will be taken over by 2/2nd Bn.
   The Reserve sub-section to be known as No.4 will be taken over by 2/1st Bn.

6. Brigade Headquarters will close at G.4.a.15.60. at 12 noon on 12th May and will re-open at H.6.a. at 4 p.m. till 8 p.m. and will re-open at C.5.a.3.3. at 10 p.m.

7. Acknowledge.

Issued to Signals at 11.45 p.m.

A.G. Ford
Major,
Brigade Major,
173rd Infantry Brigade.

Copy No.
1. 2/1st Bn. London Regt.
2. 2/2nd Bn. London Regt.
3. 2/3rd Bn. London Regt.
4. 2/4th Bn. London Regt.
5. 173rd Light Trench Mortar Batty.
6. 206th Machine Gun Company.
7. "G" 58th Division.
8. "Q" 58th Division.
9. 510th Co. A.S.C.
10. G.O.C.
11. Staff Captain.
12. Brigade Signalling Officer.
13.) War
14.) Diary.
15. File.
16. 504th Fd. Co. R.E.
17. 2/1st Fld Ambce.
18. C.R.E.
19. A.D.M.S.
20. C.R.A.
21. 15th Australian Inf. Bde.
22. 5th Australian Division.

MARCH TABLE ACCOMPANYING 173RD INFANTRY BDE. ORDER NO. 18 of 11/5/17.

No.	Unit	From	To	Pass Starting Point at	Route	Remarks
1.	Bde. Hd.Qtrs. less Signal Section	Camp	H.6.a.	12 noon	Infantry track from G.4.o.6.4 - SAPIGNIES - H.6.a.	The Brigade will halt at H.6.a. until nightfall. Units will then move off to their respective sub-sections in the same order of march. Leading Battalion to start at 8.15 p.m., but will not cross VAUX ridge by day-light.
2.	2/4th Bn.	"	"	12.3 p.m.	"	
3.	2/3rd Bn.	"	"	12.19 p.m.	"	
4.	2/2nd Bn.	"	"	12.38 p.m.	"	
5.	2/1st Bn.	"	"	12.57 p.m.	"	
6.	206th M.G.Co. 173rd T.M.Batty. Signal Section	"	"	Will march independently	"	
7.	1st Line Transport (less Cookers & Water Carts).	"	H.12	10 a.m.	Route as ordered by Brigade Transport Officer.	Cookers and Water Carts will march as arranged by Brigade Transport Officer, starting not later than 1.30 a.m.

Confidential

On His Majesty's Service.

Officer i/c
War Diaries,
A.G's Office
Base

184 TUNNELLING COY, ROYAL ENGINEERS
No. 7/2033
Date 6.4.17

S E C R E T.

ORIGINAL ADMINISTRATIVE INSTRUCTIONS ISSUED WITH OPERATION
ORDER NO. 25 STANDS.

173RD INFANTRY BRIGADE.

ADDENDA TO ADMINISTRATIVE INSTRUCTIONS No.6.
Ref. Operation Order No. 30.

RATIONS & WATER.

Rations and Water for comsumption on June 16th for the Companies of the 2/1st; 2/2nd; 2/3rd and 2/4th Bn. London Regts. established in the HINDENBURG Front Line will be carried to Coy. H.Q. in that line by Carrying Parties of the 174th Infantry Brigade (10 per Company).
O.C. Companies will arrange to send 1 guide per Company to U.13.c.5.2.

Rations and Water for the Company of the 2/8th Bn. London Regt. will be delivered to Bn. Hd. Qtrs. and then carried forward to Company Headquarters under arrangements to be made by O.C. 2/8th Bn. London Regt.

Rations will be sand-bagged at Transport Lines of Battalions concerned and will be taken by 1st Line Transport to U.13.c.5.2. except rations for 2/8th Bn. London Regt.

Sandbags should be clearly marked shewing Battalion and Company by a large letter - 2/2nd Bn. "A". - 2/4th Bn. "C".

1st Line Transport, Coy. Q.M.S., Carrying Parties and Guides will be at U.13.c.5.2. at 10 p.m. 15th inst. and report to Staff Captain.

H.H. Ganaway
Captain,
Staff Captain,
173rd Infantry Brigade.

June 14th 1917.

Copies to all recipients of Operation Order No.30.

S E C R E T.

To all concerned.

Reference Para.17 173rd Brigade Order No:30.

Delete Sub-para referring to parachute lights and substitute:-

"On S.O.S. Signal being made our Guns will place protective barrage on and 50 yards in front of HINDENBURG SUPPORT LINE. This barrage will continue at varying rates of fire for 15 minutes. It will then cease, unless a further S.O.S. Signal is made when it will recommence and continue for another 15 Minutes."

C.E.Shearman Captain,
Brigade Major,
173rd Infantry Brigade.

14/ /17.

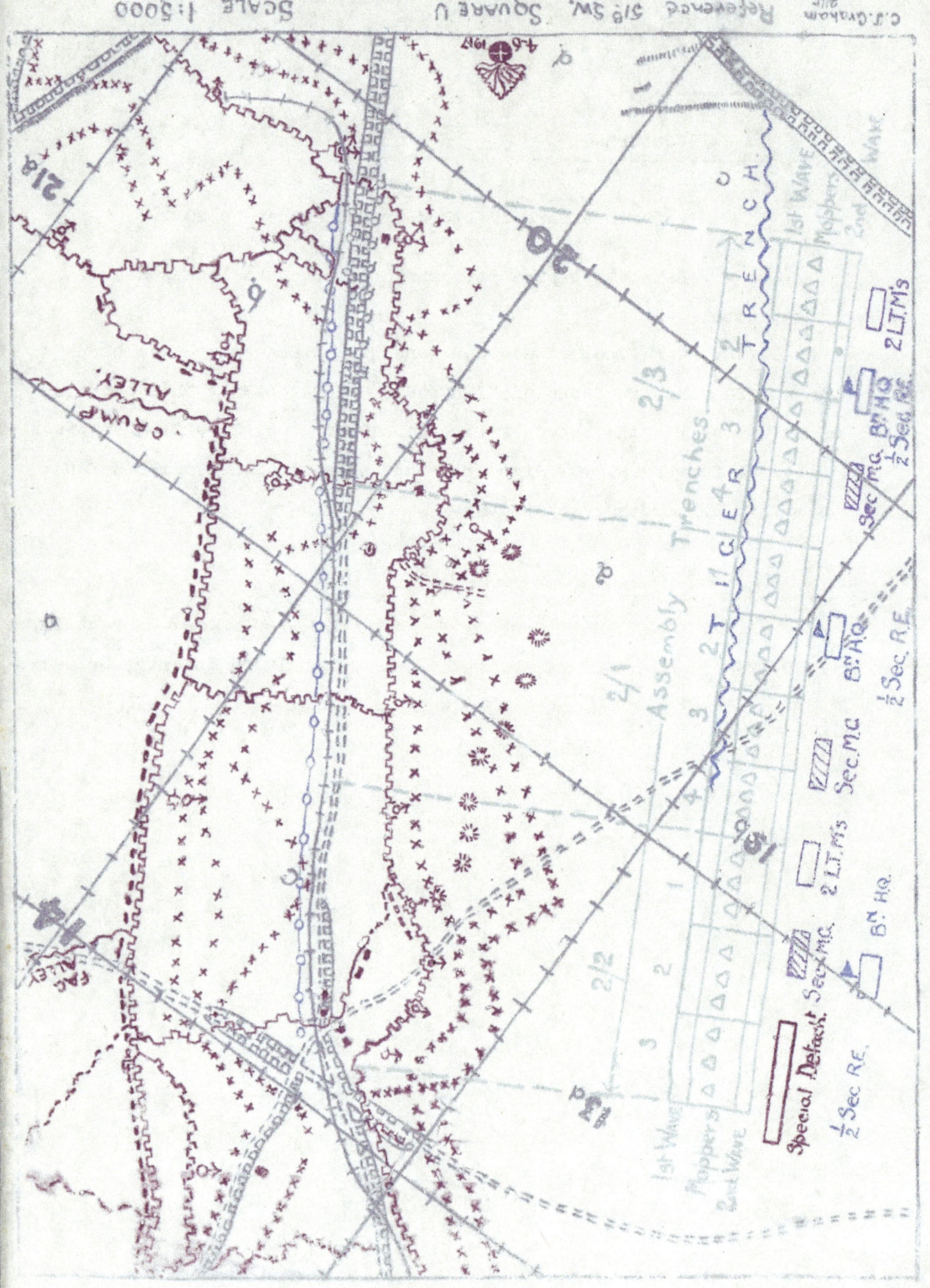

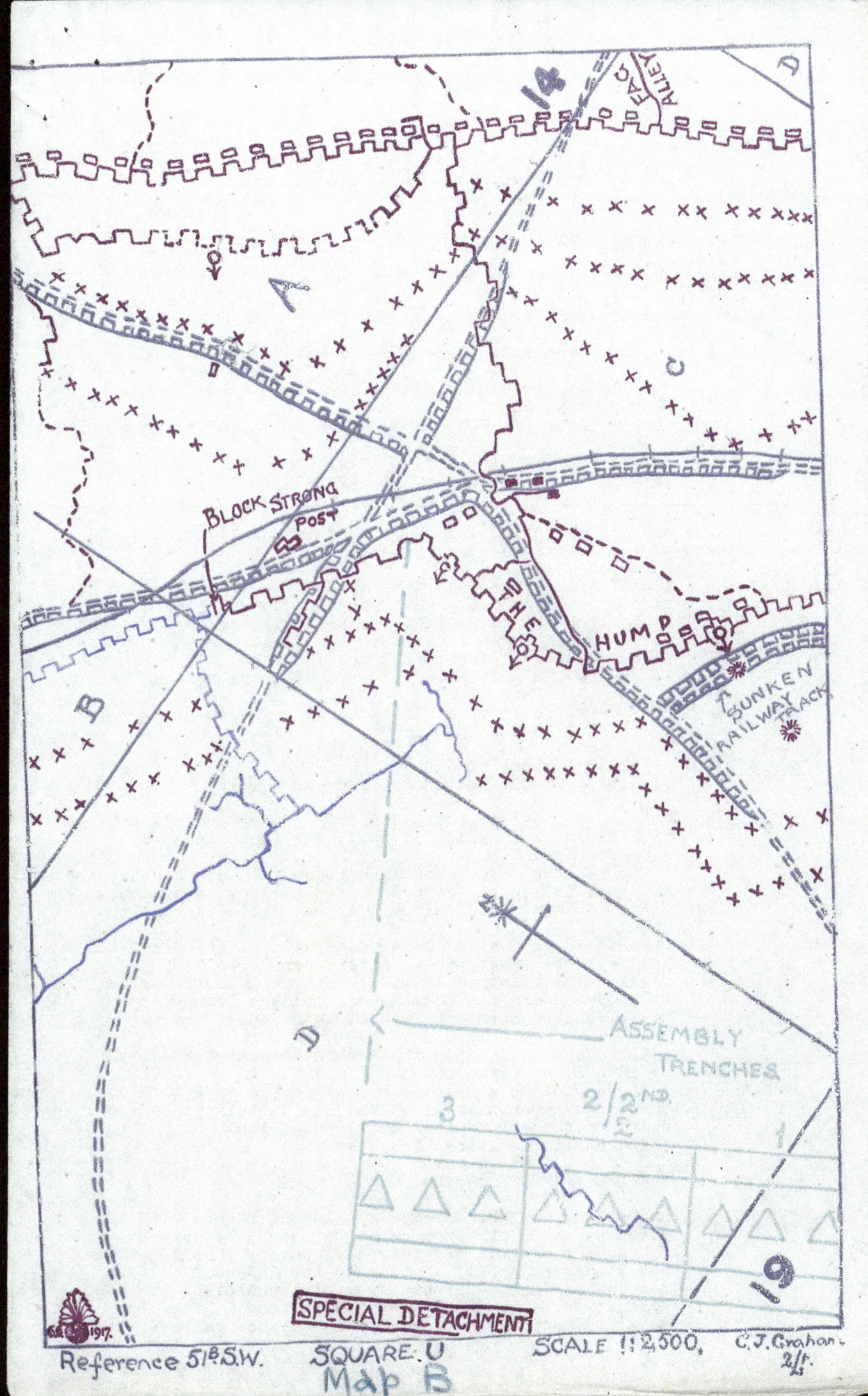

Appendix L.

SECRET   Copy No 21.

173RD INFANTRY BRIGADE OPERATION ORDER NO. 30

14th June, 1917

Reference attached maps :- BULLECOURT - 1/10,000 - 10 per Bn.
CHERISY 1/10,000.
and Operation
Map -   A. Assembly Areas &   1 to each Bn. to be issued
           objectives, 1/5,000   -   later.

        B. HUMP Position 1/2,500   - 250 to 2/2nd Bn. Lon.Regt.
                                   -   10 to 2/4th Lon.Regt.

        C. KNUCKLE Position
                         1/1,250   - A few to 2/3rd and 2/1st Lon.Rgt.

Report Map. 1. General Map   - 100 to each Bn.
            2. Pigeon Map   -   25 to each Bn.

173rd Infantry Brigade Operation Order No. 25 dated 8th June, together with amendments dated 10th June, are cancelled.

1. **PLAN.** 173rd Infantry Brigade will attack the HINDENBURG Front Line on 15th June. ZERO hour will be notified later.
   The troops on our Right and Left will co-operate with rifle, machine gun, and Lewis Gun fire.
   The objects of the attack are :-
   (a) To gain ground and to kill and harass the enemy.
   (b) To improve our tactical position.
   (c) To take prisoners.

2. **OBJECTIVES.** HINDENBURG Front Line from the MEBUS at U.20.b.52.13 to U.14.a.05.05. and cross roads in U.14.c.

3. **ASSEMBLY Areas.** Units will move to their Assembly Areas by dark, and will be in their allotted positions (see Map A) by - 30 minutes.
   The greatest care should be taken to avoid unnecessary movement and noise forward of the Railway Embankment.
   All movement into Assembly Areas will be across the open.
   To avoid confusion guide tapes will be laid from the Railway Embankment by Battalions concerned.
   All units allotted to either of the Assembly Areas will come under the Command of Officers Commanding Battalions concerned by 9 p.m. 14th June.

4. **ADVANCED BRIGADE HEAD-QUARTERS.** Will be established in the Sunken Road at T.30.c.3.9 by 10 p.m. on 14th June.
   There will be a Brigade Report Centre at U.19.b.9.2. This Report Centre will be used as Battalion Headquarters for Centre assaulting Battalion.
   There will be Runner Posts at
   (a) U.25.a.75.50
   (b) T.24.d.8.2

5. **TIME-TABLE OF ATTACK.** The attack will be carried out in accordance with attached table of barrages to be issued later.
   It must be clearly understood, however, that the times published are merely a guide to the infantry and are not orders for the exact times of assaults. It is of vital importance that the infantry should keep close up to the artillery barrage, and advance whenever it lifts.

SECRET   Appendix M.   Copy No. 23

~~See Amended order~~

173RD INFANTRY BRIGADE

Operation Order No. 25.

8th June, 1917.

Reference attached Maps:— BULLECOURT — 1/10,000
CHERISY. 1/10,000   - 10 per Battalion.
and Operation
Map.   A. Assembly Areas and
           Objectives, 1/5,000   - 300 to each Battalion.
        B. Hump Position, 1/2,500   - 250 to 2/2nd London Regt.
        C. Knuckle Position
           1/1,250   - A few to 2/3rd and 2/1st Bns.
Report Map. 1. General Map   - 100 to each Battalion.
            2. Pigeon Map   - 25 to each Battalion.

---

1. PLAN. The 173rd Infantry Brigade is to carry out an attack on the HINDENBURG Front Line.
   The attack will be made by moonlight, Z day and ZERO hour will be issued later.
   Troops on our Right and Left will co-operate with rifle, Machine Gun and Lewis Gun fire, and will undertake minor operations as outlined in para. 7.
   The objects of this attack are -
   (a) To gain ground, to kill and harass the enemy.
   (b) To improve our tactical position.
   (c) To take prisoners.

2. OBJECTIVES. 1st Objective. HINDENBURG Front line from U.20.b.40.17 to U.14.a.05.05.
   2nd Objective. A line in or commanding the Sunken road from U.20.b.5.2 to U.14.a.05.05. (This will not be a continuous line, but a continuous chain of battle patrols with Lewis Guns to act as a covering party to the main line of resistance, and to deny the Sunken road to the enemy.)

3. ASSEMBLY AREAS. Units will move to their assembly areas by dark, and will be in their allotted positions (see Map A) by - 30 minutes.
   The greatest care should be taken to avoid unnecessary movement and noise forward of the Railway Embankment.
   All movement into assembly areas will be across the open.
   To avoid confusion guide tapes will be laid from Railway embankment by Battalions concerned.
   All units allotted to either of the assembly areas will come under the Command of Os.C. Battalions concerned from 9 p.m. on Y day.

4. ADVANCED BRIGADE HEADQUARTERS Will be established in the Sunken road at T.30.c.3.9 by 5 p.m. on Z day.
   There will be a Brigade Report Centre at U.19.b.9.2. This Report Centre will be used as Battalion Headquarters for centre assaulting battalion.
   There will be Runner Posts at
   (a) U.25.a.75.50.
   (b) T.24.d.8.2.

5. TIME TABLE OF ATTACK The attack will be carried out in accordance with attached table of barrages. It must be clearly understood, however, that the times published are merely as a guide to the infantry, and are not orders for the exact times of assaults. It is of vital importance that the infantry should keep close up to the artillery barrage, and advance whenever it lifts.

2.

6.	**ARTILLERY SUPPORT.**	The 173rd Infantry Brigade will be supported by the Artillery of three Divisions - the 7th, 58th, and 62nd Divisions; assisted by the Vth Corps Heavy Artillery.

7. **SCHEME OF ATTACK.**

The Brigade will attack with the 2/3rd Battalion on the Right, 2/1st Battalion in the centre, and the 2/2nd Battalion on the Left.

The 2/3rd and 2/1st Bns. will attack on a four Company front. The 2/2nd Bn. will be on a three Company front, with the fourth Company acting as a Special Detachment, with a task which will be dealt with in para. 8.

The 1st wave of each Company will consist of two platoons in single rank. One platoon per Company, less Lewis Gun section, will follow the 1st wave at 10 paces distance to act as moppers.

The 2nd wave of each Company will be 30 paces behind the 1st wave and will consist of one platoon and the Lewis Gun section detached from the moppers.

The advance and Assault. The whole assaulting force will move forward at ZERO and get close up to the barrage. Care should be exercised to maintain the distances laid down. When the barrage lifts the 1st wave will advance and assault the 1st objective and clean it up.

The moppers up will be dropped to deal with any of the enemy who are in advance of their own front line - this should be done very thoroughly.

The 2nd wave will advance close to the barrage and assault the 2nd objective, establishing themselves as a line of battle patrols.

A Company, 2/4th Bn. will take over front line from our present Left to U.13.b.6.3 on Y night from 110th Infantry Brigade under orders to be issued later.

2/4th BN ~~This Company~~ will join up by bombing if necessary - with Left of 2/2nd Bn. as soon as 1st objective has been reached.

The 2/7th Bn. on our Right, will also seize and occupy the line of the Sunken road from U.21.c.2.3 to Right of 2/3rd Bn. as soon as 1st objective has been captured.

8. **SPECIAL DETACHMENT.**

The Company of the 2/2nd Bn. referred to in para. 7 will advance and capture enemy strong point at U.14.a.15.00 and the cross roads at U.14.c.35.85.

9. **VICKERS MAXIM GUNS.**

The advance will be supported by the Guns of the 206th, 198th, and 214th Machine Gun Cos., and the Guns of the 21st Division.

After the capture of the 2nd objective, O.C., 206th M.G.Co. will arrange for 8 M.Gs. to take up their position in captured German Line.

O.C., 206th M.G.Co. will confer with Battalion Commanders of the 2/3rd, 2/1st and 2/2nd Bns. on the placing of these Guns.

10. **LIGHT TRENCH MORTARS**

The O.C., 173rd L.T.M.Battery will arrange for four guns to move into enemy front line as soon as the 2nd objective is captured, and the hostile barrage has ceased. O.C., 173rd L.T.M.Battery will confer with Os.C. of the 2/3rd, 2/1st and 2/2nd Bns. to arrange emplacements.

11. R.E.
The O.C., 504th Field Coy. R.E. will arrange with Os.C. 2/3rd, 2/1st and 2/2nd Bns. to send R.E. personnel
(a) with mobile charges of guncotton to demolish any tunnels that may exist in the captured trenches.
(b) For supervision in constructing strong points at
U.14.c.36.95 in 2/2nd Bn. sub-sector
U.20.a.95.85 in 2/1st Bn. sub-sector
U.20.b.15.52 in 2/3rd Bn. sub-sector
U.20.b.4.2 in 2/3rd Bn. sub-sector

12. ADVANCE OF BATTALION HEADQUARTERS
Battalion Headquarters will not advance until the objective has been captured. Representatives of Headquarters will follow last wave and select a place for Headquarters and send back to notify the Bn. Commander. Bn. Commanders will immediately send back location of his new H.Q. to Brigade.

13. AEROPLANE CO-OPERATION.
Contact aeroplanes will be used at daylight to fix the positions gained by the infantry, in accordance with the principles lately practised in this Brigade.
Flares will not be used. Infantry will be issued with yellow handkerchiefs. - These will be waved whenever an aeroplane sounds its horn. Yellow handkerchiefs will mean nothing unless waved.

14. COMMUNICATIONS.
Separate orders will be issued later.

15. SYNCHRONISATION OF WATCHES
A representative from each Battalion will report at Brigade Headquarters at 6 p.m. on Y day to synchronise watches. Watches will be again synchronised at 1 hour before ZERO in assembly trenches. A representative from Brigade Headquarters will visit Battalion Headquarters for that purpose.

16. CARRYING PARTY.
Officers Commanding 2/3rd, 2/1st and 2/2nd Bns. will be required to detail a small carrying party for Vickers Machine Guns and Light Trench Mortars (numbers will be given later).

17. EQUIPMENT.
All troops will be in battle order and carry

170 rounds S.A.A.
4 Sandbags
2 Iron Rations
1 Box Respirator and P.H.G.Helmet.
1 Very Light
2 Bombs
Pick or Shovel
Full waterbottle
Aeroplane signals.

As many wire cutters as possible will be issued to the 1st waves.
20% of the men will carry "P" Bombs. S.O.S. Rockets will be carried by Company and Battalion Headquarters. Runners are to be lightly equipped and Battalion runners will not carry rifles.

18. **LIGHT SIGNALS & COMMUNICATION TRENCHES.** Instructions regarding use of Light Signals and Communication Trenches will be issued later.

19. **NOTES.**
   (a) It must be impressed upon all units that they are on no account to halt because units on their flanks happen to be held up. The best way of assisting their neighbours on such occasions will be to continue their own advance.
   (b) All Commanders must be impressed with the necessity of maintaining their direction and marching straight on to their allotted objective. With this object the ground must be carefully studied beforehand, landmarks noted wherever possible, and compass bearings taken.
   (c) No papers likely to be of value to the enemy will be taken over the parapet.
   (d) Not more than 20 officers per Battalion must take part in an assault, and a proportion of reliable N.C.Os. must also be left behind.
   (e) Officers and men will be particularly warned against retaining documents taken from prisoners as souvenirs. Very valuable information may be lost by failure to send in all documents so taken, which should be forwarded to Brigade Headquarters at the first opportunity
   (f) The word "Rotire" does not exist: anybody using it is to be immediately killed.

ACKNOWLEDGE.

[signature] Captain,
Brigade Major,
173rd Infantry Brigade.

Issued to Signals at ....

Copy No.
1. 2/1st London Regt.
2. 2/2nd London Regt.
3. 2/3rd London Regt.
4. 2/4th London Regt.
5. 173rd T.M.Battery.
6. 206th M.G.Coy.
7. 2/7th London Regt.
8. 110th Inf. Bde.
9. 174th Inf. Bde.
10. 175th Inf. Bde.
11. Left Group 58th D.A.
12. 504th Field Co. R.E.
13. "G" 58th Division
14. "A" & "Q", 58th Division
15. C.R.A.
16. G.O.C.
17. Brigade Major
18. Staff Captain
19. Brigade Signalling Officer
20. Brigade Transport Officer
21. Intelligence Officer.
22. War Diary
23. Do.
24. File.

173rd ARTILLERY BARRAGE TIME TABLE - ATTACHED OPERATION ORDER NO.25.

Zero.	Barrage opens 150 yards short of enemy front line.	Infantry leave Assembly Areas and advance across "No-Man's Land" close up to Barrage.
+0.2	Barrage lifts 50 yards.	Infantry continues to advance.
+0.4	Barrage lifts a hundred yards into enemy front line - stays there three minutes and moves back 100 yards every three minutes.	Infantry continues to advance.
+0.7"	Barrage lifts to/100 yards behind enemy front line.	Assault of front line by 1st Wave - 2nd Wave advances close up to barrage.
+0.10"	Barrage lifts 100 yards.	2nd Wave advances.
+0.13"	Barrage lifts 100 yards and forms a protective screen to Infantry during consolidation. This line will be the S.O.S. line.	Assault of 2nd Objective by 2nd Wave - Infantry mops up and consolidates 1st and 2nd Objective.

SECRET.　　　　　　　　　　　　　　　　　　　　　Copy No...... 16

Appendix O.

173rd INFANTRY BRIGADE OPERATION ORDER NO.52.

Reference Map Sheets 51B and 51C - 1/40,000.

June 19th 1917.

1. The Brigade will move to ABLAINZEVILLE area on 20th June.

2. Units will move independently via cross country tracks and will be clear of camp at the times stated below:-

    2/1st Bn. London Regt............. 9 a.m.
    2/3rd Bn. London Regt............. 9.15 a.m.
    2/2nd Bn. London Regt............. 9.30 a.m.
    2/4th Bn. London Regt............. 9.45 a.m.
    173rd L.T.M. Batty............... 10 a.m.
    206th M.G. Company............... 10.15 a.m.

3. Bde. Hd. Qtrs. will close at L'ABBAYE MORI at 10 a.m. and will re-open at ABLAINZEVILLE at the same hour.

4. Units will be distributed as follows:-

    Bde. Hd. Qtrs.   )
    Machine Gun Co.   )
    173rd T.M.Batty.   )   -   - ABLAINZEVILLE.
    2/1st Bn.Ln.Regt.   )
    2/3rd Bn.Ln.Regt.   )

    2/2nd Bn.Ln.Regt.   )
)   -   - Nr. LOGEAST WOOD.
    2/4th Bn.Ln.Regt.   )

    Advance Parties will report to the Staff Captain at the Town Major's Office ABLAINZEVILLE at 8.30 a.m. 20th instant.
    2 Train Wagons per Battalion will report at the transport lines at 7.30 a.m., on completion of the move these wagons will return to O.C. 510 H.T. Coy. A.S.C.
    2 Motor Lorries per Battalion will report at Transport Lines at 8 a.m. 20th instant.
    Stores etc of Trench Mortar Batty. will be carried under Brigade arrangements.
    Brigade Transport Officer will notify units direct of position of Wagon Lines, Watering Place and Manure Dump.
    Refilling Point will be notified later.
    Each Unit will detail a small rear party to clear up the camp after units have marched off.
    Officer Commanding, 2/3rd Bn. London Regt. will detail an Officer to take charge of this party, this officer will hand over the camp at 12 noon to a representative of the 58th Divisional Company and obtain a certificate that the camp and wagon lines are in a clean condition. This certificate will be forwarded to Bde. Hd. Qtrs. The party will then proceed to rejoin their units.

5. The following orders in force in the area are repeated for information and necessary action:-

    FIRE:- Each unit will detail a fire picquet.
            Tins of dry earth, sand or water will
            be kept ready to throw on a fire
            immediately it breaks out.

5. (Continued).

All Battalions in the area will supply each day 1 N.C.O. and 1% of their strength for the use of the Town Major.
These men are to report at 8.30 a.m. and 1.30 p.m. outside the Town Major's Office, ABLAINZEVILLE.

[signature] Captain,
Brigade Major,
173rd Infantry Brigade.

Issued to Signals at 6.15 p.m.

Copy No.
1. 2/1st Bn. London Regt.
2. 2/2nd Bn. London Regt.
3. 2/3rd Bn. London Regt.
4. 2/4th Bn. London Regt.
5. 173rd Trench Mortar Batty.
6. 206th Machine Gun Company.
7. 174th Infantry Brigade.
8. 175th Infantry Brigade.
9. 510th H.T. Coy. A.S.C.
10. 504th Field Coy. R.E.
11. "G" 58th Division.
12. "A" & "Q" 58th Division.
13. Brigade Major for G.O.C.
14. Staff Captain,
15. Brigade Signalling Officer.)
    Brigade Transport Officer.) To note and return to
    Brigade Intelligence Officer.)   last named.
16. War Diary.
17. War Diary.
18. File.
19. ~~Spare.~~
20. Spare. 2/3rd NCO Att.

- 2 -

8. Contact aeroplanes will be used at daylight to fix the position gained by the Infantry in accordance with the principles practised in this Brigade.
RED Flares will be used also yellow handkerchiefs whenever an aeroplane sounds its horn or fires a white very light.
Yellow handkerchiefs will mean nothing unless waved.

9. Synchronisation of Watches. A representative of the 2/1st; 2/2nd and 2/3rd Battalions, 208th Machine Gun Company and 173rd L. T. M. Batty. will report at Advanced Brigade Headquarters at 7.30 p.m. to-day.
Watches will be again synchronised 1 hour before ZERO at the Advanced Report Centre. A representative from Bde. Hd. Qtrs. will be there for that purpose.

10. Troops should be reminded that if shelled while assembling this will not necessarily mean that the enemy have discovered them.
In the event of casualties being experienced while assembling, troops will push on to the HINDENBURG Front Line and reorganise there. In this case the whole of the garrison (less Vickers guns) of this line will assault together at ZERO. Should such action become necessary Bde. Hd. Qtrs. will be informed by the senior officer on the spot and arrangements will be made to regarrison the HINDENBURG Front Line.

SEVERE

11. ACKNOWLEDGE.

Captain,
Brigade Major,
173rd Infantry Bde.

Issued to signals at ......

Copies to.
Copy No.
1. 2/1st Bn. London Regt.
2. 2/2nd Bn. London Regt.
3. 2/3rd Bn. London Regt.
4. 2/4th Bn. London Regt.
5. 173rd L. T. M. Batty.
6. 203rd Machine Gun Company.
7. 2/8th Bn. London Regt.
8. 110th Infantry Brigade.
9. 174th Infantry Brigade.
10. 175th Infantry Brigade.
11. Left Group 58th D.A.
12. 504th Field Coy. R.E.
13. 510th Coy. A. S. C.
14. "G" 58th Division.
15. "A" & "Q" 58th Division.
16. C. R. A.
17. Brigade Major for G.O.C.
18. Staff Captain.
19. Brigade Signalling Officer)
    Brigade Transport Officer.) To note and return to last named.
    Bde. Intelligence Officer.)
20. War Diary.
21. War Diary.
22. File.
23)
to) Spare.
28)

THE WORD

"RETIRE" DOES NOT EXIST

ANY MAN

MAKING USE OF THIS WORD IN ACTION

WILL BE TREATED

AS AN ENEMY AND SHOT

By Order of Brig. General
Commanding
173 Inf. Bde

SECRET

173RD INFANTRY BRIGADE

Administrative Instructions No. 6 issued with
reference to Operation Order No. 25.

TRANSPORT.	Will remain as at present.
RATIONS, WATER, S.A.A., BOMBS, ETC.	Each man will carry two Iron Rations and a full waterbottle. All necessary Grenades, sandbags, etc., for the attack will be delivered to units' Q.M.Stores. Dumps will be established in accordance with attached schedule in accordance with arrangements to be made by the Staff Captain; when established, units concerned will be notified, and will take same over.. O.C., 2/4th London Regt. will detail one complete platoon as carrying party. This party will be earmarked ready to report to Staff Captain as required. In addition O.C., 2/4th London Regt. will detail 1 N.C.O. and 3 men as Guard for the Brigade Dump - this party will report to the Brigade Storeman at T.23.d.9.4, when called for.
STORAGE OF PACKS.	All packs, etc., will be stored at the present Q.M. Stores. Q.M.Stores must be prepared to move on Z + 1 day.
REPLACEMENT OF ORDNANCE STORES.	The quick replacement of Lewis Guns, etc., is important. Units will report to Brigade Headquarters at once any deficiencies.
OFFICERS & OTHER RANKS.	Officers and other ranks not going into the attack will remain in the transport lines - when any of these Reserve Officers are required, Brigade Headquarters will be informed.
STRAGGLER POSTS.	Straggler Posts will be established at T.23.d.8.3 U.25.b.5.2 U.26.c.4.5 O.C., 2/4th London Regt. will detail 1 N.C.O. (Sergt.) and 8 men to take charge of these posts. Instructions for this party will be issued from this office..
PRISONERS OF WAR.	A Brigade Prisoner Collecting Post will be established at B.11.a.5.2 in charge of an N.C.O. and 2 men to be detailed by O.C., 2/4th London Regt. Prisoners captured will be sent back with as small an escort as possible. The N.C.O. i/c of the Station will keep as many men of the escort as he requires, and will send the remainder back with a receipt for the prisoners handed over. When parties of 20 or 30 have been collected they will be sent back to the Divisional Cage at MORY - B.16.d.4.2. Officer prisoners will be kept separate from the men.
SALVAGE.	As at present.
MEDICAL.	Arrangements will be notified later.
CASUALTIES.	The following instructions with regard to reporting casualties during the operation are issued :- The ordinary detailed casualty return will be rendered up to and including 12 noon on the day before the assault, after which a system of "estimated" casualty returns will come into force. This will be rendered twice daily to reach Brigade

Headquarters at 12 noon and 7 p.m..
(Estimated casualties however exceeding 10% of any unit will be reported at once.)

The following information will be given in reporting casualties :-
    (a) Total estimated loss of Officers since the commencement of operations.
    (b) Total estimated loss of O.Rs. since the commencement of operations.

All wires will commence "Total estimated aaa" and the total will be accumulative.

At the termination of the operation, or as soon as a unit is withdrawn from the line, an accurate return of the casualties sustained during the preceding period will be rendered.

This return must give the dates covered, ranks, initials, and names of officers, and total numbers of O.Rs. killed, wounded, or missing.

Accuracy is essential in this return.

H. Garraway
Captain,
Staff Captain,
173rd Infantry Brigade.

th June, 1917

SECRET   173RD INFANTRY BRIGADE   Copy No. 14

Administrative Instruction No. 5.

(Ref. Map Sheet 57C N.W. 1/20,000).   27/5/17

With reference to 173rd Infantry Brigade Operation Order No. 20 dated 27th inst., the following will be the administrative arrangements :-

TRANSPORT AND Q.M. STORES
All Transport lines and Q.M.Stores will be at B.13.b.
Transport Officers and Quarter Masters will take over the lines and Q.M.Stores of the units they relieve.

RATIONS.
The unconsumed portion of the day's ration will be carried on the man.
Battalions in the line will carry three days rations on the man.
Rations and fuel will be delivered to ERVILLERS by 510 H.T.Co., A.S.C.
Position of Brigade Supply Officer will be notified later.
Rations will be delivered by 1st Line Transport as follows :-
Right Battalion
     To Battalion Headquarters at U.25.b.5.2.
Left Battalion
     To Battalion Headquarters at T.30.a.15.60.
Support Battalion
     To Battalion Headquarters at T.30.a.2.0.
Supplies from these points will be forwarded under arrangements made with O.C. Units.
Reserve Battalion
     To Camp at B.15.d.3.5

FIELD KITCHENS & WATER CARTS
The Battalions in Reserve will use their Field Kitchens and Water Carts.

WATER.
Water will be drawn at ERVILLERS - B.13.b., and carried forward to units in the line and support by 1st Line Transport.
These units should maintain a water reserve at Battalion Headquarters. Every effort must be made to return all empty petrol tins to 1st line transport each day, otherwise the supply of fresh water cannot be maintained.

S.A.A. & R.E. MATERIAL
Demands for Ammunition, Very Lights, and R.E.Material should be sent to Staff Captain to reach Brigade Headquarters at L'HOMME MORT - B.17.a.8.8 - by 10 a.m. each day.
All ammunition and R.E.Material will be sent to Battalion Headquarters by 1st line transport.

DUMPS.
The following ammunition dumps will be maintained by
     Brigade   at   B.17.a.8.8
     Right Bn.   at   U.25.b.6.2
     Left Bn.   at   T.23.d.9.3

BRIGADE POST OFFICE
Will be at ERVILLERS - B.13.b.

2.

"C" SOLUTION.   Battalions will keep a supply of "C" Solution to be
                  used when necessary.

MEDICAL.   Battalions will establish Regimental Aid Posts.

                  Location of Relay Posts will be notified later.

PACKS.   Will be dumped at Q.M.Stores by 6.30 a.m. on the day
                  the Battalion moves, and conveyed to Q.M.Stores,
                  ERVILLERS, by lorry.

REAR PARTIES.   Each unit will leave a small rear party to hand over
                  Camp to Units of 187th Infantry Brigade. Three days'
                  rations will be left with these parties.

                                                  H. J. KING, 2/Lieut.
                                                           A/Staff Captain,
                                                  173rd Infantry Brigade.

Issued to Signals at 3 p.m.

Copy No.
1. 2/1st Lon. Regt.
2. 2/2nd Lon. Regt.
3. 2/3rd Lon. Regt.
4. 2/4th Lon. Regt.
5. 173rd T.M.Battery
6. 206th M.G.Co.
7. "G" 58th Division
8. "A" & "Q" 58th Division
9. 510 H.T.Co. A.S.C.
10. G.O.C.
11. Staff Captain
12. Brigade Signalling Officer
13. War Diary
14.   Do.
15. File
16. 504 Field Co. R.E.
17. 2/1st Field Ambulance
18. C.R.A.
19. C.R.E.
20. A.D.M.S.
21. 187th Infantry Brigade.
22. 174th Infantry Brigade.
23. 175th Infantry Brigade.

173RD INFANTRY BRIGADE

AMMUNITION DUMPS

	Map Reference	S.A.A. (Boxes)	Grenades Hand (Boxes)	Grenades No. 23 (Boxes)	No. 20 (Boxes)	Very Lights	S.O.S. Red	S.O.S. Green
Bde. Forward Dump	T.23.d.9.4	100	100	30	5	600	50	50
Right Bn.	U.25.a.7.5	30	30	16	5	150	20	20
Centre Bn.	T.24.d.8.2	30	60	16	5	150	20	20
Left Bn.	U.19.a.5.9	30	60	16	5	150	20	20
M.G. Co.	U.25.a.4.8	100	-	-	-	-	-	-

WATER DUMPS

	Map Reference	Quantity (Tins)
Brigade	T.23.d.9.4	200
Right Bn.	U.19.d.7.2	60
Centre Bn.	U.19.d.8.7	60
Left Bn.	U.13.d.7.7	30

RATIONS

	Map Reference	Number
Brigade	T.23.d.9.4	1000
Right Bn.	U.25.a.7.5	400
Centre Bn.	T.24.d.8.2	400
Left Bn.	U.19.a.5.9	400

Battalions will supply details of M.G.Coy. and L.T.M.B. under their Command, with rations and water.

SECRET.   Copy No. 23

AMENDMENTS TO
173RD INFANTRY BRIGADE OPERATION ORDER NO 25.

10th June 1917.

Para 1. will now read:- PLAN. The 173rd Infantry Brigade, supported by the 174th Infantry Brigade, is to carry out an attack on the HINDENBURG Front and Support Lines.
   The attack will be made by moonlight, Z day and ZERO hour will be issued later.
   Troops on our Right and left will co-operate with rifle, machine gun and Lewis Gun fire, and will undertake minor operations as outlined in para 7.
   The objects of this attack are:-
   (a). To gain ground, to kill and harass the enemy.
   (b). To improve our tactical position.
   (c). To take prisoners.

Para 2. will now read:- OBJECTIVES.
   1st Objective. HINDENBURG Front Line from U.20.b.40.17. to U.14.a.05.05.
   2nd Objective. HINDENBURG SUPPORT LINE from U.20.b.45.72. to U.14.a.8.1.

Para 7. will now read:- SCHEME OF ATTACK. The Brigade will attack with the 2/3rd Bn. London Regt. on the Right, 2/1st Bn. London Regt. in the centre, and the 2/2nd Bn. London Regt. on the Left.
   The 2/3rd; 2/1st and 2/2nd Bn. London Regts. will attack on a four company front.
   A Company from the 2/7th and 2/4th Bns. will be attached to the 2/3rd and 2/2nd Bns. respectively, and will be given the task of making good our flanks.
   The attack will be launched in two waves. Moppers will accompany the first wave.
First Wave. of each Company, will consist of two platoons in single rank. One platoon per Company will follow the first wave at 10 paces distance, to act as moppers.
2nd Wave will be 30 paces distance from the front wave and will consist of One platoon.
Special Moppers. Light Trench Mortar Personnel, with three L.T.M. Bombs each, will follow the front wave to deal with dug-out shafts, which are near the Enemy's Support Line.
The Advance and Assault. The whole assaulting force will move forward at ZERO and get close up to the barrage.
Great care should be exercised:-

   (a). To maintain the distances laid down.
   (b). To lose no chance of reorganisation during advance.
   (c). To use compasses whenever a chance occurs; even when waiting a few seconds for the barrage to lift (This is vital).

NOTE:- The responsibility for the direction after the assault is launched lies with every man with a compass.
The First Wave. Will advance close up to the barrage, assault the first objective and push forward behind the barrage to assault, clean up and consolidate the Second Objective, dropping the moppers to deal with the situation in the first objective. The special Moppers with the L.T.M. Bombs will follow the first wave to the second objective where they will deal with dug-out shafts as instructed in training.

2.

7. Scheme of Attack - continued:-
The Second Wave will advance at 30 paces distance from the first wave until after the first objective, when they will mop up the Sunken Road and any places between the first and second objectives. They will then push forward into the second objective and assist with mopping up and consolidation.

Para 8. will now read:- SPECIAL DETACHMENTS. O's. C. 2/2nd and 2/3rd Bns. will detail the Companies attached to them from 2/4th and 2/7th Bns. to form Left and Right defensive flanks respectively, as shown on Map

Para 9. will now read:- VICKERS MAXIM GUNS. The advance will be supported by the guns of the 206th; 198th and 214th M. G. Companies and the guns of the 21st Division.
O.C. 206th M. G. Company will arrange for two guns to follow the second waves of each Company of the 2/3rd; 2/1st and 2/2nd Bns. These guns will occupy the mebus positions in the first objective during hostile bombardments but will fire over the heads of our men in the second objective during a counter attack.
The remainder of the guns will employ indirect fire under orders of the O.C. 206th M. G. Coy.

Para 10. will now read:- LIGHT TRENCH MORTARS. O.C. 173rd L.T.M. Batty. will detail his personnel equally to the 2/3rd; 2/1st and 2/2nd Bns. to act as special moppers as detailed in para. 7. He will be responsible that they are handed over fully equipped.

Captain,
Brigade Major,
173rd Infantry Bde.

Issued to Signals at:- ......

Copy No.
1. 2/1st Bn. London Regt.
2. 2/2nd Bn. London Regt.
3. 2/3rd Bn. London Regt.
4. 2/4th Bn. London Regt.
5. 173rd Trench Mortar Batty.
6. 206th Machine Gun Company.
7. 2/7th Battalion London Regt.
8. 110th Infantry Brigade.
9. 174th Infantry Brigade.
10. 175th Infantry Brigade.
11. Left Group 58th D.A.
12. 504th Field Coy. R. E.
13. "G" 58th Division.
14. "A" & "Q" 58th Division.
15. C. R. A.
16. G. O. C.
17. Brigade Major.
18. Staff Captain.
19. Brigade Signalling Officer.
20. Brigade Transport Officer.
21. Intelligence Officer.
22. War Diary.
23. War Diary.
24. File.

1/73RD BRIGADE AMENDED BARRAGE TIME-TABLE ATTACHED TO OPERATION ORDER NO. 25

ZERO	Barrage opens 150 yards short of first objective.	Infantry leaves Assembly Areas and advances across "No Man's Land" close up to Barrage.
+ 0.2	Barrage lifts 50 yards.	Infantry continues to advance.
+ 0.4	Barrage lifts 100 yards on to 1st objective, stays there three minutes and moves back 100 yards.	Infantry continues to advance.
+ 0.7	Barrage lifts to 100 yards beyond 1st objective.	Assault of 1st objective.
+ 0.10	Barrage lifts 100 yards.	Infantry continues to advance close to barrage.
+ 0.13	Barrage lifts on to second objective.	Infantry advances very close to barrage.
+ 0.15	Barrage lifts clear of second objective and creeps back to 250 yards beyond second objective at the rate of 100 yards every three minutes and forms a protector during consolidation. This will be our S.O.S. Line.	Infantry follows the barrage in at the double and commences to clean up. This must be done thoroughly.

SECRET. Appendix K Copy No. 24

173rd INFANTRY BRIGADE ORDER NO. 29.
Reference Map - BULLECOURT 1/10,000.

June 13th 1917.

1. The 2/7th Bn. London Regt. and one Coy., 2/1st Bn. Lon. Regt. will be relieved in right sub-sector by 2/8th Bn. London Regt. and one Coy. 2/6th Bn. London Regt. during night 13/14th June.

2. 1 Coy. 2/1st Bn. London Regt now under orders of O.C., 2/7th Bn. London Regt. will revert to O.C. 2/1st Bn. on completion of relief.

3. Orders for move of 2/7th Bn. London Regt. subsequent to relief have already been issued by 174th Infantry Bde.

4. 2/8th Bn. London Regt. and 1 Coy. 2/6th Bn. London Regt. will come under orders of B.G.C., 173rd Infantry Bde. at 9 p.m. 13th June.
2/7th Bn. London Regt. will revert to command 174th Infantry Bde. on completion of relief.

5. All Trench Stores will be handed over and duplicate receipts forwarded to Bde. Hd. Qtrs. in due course.

6. 2/1st; 2/7th and 2/8th Bn. London Regts. will please acknowledge.

                         Captain,
                         Brigade Major,
                         173rd Infantry Brigade.

Issued to Signals at :-

Copy No.
1. 2/1st Bn. London Regt.
2. 2/2nd Bn. London Regt.
3. 2/3rd Bn. London Regt.
4. 2/4th Bn. London Regt.
5. 173rd Trench Mortar Batty.
6. 206th Machine Gun Company.
7. 2/6th Bn. London Regt.
8. 2/7th Bn. London Regt.
9. 2/8th Bn. London Regt.
10. 174th Infantry Bde.
11. 175th Infantry Brigade.
12. 504th Field Coy. R.E.
13. 510th Coy. A.S.C.
14. Left Group 58th D.A.
15. 58th Division.
16. A.D.M.S.
17. G.O.C.
18. Brigade Major.
19. Staff Captain.
20. Bde. Signalling Officer.
21. Bde. Transport Officer.
22. Intelligence Officer.
23. War Diary.
24. War Diary.
25. File.

SECRET.   Appendix 1.   Copy No. 21

173rd Infantry Bde. Operation Order No. 28.

Reference Map Sheet 51B S.W.)
&) 1/20,000.
57C N.W.)

June 11th 1917.

---

1. 2/4th Bn. London Regt. will be relieved in the line by 2/1st Bn. London Regt. and 1 Coy. 2/7th Bn. London Regt. during night 11/12th June. All details will be arranged direct between C.O's concerned.

2. Relief will be completed by 3 a.m. 12th June and Bde. Hd. Qtrs. notified by code word "GORY".

3. Trench Stores will be taken over and duplicate receipts forwarded to Brigade Hd. Qtrs. in due course.

4. As a temporary measure O.C. 2/7th Battalion London Regt. will detail one of his support companies to take over those posts at present held by Right front Coy. of 2/4th Bn. London Regt.

5. Till further orders the following will be the distribution of the two front line Battalions.
   No. 1 Sub-sector.
      Front Line.   3 Companies.
      Support.   1 Company.
   No. 2 Sub-sector.
      Front Line.   1 Company.
      Support.   3 Companies.
   Detailed distribution and approximate inter-Battalion boundary will be forwarded to Bde. Hd. Qtrs. by O's. C. 2/1st and 2/7th Battalions.

6. O.C. 2/1st Bn. London Regt. will make his own arrangements as to positions to be occupied by the extra support company.

7. In case of attack against Right Sub-sector O.C. 2/1st Bn. will place one Company at disposal of O.C. 2/7th Bn. London Regt.

8. On completion of relief 2/4th Bn. London Regt. will withdraw to ST LEGER under Battalion arrangements.

9. 2/2nd and 2/3rd Bn. London Regts. will withdraw under Battalion arrangements to original bivouacs near MORY - 2/2nd Bn. Lon. Regt. leading. 2/3rd Bn. London Regt. will be clear of ST LEGER by midnight 11/12th June.

10. ACKNOWLEDGE.

                                        Captain,
                                        Brigade Major,
                                        173rd Infantry Brigade.

Issued to Signals at ......
Copy No.
1. 2/1st Bn. London Regt.
2. 2/2nd Bn. London Regt.
3. 2/3rd Bn. London Regt.
4. 2/4th Bn. London Regt.
5. 173rd Infantry Bde. T.M.Batty.
6. 206th Machine Gun Coy.
7. 2/7th Bn. London Regt.
8. 110th Infantry Bde.
9. 174th Infantry Bde.
10. 175th Infantry Bde.
11. Left Group 58th D.A.

Copy No.
12. 504th Field Coy. R.E.
13. 58th Division.
14. G.O.C.
15. Brigade Major.
16. Staff Captain.
17. Bde. Signalling Offi'r
18. Bde. Transport Officer
19. Intelligence Officer
20. War Diary.
21. War Diary.
22. File.

Appendix H

SECRET.   Copy No. 14

173RD INFANTRY BRIGADE OPERATION ORDER NO.27.

Reference Map Sheet BULLECOURT - 1/10000.

June 10th 1917.

---

1. 2/2nd and 2/3rd Bn. London Regts. will concentrate in ST LEGER during night 10/11th June under Battalion arrangements. Billets will be allotted by Staff Captain in consultation with Town Major.

2. Every precaution will be taken to avoid all unnecessary movement during the daylight on June 11th.

3. 2/4th Bn. London Regt. will take over front line trenches from their present left to U.13.b.6.3. during night of 10/11th June from 110th Infantry Brigade.
Relief complete will be notified to Brigade Headquarters by code word "SWELTERING".

4. One Officer per Battalion and one Officer of 504th Field Co. R.E. and 206th Machine Gun Coy. will be detailed to visit to-morrow and report on the trenches and dug-outs of that portion of the HINDENBURG SUPPORT LINE, which is held by 21st Division. Guides are being arranged by 110th Infantry Brigade and time and rendezvous will be notified later.

5. ACKNOWLEDGE.

                                         Captain,
                                         Brigade Major,
                                         173rd Infantry Brigade.

Issued to Signals at :- 9am

Copy No.
1. 2/1st Bn. London Regt.
2. 2/2nd Bn. London Regt.
3. 2/3rd Bn. London Regt.
4. 2/4th Bn. London Regt.
5. 173rd Trench Mortar Batty.
6. 206th Machine Gun Company.
7. 58th Division.
8. 110th Infantry Brigade.
9. 504th Field Company R.E.
10. G. O. C.
11. Brigade Major,
12. Staff Captain.
13. Brigade Transport Officer.
14. Intelligence Officer.
15. Signalling Officer.
16. War Diary.
17. War Diary.
18. File.

SECRET. Copy No. 19

173rd INFANTRY BRIGADE
OPERATION ORDER NO.26.

Reference Map Sheet 57c N.W. - 1/20,000.
and TRENCH MAP ECOUST ST MEIN - 1/10000.

9th June 1917.

---

1. 8th Bn. London Regt will be relieved in No.1 Sub-sector by 7th Bn. London Regt. during night June 9/10. Relief to be completed by 3 a.m.

2. 7th Bn. London Regt. will come under orders of B.G.C., 173rd Infantry Brigade from 9 p.m. June 9th.
   8th Bn. London Regt. will revert to 174th Infantry Bde. on completion of relief.

3. Completion of relief will be notified to this Headquarters by code word "HOT".

4. All trench Stores will be handed over and duplicate copies of receipts forwarded to this office.

5. ACKNOWLEDGE.

                                                    Captain,
                                                   Brigade Major,
                                          173rd Infantry Brigade.

Issued to Signals at 9 a.m.

Copy No.
1. 2/1st Bn. London Regt.
2. 2/2nd Bn. London Regt.
3. 2/3rd Bn. London Regt.
4. 2/4th Bn. London Regt.
5. 173rd Trench Mortar Batty.
6. 206th Machine Gun Company.
7. 2/8th Bn. London Regt.
8. 2/7th Bn. London Regt.
9. 174th Infantry Brigade.
10. 175th Infantry Brigade.
11. 58th Division.
12. G. O. C.
13. Brigade Major.
14. Staff Captain.
15. Transport Officer.
16. Signalling Officer.
17. Intelligence Officer.
18. War Diary.
19. War Diary.
20. File.

Appendix F

SECRET.   Copy No. 16

173rd Infantry Brigade Order No.22.

Reference Map Sheets 1/20000 - 51B S.W. and 57C N.W.

---

1. The 2/1st Bn. London Regt. will carry out a raid against the enemy's defences known as the KNUCKLE (U.20.b.0.5. - U.20.a.8.8.).

2. Date and Zero hour will be notified later.

3. The objects of the raid will be :-

    (a). The destruction of M.G. Emplacements at U.20.a.75.65., U.20.a.8.8., U.20.a.83.64., U.20.a.86.59., U.20.b.0.5.

    (b). Obtaining information as to the state of the enemy's defences and his wire.

    (c). Obtaining identifications.

    (d). Killing of Germans.

4. O.C., 2/1st Bn. London Regt. will make all plans and issue orders in consultation with the Brigadier. A detailed scheme will be submitted to this office as soon as possible.

5. No reference whatever to this operation will be made over the Telephone.

6. 2/1st Bn. will acknowledge.

                                                    Captain,
                                                    Brigade Major,
                                                    173rd Infantry Brigade.

Issued to Signals at:- ......

Copy No.
1. 2/1st Bn. London Regt.
2. 2/2nd Bn. London Regt.
3. 2/3rd Bn. London Regt.
4. 2/4th Bn. London Regt.
5. 173rd Trench Mortar Batty.
6. 206th Machine Gun Company.
7. 175th Infantry Brigade.
8. 82nd. Infantry Brigade.
9. 58th Division.
10. 504th Field Coy. R.E.
11. O.C., Left Group, 58th D.A.
12. G.O.C.
13. Brigade Major,
14. Staff Captain.
15. War Diary.
16. War Diary.
17. File.

Appendix F.

SECRET.   Copy No. 16

173rd INFANTRY BRIGADE ORDER NO.24.

Reference Map Sheet 57c N.W. 1/20,000

June 6th 1917.

---

1. The 2/3rd Bn. London Regt. will be relieved in No.1 Sub-sector by 2/8th Bn. London Regt. during night of 7/8th June. Relief to be completed by 3 a.m. 8th June. Completion to be wired to Bde. Hd. Qtrs. using code word SULTRY.

2. Representatives of 2/8th Bn. will reconnoitre No.1 sub-sector during night 6/7th June, reporting to Hd. Qtrs., 2/3rd Bn. at 10 p.m. O.C., 2/3rd Bn. will arrange all necessary guides.

3. 2/8th Bn. will come under orders of B.G.C., 173rd Inf. Bde. at 9 a.m. 7th June.

4. All details of relief will be arranged between C.O's. concerned.

5. On completion of relief 2/3rd Bn. will move to Bivouacs in vicinity of HORY.

6. All Trench Stores will be handed over and copies of receipts forwarded to Bde. Hd. Qtrs.

                                              Captain,
                                         Brigade Major,
                                    173rd Infantry Brigade.

Issued to Signals at 5 pm

Copy No.
1. 2/3rd Bn. London Regt.
2. 2/4th Bn. London Regt.
3. 58th Division.
4. 175th Infantry Brigade.
5. 174th Infantry Brigade.
6. 2/8th Bn. London Regt.
7. O.C. Left Group, 58th D.A.
8. O.C. 504th Field Coy. R.E.
9. G. O. C.
10. Transport Officer.
11. Staff Captain.
12. Brigade Major.
13. Intelligence Officer.
14. Signalling Officer.
15. War Diary.
16. War Diary.
17. Field.

S E C R E T.   Copy No. 15.

Appendix D

173RD INFANTRY BRIGADE ORDER NO. 23.

Reference Map Sheet 51B S.W. - 1/20,000.

4/6/17.

---

1. Under instructions from 58th Division, 173rd Brigade will take over the front from 62nd Brigade up to U.14.a.0.1. exclusive.

2. The readjustment, details of which will be carried out under arrangements to be made direct between O.C. 2/4th Bn. London Regt. and O.C. 12th Bn. Northumberland Fusiliers, will be completed by 6 a.m. 5th June at which hour the Command of the extra line will be assumed by B.G.C., 173rd Infantry Brigade.

3. The completion of the readjustment will be wired to Bde. Hd. Qtrs. code word "FOX" being used.

4. O.C. 2/4th Bn. London Regt. will make all arrangements for evacuation at any time of posts etc. in the immediate vicinity of U.14.c.2.9. to enable the Heavy Artillery to bombard this locality as soon as possible after the readjustment ordered above is complete.
O.C. 2/4th Bn. will inform Bde. H.Q. when the necessary arrangements have been made.

Captain,
Brigade Major,
173rd Infantry Brigade.

Issued to Signals at .....
Copy No.
1. 2/1st Bn. London Regt.
2. 2/2nd Bn. London Regt.
3. 2/3rd Bn. London Regt.
4. 2/4th Bn. London Regt.
5. 173rd Trench Mortar Batty.
6. 206th Machine Gun Coy.
7. 62nd Infantry Brigade.
8. O.C. Left Group 58th D. A.
9. O.C. 504th Field Coy. R. E.
10. G. O. C.
11. Brigade Major.
12. Staff Captain.
13. Signalling Officer.
14. War Diary.
15. War Diary.
16. File.

S E C R E T.

SECRET   Copy No. 17

173RD INFANTRY BRIGADE ORDER NO. 21

Reference Map Sheets 1/20,000 - 51B. S.W. and 57C. N.W.

2nd June, 1917

1. The following reliefs will be carried out during night of 3/4 June.

    2/3rd Bn. will relieve 2/1st Bn. in No. 1 sub-sector.

    2/4th Bn. will relieve 2/2nd Bn. in No. 2 sub-sector.

    Reliefs to be completed by 3 a.m. 4th June. Code word for completion will be GLORIOUS.

2. On completion of relief 2/1st and 2/2nd Bns. will proceed in accordance with attached March Table.

3. All details will be arranged between C.Os. concerned.

4. ACKNOWLEDGE.

                                        Captain,
                                    Brigade Major,
                                 173rd Infantry Bde.

Issued to Signals at ....

Copy No.
1. 2/1st Bn. London Regt.
2. 2/2nd Bn. London Regt.
3. 2/3rd Bn. London Regt.
4. 2/4th Bn. London Regt.
5. 173rd Trench Mortar Batty.
6. 206th Machine Gun Coy.
7. O.C. Loft Group.
8. 58th Division.
9. 62nd Infantry Bde.
10. 174th Infantry Bde.
11. 175th Infantry Bde.
12. Brigade Signalling Officer.
13. G. O. C.
14. Brigade Major.
15. Staff Captain.
16. War Diary.
17. War Diary.
18. File.

MARCH TABLE.

UNIT.	FROM.	TO.	ROUTE.	REMARKS.
3rd Bn.	ST LEGER.	No.1. Sub-sector.	Via TEN TREES in B.4.d. – Cross roads in B.5.d.	To be clear of TEN TREES by 9.30 p.m.
4th Bn.	ST LEGER.	No.2. Sub-sector.	Via TEN TREES in B.4.d. – N. side of valley through B.5. & T.30.	Head of Column not to reach TEN TREES before 9.30 p.m.
1st Bn.	No.1. Sub-sector.	ST LEGER.	Via S. side of valley through B.5. & T.30 till cross roads B.5.d. are reached, thence ST LEGER.	
2nd Bn.	No.2. Sub-sector.	MORY BIVOUAC	N. side of valley through B.5. and T.30. – junction of roads – B.4.d. 5.0. – MORY COPSE – BIVOUAC.	

Particular care will be taken to avoid undue concentration of Troops at any time in valley running N.E. and S.W. through T.30.

SECRET   Copy No...... 14

173RD INFANTRY BRIGADE OPERATION ORDER NO. 20.

(Reference Map Sheet 57C N.W. 1/20,000).

Appendix A.

27/5/17.

1. The Brigade will relieve the 187th Brigade in the Line - Sector U.27.b.05.90. - road in U.13.c and d., and will move in accordance with attached March Table.

2. Relief will be carried out as follows :-

    Night 28th/29th, 1st and 2nd Bns. take over Nos. 1 and 2 Sub-Sectors respectively.
    Brigade H.Q. move to L'HOMME MORT and assume command of whole Sector on completion of above relief.

    Night 29th/30th, 3rd and 4th Bns. take over Nos. 3 and 4 Sub-Sectors respectively.
    206th M.G. Coy. take over M.G. defence of Sector.
    173rd L.T.M.B. relieve 187th L.T.M.B.

    The Relief will be completed by 9.am. May 30th.

3. All details as to provision of guides, retention of proportion of personnel of 187th Brigade, for 24 hrs. will be arranged direct between Bn. Commanders concerned.

4. All maps, plans etc, and Trench Stores, will be taken over and a list of the latter forwarded to Bde.H.Q.

5. As soon as possible after relief, all Units will forward a sketch map, to Bde. H.Q. shewing detailed dispositions.

6. Completion of reliefs will be wired to Bde. H.Q., the code word APPLE being used.

7. Administrative Instructions will be issued later.

8. ACKNOWLEDGE.

C.E.G. SHEARMAN, Captain,
Brigade Major,
173rd Infantry Brigade.

Issued to Signals at 3.pm.

Copy No.
1. 2/1st London Regt.
2. 2/2nd London Regt.
3. 2/3rd London Regt.
4. 2/4th London Regt.
5. 173rd T.M. Battery.
6. 206th M.G. Company.
7. "G" 58th Division.
8. "A & Q" 58th Divsn.
9. 510th H.T.Co.A.S.C
10. G.O.C.
11. Staff Captain.
12. Brigade Signalling Officer.
13. War Diary.
14. "
15. File.
16. 504 Field Co.R.E.
17. 2/1st Field Ambulance.
18. C.R.A.
19. C.R.E.
20. A.D.M.S.
21. 187th Infantry Brigade.
22. 174th Infantry Brigade.

MARCH TABLE -- APPENDIX A.

Units.	Date.	From	To	Route	Remarks.
2/1st Bn.	28th	Camp G.12.	No. 1 Sector	Divl. Track to MORY - L'ABBAYE - L'HOMME MORT.	Not to reach L'HOMME MORT before 8.45.pm.
2/2nd Bn.	28th	"	No. 2 Sector	Divl. Track to MORY - MORY Copse - Junction of roads B.10.b.	Not to pass MORY Copse before 8.45.pm.
2/3rd Bn.	29th	"	No. 3 Sector	- do. -	- do. -
2/4th Bn.	29th	"	No. 4 Sector	Divl. Track to MORY.	Time of commencement of Relief to be arranged direct between Bn. Commanders concerned.

The usual intervals will be maintained on the march.
1st Line Transport will move to ERVILLERS und arrangements to be made by Brigade Transport Officer.
Arrangements for move of 308th M.G. Company and 173rd L.T.M.Battery will be made direct between the Officers Commanding Companies and Batteries concerned.
No vehicles to pass the VRAUCOURT - St. LEGER Road by daylight. Single vehicles only will use this road between 4.am. and 9.pm.

AMENDMENTS TO 173RD INFANTRY BRIGADE ADMINISTRATIVE INSTRUCTION NO. 5

Secret

27/5/17.

TRANSPORT AND Q.M.STORES Should read :-
"All transport lines and Q.M.Stores will be at B.15.central. Brigade Transport Officer will allot lines and Q.M.Stores. 4 tents per Bn. will be taken for Q.M.Stores".

RATIONS. Line 5 - for "ERVILLERS" read "B.15.central".

WATER. Line 1 - for "ERVILLERS - B.13.b." read "MORY".

BRIGADE POST OFFICE. Will be at B.15.central.

PACKS. Line 3 - for "ERVILLERS" read "B.15.central".

H.J.KING, 2/Lieut.
A/Staff Captain,
173rd Infantry Brigade.

Copies to all recipients of 173rd Infantry Brigade Administrative Instruction No. 5 dated 27/5/17.

Army Form C. 2118.

HQ 173rd Inf. Bde.

WAR DIARY
or
INTELLIGENCE SUMMARY
(Erase heading not required.)

Instructions regarding War Diaries and Intelligence Summaries are contained in F.S. Regs., Part II. and the Staff Manual respectively. Title pages will be prepared in manuscript.

Place	Date	Hour	Summary of Events and Information	Remarks and references to Appendices
BIHUCOURT	28/5/17		The Brigade moved to L'Homme Mort taking over the command of the left sector of the Divisional front from the 187th Inf. Bde. relief being completed at 2.30 A.M. on the 29th.	C.f.g.
	29/5/17			See O.O. 20 Attack in A & B Inf. Survey After in B C/g Inf. Survey B.
L'HOMME MORT	29th		Quiet day	C.f.g. Inf. Survey B.
"	30.5.17 to 3/6/17		Quiet days	
"	3/4 6.17		Internal Relief & Gas projected from Livens Projectors	C.f.g. O.O. 21. C.
"	4/5/6		173 Bde. took over additional frontage on the left from 62nd Bde.	C.f.g. 0023 'B
"	5/7/6		No unusual activity	C.f.g. 1. Survey B.
"	7/8		Relief of 2/3 by the 2/6 Battn which came under orders of G.O.C 173 Bde. at 9 am 7th	0024 E.150 C.f.g.
"	8/9		Raid on that part of the enemy's line known as the Knuckle successfully carried out by the 2/1st Bn. London Regt with heavy loss to the enemy & capture of one prisoner who gave valuable information	1. S. B. 0022 F. C.f.g. 1. S. B.
	9/6/17 10th		Relief of 2/8 Bn. by 2/7 Bn. which came under orders of G.O.C 173 Inf. Bde. 9 Pm. June 9th	C.f.g. O.O. 26. 15B
	10/11th		Concentration in St Leger 2/5 & 2/4 Bns. & additional front taken over by 2/4 Bn. from 110th Inf Bde. Quiet day	OO 27 15. B.

WAR DIARY
or
INTELLIGENCE SUMMARY.
(Erase heading not required.)

Army Form C. 2118.

Place	Date	Hour	Summary of Events and Information	Remarks and references to Appendices
L'HOMME MORT	12		Internal Relief. Enemy Quiet. Our own artillery Active	I.S. "B" O.O.25/
"	13/13		Quiet Day	I.S. "B."
"	13/14		Relief of 2/1st Bn & 1 coy 2/1st Bn by 2/6th Bn & one coy 2/6th Bn which came under orders G.O.C. 173 Inf Bde 9 p.m. 13th June. Quiet day.	O.O.29 and I.S. "B."
"	14th		O.O. No 25 dated June 8th cancelled & O.O.30 substituted. Quiet day.	G.S.G. Attached L & M
"	15th		In accordance with O.O.30 the 173 Inf Bde attacked and captured the Hindenburg Front line on a frontage of 1100 yards at 2.50 a.m. on the 15th June. The attack was carried out by one Coy of the 2/1 Bn and 1 Coy of the 2/3rd Bn. under command of the O.C. 2/1 Bn. on the right & 6 platoons of the 2/2nd & one coy 2/4th under the command of O.C. 2/2nd Bn. on the left. Heavy losses were sustained by the enemy & 43 prisoners captured worthy surrender after stiff fighting.	O.O.30 L.
"	16th		In accordance with O.O.31. the 173 Inf Bde attacked in conjunction with the 31st Div on our left. The Hindenburg Support line at 3.10 A.M. on the 16th June. The attacking troops were composed as shown in O.O.31. under the command of O.s.C. 2/2/1d & 2/3rd Bns. Owing to the fact	

WAR DIARY
or
INTELLIGENCE SUMMARY.
(Erase heading not required.)

Army Form C. 2118.

that the enemy had succeeded by means of artillery barrage & strong bombing attacks by Sturmtruppen in reoccupying part of the front line captured by us on the 13th & maintaining themselves in numbers in this part of the line. It was necessary for the troops taking part in the attack to eject these parties of the enemy during the process of assembly in this part of the line. The alarm was given by these enemy bodies & the enemy barraged our troops in assembly causing heavy enemy casualties. Notwithstanding these difficulties the attack was launched punctually at 3.10 A.M. and we succeeded in occupying our objective. Throughout the day stubborn fighting in the Hindenburg support line took place & heavy casualties were inflicted on the enemy who brought up fresh troops and introduced a Battalion of special Sturmtruppen. It was impossible to reinforce our own men or to take up supplies of bombs or ammunition & the constant

WAR DIARY
or
INTELLIGENCE SUMMARY.
(Erase heading not required.)

Army Form C. 2118.

Place	Date	Hour	Summary of Events and Information	Remarks and references to Appendices
			reinforcement of the enemy, who was able to supply his men constantly with bombs and ammunition by means of the continuous gallery dugout under the support line, added to the enfilade fire of m.mors Machine Guns from both flanks, reduced our troops to a handful. On the evening of the 16th heavy bomb fighting was still in progress at 9.30 p.m. but the relieving troops of the 174th Inf. Bde. found the Hindenburg Support Line strongly held by the enemy, when they took over the sector on the night of the 16th/17th. The Command of the Brigade sector passed to G.O.C. 174 Inf.	O.O.31. Appendix N. C.J.G.
	16/17		Bde. at 9 p.m. on the night of the 16th June. the Battalions in the Hindenburg Front Line and in the Sunken Road between the Front & Support Line being relieved during the night of the 16/17 & B.G. Feryberg V.C. DSO was removed to Hospital suffering from fever.	C.J.G.
17K. 17/6/20			Bde. H. Qrs moved to L'ABBAYE MARY. Lt Col. Beauford assuming Command of the Bde during Gen Freyberg's illness. In rear	C.J.G.

Army Form C. 2118.

WAR DIARY
or
INTELLIGENCE SUMMARY.
(Erase heading not required.)

Instructions regarding War Diaries and Intelligence Summaries are contained in F. S. Regs., Part II. and the Staff Manual respectively. Title pages will be prepared in manuscript.

Place	Date	Hour	Summary of Events and Information	Remarks and references to Appendices
ABLAINZEVILLE	20th		In accordance with O.O. 32 moved to ABLAINZEVILLE.	O.O. 32 C/g App. O.
	20th to 30th		Training & working parties in ABLAINZEVILLE Area.	C/g

173RD INFANTRY BRIGADE

Intelligence Summary for Period of 24 hours ending 9 a.m., 29/5/17

A. OPERATIONS

1. **Enemy's attitude and general activity.** The situation is unchanged, the front being very quiet and the enemy displaying little activity beyond a frequent use of Very Lights and intermittent shelling with H.V. shells of the road at L'HOMME MORT and occasional heavy bursts on posts U.20.d.4.4, U.20.d.1.6, and U.20.c.3.4 with H.E. from direction of HENDECOURT. From 11.30 a.m. to 12.30 p.m. the Sunken road from U.27.a.5.9 to U.20.d.5.4 was heavily shelled by 5.9 howitzers, 15 shells falling here between 12 noon and 12.2 p.m. Intermittent shelling of the railway embankment with 5.9 howitzers at irregular intervals also took place. The night was quiet except for some activity with H.V. and a few shells on PELICAN ALLEY in U.27.a. and U.25.b. No M.G., T.M. or rifle fire during the night. The O.P. at U.25.b.6.3 has apparently been spotted as it was the target for some shelling, to which our artillery replied.

2. **Our own activity on same lines and where it influences enemy Action.** During the night the 2/1st Bn. London Regt. relieved a Battalion of the 187th Infantry Brigade in the Right sub-section and the 2/2nd Bn. London Regt. relieved a Battalion of the same Brigade in the Left sub-section. Relief was complete at 1.45 am. and was carried out without interference by the enemy. The Command of the Brigade sector passed from the 187th Brigade to the 173rd Brigade at 2.30 a.m. on the 29th

B. INTELLIGENCE

1. **Movement.** 11.55 a.m. seven men seen at U.9.d.7.7. and two parties of three each at same point ½ hour later. Fire was opened by our Lewis Guns on each occasion and the enemy entered their trench at the junction of MATCH ALLEY and HOOP TRENCH.

2. **Work.** At U.21.c.86 where a sniper was observed on the 27th fresh earth was noticed. It is thought that a M.G. emplacement may be in course of construction here. At 6.20 a.m. and at 11.35 a.m. parties of 9 and 4 men were seen carrying timber and working in the vicinity of UPTON WOOD and at intervals during the day men were seen working on the ridge N.W. of this Wood.

3. **Signals.** At 3 a.m. the enemy sent up 12 green lights which burst into two. No action apparently followed but at this hour their artillery was active and it is thought the signal may have been to lengthen range.

4. **Aerial Activity.** At 6.50 a.m. on the 28th and again at 10.30 and 11.30 a.m. and 1.30 p.m. enemy aeroplanes attempting to cross our lines were repulsed with A.A. gunfire.

2/Lieut.
I.O., 173rd Infantry Brigade.
for Brigade Major.

173RD INFANTRY BRIGADE

Summary of Intelligence for Period of 24 hours ending
9 a.m., 20/5/17

A. OPERATIONS

1. **Enemy's attitude and general activity.** The situation is unchanged. Enemy artillery has been rather more active during the day, shelling U.13.c. and d. and 19 a.,b., d., indiscriminately with 15 cm. from the direction of HENDECOURT. Observers report that the shelling in this area appeared to be at random, and had very poor results. The rate of fire varied between two and eight per minute but was fairly continuous throughout the day. One incendiary shell is reported to have fallen in CROISILLES at 10.5 p.m.
   On the Right sub-sector the shelling was more concentrated, the enemy firing principally on the Railway Cutting in U.26.b., particularly around U.26.b.35 to 85. Firing here was intermittent until 5 p.m., when heavy crashes of 15 cm. were fired at intervals until 9 p.m., when retaliation was asked for and obtained with satisfactory results. The direction was reported to be from BULLECOURT. At midnight a few shells were dropped on O.P. in U.26.b. and c. and at 3 a.m. to 4.20 a.m. moderate shelling of U.19.b. again occurred. Visibility has been fair. Marked absence of M.G., T.M., and rifle fire.

2. **Our own activity on same lines and where it influences Enemy Action.** Our artillery kept the enemy under constant fire throughout the day and were especially active during the afternoon.

B. INTELLIGENCE.

1. **M.G.Emplacements (located or suspected).** Patrol confirms existence of M.G.emplacement at U.20.a.70.87.

2. **Movement.** 3 to 5 p.m. U.8.a. and b. movement of small parties near UPTON WOOD and at 6.30 to 7 p.m. two men seen carrying guns into UPTON WOOD.

3. **Wire** (see Patrol report)

4. **Signals** (see Patrol report). A searchlight was active apparently from some point N.E. of BULLECOURT, but its location cannot be determined from this section of the front.

5. **Aerial activity.** No enemy planes were observed, and from 2 to 6 observation balloons were up throughout the day well in rear of the enemy lines. Our own aeroplanes were busy throughout the day.

6. **General.** A large explosion was observed at HENDECOURT in the neighbourhood of the CHATEAU at 1 p.m. No report was heard, but the smoke was unmistakeably that of an explosion and apparently that of a mine.

7. **Patrol Reports.** 2/2nd London Regt. 2/Lt. Harper and 2 O.R. left U.20.a.10.10 at 1 a.m. and proceeded N.E. to U.20.a. 10.60 where further progress became impossible as the enemy was found to be occupying a line of shell holes in front of his wire from which he fired Very Lights at 50 yards intervals every few minutes. At U.20.a.70.90 the earthworks previously reported as an M.G. emplacement was plainly seen and its appearance confirms the opinion formed as to its nature. The patrol then moved S.E. to U.20.a.80.35 and along the wire to U.20.b.10.30. The wire here is very thick and unbroken and without gaps; further advance was prevented by our artillery who were shelling the wire to the East. Red and green lights were constantly sent up from the enemy's main line while the patrol was out, but with no apparent result. The ground N.E. of U.20.a.10.30 was found to be quite flat, but broken by shell fire in U.20.a. and it then falls away at a moderate slope in a N.E. direction.

C J Graham 2/Lt I.O. 173 Bde

War Diary

173rd INFANTRY BRIGADE.
Summary of Intelligence for 24 hours ending 9 a.m.
31/5/17.

A. **OPERATIONS.**

1. <u>Enemy's attitude and general activity.</u>   The enemy's Artillery was somewhat more active throughout the day. Gas shells were fired into area T.29.a/b. and on the North edge of ST. LEGER WOOD.   The EMBANKMENT line in T.24.d. and T.25.a. & d. and posts in Right Sub-sector were shelled intermittently from 1.30 p.m. to 10.30 p.m. with various calibres mainly from direction of RIENCOURT and HENDECOURT.
Enemy M.G's. active between 5 and 6 p.m. against our O.P. at U.25.b.7.5.   There was little rifle fire, but at 5.30 p.m. a Medium Trench Mortar Batty. fired 20 rounds on our posts in U.27.a.

2. <u>Our own activity on same lines, and where it influences enemy action.</u>   Our artillery was active throughout the day.   At 3.40 a.m. our artillery fired a barrage on enemy trenches from U.20.a.60.10 to U.14.c.60.20. which lasted for 8 minutes.   The enemy's retaliation was slow and weak, a few shells being fired on Cutting between U.25.a. and b. and U.26.c.3.5 at intervals of 1 minute from 4.10 a.m. to 4.25 a.m. On the ~~xxxxxix~~ left sub-sector the enemy's barrage opened at 3.44 a.m. and lasted until 4.10 a.m. The fire was of a steady nature but of no great strength.

B. <u>INTELLIGENCE</u>

1. <u>Movement</u>. 2 of the enemy were seen to jump out of trench at U.25.b.50.30 at 7.25 p.m., 1 of whom got back into the trench but other walked along top of C.T., finally disappearing over sky line.
2. <u>Smoke</u>. At 4.10 p.m. smoke was seen rising in large volumes in area U.16.c.50.40
3. <u>Signals</u>. During our barrage at 3.40 a.m. on 31st May the enemy sent up a number of golden rain lights. During the bombardment to the N.W. of our line between 11 p.m. and 12 midnight on 30th the enemy discharged every variety of coloured lights at frequent intervals.
3. <u>Aerial Activity</u>. Enemy's aerial activity nil. Our planes were active throughout the day. Three of our planes flying very low flew over our line in the railway cutting and passed beyond CROISELLES.
4. <u>General</u>. Visibility was fair throughout the day.
5. <u>Patrols</u>. 2/2nd Bn. London Regt. - Lt. M.L.Harper, 2/2nd Lon. Regt. and 2 O.R. left No. 5 Post at U.20.a.15.20. at 10.20 p.m. on 30th inst. and proceeded to U.20.a.70.50. at which point they were sniped from their left. A Machine Gun approximately at U.20.a.60.60. was firing in N.E. direction.   The German wire from U20.a.80.50. to U20.b.10.40. is about two feet high and very strong, but cut in places by shell fire - From U20.b.10.40 to U20.b.15.15 the wire is in same condition and of same height. The depth of the wire could not be ascertained because of the tall grass, but no great damage appeared to have been done to it by shell fire.   At no point were the enemy trenches distinguishable.   When at U20.a.80.40. an enemy party could be heard working behind their wire, and from the sounds they were using picks and hammering.   Immediately behind the party a reddish green signal rocket was exploded followed by a burst of reddish green flame and much smoke. The patrol returned through post 5 at 1.30 a.m. 31/5/17 at which time our shells were falling on enemy's wire at U20.b.10.40.

Page 2.

5. Patrols Continued. 2/1st Bn. London Regt. 1 N.C.O. and 3 Other Ranks left U.21.c.5.4. at 11.30 p.m. and returned at 2 a.m. and proceeded north to enemy wire which was patrolled to the West for 200 yards. The wire is still strong though cut in places by our artillery. Shell holes in front of the wire are occupied by enemy who fire very lights from them at intervals and a second patrol of the 2/1st Lon. Regt. was unable to examine wire between midnight and 2 a.m. to the east of the SUNKEN Road in U.21.c. This patrol was fired on by a single rifle.

2/Lt.,
I.O. 173rd Infantry Bde.
for Brigade Major.

173rd Infantry Brigade.
Summary of Intelligence for
24 hours ending 9 a.m. 1/6/17.

A. OPERATIONS.

1. <u>Enemy's attitude and General Activity.</u> The period under review has been marked by no special activity on enemy's part; except for occasional burst of Machine Gun fire. The cutting and area U.20.c. and d. have been occasionally shelled, apparently from UPTON WOOD, but a large percentage of enemy shells were "blinds". At 1 a.m. six 15 cm. shells at 5 minute intervals fell in valley in rear of embankment at T.24.d.55 at 12.15 a.m. 12 gas shells fell in U.19.a., fired from direction of RIENCOURT. Between 2.30 a.m. and 3 a.m. 18 15 cm. shells, fired from direction of RIENCOURT, at one minute intervals fell in area U.19.c. and d.

2. <u>Our own Activity on same lines and where it influences enemy action:-</u> Our artillery and aeroplanes were active throughout the day.

The enemy made no reply to our burst of fire at 8 p.m. 31st May, but in response to our artillery fire at 2.30 a.m. he fired at 2.34 a.m. shrapnel over ridge at U.19.b. and d. Further reports confirm the fact that the enemy shelling in reply to our barrage at 3.40 a.m. 31st May, was light.

B. INTELLIGENCE.

1. <u>M.G. Emplacements.</u> (Located or Suspected. M.G. Emplacements known to be at U.20.b.33. and U.20.b55.15 confirmed by ground observers. What appears to be new concrete work has been observed on known M.G. Emplacements plainly shewn on aeroplane photographs at U.20.b.13.50 XXXXX and U.20.b.05. U.20.a.9.6. Two or three of the enemy have been seen by these posts.

2. <u>Movement.</u> At 4.5 p.m. One German was seen to walk along left of UPTON WOOD.

3. <u>Signals.</u> At 5.5 p.m. 31st May two white light seen descending from cloud as if dropped by aeroplane over T.2.a.80. During heavy bombardment at 2.30 a.m. on 1st June on right sub-sector alternate red and gold rain lights sent up from direction of RIENCOURT. 20 red lights sent up from enemy's lines opposite right sub-sector at 2.40 a.m. without any marked result.

4. <u>Aerial Activity.</u> Enemy planes showed more activity than during previous day. One plane crossed our lines at 8.15 a.m. but was engaged by our A.A. Guns and flew back after five minutes.

5. <u>General.</u> Enemy O.B's observed to rise at following bearings from O.P. at T.29.c.70.90.

Time.	Bearing.	
5 a.m.	38° T.B.	
5.12 a.m.	68° T.B.	
5.15 a.m.	38° T.B.	O.B. Came down.
5.25 a.m.	70° T.B.	
5.30 a.m.	38° T.B.	

6. <u>Patrols.</u> Patrols and listening posts reported enemy movement near his wire in U.20.a.4.9. at 1.45 a.m. A patrol sent out to clear situation up reported no sign of enemy.

2/Lt. Heading, 2/2nd London Regt. with 2 O.R. left posts ?.c. at U.13.d.9.3. at 10.15. p.m. and proceeded due north to trench occupied by K.R.R. at U.13.d.8.8. The patrol then turned east and ran into enemy wire at U.14.c.0.7. and found screw pickets and thick wire 15 feet deep, partly knocked down in seven or eight places but not practicable for troops to U.14.c.12.

From there to U.20.a.7.8. the wire is fifteen feet deep and practically untouched by shell fire. Very lights were put up from point U.20.a.7.5. and it was not possible to get close, but the wire appeared to be only slightly damaged by shell fire.

173RD INFANTRY BRIGADE

War Diary

Summary of Intelligence for the Period of 24 hours ending
9 a.m., 2/6/17

A. OPERATIONS

1. <u>Enemy's attitude and general activity</u>. The enemy artillery was extremely quiet during the day with the exception of a few rounds from H.V.guns on L'HOMME MORT road during the afternoon. This inactivity continued until our artillery activity at 10.55 p.m. and 2.10 a.m., when the enemy opened rapid fire with 77 mm guns on the ridge in U.13.d. and U.19.b. for about 15 minutes. In response to two green lights the enemy's fire slackened but the Sunken road in T.24.d. - U.19.c. was shelled with 5.9 inch shells for from about an hour. Throughout the morning and afternoon there was intermittent shelling of U.19.d., T.30.b. and U.19.b. and d.

2. <u>Our own Activity on same lines and where it influences enemy Action</u>. Our artillery and aeroplanes were active throughout the day. Enemy M.G.emplacements at U.20.a.79.65, U.20.a.9.6, and U.20.b.13.50 were successfully bombarded by our artillery, and badly damaged. It was observed this morning that the enemy had already started to repair these emplacements.

B. INTELLIGENCE

1. <u>Movement</u>. Six men seen at U.21.c.central at 0.30 p.m. were dispersed by our rifle fire.

2. <u>Smoke</u>. 9.40 a.m. at U.17.d.70.76 dense black smoke seen to rise. 9.55 a.m. at U.17.d.35.50 dense white smoke seen to rise.
XXXXXXXXXXXXXXXXXXXXXXXXXXXXXXXXXXXXXXX

3. <u>Wire</u>. Patrol reported enemy wire between and along U.20.c.2.5 - U.20.a.2.5 - U.20.b.00.59 - U.20.b.4.0, is cut in places but still forms an efficient barrier.

4. <u>Signals</u>. Two reds followed by two reds and a white sent up several times by enemy with no apparent result. Red and golden rain sent up at 10.55 p.m. and 2.10 a.m. resulted in rapid fire by 77 mm. guns on ridge in U.13.d. and U.19.b. Large number of whire Very Lights ssnt up from U.20.b. between 11 p.m.on 1st and 1.30 a.m. on 2nd June.

5. <u>Aerial Activity</u>. At 11 a.m. an enemy plane flew over CROISILLES. At 7 p.m. an indecisive fight took place between 5 British and 5 enemy planes without any casualties on either side. Baloons seen to rise at following True Bearings from O.P. at T.29.c.70.90 :-   88°, 79°, 72°, 70°, 55°, 44°.

6. <u>General</u>. One of our snipers at No. 2 post U.21.c.25.26 claims to have silenced enemy sniper at about U.20.b.3.3.
<u>Visibility</u> - fair to good.

7. <u>Patrols</u>. 2/Lieut. Denton and 2 O.R. left post 6a at U.19.b.9.9 at 10.15 p.m. and proceeded to U.14.c.2.2 and patrolled along the enemy's wire from that point to U.20.a.8.8 The wire was only slightly damaged from shell fire and impassable for infantry. The wire has a depth of 6 - 9 yards and is supported on iron stakes about 3 feet high. Most of our shells appear to have fallen just short of the enemy's wire, and from the Very Lights sent up the consolidated shell holes in U.20.a. are still held by the enemy. The patrol returned at 12.15 a.m. 2/6/17.

2/Lieut.,
I.O.,173rd Infantry Bde.
for Brigade Major.

War Diary

173rd Infantry Brigade.
Summary of Intelligence for 24 hrs. ending 9 a.m. 3rd June 1917.

A. OPERATIONS.

1. <u>Enemy's attitude and General Activity.</u> Enemy shelling was normal for first half of period under review. During the afternoon and evening the valley behind the Railway Embankment in T.30.b. was occasionally shelled by 15 cm. from direction of RIENCOURT. At 11.40 p.m. enemy heavily bombarded our posts in U.26.b. - U.21.c. and U.21.d., inflicting four casualties, one being fatal. An enemy Machine Gun traversed the front of right sub-sector continually from 5.15 a.m. and it appears as if new M.G.s. have been brought up.
The enemy continued to work on repairs to M.G. Emplacements at U.20.a.79.65.; U.20.a.96. and U.20.b.15.50. and great working activity was noticeable in this area.
          generally
2. <u>Our own Activity on same lines and where it influences enemy action</u>:- Our Artillery was active throughout the day. At 2.10 a.m. according to plan Gas was projected. The enemy replied by a moderate rifle fire and by sending up Golden Rain Light followed in 4 - 5 minutes by a barrage on front line with shells of heavy calibres. A great number of many coloured lights Orange, red, white, green were sent up by enemy on flanks and front of section against which gas was launched.

B. INTELLIGENCE.

1. <u>Machine Gun Emplacements (Located or Suspected).</u> At 11 p.m. three M.Gs. were firing over our posts 6c. at U.13.d.9.3. and 6a. at U.19.b.90.85. from about U.14.a.0.9. Listening Post in TIGER TRENCH report TIGER TRENCH is swept by M.G. fire.
2. <u>Smoke.</u> At 5 p.m. 2/6/17, an explosion was seen in FONTAINE.
3. <u>Wire.</u> In patrol report on enemy wire forwarded in this office Intelligence Summary for period of 24 hours ending 9 a.m. 2/6/17, map co-ordinates should read U.20.a.90.45. and U.20.b.30.05
4. <u>Signals.</u> Enemy observed signalling in code with light ~~from xxxxxxxxxx of church behind right of xxxxx xxxxxxxx~~ at a T.B. of 38° from O.P. at T.29.c.70.20. Signallers ~~xxxxx~~ read last part of message as follows:-
   "MIN AAA WIROUNGER AAA UFEN AAA LUTZ AAA
       HATWOHL AAA"
5. <u>Aerial Activity.</u> Our planes active patrolling and observing. Enemy planes more active and those endeavouring to cross our lines heavily engaged by our A.A. Guns and driven back.
6. <u>General.</u> Enemy O.B's. seen at following True Bearings from O.P. at T.29.c.70.20.

           56°
           55°
           66°
           70°
           88°

                                            (signed) Graham
                                                     2/Lieut.,
                                                Intelligence Officer,
                                 for   Brigade Major,
                              173rd Infantry Brigade.

War Diary

173rd Infantry Brigade.
Summary - of - Intelligence.
for 24 hours ending 9 a.m. 4/5/17.

A. OPERATIONS.
1. Enemy's attitude and General activity. Enemy's artillery has been fitfully active throughout the period - U.19.D, and the embankment in U.24.d. were lightly shelled by 15 cm. and at midnight the enemy sent some shrapnel on U.25.d.9.9. fired from direction of HERMICOURT. Our posts in U.21.c. were lightly shelled by 77 mm. and about 5 a.m. 6 or 7 shells - all "blinds" - fell on U.25.b.8.8. Area U.13.c. and d. - U.19.a. and b. were shelled intermittently with shrapnel and H.E. during the night.
At 8.30 p.m. camp at S.18.central shelled by 35 cm. gun - eight shells in all fired at 8 minutes interval were fired.
2. Our own activity on same lines, and where it influences Enemy Action. The 2/3rd Bn. London Regt. relieved the 2/1st Bn. London Regt and the 2/4th Bn. London Regt. relieved the 2/2nd Bn. London Regt. in the right and left sub-sectors respectively.
   The 2/1st Bn. moved into support.
   The 2/2nd Bn. moved into reserve.
About 11 p.m. a number of golden rain rockets were put up by the enemy which were observed from L'HOMME MORT. As the above relief was in progress neutralising fire was asked for from our counter batteries and promptly obtained. The enemy did not develop any serious volume of fire and the shelling of left of our right sub-sector which had been moderate about 10.30 p.m. ceased. It is not thought from later reports that our relief was spotted, and the signals observed on our front and to our right may have had some connection with an artillery strafe which was in progress apparently about a mile to our left.
   Our artillery has been active throughout the day, firing chiefly on the enemy's front line and wire.

B. INTELLIGENCE.
1. Signals. The enemy sent up the usual profusion of red, white and green very lights. One light varied from the ordinary golden rain bursting into a golden cascade, remained visible in the air for nearly a minute before disappearing. Double red lights followed by green sent up by enemy - without result.
2. Aerial Activity. Enemy displayed great aerial activity throughout the period, enemy aircraft crossed our lines several times. Each morning for the last week an enemy plane or planes has flown very high over the area around L'HOMME MORT. Our A.A. guns have engaged them vigorously without result.
3. General. Enemy's O.B's. were in evidence, some of which remained up throughout the day.
   Wind:- practically nil.
   Visibility:- good.
4. Patrols. Owing to internal reliefs no patrols were sent out.

C.Graham
2/Lieut. I. O.
for Brigade Major,
173rd Infantry Brigade.

173RD INFANTRY BRIGADE.

SUMMARY OF INTELLIGENCE FOR

PERIOD OF 24 HOURS ENDING 9 A.M. 5/6/17.

A. **OPERATIONS.**

1. **Enemy's attitude and General Activity.**

   Enemy's attitude quieter than during preceding period. Gas shells were fired on ECOUST from direction of HENDECOURT and at 3.30 a.m. 5th inst. three bursts of M.G. fire from direction of RIENCOURT passed over Right Sub-sector. Our posts in left sub-sector shelled intermittently and irratically, throughout the day, with 77 mm guns. Shrapnel fired on working party at U.13.d. between 10 and 11 p.m. Between 4 and 4.30 a.m. at 1 minute intervals 17 10.5 cm. shells fell in area T.29 and T.30.c.

2. **Our own activity on same lines, and where it influences Enemy Action.**

   Our artillery active throughout the day on enemy's line and wire in U.14 and U.20 ; with what result has not yet been ascertained. Our artillery activity here affectually prevented enemy from working or moving about in this sector.

B. **INTELLIGENCE.**

1. **Smoke.**

   At 1.15 a.m. 4/6/17, an explosion was seen to the left of HENDECOURT.

   At 12.45 a.m. 5/6/17, a large flare was observed to the West of HENDECOURT - apparently an ammunition dump exploded.

2. **Signals.**

   About 20 red flares sent up about 10 p.m. from U.14.a. A searchlight active at 12.30 a.m. in direction of RIENCOURT. Patrol reports enemy Very Lights sent up from behind their support line at U.21.a.central.

3. **Aerial Activity.**

   Considerable aerial activity by our planes, and those of the enemy. An enemy machine - albatross monoplane - brought down near U.13.d.5.5. and the pilot taken prisoner by Brigade on our left.

4. **Patrols.**

   At 11 p.m. 4/6/17 - 2/Lt. Seys, 2/4th Bn. London Regt. and 2 O.R. left post No.5. at U.20.a.15.10. and proceeded on T.B. of 45° until the German wire was reached - this appeared to be somewhat damaged, but owing to the moon a close examination was not possible.
   The patrol then went N. to U.20.a.45.95. (approx). The wire here was more knocked about and some gaps were visible. The patrol returned to post= G at U.13.d.8.2. at 12.55 a.m. and were fired at without effect by a sniper from enemy front line about U.14.c.7.1.
   The enemy sent up less very lights than usual.

   A patrol of 1 N.C.O. and eight men left U.20.d.3.4 at 11 p.m. on 4/6/17 - returned at 1 a.m. to U.20.d.30. Their instructions were to reconnoitre ground in front of U.20.d.34. U.20.d.10 and 5, with a view to future work in this area and to locate suspected enemy night post about U.20.d.3.9.

   They report that no enemy posts or patrols were seen. That the enemy were firing very lights considerably in rear of his line at U.31.a.central and that a number of dead bodies of Australian troops are lying from U.20.d.9.4. to U.20.d.10.90.

War Diary

173rd INFANTRY BRIGADE
SUMMARY OF INTELLIGENCE
for 24 hours ending 9 a.m. 6th June 1917.

A. **OPERATIONS.**

1. <u>Enemy's attitude and General Activity</u>. Enemy's artillery was quiet during the period under review. About 9.15 p.m. burst of shrapnel and H.E. were fired on paths in U.19.a. and T.24.b. and continued intermittently throughout the night.
Our posts from U.20.d. to U.13.d. lightly shelled with 10.5 c.m. and 15 cm. Howitzers about 9 p.m.
CROISILLES and the valley in T.30 was irregularly shelled throughout the period with shrapnel and H.E.

2. <u>Our own Activity on same lines, and where it influences Enemy Action</u>. Aour artillery active throughout the day on enemy's front line and wire.

B. **INTELLIGENCE.**

1. <u>Observation Posts (located or suspected)</u>. Snipers posts suspected at U.14.c.30.90. Fire from this point ceased after retaliation by our snipers.

2. <u>Movement</u>. The activity of our artillery prevented work or movement in enemy front and support lines.
At 2.30 a.m. 6 men observed at U.14.c.30.90. were dispersed by our rifle fire.

3. <u>Signals</u>. Enemy continues to send up a large number of very lights from U.14.c.

4. <u>Aerial activity</u>. Enemy aircraft active. A patrol of 8 enemy planes flying high, at 7.15 p.m. endeavoured to cross our lines but were driven back by our A.A. Guns. Our machines constantly patrolled our lines and at intervals crossed over the enemy lines.

5. <u>Patrols</u>. Patrols were sent out from No.5 post at U.20.a.15.10. and U.21.c.14 at 11.45 p.m. and U.20.c.80.75. at 10.30. p.m. respectively, but owing to our artillery shelling enemy front line and wire the patrol could not approach close to enemy wire. No hostile patrols were encountered and no movement observed either behind or in front of enemy's wire, except that 2 men were momentarily seen on sky line from point U.21.c.8.2. The enemy sent up a number of very lights of various colours.

C.J.Graham 2/Lt. I.O.
for Brigade Major,
173rd Infantry Brigade.

B.C.I. War Diary

173RD INFANTRY BRIGADE
SUMMARY OF INTELLIGENCE.

Period 24 hours ending 9 am.
June 7th 1917.

A. OPERATIONS.

1. Enemy's attitude and General Activity. The enemy's artillery during the period under review was very quiet. On our right subsector our posts in U.20.d. were shelled at "Stand to" last night. On our left subsector sniping was carried on by enemy from front of LONE TRENCH and M.G. fire from the HUMP fairly active throughout the night. At 11.15 p.m. a T.M. fired 20 rounds from a point about U.14.c.25.55. CROISILLES was shelled with H.E. both in the morning and evening and the batteries N.W. of ST LEGER were shelled with shrapnel. Enemy shelling during the day throughout the sector was erratic and intermittent and on sector from U.20.b.3.3. to U.21.a.2.2. it was noticed that the enemy sent up considerably less Very Lights, than he usually does. Batteries near L'HOMME MORT were fairly heavily shelled from midnight to 12.15 a.m.

2. Our own activity on same lines, and where it influences enemy action. Our artillery active throughout the day on enemy line and wire without much retaliation by the enemy.

An enemy sniper at U.14.c.20.85. was knocked out by one of our snipers from LONE TRENCH.

B. INTELLIGENCE.

1. M.G. Emplacements (located or suspected). Enemy M.G. Emplacement at U.20.b.57. is still intact.

2. Observation Posts (located or suspected). Considerable work appears to have been done on enemy Strong Point at U.21.a.2.5. 18 pdrs. registered on this point during the day.

3. Movement. At U.8.a.25.65. at 5.45 a.m. two men carrying sacks proceeded along road to S.W. Two men seen here again at 7.30 a.m. A considerable sized enemy working party in U.7.d. were dispersed by our 60 prs.

4. Signals. Red lights sent up by enemy in some profusion from U.14.c. between 9.55 and 10.15 p.m. and 2.15 to 2.45 a.m. but no action followed. At 9.20 p.m. a light bursting into 10 - 12 smaller lights of a bright yellowish colour was sent up. A green light which after bursting decended with a golden tail was observed.

5. Aerial Activity. Enemy planes endeavoured to cross our lines but were driven back by A.A. Guns.
From O.P. at U.26.b.80.50. Enemy O.B's. seen rise at following T.B.

Time.		
4.54 a.m.	$47°$	
5.30 a.m.	$30°$	
5.55 a.m.	$68°$	
-	$80°$	

Several enemy planes were active over L'HOMME MORT at 3.45 - 4 a.m. and were heavily engaged by A.A.G. and M.G. fire.

6. General. Visibility. Fair.
Wind. Light - S.E.

7. Patrols. 2/3rd Bn. London Regt. 2/Lt. P.W. Herepath and 4 men left U.26.c.7.1. at 11.50 p.m. on 6/6/17 to report on depth and condition of river bed from U.26.c.7.1. to U.20.d.80.65. The river bed is dry throughout and for the first 300 yds. is about 4 feet deep, but thence its depth gradually decreases until just before PELICAN AVENUE it is almost level with the ground. There is cover from view along the river bed as far as PELICAN AVENUE.

The enemy artillery does not appear to have been active along this stretch and three telephone wires run along the bed.

2/4th Bn. London Regt. 2/Lt. Croll and three Scouts left U.13.d. 80.20. at 11 p.m. on 6/6/17 and proceeded East for 180 yards. Enemy flares were numerous and an enemy post located at U.14.c.20.40 No enemy patrols were encountered and the party returned at 12.20 a.m. 7/6/17 to U.13.d.80.20.

Captain Spear, 2/3rd London Regt. and 1 O.R. left U.21.c.22. at 12.30 a.m. 7/6/17 and established liason with posts of 2/9th London Regt. at U.27.b.2.7. - U.21.d.2.5. and Crucifix and post at U.27.b.19.

London Regt. at U.27.b.2.7., U.21.d.2.3. and CRUCIFIX, and
M.G. post at U.27.b.1.9.
Patrol returned to U.21.c.2.2. at 1.30.a.m. 7/6/17.

C.J.Graham
2/Lt. I.O.
for Captain,
Brigade Major,
173rd Infantry Brigade.

5. **Patrols.** (Continued). 2/Lt. Taylor, 2/8th Bn. London Regt., 11 Riflemen and 2 Lewis Gunners, with Lewis Gun, left post at U.21.c.20.40. at 1.30 a.m. to locate and engage any enemy patrols and discover condition of enemy wire and condition of ground in front of Company Sector. No enemy patrols were encountered. German wire consists of low entanglement and ground level and free from brush.
Party returned at 2.45 a.m. at U.21.c.40.20.
2/Lt. Tregelles, 2/8th Bn. London Regt., 1 N.C.O. and 3 riflemen left post at U.20.c.25.45. Number of very lights sent up from U.20.a.66.55. Enemy M.G. firing - longish bursts from U.20.a.90.60. No enemy patrols encountered. Party returned at 3.50 a.m. to U.25.a.80.60.

2/Lieut. I. O.
for Brigade Major,
173rd Infantry Brigade.

War Diary

173RD INFANTRY BRIGADE.

Summary of Intelligence for 24 hours ending 9 a.m. 8/6/17.

A. OPERATIONS.

1. **Enemy's Attitude and General Activity.** Enemy's artillery showed more activity throughout the day. In our right subsector the junction of PELICAN AVENUE and TIGER TRENCH was shelled at midnight by 5.9 cm. from direction of HENDECOURT. Three direct hits were obtained on PELICAN AVENUE and the O.C. H.T.M. was killed and gun buried. Sunken road at U.21.c.35.15 shelled at 3.15 a.m. with 5.9 cm. H.E. from HENDECOURT. U.21.c.10.40. shelled by 77 mm. gun from about U.9.c. - The CEMETERY at C.2.a. shelled with 4.2 c.m. and 5.9 cm. 4.5 How. Batt. in C.7.a. received 45 rounds, a large percentage of which were "blinds".

M.G. fire directed at intervals on track U.19.d.50.10. - from an M.G. position not yet located.

On left sub-sector enemy's artillery was quieter - Heavy bursts of H.E., 77 mm. and shrapnel were fired on our front posts at 9.30 p.m. T.29.b. and T.30.a. were shelled with 10.5 cm. Short burst of M.G. were fired during night on to Railway Embankment and road in T.24.d.

2. **Our own Activity on same lines, and where it influences Enemy Action.** Our artillery was active throughout the day on usual targets. Shooting on enemy's line and wire appeared to be good.

2/3rd Bn. London Regt. was relieved by 2/8th Bn. London Regt. in Right Subsector during night of 7/8th. Relief was completed by 1.30 a.m. on 8th inst.

B. INTELLIGENCE.

1. **M.G. Emplacements (suspected or located.).** At 7.15 p.m. during a bombardment of the enemy line a Hun was observed to run from Sunken road about U.20.b. to the entrance of a M.G. Emplacement or O.P. at about U.20.b.5.3. which is some distance from the actual emplacement at U.20.b.51.18. and probably connected to it by a subterranean passage. A shell exploded close to this entrance and exposed the walls of the tunnel or passage which appears to be of concrete and measuring approximately 10' x 10'.

2. **Movement.** At 10.47 a.m. 30 enemy and 11.5 a.m. 10 enemy seen at U.16.c. moving towards HENDECOURT.

From 8 a.m. to 10 a.m. small parties seen on track U.16.a.90.60.

At 4.20 a.m. and 4.25 a.m. parties of two men and six men seen at U.15.a.80.80. they approached from NORTH and returned in same direction in pairs. It appears to be a dump and was shelled by our artillery at 4.35 a.m. T.B. from U.21.c.10.40. is 3°.

3. **Signals.** Enemy sent up more lights than usual from U.20.a. and U.20.b. and U.21.a. Search light observed from U.25.a.80.40 on a true bearing 95° and 90°.

4. **Aerial Activity.** Enemy patrols endeavoured to cross our line but were driven back by our A.A. Fire.

5. **Patrols.** 2/Lt. Croll, 2/4th Bn. London Regt. and 3 scouts left U.13.d.75.20. at 11 p.m. on 7/6/17 and proceeded to enemy wire at U.14.c.25.15. and worked S.E. alongside the wire to a point at U.20.a.60.82. The front belt of wire is considerably damaged and beaten down, especially at U.20.a.60.82. It was not possible to view closely the state of the second belt but at a distance it appeared to be in the same condition as the front belt. No enemy working parties were out and their trenches seemed very quiet. Movement of the enemy heard occasionally - the click of very light pistols being distinctly audible. Many lights were sent up in a diagonal direction so as to fall by front wire belt. Lights were sent up from sunken road at U.14.c.2.4. The shell hole reached at U.20.a.6082 had a pathway running back through the enemy wire but there was no sign of occupation. Only M.G. fire encountered was overhead from approximately U.14.c.50.80. Patrol returned at 1 a.m. to U.20.a.20.70.

173rd INFANTRY BRIGADE.

War Diary

Summary of Intelligence for 24 hrs. ending 9 a.m. 9.6.17.

A. Operations.

1. **Enemy's attitude and General Activity.** The front has been quiet up to 11.30 p.m. 8th inst. Enemy's artillery rather more active than yesterday. 9 a.m. to 11.30 a.m. Enemy shelled cemetery in C.2.a. with 10.5 cm. H.E. Hows. also placed salvoes of 10.5 cm shrapnel over Cemetery at 4 minute intervals, firing estimated to be from a bearing of 85° true from O.P. at U.25.b.80.30. At 4 p.m. enemy shells at 1 minute intervals on U.26.b.central. At 7.10 to 7.15. p.m. a dozen 10.5 cm. Hows. at U.20.c., 7.40 p.m. 13 - 10.5 cm. H.E. Hows. in U.20.c., 11.40 p.m. to 12.30 am. in response to our fire the enemy placed a barrage on our front line of posts and between front and support lines in Right Sub-sector. All calibres and rifle grenades were used on posts and sunken road in U.21.c. 12.30 a.m. artillery was active on both sides dying down in about ½ hour. The usual erratic and intermittent shelling of posts in Left Sub-sector with 77 mm, during the day. Bearings were taken on big gun flashes from U.25.b.80.30. of 48° true, at 9.25 pm. and from C.2.b.02.92. of 55° true, at 11 p.m. to 12.30 a.m. A Machine Gun was active during the night from U.14.c.25.85. traversing LONE TRENCH. Snipers were very active in the HUMP during the morning against LONE TRENCH.
A report on minor operations carried out is attached.
An enemy dump was blown up at 11.45 p.m. on a true bearing of 35° from U.26.c.6505.

B. INTELLIGENCE.

1. **M.G. Emplacements (suspected or located).** Enemy M.G. reported firing from direction U.20.b.40.20.
2. **Observation Posts (located or suspected).** See movement.
3. **Movement.** 6.17 a.m. 1 man seen in holes on ridge true bearing 7° from U.26.c.65.06. apparently observing. 9.15 a.m. 3 men moving along trench U.20.b.80.20. 3.25 p.m. working party of ten men U.20.b.80.10. 12 men at U.21.a.10.82 believed to be mouth of C.T.
4. **Smoke.** Smoke seen issuing from holes on ridge 6.15 a.m. true bearing 7° from U.26.c.65.06. 6.21 a.m. smoke issuing from holes on ridge true bearing 24° from U.26.c.65.06. 6.15 p.m. three explosions were seen East of BULLECOURT.
5. **Signals.** See also Raid Report. It is generally agreed in spite of Prisoners statement as to S.O.S. that a twin green light was the signal for barrage last night, and at 1.50 a.m. on a true bearing of 78° from U.25.b.80.30. this signal was again observed and appeared to draw enemy barrage on to front of our unit well to our right. Further the orange lights fired during our barrage were from the flanks of position raided.
The Green and Red from the Support Line and the Golden Rain from the Support Line immediately in rear of KNUCKLE.
6. **Aerial Activity.** Only one enemy plane reported during the day at 9.9 a.m. the 8th, fired at by A.A. Guns and disappeared to the East.
Our aircraft displayed their usual activity.
Enemy O.B's. were observed from following true bearings:-

From U.25.b.80.30.			From U.25.a.80.50.	
85°	40°	78°	2 at 62°.	)
35°	68°	31°		) All were
66°	25°	53°		) withdrawn
19°	52°			) by 12.10 p.m.

They were first observed at 6.45 a.m.

7. Patrols. 2/7th London Regt. 2/Lt. Weiss, 2/Lt. Barnes, Sgt. Knight, 8 Bombers, 2 Lewis Gunners with 1 Lewis Gun, left Coy.H.Q. at U.21.c.50.20 at 9.50 p.m. to gain information of enemy movements, locate and capture enemy patrol; they returned to point of departure at 11.30 p.m., having heard voices in enemy Front Line and made certain there was no enemy patrol out on frontage of Right Sub-sector.

2/Lt. Tregelles, 1 N.C.O. and 5 Riflemen left U.19.d. 50.00. at 12.45 a.m. to erect guide wire between posts, which was done. They returned at 4.15.a.m. and report that enemy appears to have pushed posts forward about 100 yds. in U.20.d.

C J Graham
2/Lieut. I.O.
for Brigade Major,
173rd Infantry Brigade.

War Diary

173RD INFANTRY BRIGADE.
Summary of Intelligence for period of 24 hours 9 a.m. 10/8/17.

A. OPERATIONS.

1. **Enemy's attitude and General Activity.** Enemy's attitude quiet. U.25.b.6.9. - U.25.b.9.8. shelled with H.E. and Shrapnel put over U.26.c. At 6.28 p.m. posts in right sub-sector shelled for 5 minutes with 77 mm guns in retaliation for our bombardment at 6.20 p.m. About 5 a.m. 10th, 20 10.5 cm shells dropped left of O.P. at U.25.b.7.32. Between 11 p.m. and 12.30 am. on night of 9/10th 30 gas shells dropped in and around valley in T.30.b. At 5.40 a.m. 48 77mm shells at minute intervals in T.30.a. M.G. at U.14.c.20.95 active throughout night. At 12 midnight 12 Light Trench Mortars fired from approx. U.14.c.5.6. fired in direction of U.13.d.central.

2. **Our own activity on same lines, and how it influences Enemy Action:-** Our artillery was less active but fired occasional heavy burst on enemy front and support lines, at irregular intervals throughout the period.

B. INTELLIGENCE.

1. **Movement.** 4.40 p.m. 3 men seen walking towards FONTAINE at U.8.a.8.5. and at 5.5 and 5.20 p.m. more men observed in same place. 5.2 p.m. 2 men seen walking along line of trenches at U.8.a.5.5. 7.32 p.m. 2 men walking from FONTAINE towards Sunken Road at U.8.a.8.2.

2. **Smoke.** 3.10 p.m. smoke seen issuing from U.8.a.2.7. and dense smoke from about U.2.b. - which appeared to be a dump set on fire. 4 p.m. Fire seen burning in RIENCOURT. 4.52. p.m. Tall column of smoke lasting 15 minutes at HENDECOURT.

3. **Signals.** Two golden rain fired from U.14.c. 5.5. about midnight About 8.10 p.m. one blue light fired which was followed by 77 mm shells on our front line in Right Sub-sector.

4. **Aerial Activity.** No enemy aerial activity but our planes were active throughout the period.

5. **Patrols.** 2/Lt. Croll, 2/4th Bn. London Regt. and 3 scouts left U.20.a.11 at 10.45 p.m. and worked N.E. and then N.W. till enemy was reached and thence to U.14.c.1.2. Although enemy movement heard - enemy was very quiet and nothing was seen. Very Lights active but no Machine gun fire except from U.14.c.20.95. Patrol returned to U.20.a.11. at 12.15. a.m.
2/Lieut. Sheffield, 2/3rd Bn. London Regt. and 11 men left Sunken Road at U.20.c.35.50 proceeding to enemy wire about U.20.a.7.5. Thence to U.20.a.10.50. enemy wire is cut off pickets and rolled, apparently by shell fire, into rolls about 10" x 2" These rolls are close together but it is passable almost everywhere - Thence to U.20.b.01.02. - screen pickets are standing but wire is cut off them and forms slight trip entanglement on ground. Thence U.20.a.32.15. wire is in same condition. Ground for 100 yards this side of enemy wire much broken with deep shell holes. Number of very lights sent up and occasional M.G. and Minenwerfer fire - Patrols returned at 12.35 a.m. to Sunken road at U.20.c.80.45.
2/Lieut. Walker and 2 P.R. at 12.30 a.m. left C.2.b.40.75. and proceeded to No.7 post U.27.a.17 and got in touch with O.C. Right forward Coy. H.Q. Thence patrol went via Sunken Road to CRUCIFIX and got in touch with D Coy., 2/10th London Regt. returning thence by direct road to starting point at 3.15 a.m.

J Graham
2/Lt
for Brigade Major,
173rd Infantry Brigade.

173RD INFANTRY BRIGADE.
Summary of Intelligence for the period of 24 hours ending 9 a.m. 11/6/17.

War Diary

A. **OPERATIONS.** 1. *Enemy's Attitude and General Activity.* Enemy artillery was more active on our front line during the day. Between noon and 1.35 p.m. area U.19.b. and d. was shelled with salvoes of H.E. and again between 2 p.m. and 3 p.m. U.25.b.57. was shelled rather heavily with H.E. between 8 and 8.15 p.m. Heavy bursts were fired on our left sub-sector. 30 gas shells on T.24.c. from 7.50 p.m. to 8.15 p.m. and 60 10.5 cm along ridge and C.T. and front line posts in U.13.d. and U.19.b.

2. *Our own Activity on same lines, and where it influences the Enemy Action.* Our artillery was normal — U.20.b. and CRUMP ALLEY were constantly shelled.

B. **INTELLIGENCE.** 1. *General.* Visibility poor. No enemy movement observed. Very lights were active during the night.

2. *Patrols.* 2/Lt. Seys, 2/4th Bn. London Regt. and 6 scouts left post No.5. at U.20.a.15.10. and proceeded on a T.B. of 45° until the German wire was seen and keeping about 50 yards from it worked north to point U.14.c.21. and then returned to starting point. No enemy movements seen or heard or any patrols encountered. Very Lights sent up than usual from a point about U.29.a.99. No M.G. fire but enemy sniper, location unknown, was active.

C J Graham
2/Lt. I.O.
for Brigade Major,
173rd Infantry Brigade.

War Diary

173RD INFANTRY BRIGADE

Summary of Intelligence for period of 24 hours ending 9 a.m.
June 12th 1917.

-*-

A. OPERATIONS.

1. **Enemy's Attitude and General Activity.** The enemy's attitude was quiet throughout the period. Between 11.45 a.m and 1.15 p.m there was desultory shelling of Area U.21.c. with H.E. and throughout the day salvoes of 77 mm and 10.5 cm. were fired on U.19.d. and U.20.c. from direction of RIENCOURT. About 2.30 a.m. shells of large calibre fell in vicinity of post at U.26.c.25.55., a sap leading to this post received a direct hit. There was M.G. fire at intervals throughout the night apparently from about U.20.a.90.45. and U.14.c.38. Indirect M.G. fire sweeps U.25.d. especially in neighbourhood of Railway Crossing in U.26.c. Some T.Ms. fell about U.21.c. in advance of Sunken Road position.

2. **Our own Activity on same lines and where it Influences Enemy Action:-**
Our own artillery was active throughout the day, firing on enemy front and support lines. In the left sub-sector 2/1st Bn. relieved 2/4th Bn. London Regt. and 1 Company, 2/7th Bn. London Regt. took over the posts previously held by the Right Front Coy. of the left Battalion.
No patrols were sent out owing to the relief.

B. INTELLIGENCE.

1. **Movement.** Two men were seen working on ridge about U.14.b. at 10.45 a.m.
2. **Smoke.** At 12 mid-day was seen issuing from centre of wood East of HENDECOURT.
3. **Aerial Activity.** Several enemy planes came over our lines at intervals between 4.30 p.m. and 9. a.m. this morning

C J Graham

2/Lt. I.O.

for Brigade Major,
173rd Infantry Brigade.

War Diary

173rd Infantry Brigade.

Summary of Intelligence for period of 24 hours ending
9 a.m. 13/6/17.

A. OPERATIONS.
1. Enemy's Attitude and General Activity. Enemy was quiet throughout the period. U.20.c., U.25.central were occassionally shelled and between 11.25 a.m. and 11.45 a.m. about 100 gas shells which appeared to be from 77 mm guns, fell around T.24.a. & c. Junction of Pelican Avenue and Tiger Trench was shelled during the day and during the night Tiger Trench was shelled with 10.5 cm. and swept by M.G. fire. Gas shells were fired in region of U.20.c. and in rear of embankment about U.25.a. between 1 and 2 a.m. M.G's. were active throughout the night with indirect fire on U.25.a.7.6. near ECOUST - CROISILLES Road. Two snipers were active apparently from U.20.b. about junction of front line trench and sunken road. ST LEGER was shelled at 6.15 a.m. and 8.45 a.m. apparently by H.V. Gun firing from direction of U.15.a.

2. Our own activity on same lines and where it influences enemy action. Our artillery were consistantly active firing on enemy front system and our aircraft were active patrolling and observing.

B. INTELLIGENCE.
1. Signals. Fewer Very Lights than usual. Golden sent up from U.20.b. resulting in enemy's artillery fire considerably slackening.
~~Visibility - Fair.~~
2. General.
Visibility - Fair.
Wind - Practically nil.

Graham
2/Lt. I.O.
for Brigade Major.
173rd Infantry Brigade.

War Diary

173rd INFANTRY BRIGADE.

Summary of Intelligence for Period of 24 hours ending
9 a.m. 14/6/17.

A. **OPERATIONS.**
1. **Enemy's attitude and General Activity.** The enemy's artillery was normal during the period. Except in answer to our barrage on BOVIS TRENCH, to which he replied with shrapnel barrage, a section of which was placed along Sunken Road to cross roads in U.20.d. with great accuracy. CROISILLES was shelled intermittently and a large calibre shell fell near the TOOTH. Our front and Support lines shelled at intervals throughout the day.
Enemy bombarded the line of the RAILWAY EMBANKMENT and CUTTING, during raid by 175th Inf. Bde. on BOVIS TRENCH.
M.G. fire indirect in short bursts trained on level crossing - but the elevation was high. M.G. Fire directed on Railway Embankment U.25.a.55.555 - U.26.c.80.00 - M.G. fire appeared to come from U.20.b.50.80.
2. **Our own activity on same lines and where it influences Enemy Action.** Our artillery was very active on enemy front system.

B. **INTELLIGENCE.**
1. **Movement.** At 2.30 p.m. 2 enemy seen in rear of COPSE TRENCH U.15.a. walking towards HENDECOURT.
At 1.30 p.m. 3 men carrying rifles and one with field glasses seen at U.20.b.35.85. and were shot at by our snipers.
2. **Smoke.** Smoke reported approximately at U.21.c.00.95. apparently a ruse to draw observation as it was followed by bursts of shrapnel over R.5. post and posts in U.20.c. & d.
3. **General.** Enemy A.A. Guns appeared to use more rounds per target than customary.
   Ladder or top of steps seen at 5 p.m. in a shell hole at U.20.b.55.75.
   Tail of T.M.Bombs seen fired from enemy front line about U.21.central.

C J Graham

2/Lieut. I.O.
for Brigade Major.
173rd Infantry Brigade.

SECRET.　　　　　　　　　　　　　　　　　　　　　　　Copy No...... 21

Appendix N.

173rd INFANTRY BRIGADE OPERATION ORDER NO.31.

Reference Map Sheets - BULLECOURT 1/10,000
- CHERISY 1/10,000 and A.2.　　　　　　　June 15th 1917.

---

1. As far as can be ascertained the situation at present is as follows. Our troops have captured and occupied the whole of this morning's objective with the exception of a small portion of the HINDENBURG FRONT LINE about the MEBUS at U.14.c.67.11. Orders have been given for this portion to be cleard up under arrangements to be made between O.C's. 2/1st and 2/2nd Bn. Lon. Rgts.
   In co-operation with us the 21st Division on our left will assault the HINDENBURG LINE from U.14.a.45.45. (Exclusive) north-westwards.
   The boundary b.' between us and 21st Division will be a line joining U.14.a.45.45. to U.14.a.00.15.(inclusive to us).

2. The attack will be resumed in the early hours of to-morrow. Zero hour will be notified later. The objective will be the HINDENBURG Support Line from U.20.b.50.70. to U.14.a.45.45., a defensive flank being formed along line U.20.b.50.70. - U.20.b.45.52. - U.20.b.50.00.

3. Assaulting troops as shewn below will be in assembly positions in HINDENBURG Front Line by 2.10 a.m. (MOONRISE) and Os. C. concerned will report assembly complete to Bde. H.Q. by using code word "BANANA".

   3 Companies, 2/3rd London Regt. - 1 Coy. 2/8th London Regt.
   　　　　　　　　　　　　　　　　　　　　(under O.C. 2/3rd Bn.)

   3 Companies　2/1st Bn. London Regt.

   2½ Companies　2/2nd Bn. London Regt.

   2 Companies　2/4th Bn. London Regt.　(under O.C. 2/2nd Bn.)

   In addition each assaulting party will be accompanied by a proportion of L.T.M. personnel with Stokes Bombs for dealing with dug-outs and R.E. for assistance in consolidation and blocking of the tunnels known to exist underneath HINDENBURG SUPPORT LINE.
   All units allotted to either of the assembly areas will come under the command of Officers Commanding Battalions concerned by 9 p.m. to-day.
   Detailed disposition and assembly areas are shown on attached map A2.

4. <u>Scheme of attack.</u>　The attack will be carried out in one wave supported by mopper up and detachment of R.E. and L.T.M. personnel mentioned above.
   The proportion of assaulting troops to mopper up will be 3 to1.
   Barrage time table will be forwarded as soon as received.

5. All posts in advance of HINDENBURG Front Line will be withdrawn by 3 a.m.
   Any alteration in localities selected for Bn. Battle H.Q. will be notified to Bde. Hd. Qtrs. immediately.

6. The arrangements and instructions outlined in paras. 4; 5; 6; 13; 16; 17; and 18 of 173rd Infantry Brigade Order No.30 of 14th June will stand.

7. VICKERS GUNS.　The advance will be supported by the guns of the 206th; 198th and 214th Machine Gun Companies.
   O.C. 206th Machine Gun Company will arrange that 8 Machine Guns are in position and ready for action in HINDENBURG FRONT LINE as soon as possible after receipt of this order.　No Vickers Guns will be sent forward of this line till further orders.

2.

6. ARTILLERY SUPPORT. The 173rd Infantry Brigade will be supported by the Artillery of three Divisions - the 7th, 58th, and 62nd Divisions; assisted by the Vth Corps Heavy Artillery.

7. SCHEME OF ATTACK. The attack will be carried out by one Company of each of 2/3rd, 2/1st, and 2/4th Bns. and 1½ Companies of 2/2nd Bn. - detailed disposition and assembly areas are shewn on attached map A.1.

O.C., 2/8th Bn. will establish a line of posts from U.20.b.40.16 S.E. along line of Sunken Road, connecting up with the existing post R.5 at U.21.c.2.3, and will detail one platoon to report to O.C., 2/1st Bn. before noon, 14th June.

For the purposes of this operation the Companies of the 2/3rd and 2/4th Bns. mentioned above, will be under the orders of Officers Commanding 2/1st and 2/2nd Bns. respectively.

Upon gaining the objective, Companies will "mop up" and consolidate under the protective barrage. - Battle patrols being pushed on to the line of the Sunken Road in U.14.c. and U.20.b.

8. DEFENCE OF CAPTURED OBJECTIVES. In the event of enemy bombarding the captured line, the S.O.S. signal will be made, when our artillery will barrage enemy line with 4.5 howitzers, and will place a strong barrage of 18 pounders 50 yards short of the HINDENBURG Support Trench.

9. SPECIAL DETACHMENT The Company of the 2/2nd Bn. referred to in para. 7 will advance and capture enemy strong point at U.14.a.15.00 and the cross roads at U.14.c.35.85.

10. VICKERS MAXIM GUNS. The advance will be supported by the guns of the 206th, 198th, and 214th Machine Gun Cos. and the guns of the 21st Division.

The O.C., 206th Machine Gun Co. will place one section at the disposal of the O.C., 2/2nd Bn. and one section at the disposal of O.C., 2/1st Bn.

These guns will accompany the assaulting troops taking up previous selected positions as soon as the objective is reached. O.C., 206th Machine Gun Co. will confer with battalion Commanders concerned as to the placing of these guns.

11. BATTALION HEADQUARTERS. Battalion H.Q. for 2/1st and 2/2nd Bns. will be at Railway Embankment in T.24.d.

12. AEROPLANE CO-OPERATION. Contact aeroplanes will be used at daylight to fix the positions gained by the infantry, in accordance with the principles practised in this Brigade.

Flares will not be used. Infantry will be issued with yellow handkerchiefs - these will be waved whenever an aeroplane sounds its horn. Yellow handkerchiefs will mean nothing unless waved.

13. COMMUNICATIONS (i) Advanced Report Centre will be at U.19.b.9.2. Communications established by means of
    (a) Wire.
    (b) Power Buzzer.
    (c) Visual.
    (d) Pigeons.
    (e) Runners.

3.

  (ii) Telephone Stations and Relay Posts for Runners will be established at U.25.a..75.60 and at T.24.d.8.2.
  (iii) Power Buzzers will be installed at Advanced Report Centre and at a place in U.13.b. to be notified later.
  (iv) A Wireless Station will be installed at T.24.d.8.2.
  (v) Visual Stations at U.19.b.30.85, T.24.d.8.2 and T.30.c.7.9., will be manned by 2/4th Bn. London Regt. signallers as at present.

14. SYNCHRONISATION OF WATCHES.
A representative from 2/1st and 2/2nd Bns. and 206th Machine Gun Co. will report at Brigade Headquarters at 7 p.m. 14th June to synchronise watches.

Watches will again be synchronised at 1 hour before ZERO at the Advanced Report Centre. A representative from Brigade Headquarters will be there for that purpose.

15. CARRYING PARTY.
Officers Commanding 2/1st and 2/2nd Bns. will be required to detail a small party for Vickers Machine Guns (two per gun).

16. EQUIPMENT.
All troops will be in battle order, and carry :-
  170 rounds S.A.A.
  4 Sandbags
  2 Iron Rations
  1 Box Respirator & P.H.G. Helmet
  1 Very Light
  2 Bombs
  Pick or Shovel
  Full water-bottle.
  Aeroplane signals.

As many wire cutters as possible will be issued to the 1st waves.

S.O.S. Rifle Grenades will be carried by Company and Battalion Headquarters. Runners are to be lightly equipped, and Battalion Runners will not carry rifles.

17. LIGHT SIGNAL.
S.O.S. - Special Rifle Grenade bursting into four red stars.
The ordinary S.O.S. signal will again be taken into use after 6 a.m. 17th June.

Resume normal rate of fire - Two white parachute lights.

These signals will be carried by each Company Headquarters.

18. NOTES.
(a) It must be impressed upon all units that they are on no account to halt because units on their flanks happen to be held up. The best way of assisting their neighbours on such occasions will be to continue their own advance.
(b) All Commanders must be impressed with the necessity of maintaining their direction and marching straight on to their allotted objective. With this object the ground must be carefully studied beforehand, landmarks noted wherever possible, and compass bearings taken.
(c) No papers likely to be of value to the enemy will be taken over the parapet.

4.

- (d) Not more than 4 officers per Company must take part in an assault, and a proportion of reliable N.C.Os. must also be left behind.
- (e) Officers and men will be particularly warned against retaining documents taken from prisoners as souvenirs. Very valuable information may be lost by failure to send in all documents so taken, which should be forwarded to Brigade Headquarters at the first opportunity.
- (f) The word "Retiro" does not exist; anybody using it is to be immediately killed.
- (g) No reference to this operation will be made over the telephone until after ZERO hour.

ACKNOWLEDGE.

[signature] Captain,
Brigade Major,
173rd Infantry Brigade.

Issued to Signals at 6 a.m.

Copy No.
1. 2/1st London Regt.
2. 2/2nd London Regt.
3. 2/3rd London Regt.
4. 2/4th London Regt.
5. 173rd T.M.Battery
6. 206th Machine Gun Co.
7. 2/8th London Regt.
8. 110th Infantry Brigade
9. 174th Infantry Brigade.
10. 175th Infantry Brigade.
11. Left Group 58th D.A.
12. Brigade Major for G.O.C.
13. 504th Field Co. R.E.
14. 510 Co. A.S.C.
15. "G", 58th Division
16. "A" & "Q", 58th Division
17. C.R.A.
18. Staff Captain.
19. Brigade Signalling Officer)
    " Transport Officer) To note and return to last
    " Intelligence Officer)   named.
20. War Diary
21. War Diary
22. File
23)
to) Spare
28)

Confidential

War Diary of
J.G. 123 Inf. Bde.
from 28/5/17 to 30/6/17

Army Form C. 2118.

JULY 1917

WAR DIARY
or
INTELLIGENCE SUMMARY.
(Erase heading not required.)

Place	Date	Hour	Summary of Events and Information	Remarks and references to Appendices
ABLAINZEVELLE – LOG EAST WOOD	1st		Intermittent training etc	Cees
BANCOURT	6th			
"	7th		Bn marched to BANCOURT CAMP – via GOMIECOURT – SAPIGNIES – BAPAUME	
BANCOURT	8th			
"	9th		1st, 2nd & 4th Bns London Regt; 173 & 174 M.G. marched to PUYSIEULCOURT and YPRES	OO.33 APPEN: "A" Cees
NEUVILLE BOURJONVAL	10th		Bn Hy and 3rd Bn moved to NEUVILLE by road.	
"	11th		Brig Commander inspected Bn in afternoon	Cees
YPRES Area	12 & 13		Training	Cees
"	14th		Bn inspected by Col. Ty Corps (Lt Gen Smith Dorrien)	Cees
"	15th		Lt Col Spragge Ty Corps arrived in Ypres in afternoon. Relief completed 10pm	Cees
(PROVENCOURT)	16th		Bn took over BEAUCAMP SECTION from 17th J.B. Dispositions as follows – 2/3rd 9Bn Right Front – (+ 1 Coy 2/4 Bn)	OO.34
BEAUCAMP SECTION.			2/1st 13th Left "	"B" Cees
			2/4th (less 1 Coy) "B" in Support (GOUZEUCOURT & DEZART WOODS)	
			2/2 13th in Div Reserve – YPRES	

Army Form C. 2118.

WAR DIARY
or
INTELLIGENCE SUMMARY.
(Erase heading not required.)

Instructions regarding War Diaries and Intelligence Summaries are contained in F.S. Regs., Part II. and the Staff Manual respectively. Title pages will be prepared in manuscript.

Place	Date	Hour	Summary of Events and Information	Remarks and references to Appendices
BERTINCOURT Front Section	16th to 21st		Quiet and normal Trench warfare. Owing to lack of steam bath covered in inclement weather a C.T. was dug to Bertincourt and work of outpost line and Support line in Right Subsection was begun.	Intell Summary. C. D. E. F.
	22nd		2/4th relieved 2/3rd in Right Subsection. 2/2nd relieved 2/1st in Left Subsection.	OO.35 G.CW TS CW H TS II TJX CW M N appx.
	23rd		Normal Trench warfare - Section very quiet on carrying continued.	
	28th			
	29th		1 Officer and 38 OR 2/7 2/8 5th raid. Plush TR opposite Ryan Subsection. Party entered trench but found same empty. Our casualties - 2 OR lightly wounded.	CW IS P
NEUVILLE BOURJONVAL	30th		Bde relieved by 27 JB, 9th Bde. (Brig Gen Oz surrendered H.C. D.Sc) Relief completed by 7 p.m. on relief. Bde HQ moved to Neuville and Bde H Staff open BERTINCOURT- RUYAULCOURT- NEUVILLE en route for MAROW- 13th coy reported arra.	OO.36 Q CW

WAR DIARY or INTELLIGENCE SUMMARY

Army Form C. 2118.

Place	Date	Hour	Summary of Events and Information	Remarks and references to Appendices
MANIN	3.		Bn moved to as follows.	
			Bn HQ by rail to SAULTÉ Bque and to MANIN	0036 Q
			2/1 s/Bn - to 12ep LES HAMEAU ditto	
			2/2 " /Bn " ditto	
			2/4 " /Bn " ditto	
			2/3 " /Bn to MANIN	
			173 LTM13 " "	Defence Sch Appx R
			208 Inf Coy " "	

J Sherman Capt
Bde Major
173 I.B.

#2173 July Rpt
1916
June 1917
(58 pi)

S E C R E T   Copy No. 21

173RD INFANTRY BRIGADE OPERATION ORDER NO. 33

(Reference Map Sheet 57C - 1/40,000)

6th July, 1917

The 58th Division will take over the line from CANAL DU NORD to VILLERS PLOUICH, exclusive, in relief of the 42nd and 59th Divisions.

The 174th Inf. Bde. will take over the front now held by the 59th Division, with their Headquarters at Q.15.c.7.3.

The 175th Inf. Bde. will take over the front now held by the 42nd Division, with their Headquarters at Q.14.d.1.9.

The 173rd Inf. Bde. will be in reserve, with their Headquarters at NEUVILLE-BOURJONVAL.

Headquarters, 58th Division, will be established at 10 a.m., 9th inst., at LITTLE WOOD, YTRES.

---

1. The Brigade Group (less Artillery) will move on the 8th and 9th July in accordance with attached March Tables.

2. Starting Point on the 8th will be F.23.d.5.5 (sheet 57D) Cross roads E. of ABLAINZEVILLE.

3. Starting Point for the 9th will be notified later.

4. O.C., 2/4th London Regt. will detail one platoon to march in rear of the column to collect stragglers on the 8th instant. O.C., 2/1st London Regt. will detail a similar party on the 9th instant.

5. Brigade Headquarters will close at ABLAINZEVILLE at 2 p.m. on the 8th inst. and open at BANCOURT Camp at 3.30 p.m.

6. Administrative Instructions attached.

7. ACKNOWLEDGE.

H H Ganaway
Captain,
A/Brigade Major,
173rd Infantry Brigade.

Issued to Signals at ..9am..

Copy No.
1. 2/1st London Regt.
2. 2/2nd London Regt.
3. 2/3rd London Regt.
4. 2/4th London Regt.
5. 173rd Trench Mortar Bty.
6. 206th Machine Gun Coy.
7. 174th Infantry Brigade
8. 175th Infantry Brigade
9. 510th H.T.Co., A.S.C.
10. 504th Field Co. R.E.
11. "G" 58th Division
12. "A" & "Q" 58th Division

Copy No.
13. Brigade Major for G.O.C.
14. Staff Captain
15. Brigade Signalling Officer
16. Brigade Transport Officer
17. Brigade Intelligence Officer
18. 59th Division
19. 2/2nd Field Ambulance
20. War Diary
21. War Diary
22. File
23. Spare

MARCH TABLE ISSUED WITH 173RD INFANTRY BRIGADE OPERATION ORDER NO. 55

Date	Unit	From	To	Time of Passing Starting Point	Route	Remarks
8th July	2/1st London Regt.	ABLAINZEVILLE	BANCOURT CAMP at H.36.d.9.9	1.0 p.m.	COURCELLES - SAPIGNIES - BAPAUME	
"	2/3rd London Regt.	"	"	1.15 p.m.	"	
"	2/2nd London Regt.	LOG-EAST WOOD	"	1.30 p.m.	"	
"	2/4th London Regt.	"	"	1.45 p.m.	"	
"	Bde. Hd. Qtrs.	ABLAINZEVILLE	"			
"	173rd T.M. Batty.	"	"	2.0 p.m.	"	
"	203rd M.G. Coy.	"	"			
"	504 Field Co. R.E.	"	"	2.15 p.m.		
"	1 Section 2/2nd H.C. Field Amb.	"	"	2.25 p.m.		
"	510 H.T.Co. A.S.C.	LOG-EAST WOOD	ROCQUIGNY	Under arrangements of O.C., 510 H.T.Co., A.S.C.		

2.

Date	Unit	From	To	Time of passing Starting Point	Route	Remarks
9th July	Bde. Hd.Qtrs.	Camp at BARCOURT	NEUVILLE-BOURJONVAL	(5.10 p.m.	HAPLINCOURT - BERTINCOURT - YTRES	An interval of 100 yards will be maintained between Companies.
	2/3rd London Regt.			(5.20 p.m.		
"	2/2nd London Regt.	"	YTRES	5.35 p.m.	"	
"	2/4th London Regt.	"	YTRES	5.50 p.m.	"	
"	2/1st London Regt.	"	RUYAULCOURT	3. 5 p.m.	"	
"	173rd T.M.Battery	"	"	3.10 p.m.	"	
"	206th M.G.Coy.	"	"	6.15 p.m.	"	
"	504 Field Co. R.E.	"	NEUVILLE-BOURJONVAL	3.25 p.m.	"	Transport to YTRES
"	1 Section 2/2nd R.O. Field Amb.	"	As detailed in A.D.M.S. A.O. No. 24			This section will not leave column until 2/2nd and 2/4th Bns. have entered YTRES.

[signature]

2.

Date	Unit	From	To	Route	Time of passing Starting Point	Remarks
9th July	2/2nd London Regt.	Camp at BARCOURT	YTRES	HAPLINCOURT - BERTINCOURT - YTRES.	5.10 p.m.	
"	2/4th London Regt.	"	YTRES	"	5.25 p.m.	) An interval of 100) yards will be main-) tained between) Companies.) No troops to pass) HAPLINCOURT before) 5.30 p.m.
"	2/1st London Regt.	"	RUYAULCOURT	"	5.40 p.m.	
"	173rd T.M.Battery	"	"	"	5.45 p.m.	
"	206th M.G.Co.	"	"	"	5.50 p.m.	
"	504 Field Co. R.E.	"	NEUVILLE-BOURJONVAL	"	6. 0 p.m.	Transport to YTRES
"	1 Section 2/2nd H.C.Field Amb.	"	As detailed in A.D...S. A.O.No.24	"	6.10 p.m.	This section will not leave column until 2/2nd and 2/4th Bns. have entered YTRES.
10th July	Bde. Hd.Qtrs.) 2/3rd London Regt.)	"	NEUVILLE-BOURJONVAL	"	(7. 0 a.m. (7.10 a.m.	An interval of 100 yards will be main- tained between Cos.

S E C R E T

173RD INFANTRY BRIGADE

ADMINISTRATIVE INSTRUCTION NO. 7
Issued with Brigade Operation Order No. 33

6th July, 1917

---

1. Units will be accompanied by 1st Line Transport and one baggage wagon.

2. All canvas and shelters now occupied by units of this Brigade will be struck, and collected at road junction F.30.a.2.6 (57D) by 12 noon, 8th instant. O.C., 2/2nd Bn. will detail a small guard, which will be mounted at 9 a.m., to take charge of this canvas, etc. at F.30.a.2.6 until collected (under Divisional arrangements) during the afternoon of the 8th - the guard will then proceed to rejoin its unit.
   In the event of wet weather no canvas will be struck, but guards will be left over various camps and a notification sent to this office of the number of personnel comprising the guards.

3. Units now occupying billets will obtain a certificate from the Town Major, ABLAINZEVILLE that billets are left in a clean condition - this certificate will be forwarded to Brigade Headquarters.

4. O.C., 2/3rd London Regt. will detail a guard of 1 N.C.O. and 3 men to proceed to BANCOURT Camp to relieve the Guard of the 174th Inf. Bde. - this guard is to report to the Staff Captain, 174th Inf. Bde. not later than 3 p.m. on the 7th instant.

5. A small advance party from each unit will report to the Staff Captain at BANCOURT Camp at 3.30 p.m. on the 8th inst.

6. One baggage wagon per Battalion will report at Battalion Headquarters at 9 a.m., 8th instant. The drivers and horses will be rationed by the Unit concerned up to midnight, 9th instant. On completion of the move baggage wagons will report to O.C., 510 H.T.Co., A.S.C., at 0.27.a.5.4 (ROCQUIGNY).
   2 lorries per Battalion will report to Battalion Headquarters at 7.30 a.m., 8th instant. These lorries will proceed direct to the new area. O.C., Units will arrange for advance parties to be sent with these lorries. Os. C., M.G.Co. and T.M.Battery will each detail 1 N.C.O. as advance party - these N.C.Os. will travel on the lorries of the 2/1st Bn.
   Extra transport for M.G.CO., and T.M.Battery will be arranged for by Bde. Transport Officer.
   Advance parties will report on arrival as under :-

   <u>2/2nd and 2/4th</u> parties to Town Major, YTRES. They will take over billets and camp now occupied by the 1/6th Lancs.Fusiliers and 1/8th Lancs. Fusiliers respectively. (As 2/2nd Bn. will be taking over a scattered area the advance party must necessarily be large.)

2.

       2/1st., M.G.Co., T.M.Battery parties to Town Major,
       RUYAULCOURT, and will take over Camp
       and billets now occupied by the 8th
       Manchester Regt., 127th M.G.Co., and
       127th T.M.Battery respectively.

       Bde. Headquarters, 2/3rd Lon.Rgt. & 504 Field Co. R.E.
       parties will report to Town Major,
       NEUVILLE-BOURJONVAL, and will take over
       billets, etc. now occupied by a Brigade
       Headquarters, 2/4th Lincs. Regt. and a
       R.E. Coy. respectively.

7. All canvas at BARCOURT Camp will be struck prior to departure and handed over to the guard mentioned in para. 4, who will be relieved under arrangements to be notified later. 2/3/2
    O.C., 2/3/2 Battery will detail sufficient men to strike Brigade Headquarters Camp.

8. Refilling Point, 9th instant and onwards, O.28.b.1.8.
Rations for consumption on the 9th instant will be delivered at BARCOURT Camp.
    Rations for consumption on the 10th instant and onwards will be delivered at Units' Transport Lines by 510 H.T.Co., A.S.C.

===========

For information :-

    (a) Water for men and animals in new area - good.

    (b) All sick in the new area will be sent to the 2/3rd H.C. Field Ambulance at BUS.

    (c) A section of the 2/2nd H.C. Field Ambulance will follow the column on the march.

    (d) D.A.D.O.S. will be at O.27.a.5.4.

    (e) O.C., 510 H.T.Co., A.S.C. will be at O.27.a.5.4.

    (f) Railhead from 8th instant - ROCQUIGNY.

    (g) Expeditionary Force Canteen at YTRES.

To all recipients of 173rd Inf.Bde. Operation Order No. 53

Cancel March Table 2 (9th July), and substitute attached.

Delete last two lines of para. 7, page 2, of Administrative
    Instruction No. 7 and substitute "O.C., 2/3rd Bn. will
    detail sufficient men to strike Bde. Hd.Qtrs Camp."

                                                     H H Garraway
                                                          Captain,
                                                     A/Brigade Major,
7/7/17   173rd Infantry Brigade.

SECRET. Copy No...... 20....

173RD INFANTRY BRIGADE OPERATION ORDER
NUMBER 34.

Reference Map Sheet 57c S.E. - 1/20,000
& Map No. 1 - 1/10,000 (attached.).

July 14th 1917.

---

1. The Brigade will take over that portion of 174th Infantry Brigade's Front between the Divisional Right Boundary and QUEEN'S LANE, exclusive, on the night of 16/17 July. Relief to be completed by 9 a.m. 17th inst.

2. On completion of the relief the Brigade will be distributed as follows -

    <u>Front System</u> - 2/3rd Bn. London Regt. + 2 Coys. 2/1st Bn. London Regt. under Command of O.C. 2/3rd Bn.

    <u>Intermediate Line.</u> - 2/1st Bn. Lon. Regt. (Less 2 Coys.).

    <u>In Support.</u> - (GOUZEAUCOURT WOOD - 2 Coys.)   ) 2/4th Bn.
    (DESSART WOOD - 2Coys. & Bn. H.Q.)) Lon. Regt.

    <u>In Divisional Reserve</u> - (YTRES) - 2/2nd Bn. London Regt.

3. Officers Commanding Battalions, 206th Machine Gun Coy. and 173rd Light Trench Mortar Batty. will inform Bde. Hd. Qtrs. as soon as possible as to the size and description of reconnoitring parties they wish to send up to their sectors.

4. A Map of the Brigade Sector is forwarded Herewith.

5. Detailed orders for the relief and Administrative Instructions will be issued later.

                                                  Captain,
                                            Brigade Major,
                                        173rd Infantry Brigade.

Issued to Signals at:- 8.15 p.m.

Copy No.
1. 2/1st Bn. London Regt.
2. 2/2nd Bn. London Regt.
3. 2/3rd Bn. London Regt.
4. 2/4th Bn. London Regt.
5. 173rd L.T.M. Batty.
6. 206th Machine Gun Coy.
7. 174th Infantry Brigade.
8. 175th Infantry Brigade.
9. 58th Division, "G".
10. 58th Division, "A" & "Q".
11. S.S.O.
12. 510th Coy. A.S.C.
13. 504th Field Coy. R.E.
14. Brigade Major for G.O.C.
15. Staff Captain.
16. Brigade Signalling Officer.
17. Brigade Transport Officer.
18. Brigade Intelligence Officer.
19. War Diary.
20. War Diary.
21. File.
22. Spare.

Secret

173RD INFANTRY BRIGADE

Administrative Instruction No. 7
(Issued in connection with 173rd Inf. Bde. Operation Order No. 34).

15th July, 1917.

TRANSPORT & Q.M.STORES. Will be at V.6.a. for all units except 2/2nd Bn. London Regt., which will remain as at present.
Brigade Transport Officer will allot lines.

RATIONS Rations will be delivered by 510 H.T.Co., A.S.C, to units' wagon lines.
Rations for units in the front system will be delivered by 1st Line transport (at night) to Q.12.d.6.0. From this point they will be taken over by carrying parties under unit arrangements.
Rations for Battalions in the intermediate line and support will be delivered under units' arrangements.

WATER. Water carts can be filled at METZ and DESSART WOOD.
A tank (capacity 400 gallons) is situated at Q.12.d.6.0. O.C., 2/3rd Bn. will be responsible for seeing that this tank is kept filled.

S.A.A. ETC. Demands for S.A.A., Very Lights, R.E. Material, etc., will be sent to the Staff Captain at Bde. Hd.Qtrs. by 10 a.m. each day.
Battalions in the front system will maintain a dump of ammunition, etc., as laid down in the attached table.
Brigade Dump at Q.28.a.2.8.

MEDICAL. Regimental Aid Posts under Units' arrangements. Evacuation of sick and wounded will be carried out in accordance with A.D.M.S., 58th Division circular M.1705 forwarded to units on 10th July.

BRIGADE POST OFFICE. Will be at Brigade Headquarters' Wagon Lines at V.6.a.

TENTS & SHELTERS. Particulars of Tents and Shelters for Transport Lines and the Battalion in Support (2/4th London Regt.) will be notified later.

H H Garaway
Captain,
Staff Captain,
173rd Infantry Brigade.

Copies to all recipients of 173rd Inf. Bde. Operation Order No. 34.

S.A.A., GRENADES, ETC., TO BE MAINTAINED BY BATTALION IN FRONT SYSTEM

	S.A.A. (rounds)	Hand Grenades	Rifle Grenades	1" Very Lights	Rockets
1. Platoons in front and Support lines.	4,000	3 Boxes	2 Boxes		
2. Companies in front and support lines	20,000	20 "	12 "	150	
3. Battalion in front and Support lines	30,000	100 "	20 "	150	
4. Each Lewis Gun	6,000	This in addition to S.A.A. in magazine.		500	60 S.O.S.
5. Each Vicker's Maxim	10,000	This in addition to S.A.A. in belts.			

15/7/17

SECRET.   Bm/S.56/1.

To all recipients of 173rd Infantry Brigade Operation Order
                    Number 34 dated 14/7/17.

1. Reference 173rd Infantry Brigade Operation Order No.34 dated 14th July, relief will be carried out in accordance with attached Relief Table - further details being arranged between Unit Commanders direct.

2. Administrative Instructions have already been issued.

3. Brigade Headquarters will close at NEUVILLE at 6 p.m. opening at Q.34.a.20.85. at the same hour.

4. A List of all Trench Stoves, Maps, Aeroplane Photographs, etc. xxxxxxxxxx taken over will be forwarded to Brigade Headquarters in due course.

                                      C.J.Shearman Captain,
                                                    Brigade Major,
                                                    173rd Infantry Brigade.

15/7/17.

RELIEF TABLE

Date.	Relieving Unit.	Outgoing Unit.	Relief to be complete by	Remarks.
16th.	2/3rd Bn. Ln. Regt. + 3 Coys. 2/1st Bn. London Regt.	2/5th Lon. Rgt. + 2 Coys. 2/7th Bn. Lon. Regt.	7 p.m.	Front System - Via LINCOLN AVENUE (covered approach to Southern end of this C.T. must be reconnoitred before hand).
16th.	2/1st Bn.Ln.Rgt. less 3 Coys. + 1 Coy. 2/4th Bn. London Regt.	3 Coys. 2/6th Bn. London Rgt.	7 p.m.	Intermediate Line - Via H.Q. 174th Infantry Brigade and SHAFTESBURY AVENUE.
16/17th	2/4th Bn. Lon. Regt. less 1 Coy.	-	9 a.m.	(2 Coys. Q.27.d.8.1. (1 Coy. DESSART WOOD.
17/18th	203rd M.G. Co.	198th M.G. Co.	-	206th Machine Gun Coy. will select site for Headquarters about Q.23.c.65.20.
17/18th	175rd Light Trench Mortar Batty.	174th Light Trench Mortar Batty.	-	H.Q. Q.25.c.5.5.

2/2nd Bn. London Regt. will remain in present location at YPRES.

173RD INFANTRY BRIGADE

Summary of Intelligence for Period 9 a.m. 16/7/17
to 9 a.m. 17/7/17

A. **OPERATIONS.**

1. Enemy's attitude and General Activity.
   Hostile Artillery fairly quiet. The following areas were shelled during the period.

Place	Time	Calibre	No. of Shells
GOUZEAUCOURT WOOD (N.End)	7 - 7.30 p.m.	15.0 cm	About 20
Q.12.b.6.0	5.30 p.m.	7.7 cm	4
BEET FACTORY BEAUCAMP	5.30 a.m.	10.5 cm	5
Q.18.b.9.9	5.35 a.m.	H.E.	6

   BEAUCAMP was shelled at intervals. At 8 a.m. four L.T.M. shells fell in front of posts at R.7.b.1.6.
   Hostile M.Gs. fired occasional bursts during the night, traversing road at R.7.b.02.50 and around Q.12.d.9.9.
   Few Very Lights were used by the enemy. At 11.14 p.m., 11.42 p.m., 11.55 p.m., 12.20 a.m. and 1.52 a.m. a searchlight was visible in the direction of R.3.
   A Sniper was active in PLUSH TRENCH at R.8.a.1.9. during the morning. He was fired on by our snipers and silenced.

B. **INTELLIGENCE.**

   Movement. At 6 a.m. sentry observed at R.1.c.9.6.
   At 7.20 a.m. 2 Officers accompanied by 2 runners seen in PLUSH TRENCH.
   At 8.10 a.m. Two Companies of infantry observed proceeding E. from FONTAINE-NOTRE-DAME.
   At 8.45 a.m. three parties of seven men each were seen propelling three small trucks along light railway at L.25.b. They were wearing white fatigue dress.
   At 10.30 a.m. party of 7 men with single horse wagon collected hay at L.9.c.2.5.
   From 5.5 - 5.30 p.m. 3 men were observed at RIBECOURT STATION.
   At 7.55 a.m. a light engine was seen leaving FONTAINE-NOTRE-DAME proceeding West. A train passed FONTAINE-NOTRE-DAME going W. at 7.20 p.m.

   Work. Trench at R.1.d.2.3 appears to have been deepened.

   Signals. Two red lights discharged from PLUSH TRENCH at 1.52 a.m. with no apparent result.

   Aerial Activity. Enemy aeroplanes active between 5 and 6 p.m. over our lines. They were driven off by M.G. fire.

   Patrols.
   At 11 p.m. last night 2/Lt. Arnold, 1 N.C.O. and 19 O.R. left the trenches at junction of ASHBY ALLEY and front line. Patrol proceeded in a N.W. direction in front of our wire as far as R.7.b.1.7. When close on this point an enemy patrol 5 strong was observed on their right. On turning N. to engage them the BOSCHES doubled back along the road to PLUSH

TRENCH. Our patrol continued due North until they reached the wire in front of PLUSH TRENCH at R.1.b.1.1. The patrol then proceeded along the wire in an Easterly direction to R.8.a.1.7 No sign or sound was heard to shew if trench was occupied. Patrol returned from R.8.a.1.7 turning S. down road, re-entering trench at ASHBY ALLEY.

Patrol of 20 men under 2/Lt.A.Ward, 2/1st Lon.Rgt., supported by an Officer and Lewis Gun team of 1 N.C.O. and 3 men with gun from 2/7th Lon.Regt., left our trenches at 9.45 p.m. on 16th July at Q.6.c.4.3, and proceeded to BOAR COPSE and took up their night position. The patrol remained out until 2.15 a.m. They returned by same route to our trenches after posting the Day Post. No sign of the enemy was observed.

No casualties in either of the parties.

2/Lt., I.O.,
for Brigade Major,
173rd Infantry Brigade.

173RD INFANTRY BRIGADE.
SUMMARY OF INTELLIGENCE
Period from 9 a.m. 18th July, 1917 to 9 a.m. 19th July, 1917.

A. OPERATIONS:-

1. **Enemy's Attitude and General Activity.** Hostile Artillery activity was normal. The following areas were shelled during the period.

TARGET.	TIME.	NO. OF ROUNDS.	CALIBRE ETC.
LOUGHBOROUGH LANE)	12 "		
& COALVILLE LANE.)	1 p.m.	-	7.7 cm. H.E.
LEICESTER AVENUE &)			
BEAUCAMP.)	6 p.m.	10.	10.5 cm. H.E.
R.7.c.1.9.)	9 p.m.		Gas Shells in salvoes
)	12.30 am.	-	of 5 at ½ hour intervals.

T.M.B. active during morning and evening, particularly at 8 p.m. on front line between LOUGHBOROUGH LANE and COALVILLE LANE.
RIFLE GRENADES were fired from 9 p.m. to 12.30 a.m. on R.7.b.1.7.
MACHINE GUNS usual intermittent fire by night, but none by day.
2. **Our Own Activity on same lines and where it influences Enemy Action:-** Our L.T.M.B. retaliated against hostile T.M.B. Our field guns were active during the night and at 9.30 p.m. a heavier discharge was noticed.

B. INTELLIGENCE:-

(a). Enemy appears to bring M.G. out at night to about point R.1.d.1.0.
(b). T.M. Emplacement suspected at about R.1.d.3.7.
(c). Movement. Considerable movement along road at L.13.b.9.0. all day chiefly towards FLESQUIERES in parties of two and three.
   10 a.m. 7 men repairing overhead wire at L.19.a.
   10.25 a.m. 2 men walking along railway cutting at L.20.c.5.0. towards RIBECOURT.
   10.50 a.m. 2 men leave trench at R.1.d.6.7. with small dixies returning at 11.10 a.m. with dixies.
   1.45 p.m. Red Cross motor ambulance going from FLESQUIERES in easterly direction.
   4 p.m. 2 men in grey uniforms seen at L.32.c. walking in direction of RIBECOURT
   5.30 p.m. 3 men carrying maps and papers seen in trenches at L.20.c. observing our lines. Artillery was informed but failed to reach them.
   9.10 p.m. 4 men got out of trench at R.1.d.1.8. and proceeded to RIBECOURT.
   During early morning men observed in PLUSH TRENCH especially around R.1.d. were fired on.
(d). Smoke:- at 7.30 p.m. an explosion was seen at L.25.central.
(e). Signals. At 10.15 p.m. 5 red lights were seen at K.35.c. but no result followed.
(f). Aerial Activity. At 7.20 p.m. our A.A. guns drove back two enemy biplanes in the direction of HAVRINCOURT.
VISIBILITY - Fair.
PATROLS. (1). 2/Lt. R. L. ASLIN, 2/3rd London Regt. and 21 O.R. left our trenches at R.7.a.4.5. at 11.30 p.m. to find if enemy were holding PLUSH TRENCH and to engage any BOSCHE Patrol. Patrol proceeded in a N.E. direction for 3 to 4 hundred yards and then turned N.W. about point R.1.c.1.5. Patrol then proceeded S.W. to S. and returned to our lines at 1.0 a.m. at R.7.a.4.5. No sound or sign of enemy in PLUSH TRENCH and no Bosche Patrols encountered.
(2). At 9.45 p.m. the usual patrol left our lines under 2/Lt. A. WARD and took Post in BOAR COPSE. Nothing was seen or heard of the enemy and the party returned at 3.50 a.m.

L. C. ?
2/Lieut.,
A/I.O. for Brigade Ma?
173rd Infantry Brigade.

173RD INFANTRY BRIGADE.
SUMMARY OF INTELLIGENCE.

Period from 9 a.m. 19th July to 9 a.m. 20th July.

A. OPERATIONS:-

1. <u>Enemy's Attitude and General Activity.</u> Hostile Artillery was more active than usual, particularly between 12.30 p.m. and 2 p.m. and from 5 p.m. to 7 p.m. The principal areas shelled were Q.11.d. - Q.11.a. - Q.17.c. - BEAUCAMP and BEAUCAMP VALLEY. DESSART WOOD received 15 shells of small calibre between 10 p.m. and 11 p.m., of which 5 were blinds, from the direction of HAVRINCOURT.
L.T.M.B. was active at 11.50 p.m. on LOUGHBOROUGH LANE, also during the early part of the evening.
M.G. activity was normal.

2. <u>Our own Activity on same lines, & where it influences Enemy Action:-</u> Our L.T.M.B. replied to enemy T.M. and silenced it. An enemy M.G. which was active at intervals from 10 p.m. to 11.50 p.m. and again at 5.55 a.m. was silenced on both occasions.
Our artillery was active during the evening.

B. INTELLIGENCE:-

(a). M.G. Emplacement suspected at R.1.d.2.2.
(b). T.M. Emplacement located at R.1.d.3.1.
(c). Movement. The usual movement along road to FLESQUIERES at L.14.a. and B. was observed.
  9.35 a.m. 3 men walking on top of trench at L.31.c.5.4. for 20 yards.
  11.5 a.m. Motor Lorry on road from NINE WOODS to MARCOING.
  8.45 p.m. - 9.15 p.m. Transport observed on road at L.14.a. going towards FLESQUIERES.
  9.10 p.m. 3 men seen on parapet of PLUSH TRENCH at R.1.c.5.8 three rounds were fired at them, and one man believed to be hit.
  6.50 a.m. 8 men seen pushing two trucks into RIBECOURT on Light Railway.
  7 a.m. Officer and orderly inspecting wire in front of PLUSH TRENCH at R.1.c.5.8 were fired at and disappeared.
  7.45 a.m. 4 men seen on parados of trench at L.31.c.7.6.
(d) Smoke. At 4.35 p.m. smoke was seen rising from behind RIBECOURT STATION.
(e) Dug-out suspected at R.1.a.3.8.
(f) Aerial Activity. One of our aeroplanes patrolled the enemy's lines at 4.30 a.m.
(g) General. Very Lights were fired from various parts of PLUSH TRENCH about 100 to 200 yards apart.

PATROLS

2/Lt. W.Gabony and 22 O.R. left our lines at Q.6.d.25.00 at 12 midnight and returned to same place at 2 p.m.
  Patrol proceeded N.N.E. until they reached wire of PLUSH TRENCH. Wire was found to be six feet deep and very thick. Patrol then proceeded S.E. along wire of PLUSH TRENCH to about point R.1.c.5.7 and then returned to our lines bringing back with them a piece of Bosche wire and one of his pickets. No sign of the occupation of that part of PLUSH TRENCH was observed, and no enemy patrol was encountered.

2/Lieut.
A/I.O., for Brigade Major,
173rd Infantry Brigade

War Diary

173RD INFANTRY BRIGADE.
SUMMARY OF INTELLIGENCE
Period from 9 a.m. 20th July to 9 a.m. 21st July.

A. OPERATIONS:-
   1. <u>Enemy's Attitude and General Activity</u>. Hostile Artillery again more active than usual.
   The following Table shows the principal areas shelled:-

TARGET.	TIME.	NO. OF ROUNDS.	CALIBRE ETC.
R.7.b.1.3.	9.45 a.m.	3	7.7 cm. H.E.
R.7.a. (S.E.sector)	12 noon – 1 p.m.	30	ditto.
R.7.central.	10 p.m. – 11 p.m.	-	77 cm. H.E. & 15 cm.

At 5.15 p.m. shells of heavy calibre were fired on Q.11.b., about 1/3rd of which seemed to explode only partially.
   Hostile T.M.B. fired intermittently during the afternoon on our front line around R.7.b.1.3.
   M.G. activity was normal, chiefly active from 10 - 11 p.m.
   From 10.30 - 11 p.m. our front line received a few Rifle Grenades.
   2. <u>Our own activity on same lines, & where it influences Enemy Action</u>:- Our Artillery fired on PLUSH TRENCH about 11.30 p.m. and 10.30 p.m.
   An enemy working party, who had evidently lost themselves, was fired at by one of our M.G's., result not known.
   <u>General</u> - This sector was practically unaffected by the heavy bombardment on our left from 10.30 p.m. to 12.30 a.m.

B. <u>INTELLIGENCE</u>:-
   (a). M.G. Emplacements suspected at K.35.d.20.75. and K.36.a.45.10
   (b). <u>Movement</u>. Usual movement along road at L.14.a. and b.
       4.30 p.m. 4 men seen carrying rifles and equipment at L.31.d.3.1.
       5.20 p.m. 3 men seen standing on parapet about L.21.
       5.40 p.m. 1 man seen at L.31.d.5.0. wearing peaked cap, joined by 2 other men wearing round soft caps, they appeared to be examining wire.
       7.5 p.m. 2 men seen working at L.20.d.3.6.
       Considerable movement was observed in PLUSH TRENCH. At 5.30 a.m. 1 man standing on parapet at R.1.d.7.1. was fired at and disappeared.
       5.30 a.m. working party seen in PLUSH TRENCH at R.1.c.60.75.
       6.15 a.m. 2 men seen walking along light railway towards RIBECOURT.
   (c). <u>Work</u>. Fresh work is noticed at R.1.c.60.75. and more wire put up at R.1.c.7.7.
       At. 4.1.c.3.8. near gap in wire there is an emplacement of some sort.
   (d) <u>Transport</u> heard about 1 a.m. in direction of L.14.
   (e) <u>Wire</u>. Enemy heard wiring from time to time on right of sector.
   (f) <u>Signals</u>. During heavy shelling of PLUSH TRENCH by our artillery at 10.30 p.m. 2 green stars were sent up at 100 yards intervals along PLUSH TRENCH from left to right. After a short interval enemy began shelling on left of our sector.
   (g) <u>Aerial Activity</u>. Enemy aircraft were seen over our lines at 6 p.m. at a great height. At 11.45 a.m., 4 p.m. and 7 p.m. one of our planes flew low over Bosche lines.
   (h) <u>General</u>. At 7.10 p.m. Goods train left FONTAINE in direction of CAMBRAI.
   A 4" iron pipe has been found running through our lines towards PLUSH TRENCH cutting front line at its junction with BEAUCAMP - RIBECOURT road.
   A C.T. 3' deep was dug from our front line to BOAR COPSE during the night.

2.

PATROLS

2/Lt. C.C.Gillbanks and 25 other ranks left our lines at R.7.b.2.5 at 11 p.m.

Patrol proceeded due N. until they reached wire outside PLUSH TRENCH, then turned E. along wire to about point R.1.d.8.1. A large working party about 30 strong was heard at work in the trench along that front. Wire was found to be in good condition consisting of one belt 12' to 15' deep, 2' 6" high about 30 yards in front of trench. A small gap in wire was found at R.1.d.5.1.

Round the small salient at R.1.d.3.1 there were signs of permanent occupation.

No Bosche patrol was encountered.

Patrol returned to our lines from R.1.d.8.1 and entered our trench at ASHBY ALLEY at 1.15 a.m.

S.A.Seys
2/Lieut.
A/I.O., for Brigade Major,
173rd Infantry Brigade.

SECRET.   Copy No. 22

173RD INFANTRY BRIGADE
OPERATION ORDER NO. 35.

Reference Map Sheets 57c. N.E. & S.E. - 1/20,000.

July 22nd 1917.

---

1. Reference 173rd Infantry Brigade Warning Order No. 1. dated 21st July.
   Reliefs will be carried out in accordance with attached RELIEF TABLE.

2. All Maps, Defence Schemes, Photographs, Trench Stores, etc. will be handed over.
   Duplicates of receipts being sent to these Headquarters in due course.

3. Administrative Instructions are attached.

4. Troops moving between GOUZEAUCOURT & DESSART WOOD will keep an interval of 300 yards between Platoons.

5. All details will be arranged between Battalion Commanders concerned.

                                            Captain,
                                         Brigade Major,
                                      173rd Infantry Brigade.

Issued to Signals at 6.30.am.

Copy No.
1. 2/1st Bn. London Regt.
2. 2/2nd Bn. London Regt.
3. 2/3rd Bn. London Regt.
4. 2/4th Bn. London Regt.
5. 173rd Light Trench Mortar Batty.
6. 206th Machine Gun Company.
7. 174th Infantry Brigade.
8. 175th Infantry Brigade.
9. 510th Coy. A.S.C.
10. 504th Field Coy. R.E.
11. "G" 58th Division.
12. "A" & "Q" 58th Division.
13. Brigade Major for G.O.C.
14. Staff Captain.
15. Brigade Signalling Officer.
16. Brigade Transport Officer.
17. Brigade Intelligence.
18. S.S.O.
19. 120th Infantry Brigade.
20. 291st Bde. R.F.A.
21. War Diary.
22. War Diary.
23. File.
24. Spare.

175RD INFANTRY BDE.
RELIEF TABLE

Outgoing Unit.	Move to -	Relieving Unit.	Sub-Sector.	Complete Relief by.	Proportion of Outgoing unit to be left behind.	Remarks.
2/1st Bn. London Regt.	YPRES. (Div. Reserve)	2/2nd Bn. Lon. Regiment.	Left.	3 p.m.	1 Officer and 1 Lewis Gun Team for BOAR COPSE.	Coy. of 2/2nd Bn. relieving Right Front Coy. of 2/1st Bn. will use LINCOLN AVENUE. Remainder of 2/2nd Bn. will use SHAFTESBURY AVENUE. 2/1st Bn. will move out in corresponding manner and will be clear of S. end of LINCOLN & SHAFTESBURY AVENUES by 3.30 p.m.
2/3rd Bn. London Regt.	1 Coy. & H.Q. DESSART WOOD. 2 Coys. GOUZEAU-COURT WOOD. 1 Coy. Intermediate Line.	2/4th -n. Lon. Regiment.	Right.	9 p.m.	1 N.C.O. per Platoon.	Both units will use LINCOLN AVENUE.

173RD INFANTRY BRIGADE

Administrative Instruction No. 8
Issued with Brigade Operation Order No. 35.

22/7/17

1. The 2/1st Bn. will take over billets and transport lines now occupied by 2/2nd Bn. at YTRES at P.20.b.1.S.
    2/2nd Bn. will take over transport lines now occupied by 2/1st Bn. at V.6.a.
    O.C., 2/1st Bn. will detail a small advance party to take over the billets, etc.

2. 2/3rd Bn. will take over billets, etc., now occupied by 2/4th Bn., viz:- Bn. Hd.Qtrs and 1 Coy., DESSART WOOD (W.2.a.5.4), 2 Companies GOUZEAUCOURT WOOD, remaining Coy. Intermediate Line.
    O.C., 2/3rd Bn. will detail a small advance party to take over billets, etc.

3. 2/2nd Bn. will entrain at P.20.c., as follows :-

    1 Coy. at 9 a.m., proceeding to DESSART WOOD W.1.c.
    Bn.Hd.Qtrs and 3 Coys. at 9.10 a.m., proceeding to Q.14.c.

    2/1st Bn. will entrain as follows :-

    Bn.Hd.Qtrs. and 3 Coys. at Q.14.c. at 3.30 p.m. and proceed to YTRES, P.20.c.
    1 Coy. at DESSART WOOD (W.1.c.) at 3.30 p.m., proceeding to YTRES, P.20.c.

    Os.C., 2/1st and 2/2nd Bns. will each detail an entraining Officer.

H.Caraway

Captain,
Staff Captain,
173rd Infantry Brigade.

Copies to all recipients of Bde. Operation Order No. 35.

173RD INFANTRY BRIGADE.
SUMMARY OF INTELLIGENCE.

Period from 9 a.m. 21st July to 9 a.m. 22nd July.

A. OPERATIONS:-
   1. <u>Enemy's Attitude and General Activity.</u> There has been no marked change in Enemy's Artillery activity.
   The following Table shows the volume of his fire during the period.

No. of Rounds.	Time of Fire.	Calibre.	Where Striking.	Type.
6	8.35 a.m.	7.7 cm.	PLOUGH SPT.	H.E.
9	8 a.m.	10.5 "	R.7.d.1.7.	H.E. (5 Blinds).
24	12 a.m.	15 c.m.	HAVRINCOURT WOOD.	H.E.
10	8.30 p.m.	10.5 c.m.	BEET FACTORY.	H.E.
50	8.30 to 9.30 p.m.	10.5 cm.	Q.12.a.9.4.	H.E. (appeared from direction of F.14.

Between 9.45 and 10 a.m. Pineapple Bombs were fired on R.7.b.1.7. Our Trench Mortars replied and silenced.
A Battery was observed firing from about F.14.c.5.5.
   2. <u>Our Own Activity on Same Lines, and where it influences Enemy Action:-</u> Our Artillery actively retaliated with Shrapnel on PLUSH TRENCH at 10 p.m. At this time and place shouts were heard.

B. <u>INTELLIGENCE.</u>
   (a). <u>Movement.</u> 5.40 a.m. man seen, apparently inspecting wire at R.1.c.7.7. (PLUSH TRENCH) was fired on and disappeared.
   6.50 a.m. a party of about 10 men seen loading hay on a wagon at L.13.d. Wagon then moved at 6.45 towards FLESQUIERES.
   The usual movement was noticed on the FLESQUIERES Road throughout period.
   At 5.15 p.m. 6 men were seen to leave Trench at L.31.d.2.5. and walk along towards RIBECOURT.
   9 p.m. 10 men were seen about L.31.d.2.5. They were dispersed by our M.G. fire.
   5.30 a.m. at R.1.c.9.9. 4 men were seen. Our Lewis Guns fired on them when one was seen to fall whilst others ran away.
   (b). <u>Smoke.</u> At 1.5 a.m. what is believed to be a Dump was seen emitting smoke and flames behind RIBECOURT.
   (c). <u>Transport.</u> Heard at RIBECOURT between 2 - 2.30 a.m.
   (d). <u>Wire.</u> Wiring was heard in PLUSH TRENCH at 1 - 2 a.m. at about R.1.d.7.1.
   (e). <u>Aerial Activity.</u> Normal and undistinguished by any special feature.
   (f). <u>General.</u> The following O.B. was seen.

Time.	Direction.	Notes.
5.45 a.m.	FONTAINE.	Descended again almost immediately.
9.15 p.m.	Behind FLESQUIERES.	- - -

Leonard Selden

2/Lieut.,
A/I.O. for Brigade Major,
173rd. Infantry Brigade.

173RD INFANTRY BRIGADE

Summary of Intelligence for period 6 a.m. 22/7/17 to 6 a.m. 23/7/17

A. OPERATIONS.

1. **Enemy's Attitude and General Activity.** Diminished activity both in the enemy's artillery and signals has characterised the period. His artillery fire may be summarised as follows:-

Time	No. of Rounds	Where striking	Type	Calibre
9.25 a.m.	6	R.7.b.1.7	H.E.	77 mm
2.50 p.m.	6	R.7.a.6.5	H.E.	10.5 cm
3 - 4 p.m.	22	LOUGHBOROUGH LANE	H.E.	10.5 cm
3 - 4 p.m.	15	R.13.a.9.6	H.E.	10.5 cm
8 - 9 p.m.	30	LOUGHBOROUGH LANE	H.E.	10.5 cm
10 p.m.	6	Q.11.c.8.8 to) Q.11.c.4.4)	H.E.	10.5 cm

A few 77 mm. H.E. around front line and ASHBY ALLEY at 7.15 a.m.

2. **Our own Activity.** Our attitude quiet during period.

B. INTELLIGENCE.

(a) **Machine Gun Emplacements.** Some M.G. fire on BOAR COPSE and SUNKEN ROAD from direction of K.36.c.5.0; and also from Q.6.b.4.5. Otherwise situation unchanged and nothing to report.

(b) **Movement.** Usual occasional movement in road at L.14.a. & b. At 2.20 p.m. man seen studying a map about L.19.c.9.5. At 5.30 p.m. 4 men seen with maps at F.13.c.6.2.

(c) **Smoke.** At 7.50 a.m. large columns of smoke seen issuing from behind ridge S. of BOURLON WOOD.

(d) **Signals.** Between 10 p.m. and 3 a.m. 2 Very Lights were observed coming from PLUSH TRENCH.

(e) **Aerial Activity.** 4 a.m. 2 O.Bs. up by BOURLON WOOD, and in late afternoon many up all along the line. Aeroplanes noted at 9.30 a.m. going W. over our lines.

(f) **General.** At 7.45 a.m. a pigeon was released from PLUSH TRENCH K.36.c.6.1.

Visibility generally only fair. Wind N.E.

Leonard Selden

2/Lieut.
A/I.O., for Brigade Major,
173rd Infantry Brigade

173RD INFANTRY BRIGADE.
Summary of Intelligence for
Period from 6 a.m. 23rd July to 6 a.m. 24th July, 1917.

A. OPERATIONS.

1. **Enemy's Attitude and General Activity.** No marked change has characterised the enemy's action.

His fire may be summarised as follows:-

Time.	No. of Rounds.	Where Striking.	Calibre.	Type.
8 a.m.	14 b	LOUGHBOROUGH LANE.	-	Trench Mortar.
8 p.m.	12	ditto	-	ditto.
8.15 p.m.	15	R.7.a.	77 mm.	H.E.

From 6.30 a.m. to 8 a.m. 77 mm and 150 mm. were active & rounds not counted.
The night 23/24 was marked by increased M.G. activity on the enemy's part. Indirect fire over BROKEN TRENCH was noted. A report states that this activity was retaliation for our own Machine Gun fire.

2. **Our own activity on same lines, and where it influences enemy action:-** Our artillery shelled PLUSH TRENCH during the morning, destroying the wire in places.
M.G's. fired 20,000 rounds during the night, indirect fire.

B. INTELLIGENCE.
(a). **M.G. Emplacements.** M.G. noted firing from R.1.d.2.2. (PLUSH TRENCH). M.G. suspected at K.36.c.50.
(b). **Movement.** Noted in PLUSH TRENCH at R.1d. our snipers retaliated and claimed 1 hit.
   6.38 p.m. 2 men seen walking on track about K.28.d.
   6.56 p.m. 1 man seen walking in front of FEMY WOOD.
   7.20 p.m. Several men seen passing down PLUSH TRENCH in S.E. direction.
   8.20 p.m. 2 men seen on road at Q.6.a.
(c). **Aerial Activity.** E.A. Machine seen over our lines at 12.40 p.m. - 4.30 p.m. and 4.50 p.m.
(d). **General.** Visibility - Poor.

Leonard Selden

2/Lieut.,
A/I.O. for Brigade Major.
173rd Infantry Brigade.

Period 6.am to 6am.   Intelligence Summary.   25.7.17.

Operations The enemy has shown no marked change in his attitude during the period. His principle target appeared to be on the Right at Plough Support, & Village Support. Villers Rouvil was shelled during the day with a few 15 cm shells at a time. M.Gs. were active during the night 24/25. firing short bursts. T.Ms. also active in R.7.B (PLUSH)

Summary of Shell Fire

Time	No of Rounds	Calibre	Type	Where striking
8.15 am	6	7.7 cm	H.E.	PLOUGH Support
3.0-4.40 pm	12	15.0 cm	"	R.4.b
5.10 pm	6	15.0 cm	"	Village Support.
6.15 pm	7	15.0 cm	"	PLOUGH Support.
7 pm to 9.30 pm	14	15.0 cm	"	Q.6.c.
9.7 pm	8	7.7 cm	"	Village Support.
9.7	20	10.5 cm	"	Q.12.a.80.50

M.G. Activity. The usual activity on our part, M.Gs. active during night with overhead fire.

Intelligence) M.G. emplacements. During night M.G. fire from R.7.B.18. Q6.B.52 (PLUSH TRENCH)

Movement 10.15 am 1 man seen walking in track at L20.D.7.1
    5.45 pm 1 " " examining wire " L.20.D.7.1.
    9. pm 2 " " taking M.G. into position
    7.20 pm 3 " " examining wire " L.20.D.7.1.
Men suspected on high ground to East of BOAR Copse (located at 6pm) likely on ARGYLE ROAD. Movement in PLUSH particularly at dark. Our snipers had a shot here. Digging was heard in PLUSH TR. at Q.6.b. Work seem on a Strong Point at K.36.c.12. at 8.40 pm, again heard 3.0 and 3.30 am, 25th.

Signals Our men in BOAR COPSE saw a Searchlight from direction of K.36.c.12.

Aerial Activity Our Q.Bs no activity poor.
    10.15 am 1 E.A. over driven off by AA and M.Gs. fire
    4.45 pm 5 E.A. " engaged by " " " "
    5.15 pm 5 E.A. " " " " " " " "

PATROLS. 1 Off. and 20 O.Rs. left our lines at 10.30pm, reach within 15 y of ravine at Q.6.a.45 and Q.6.a.25. No obstacles were met ravine was found to be occupied and work was heard, no covering party was met, but a M.G. fire from PLUSH TR. E of BOAR Copse. Patrol returned at 11.45 pm.

        1 Off. and 4 O.Rs. left our lines at 11.0pm (R.7.B.73) and went out 300x till enemy wire was seen and then turned W for 200x wire is in good condition and no gaps seen
Voices heard in PLUSH TR about R.1.d.0.7.
No enemy Patrol was met. Patrol returned at 1.0 am. to R.7.B.81.

                                    Leonard Soloman
                                        2/Lt
                                    for Bde Major
                                    1/3 Infty Bde.

173RD INFANTRY BRIGADE SUMMARY OF INTELLIGENCE.

For Period of 24 hours from 6 am 25th to 6 a.m. 26th July, 1917.

OPERATIONS.

1. **Enemy's Attitude & General Activity.** No change noticed in the enemy's attitude. His M.G's. fired short bursts during the night as in previous periods. T.M. activity was noticeably diminished.

Artillery fire may be summarized as follows:-

Time. p.m.	No. of Rds.	Calibre.	Type.	Where Striking.	Remarks.
5.30 - 6.0	12	15 c.m.	H.E.	Q.12.a.3.2. and Q.12.c.2.7.	) 3 minute) intervals) Spotted by) E.A.
7.55 to 9.15.	20	15 c.m.	H.E.	35ˣ W. of and parallel with LEICESTER AV.	
9.10. to 9.45.	12	15 c.m.	H.E.	Junction of BEAUCAMP RES. and LEICESTER AV.	

2. **Our Own Activity on same lines, & where it Influences Enemy Action:-** Overhead fire from our M.G's. during night. Our artillery shelled PLUSH TRENCH at 10.15 p.m. and 2.15 a.m.

B. INTELLIGENCE.
(a). **M.G. Emplacements.** M.G. Fire from approx R.1.d.8.1. during night.
(b). **Movement.** 1.15 p.m. 2 men haymaking in Field S. of road L.13.d.7.6.

    1.45 p.m. 1 man seen sitting on parapet at L.31.a.
    7.15.p.m. 1 man seen wiring at R.1.d.95.45. He was fired on by our snipers and disappeared.

The usual movement in PLUSH TRENCH.
(c). **Smoke.** At 3.20 a.m. an explosion was heard from the direction of HAVRINCOURT.
(d). **Signals.** One Green Light from PLUSH TRENCH at 1 a.m. No apparent result. Two blasts on a whistle were twice repeated from direction of crater at K.36.c.50.60.
(e). **Aerial Activity.**
    1 E.A. over at 8.5 a.m. driven off by our A.A. Guns.
    3. " " " 4.55 " " " " " " "
    1. " " " 5.30 to 6.30 " " " " " " "
(f). **General.** Sniper is suspected at Q.6.b.8.0.
PATROLS. 2/Lt. Chilvers and 2 O.R. left our lines at Q.6.c.75.75 at 9.45 p.m. Party proceeded to BOAR COPSE thence to ravine N. of the COPSE. No obstacles met and ravine found to be unoccupied. Tape found running from bush in E. of ravine in a West direction 10 yards from and parallel with Ravine. This was followed to about Q.6.a.5.5.
Patrol returned to Q.6.c.75.75. at 12.30 p.m.

Patrols Continued. 2/Lt. Marsh and 7 O.R. left our lines at R.7.b.4.4. at 11 p.m. Party proceeded N. for 40 yards, when enemy patrol was seen. They waited 30 minutes and then went on.
   Working Party heard at R.1.d.6.0. and a green light fired from PLUSH TRENCH. No action followed.
   Wire was examined from R.1.d.5.0. to R.1.d.3.0. and found in good condition. We were then seen and M.G. fire opened on us.
   Grass in front of wire has been cleared for about 5^x.
No new wire seen as suggested by Bde. on following sketch.
Patrol returned at 1.30 p.m.

Leonard Selde
2/Lt. A/I.O.
for Brigade Major,
173rd Infantry Brigade.

War Diary

173RD INFANTRY BRIGADE.
SUMMARY OF INTELLIGENCE

Period 9 a.m. 26th July to 9 a.m. 27th July, 1917.

A. OPERATIONS.

1. **Enemy's Attitude and General Activity.** Hostile artillery was normal. BEAUCAMP & VILLERS PLOUICH wre more heavily shelled than usual.

Target.	Time.	No. of rounds.	Calibre.
BEAUCAMP.	8 a.m. - 9 a.m.	45	GAS.
VILLERS PLOUICH.	9.10 a.m. - 9.15 a.m.	8	15 cm.H.E.
Q.12.b.	10 a.m.	30	77 mm.
BEAUCAMP.	10.5 a.m. - 11.20 am.	40	15 cm.
BEAUCAMP.	3.30 p.m. - 3.45 pm.	12	15 cm.
PLOUGH SPT.	6.5 p.m.	12	77 mm.
Q.12.b.	9.15 p.m. - 9.35 p.m.	20	77 mm.
VILLERS PLOUICH.	11 p.m. - 1 a.m.	10	15 cm.

At 5.55 p.m. 12 T.M. fell near PLOUGH SPT.
M.G. Fire at night as usual.

2. Our own activity on same lines and where it influences enemy action:- Our artillery active on PLUSH TRENCH and wire cutting during day.

B. INTELLIGENCE.

(a). **M.G. Emplacements.** M.G. Emplacement suspected at R.1.c.95.15. and R.1.d.30.46.

(b). **Movement.** 10.10 a.m. 2 men seen on road L.14.b.50.15.
10.11 a.m. 1 man seen walking down Sunken road L.25.c.0.2. towards German Line.
10.20 a.m. One man sitting on bank of Sunken Road at K.36.b.35.65.
11.47 a.m. one man pulling on rope at K.36.b.35.65.
7.30 p.m. 2 men in rear of PLUSH TRENCH at R.1.d.5.2. were fired on by our snipers and disappeardd.
8.30 p.m. at R.2.b.1.9. (approx). men were seen working on parapets.

(c). **Dug-outs.** Suspected dug-out at R.1.d.12.20 was shelled by our artillery.

(d). **Wire.** Wooden pickets were heard being driven in the ground between 11 p.m. and 12 midnight in Q.6.b & d.

(e). **Signals.** Red light seen at about R.2.central between 11 p.m. and 1 a.m. (see Patrol Report.).

(f). **Aerial Activity.**
At 7 p.m. E.A. seen to ascend and descend behind wood near MARCOING and at 8.30 p.m. 2 E.A. ascended at same place.
8 p.m. - 8.40 p.m. considerable aerial activity. British and enemy machines engaged in fight.
At 8.40 p.m. one machine, believed to be British was brought down behind enemy's line.

(g). **General.** Train seen on line at F.15.a. going N.E.

PATROL REPORTS:- 2/Lt. Laithewaite and 2 O.R. left out lines at 11.30 p.m. at point Q.6.c.4.3. Patrol proceeded down Sunken Road to 50 yards past BOAR COPSE and then turned half right. at 12.20 a.m. when near the Ravine voices and tools were heard of working party, apparently from PLUSH TRENCH. Patrol proceeded along Ravine in Q.6.a. and found it to be 250 yards long, 40 yards at top and 4 to 18 feet wide at bottom. No M.G. Emplacements were seen. On leaving Ravine at 2 a.m. voices were again heard in PLUSH TRENCH Patrol then returned to our lines at 2.15. p.m.

2/Lt. Bundle H. and 5 O.R. left our lines at 11 p.m. at point R.7.b.5.4. Patrol proceeded N.N.W. until they reached wire of PLUSH TRENCH at about R.7.b.8.8., proceeded along wire as far as R.7.b.2.8. Found wire had been cut in places, but in no place was it cut. Found whell holes short of his wire. Patrol saw party of enemy about 12 patrolling behind his wire.
Signalling with red lights observed at about R.2.central. Patrol returned to R.7.b.5.4. at 12.50 a.m.

W.J. Knight
2/Lt.
A./I.O. for
Brigade Major,
173rd Infantry Bde.

PERIOD **Intelligence Summary** 28-7-17.
6 AM - 6 AM.

Operations. Enemys Attitude & General Activity.

Hostile activity was normal on Front Line system of Trenches
BEAUCAMP was more heavily shelled than usual. The wireless
installation was hit at 12.30 pm. VILLERS PLOUICH had a quieter
day. PLOUGH Spt again shelled intermittently and neighbourhood of
BROOKSBY LANE recieved attention.

TARGET.	TIME	No of ROUNDS.	CALIBRE.
Q12.C.14.	11 AM.	2.	10.5 HE
BEAUCAMP	3 to 4 pm	200.	10.5 HE
Q12.C.14	5.50 pm	4	10.5 HE
BOAR COPSE	10 pm	10	10.5 HE

TM. fired 3 shells into BOAR COPSE at 9.30 pm.
MG normally active throughout the night.

Our own Activity. Our Artillery 6" fired on wire of PLUSH TR.
all day. PLUSH TR. also shelled by our 18 lbs. Guns. M.Gs.
intermittently fired on wire of PLUSH TR. throughout the night.
T.M. believed to be in PLUSH TR in Q6B

MOVEMENT. 11.33am 4 men proceeded from RIBECOURT into sunken Rd.
in direction of enemy lines carrying bread. 6.10pm 2 men seen at
R1B.92.55 wearing grey uniforms; 6.25pm. 2 men seen at R1C 55.75 in
PLUSH TR. 6.30pm. movement observed in trenches at L31C.
6.40 pm. several men seen at L20B.45.15. 7.50 pm one man with
coil of wire seen at L20-a.65.90. man was observed to stoop and waited
an explosion followed 100 yds N of given reference. 8.10 pm one man
entered trench at L20 c 50 40. 8.55 pm. 2 men seen at R1B 55.
WORK.

Working party heard in PLUSH TR. at 12.45 am at about Q6B.

Smoke At 4.0 pm. large volume of Smoke rose just S. of Bouton Wd.

Aerial Activity E.A. more active than usual being seen over our lines
at 9.50 - 10.10 - 10.20 AM. and 3.25 - 3.55 - 4.15 pm. Enemy OB. were
also up during day. One on a true bearing of 430 and another at of
55° from Q12.B.95.42.

General Gun emplacement suspected in S edge of MARCOING
COPSE at L29b.63. Two pigeons flew from direction of enemy
lines over our lines at 6.15 pm. in a direction NE to SW.
Snipers fired on BOAR COPSE during the night from
about Q6B08. Small Slit containing a few stick Grenades
was found in front of our wire at Q6-d-12.

PATROLS. A patrol consisting of 1 offr and 3 O.Rs left our lines at R7B54
at 11.50 pm. and proceeded due N. for about 750 yds. on approaching
enemy wire German wiring party of about 25 men were seen at
work at R1B04-1. protected by covering party. Another Bosche
wiring party was heard about R1d-12. No other definite information
could be obtained regarding state of Bosche wire. Patrol returned
at 1.25 am to R7B.54.
Another patrol consisting of 1 off & 10 R. left our line at Q6.C.12
at 11 pm. and proceeded to N. along Sunken Rd. to point about
Q6-a-35. where Bosche had erected 2 light poles one on either
side of Road to support Telephone wire running approx; E-W.
wire was seen. On W side of Sunken Road from opposite
RAVINE to a point about 100 yds N. two strands of Barbed wire
had been erected two strands also crossing Sunken Rd just
N. of RAVINE. No sign or sound of enemy was heard.
Patrol returned to Q6C12 at 2 am.

W. J. Knight
2 Lt I.O.
for Bde Major
173 Infy Bde.

REPORT ON RAID carried out on PLUSH TRENCH on night of 28th/29th July 1917.

ENEMY FIRE BEFORE ZERO:- N I L.

LIGHTS SENT UP:- At no time either before, during or after the raid were any lights seen to be sent up from PLUSH TRENCH.

CONDITION OF ENEMY WIRE:- Neither at RIGHT nor LEFT points of entry had wire been effectively cut, and at both points offered great resistance. Blankets had to be used and owing to depth of wire this made the crossing a difficult task. On the right it looked as if a Working Party had been attempting to repair wire as several coils of wire were found.

CONDITION OF ENEMY TRENCH:- Trench is of an average depth of 5 feet, uneven floor and unrevetted.
A M.G. Emplacement was found at R.1.d.30.15. midway between two island traverses shewn on aeroplane Map 3L275.
At R.1.d.15.20. approx. there is an emplacement about 8 ft. by 3 ft. 6 ins. by 5 ft. 6. ins. deep, with a well bottom.

CROSS SECTION.   PLAN.

Nothing was found inside it to indicate the use to which it is put.

DUGOUTS:- No dugouts were found.

RESISTANCE OFFERED BY ENEMY:- The trench between points of entry was found to be unoccupied.

ENEMY ARTILLERY:- During the raid there was no enemy activity either Artillery or M.G.
At 1.10 a.m. enemy retaliated on our Support Line and ASHBY ALLEY and swept "No Man's Land" with M.G. fire, and heavy Minenwerfer.
By 1.45 a.m. situation was again Normal.

STORES ETC.:- Nothing Found.

GENERAL.:- Owing to the great difficulty in crossing the wire, the right party had not sufficient time to enter the trench; but 2/Lieut. L.F.C. ARNOLD got to the parapet with an N.C.O. and three men - but owing to the fact that the 'return signal' had been sent up and in view of the returning barrage, he did not deem it advisable to make an entry.
Cpl. H.V. Wayt, of the left party, entered the trench and proceeded about 250 yards down the trench to the right.

CASUALTIES:- We suffered two casualties from our own barrage. Both these occurred from shorts whilst the parties were crossing the Hun Wire.

P.T.O.

Page 2.

REMARKS:— The shrapnel barrage was good. One Howitzer firing on the right was falling short, but this was observed from the Command Posts and "checked". The tapes running to the Hun Wire were found to be of great assistance especially in getting back the two wounded men.

                Sd.   S.G. LIPSCOMB,
                       Captain,
                  O.C. "A" Company,
9.30 a.m.   2/3rd Bn. London Regt.
29/7/17.

From Headquarters
173rd Inf. Brigade.

    Herewith report of Raid on night of 28th/29th July. For your information.

29/7/17

                    W.J. Knight 2/Lt.
                    &c. I.O. for Brigade Major
                    173rd Infantry Brigade

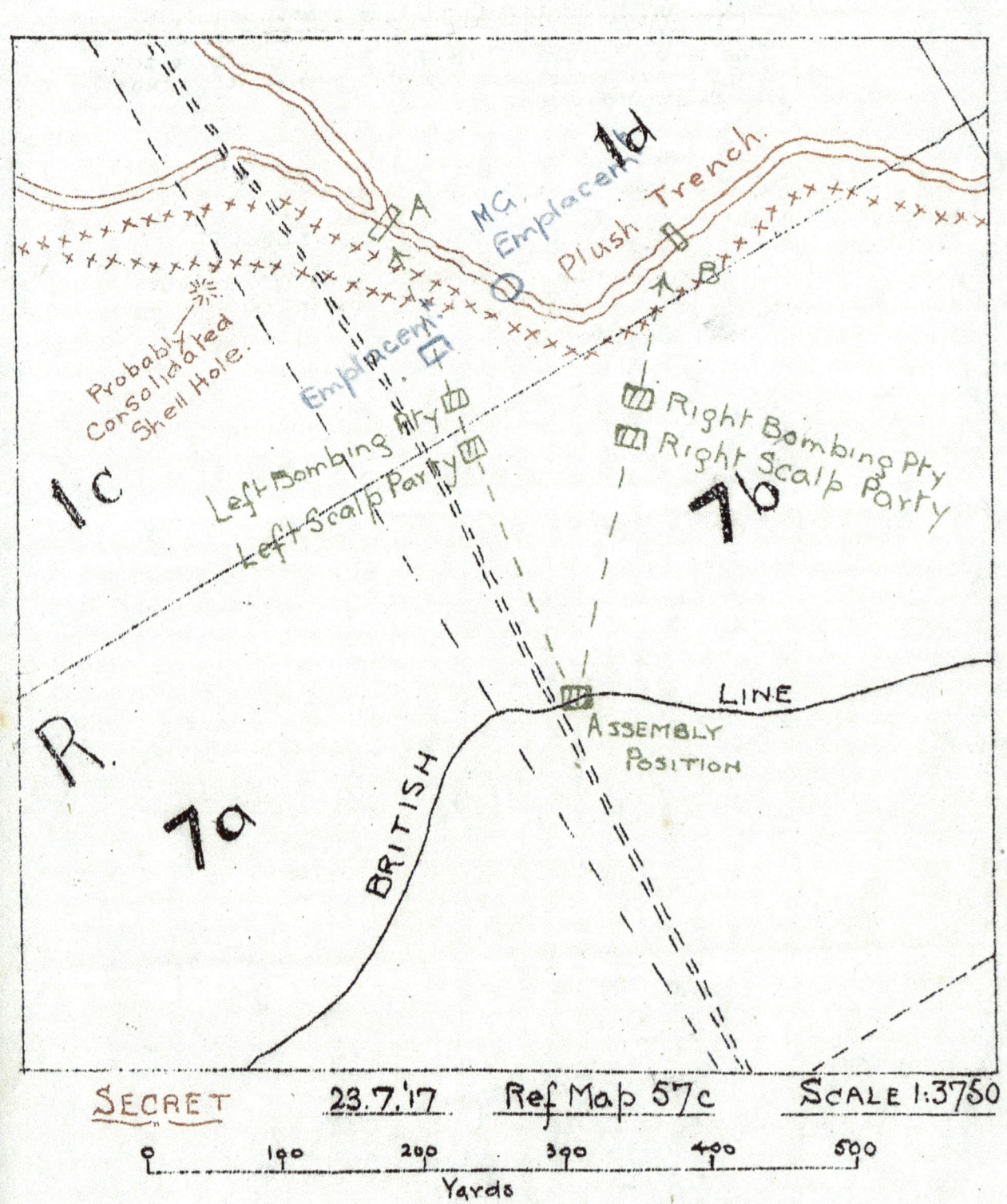

173RD INFANTRY BRIGADE.
SUMMARY OF INTELLIGENCE.
Period 24 hours ending 9 a.m. 29th July 1917.

A. OPERATIONS.

1. <u>Enemy's Attitude and General Activity</u>. Hostile Artillery was below Normal on our Trench System, excepting at 1.10 a.m. when VILLERS PLOUICH, PLOUGH SUPPORT & LINCOLN AVENUE, were rather heavily shelled, mainly 15 c.m., for about 20 minutes, in retaliation to our raid.

BOAR COPSE was also shelled at 1.30 a.m. with 10.5 cm. H.E. 80 to 90 shells falling there.

VILLERS PLOUICH was intermittently shelled throughout the day with 15 cm.

T.M. at 8 p.m. 8 shells fell round BOAR COPSE.
T.M. at 11.30 p.m. 21 shells fell round BOAR COPSE.

2. Our own Activity on same lines, and where it influences Enemy Action. Our Artillery was active on PLUSH TRENCH and its wire all day.

At 12.45 a.m. our artillery formed a barrage for raiding party on PLUSH TRENCH.

Our M.G's. fired 18,250 rounds as a barrage at 12.45 a.m. to support Raiding Party.

B. INTELLIGENCE.
  (a). <u>Movement</u>. 11.15 a.m. Man seen on parapet at L.31.a.7.4.
                      5.0 p.m. One man seen at R.1.d.2.3.
                      6.5 p.m. 5 men seen at L.31.b.5.4.
                      6.35 p.m. Movement observed at L.32.c.5.2. and L.32.c.3.2.
                      6.50 p.m. One man appeared to be observing towards PLUSH TRENCH from R.2.a.35.21.
                      6.50 p.m. Movement observed at suspected dugout at L.32.c.9.5.
                      8.0 p.m. One man seen at R.2.a.35.21.
                      At 9.15 a.m. - 11.7 a.m. - 12.22 p.m. - and 5.15 p.m. men seen at L.31.d.2.9. were fired at by k our 18 prs.
                      6-0 p.m. men seen at L.31.c.9.6. were fired at by our 18 prs.
  (b). <u>Dugouts</u>. Large Dug-out, well built with steps leading down, located at R.32.c.9.5.
  (c). <u>Aerial Activity</u>. Was not so marked as usual. E.A. over our lines at 10.5 a.m. and 5.55 p.m. and at 6 p.m. one over BOAR COPSE, which flew off in a N.E. direction.
  (d). <u>General</u>. At 8.30 p.m. a BOSCHE M.G. Section were observed taking up a position about R.1.d.0.2. was fired at and one man believed to be killed.

W. J. Knight
2/Lieut.,
A/I.O. for Brigade Major,
173rd Infantry Brigade.

SECRET. W.D. Q

To all recipients of 173rd Infantry Brigade Operation
Order Number 36 dated 25/7/17.

Herewith Amendments to 173rd Inf. Bde. Operation Order No. 36.

<u>Para 6.</u> Add - "Trench details of 174th Infantry Brigade, who will move throughout with 2/1st Bn. London Regt., joining this Battalion from the line on 30th July.

<u>Para 7.</u> - after " 1 Officer per Company" add " 1 Officer per Battalion Headquarters from each Battalion in the line".

<u>Table "B" page 1 - Serial IV.</u>

For "2/1st London Regt." read "2/1st London Regt. + Trench Details 174th Infantry Brigade".

<u>Table "B" Page 2 - Serial X.</u>

For "July 30/31" read "July 29/30".

Captain,
Brigade Major,
173rd Infantry Brigade.

27/7/17.

SECRET.   Copy No.......

173RD INFANTRY BRIGADE OPERATION ORDER

NUMBER 36.

Reference Maps Sheets 57c N.E. & S.E. - 1/20,000 & LENS 11.

25th July 1917.

---

1. 58th Division will be relieved in the Line during period 30th/31st July by 9th Division and on completion of the relief will concentrate in FOSSEUX Area with Divisional Headquarters at FOSSEUX.
   On arrival in above area the Division will be IN Third Army Reserve (XVII Corps.)

2. 173rd Infantry Brigade will be relieved in the Right Sector by 27th Infantry Brigade on July 30th and night July 30th/31st in accordance with Relief Table (A) attached.

3. Advanced Parties including C.O's. of Battalions of 27th Infantry Brigade, taking over Front Line Sectors will arrive on 28th instant and will accommodated by Battalions in the line till completion of relief.

4. All Trench Stores, Maps, Photographs, Defence Schemes etc. will be handed over on relief. Duplicate receipts for same being forwarded to Bde. H. Q. by 12 noon July 31st.

5. Code word for relief "complete" will be FOX.

6. The Brigade on relief will move in accordance with Table (B) attached, to the Area HANIN - IZEL LES HAMEAU, with Bde. H.Q. at HANIN.
   During this move the Brigade Group will be composed as follows:-

         2/1st Bn. London Regt.
         2/2nd Bn. London Regt.
         2/3rd Bn. London Regt.
         2/4th Bn. London Regt.
         206th Machine Gun Coy.
         198th Machine Gun Coy.
         214th Machine Gun Coy.
         173rd L. T. M. Batty.
         504th Field Coy. R. E.

7. The following personnel will be left behind/in the line by units for a period of 24 hours after completion of relief, and will move with 206th Machine Gun Coy. on August 1st.

         1 Officer per Company.
         1 N.C.O. per Platoon.
         1 Other Rank per Lewis Gun Section.
         1 Other Rank per L. T. M.

8. Administrative Instructions are attached.

9. Command of

9. Command of Sector will pass to G.O.C. 27th Infantry Bde. on completion of Inter-Battalion relief on evening July 30th.

10. ACKNOWLEDGE.

                                         [signature]
                                                     Captain,
                                                 Brigade Major,
                                               173rd Infantry Bde.

Issued to Signals at ......

Copy No.
1. 2/1st Bn. London Regt.
2. 2/2nd Bn. London Regt.
3. 2/3rd Bn. London Regt.
4. 2/4th Bn. London Regt.
5. 173rd L. T. M. Btty.
6. 203th Machine Gun Coy.
7. 174th Infantry Bde.
8. 510th H.T. Coy. A.S.C.
9. 504th Field Coy. R.E.
10. "G" 58th Division.
11. "A" & "Q" 58th Division.
12. S. S. O.
13. 27th Infantry Bde.
14. S. A. Infantry Bde.
15. 120th Infantry Bde.
16. 291st Bde. R. F. A.
17. 214th Machine Gun Coy.
18. 198th Machine Gun Coy.
19. Brigade Major for G.O.C.
20. Staff Captain.
21. Brigade Signalling Officer.
22. Brigade Transport Officer.
23. Brigade Intelligence Officer.
24. War Diary.
25. War Diary.
26th File.

SECRET

FILE No. G.12.

Sub-Nos. 73-

SUBJECT. Minor Enterprises

Sub-head. Report of 2 Raids by 58th Division on night 22/23 July, 1917

IV Corps

Referred to.	Date.	Referred to.	Date.

SECRET.

Third Army No.G.12/73.
IV Corps No.G.S.17/1.

Third Army.

I forward herewith the report of two raids carried out by the 58th Division on the night of July 22nd and 23rd.

The success of these raids was due to a great extent to the reconnaissance and rehearsals. They were well planned and carried out. The first raid would have been more of a surprise if it had been carried out without an artillery barrage, but the ground was covered with scrub jungle and the barrage was used to drown the noise the men made moving through it.

In the second raid the enemy working in the pits got alarmed and bolted. As regards the remark about identifications, at least two Germans are said to have been killed, but identifications were not made at the time, and when a patrol was sent out later for the purpose, the bodies could not be found, or had been removed.

(Signed) C. L. WOOLLCOMBE,

H.Q., IV Corps.   Lieutenant-General,
27th July, 1917.   Commanding IV Corps.
ECK.

Raids appear to have been very well carried out and no doubt inflicted considerable casualties.

(Signed) J. BYNG,
General.

IV Corps.

Reference Third Army No. G.14/134 dated 14th June, 1917, herewith reports on raids carried out by this Division on the night of 22/23rd July, and the following night.

Reference Map - Sheet 57.C. S.E. 1/20,000.

1. FIRST RAID - 10.30 p.m. 22/23rd July, 1917.

   (a) Name of Commander .... Sec.Lieut. H.S.PRINCE, 2/9th London Regt, 175th Inf. Brigade.

   (b) Troops employed .... 2 Officer 64 O.R. and 2 Sappers.

   (c) Objective. The scrub on the West side of SHROPSHIRE SPUR. The centre of the objective was the QUARRY at K.33.d.55.15.

   (d) Short narrative of events :-

   At dawn on 22nd, 2/Lieut. Prince and Sgt Briggs who had previously carried out several day and night reconnaissance of the approaches to the objective, passed down telephone wire from ASHTON Saphead (Q.3.b.7.7.) for 50 yards along the route to be taken.

   The raiders took up their position in ASHTON Saphead at 9 pm. and at 9.55 pm. commenced to crawl out towards their objective, in 2 lines of 5 files of 4 at 15 paces interval and distance, covering a frontage of about 70 yards and preceded at 20 yards by 3 pairs of scouts covering a frontage of 50 yards; the centre pair following the laid wire and then guiding further advance on a compass bearing and laying a tape. The advance was covered by the sound of our machine guns which fired intermittently across the objective from positions in the rear.

   At 10.26 pm. the whole of the party had reached unobserved a position 100 yards from the objective and was ready for advance under barrage as arranged at 10.30 pm. at which hour a light barrage of 18 pdrs. fell on the objective, while one battery of 4.5's opened on various usually troublesome points, in the enemy outpost line in rear and on flanks of the objective. The 18 pdr. barrage lasted from 10.30 to 10.33 p.m. and 4.5 battery carried on intermittent fire on its targets until 11.15 pm. by which time it was arranged that the patrol should have withdrawn.

   Immediately on the opening of the barrage, the party continued its advance, and at 10.33 p.m. was within 40 yards of the outpost. The enemy sent up two white lights during the barrage but was otherwise unaware of the raiders approach.

   On the scouts reaching the enemy wire in front of the outposts, the leading line of raiders deployed, cut gaps through the wire and took up positions on the far side. The order was then given to get ahead. The party thereupon proceeded to clear MOW COP and was met with rifle fire, rifle grenades and stick handle grenades from the outpost line, and heavy rifle fire from the line of fire bays in the open ground North of the Scrub. Hostile machine gun fire came from both flanks; one firing from the vicinity of OXFORD VALLEY and another from the right of SHROPSHIRE SPUR ROAD. These guns were engaged by the raiders L.G. sections placed on both flanks for this purpose. Our men were occupied

/until

- 2 -

until 11.15 pm. in close fighting clearing the scrub to its North and West boundaries. Seven of the enemy were left dead in the QUARRY and two were killed on our left. A party of eight Germans under a Corporal, attacked our men on the right but were wounded and cleared off, and Corporal and one Other Rank were taken prisoners unwounded.

At 11.15 pm. the scrub had been cleared of all living Germans and the signal for withdrawal - 3 red lights - was fired. The whole party including the wounded were back and names checked by 11.40 pm.

(e) Result :- At least 21 of the enemy accounted for - nine dead were counted.

(f) Prisoners and War material captured:- 2 O.R. unwounded - No M.G's or T.M's were found.

(g) Approximate Casualties :- 1 Officer and 3 O.R. slightly wounded - 2 O.R. seriously wounded.

(h) General remarks :- The raid was entirely successful and this was due largely to the detailed arrangements for and practice of the stealth which was to characterise the operation.

2. SECOND RAID - 11.10 pm. 23/24th July 1917.

(a) Name of Commander .... 2nd Lieut. FOUCAR.
2/12th London Regt, 175th Inf. Brigade.

(b) Troops employed .... 1 Officer 40 O.R.

(c) Objectives ...... WIGAN COPSE K.26.d. and the ground 75 yards North of it.

(d) Short narrative of events :-

Arrangements had been made for support from Artillery, T.M's and M.G's.

While getting into position along the Canal Bank, the raiding party heard distinct sounds as of work in the pits North of WIGAN COPSE. This work ceased at 10.40 pm. after a shot and some shouting.

When the raiding party assaulted at 11.10 pm. it found the pits empty both of men and material. These pits are reported to be about 12 feet wide and 7 feet deep with steep sides and apparently no parapet.

The party which went through WIGAN COPSE found five Germans and claim to have killed or wounded them all.

The COPSE itself contains thick undergrowth but no strong wire was found along the Southern edge, as reported by a previous raiding party. A few low strands of wire was all that was met with.

The enemy made no retaliation whatever, during or after the raid, either with Artillery or Machine-guns and the raiding party returned to our lines at 11.30 pm.

After the raiding party had returned, a patrol was sent out to search for identifications, but none were obtained.

(e) Result :- About five of the enemy accounted for.

(f) No prisoners or war material were captured.

(g) Casualties :- Nil.

(sd) H.S. Fanshawe
Major General,
Commanding 58th (London) Division.

25/7/17.

RELIEF TABLE (A) ISSUED WITH 173RD INF. BDE.
OPERATION ORDER NO. 36.

Out-going unit.	Incoming Unit.	Sector.	Date.	Complete Relief.	Guides.	Remarks.
2/1st London Regt.	9th Sco. Rif. from BERTINCOURT.	Reserve LINES.	30th July.	9 p.m. 30th July.	From outgoing unit in L.	O's. C. Units arrange direct as to time of relief.
2/3rd London Regt.	8th K.O.S.Bs. from BERTINCOURT.	Support, DESSART & GOUZEAUCOURT WOODS.	30th July.		1 per Platoon from Coys. in GOUZEAUCOURT WOOD to be at Bn. H.Q. in DESSART WOOD by 4.15pm	8th K.O.S.Bs. arrive DESSART WOOD at 4.30 p.m.
2/2nd London Regt.	12th Royal Scots. from BUTAUCOURT.	Left Sub-sector.	30th July.	9 p.m. 30th July.	1 per Platoon and 1 for Bn. H.Q. DESSART STA. Q.4.CENTRAL at 1.15 p.m.	12th R. Scots. arrive Q.4.CENTRAL DESSART WOOD 1.30 P.M. Both Units to use SHAFTESBURY AVENUE only.
2/4th London Regt.	11th Royal Scots. from NEUVILLE BOURJONVAL.	Right Sub-Sector.	30th July.	9 p.m. 30th July.	1 per Platoon and 1 for Bn. H.Q. at DESSART WOOD STA. W.1.c. at 1.15 p.m.	11th R. Scots. arrive DESSART WOOD Q.14.central 1.30 p.m. Both Units to use LINCOLN AVENUE only.
173rd L.T.M. Battery.	27th L. T. M. Battery. from NEUVILLE BOURJONVAL.	Line.	30th July.	10 p.m. 30th July.	1 per Gun at Q.14.central at 1.15 p.m.	27th L.T.M.B. arrive Q.14.central 1.30 pm. All guns will be left in position, 173rd L.T.M.B. taking over the guns of 27th L.T.M. B. in NEUVILLE.

RELIEF TABLE (A) - PAGE 2.

Outgoing Unit.	Incoming Unit.	Sector.	Date.	Complete Relief.	Guides.	Remarks.
206th M.G.Co.	27th M.G.Co. from NEUVILLE BOURJONVAL.	Line.	Night 30/31st July.	3 a.m. 31st July.	1 per Gun at Cross Roads METZ - EN COUTURE. Q.20.c.7.N.	Limbers to move in pairs at 400 yards interval North of an E and W Line through Q.22.central.

NOTE:- Each Unit will place an officer in charge of their Guides and this officer will be responsible that the Guides are evenly distributed.

ALL UNITS ON RELIEF MOVE TO STAGING AREA - SEE TABLE "B"

MOVE TABLE "B" ISSUED WITH 173RD INF. BDE. OPERATION ORDER NO. 36

Serial No.	Date	Unit	From	To	Road, Rail or Bus	Route	Remarks
I	July 30th	504 Field Co. R.E.	Line	NEUVILLE BOURJONVAL	Road	-	On relief by 90% Field Co. R.E.
II	July 29th	214th M.G.Co.	Line	METZ-EN-COUTURE	Road	-	-
III	July 30th	Marching Portion Brigade Transport and Transport 214 M.G.Co.	YPRES Area	ABLAINZEVILLE	Road	BAPAUME - BIHUCOURT - LOGEAST WOOD	See Note 3.
IV	July 30th	2/1st Lon.Rgt.	YPRES	BERTINCOURT	Road	-	-
V	July 30/31	2/3rd Lon.Rgt.	Brigade Reserve	BERTINCOURT	Light Railway from W.1.c.	-	Entrain W.1.c. (7 p.m., July 30th).
VI	July 30/31	2/2nd Lon.Rgt.	Left Sub-sector.	RUYAULCOURT	Light Railway from Q.14.central	-	Entrain Q.14.central (9 pm. July 30th).
VII	July 30/31	173rd L.T.M.B.	Line	NEUVILLE BOURJONVAL	Light Railway from Q.14.central	-	Move with Serial VI

MOVE TABLE "B" - Page 2

Serial No.	Date	Unit	From	To	Road, Rail or Bus Route	Remarks
VIII	July 30/31	2/4th Lon.Rgt.	Right Sub-sector	NEUVILLE BOURJONVAL	Light Railway from Q.27.b.	Entrain at Q.27.b. (9.30 p.m) W/c 30/k
IX	July 30/31	206th M.G.Co.	Line	NEUVILLE BOURJONVAL	Road	Move independently on completion of relief.
X	July 30/31	198th M.G.Co.	Line	METZ-EN-COUTURE	Road	-
XI	July 30/31	Bde.Hd.Qtrs.	Line	NEUVILLE BOURJONVAL	Road	On completion of relief.
XII	July 31st	Serial III	ABLAINZE-VILLE	IZEL-MARIE Area	Road	See Note 3. AYETTE - ADINFER - RAISART - BEAUMETZ - GOUY - FOSSEUX - BARLY - AVESNES

MOVE TABLE "B" - Page 3

Serial No.	Date	Unit	From	To	Road, Rail, or Bus	Route	Remarks
XIII	July 31st	Serials I VII XI (less marching portion)	Staging Area	(IZEL (MANIN (MANIN	Bus or DECAUVILLE Ry. to BAPAUME, thence rail to SAULTY, thence road to destination.	-	-
XIV	July 31st	Serials II X (less marching portion)	Staging Area	BERNEVILLE	Do. do. do.	-	-
XV	July 31st	Serials IV V (less marching portion)	Staging Area	(IZEL (MANIN	Bus or DECAUVILLE Ry. to BAPAUME, thence rail to BEAUMETZ, thence road to destination.	-	-
XVI	July 31st	Serials VI VIII (less marching portion)	Staging Area	IZEL	Do. do. do.	-	-
XVII	Aug. 1st	Personnel 206th M.G.Co.	NEUVILLE BOURJONVAL	MANIN	Bus	-	-
XVIII	Aug. 1st	Transport 206th M.G.Co.	YTRES Area	ABLAINZE-VILLE	Road	As for Serial III	-
XIX	Aug. 2nd	Transport 206th M.G.Co.	ABLAINZE-VILLE	MANIN	Road	As for Serial XII	-

MOVE TABLE "B" - Page 4

N O T E S

1. For particulars as to times of trains and buses, and details of marching portions of units, see Administrative Instructions.

2. One Section 2/2nd H.C. Field Ambulance will accompany marching portion of Brigade Group.

3. Marching portions will move in four columns, as follows :-

 (a) Transport - 2 Battalions
 (b)   Do.   do.   do.
 (c) Field Ambulance
 (d) Field Co. R.E.

Each column will be in charge of an Officer, and an interval of 500 yards will be kept between columns.

4. Route for buses between Staging Camp and BAPAUME will be YTRES - BUS - ROCQUIGNY - LE TRANSLOY.

****

S E C R E T   July 25th, 1917.

173RD INFANTRY BRIGADE

Administrative Instruction No. 9

(Issued with 173rd Inf. Bde. Operation Order No. 36)

****

C O N T E N T S :-

1. Instructions (Part I - General
              (Part II - Transport

2. Medical Arrangements in New Area.

3. Notes.

Table "A" - Light Railway Arrangements from Line to Staging Area.

Table "B" - Light Railway and Bus Arrangements from Staging Area to BAPAUME.

Table "C" - Transport Personnel, Animals, etc., leaving by Omnibus Trains.

Table "D" - Departure of Tactical Trains from BAPAUME to SAULTY.

****

No. 1

INSTRUCTIONS

Part I - General.

RATIONS

Units, except marching portion, will be issued with two days' rations the day before the marching portion leaves.

Rations for marching portions of transport, etc. (men and animals) will be issued at ABLAINZEVILLE on night of arrival for consumption the following day.

Rations will be delivered to units in the new area on the night of arrival in the new area for consumption the following day.

Units will notify 173rd Bde. Supply Officer direct of numbers proceeding - (a) by train, (b) by road.

O.C., 2/1st Bn. will ration the 174th Inf. Bde. trench details (10 Officers and 64 O.Rs.) for consumption on 31st July and August 1st.

O.C., 206th Machine Gun Co. will ration 173rd Bde. trench details (10 Officers and 66 O.Rs.) for consumption on August 1st and 2nd.

TRENCH DETAILS REMAINING BEHIND

Trench details of 2/5th and 2/8th Bns., 174th Inf. Bde. will report to O.C., 2/1st Bn. on the night 29/30th July, and will move throughout to SAULTY with the 2/1st Bn.

On arrival at SAULTY 2/5th Bn. details will proceed to BERNEVILLE and 2/8th Bn. details to SIMENCOURT.

Personnel as detailed in 173rd Bde. Operation Order No. 56, para. 7, when relieved will proceed to NEUVILLE BOURJONVAL, and move throughout with the 206th Machine Gun Co. to MANIN - IZEL Area, by bus.

206th MACHINE GUN CO.

Guns and personnel will proceed by bus from NEUVILLE BOURJONVAL to MANIN on 1st August. Time to be notified later.

Transport by road - see "Instructions - Part II".

ENTRAINING

Capt. J.H.Lee, 2/1st Lon. Regt. will act as Brigade Entraining Officer, and will report to R.T.O., BAPAUME, at 7.45 a.m., 31st July. He will travel on the last train from BAPAUME (5. 0 p.m.)

Each unit entraining will send a representative forward to report to the Brigade representative for instructions.

Loading parties, horses, and transport, will report to R.T.O., BAPAUME, 3 hours before the departure of each train. Remainder of troops 1½ hours before departure of train.

No horses or vehicles are to travel on Coaching Stock trains, and Table "G" must be strictly adhered to.

Breast ropes will be required for Omnibus trains.

Marching Out States will be handed in to R.T.O. BAPAUME by every unit entraining.

O.C., Train, will detail picquets at all stops for each end of the train to prevent troops leaving.

Units will arrange for L.G.Limbers to remain near SAULTY Station to await arrival of Lewis Guns, which are being carried on the Coaching Stock trains.

(O.V E R

No. 1 - Part I (Contd)

DETRAINING
2/Lieut. L. Arnold, 2/3rd Lon. Regt. will act as Bde. Detraining Officer at SAULTY. This officer will travel by the first train proceeding to SAULTY and report to the R.T.O.
Each unit will detail an officer to act as Detraining officer who will travel on the first train in each case.

ADVANCED BILLETING PARTIES
Advanced billeting parties consisting of 2/Lieut. L. Seldon, 2/1st London Regt., as Brigade representative, and one officer and one N.C.O. from each Battalion, and one N.C.O. from other units, will rendezvous at Divisional Headquarters, LITTLE WOOD, YTRES, on 27th July (hour to be notified later), and proceed by bus to MANIN, reporting on arrival at the Headquarters of the 27th Inf. Bde.
This party will be accommodated by the 27th Inf. Bde. and will carry two days' rations; rations for subsequent days will be issued under arrangements to be made by the S.S.O., 58th Division.
2/Lieut. Seldon will arrange billets at MANIN for 206th Machine Gun Co., arriving on 1st August.

CAMPS IN STAGING AREA
Each unit will send a small advance party to take over camps, etc., in the Staging Area.

2/1st Bn.	from	9th Scottish Rifles at BERTINCOURT
2/3rd Bn.	from	6th K.O.S.B. at BERTINCOURT
2/2nd Bn.	from	12th Royal Scots at RUYAULCOURT
2/4th Bn.	from	11th Royal Scots at NEUVILLE
173rd T.M.B.	from	27th T.M.B. at NEUVILLE
Bde. Hd. Qtrs.	from	27th Inf. Bde. Hd. Qtrs. at NEUVILLE

Units will see that camps are left clean and tidy.

STORES
Each Battalion will hand over to the relieving Battalion of 27th Inf. Bde. 100 Boxes of S.A.A. from the mobile reserve. 206th Machine Gun Co. will hand over 50 boxes of S.A.A. from their mobile reserve.
All petrol tins will be handed over. Units in the line will hand over _full_ tins of water.

✳✳✳✳✳✳✳✳✳✳✳✳✳✳

Part II - Movement of Transport

Part by road and part by train

TRAIN PORTION
As per attached Table "C".

ROAD PORTION
(All vehicles not mentioned in table 'C')

Two lorries per Battalion and one for Brigade Hd. Qtrs. will report at Units' transport lines at 7 a.m., 30th July, and when loaded will proceed direct to the new Area - a small party should travel with these lorries.
On completion of journey, lorries will return to their column.
Two baggage wagons per Battalion and one for Bde. Hd. Qtrs. will report at Units' transport lines on the evening of the 29th July.
One wagon for baggage and supplies for 206th Machine Gun Co. will report on 31st July.
Brigade Headquarters will arrange to carry Stores of 173rd L.T.M.B.
These wagons on completion of the journey will return to O.C., 510 H.T.Co.A.S.C. at AVESNES-LE-COMTE.

No.1.- Part II (Contd)

ADVANCE PARTY A representative from each unit will be sent forward on a bicycle or horse on the day prior to arrival at ABLAINZEVILLE, to report to Town Major to ascertain billets and position of supply dumps. Marching Portion of transport will be divided into columns. Senior officer with each column will be O.C., of his column. Each column will maintain an interval of 500 yards, and will proceed as under :-

Date	Column	Starting point	Time	Destination	Route
July 30th	A. Bde. Hd.Qtrs. 2/3rd & 2/1st Bns. transport	F.20.a.0.8	8.30 am	ABLAINZEVILLE	BAPAUME - BIHUCOURT - LOGEAST WOOD
	B. 2/2nd & 2/4th Bns. transport	Do.	8.45 am	Do.	do. do. do.
	C. 214th M.G.Co. Transport	Do.	9. 0 am	Do.	do. do. do.
	D. 504 Fd.Co.R.E. Transport and Horsed Ambulance	Do.	9.10 am	Do.	do. do. do.
July 31st	A.	Road junction immediately W. of 1st G in COURCELLES-LE-COMTE (Ref: Map Sheet LENS 11).	7. 0 am	(MANIN (2/1st - IZEL	AYETTE - ADINFER - RAMSART - BEAUMETZ - GOUY - POSSEUX - BARLY - AVESNES.
	B.		7.15 am	IZEL	
	C.		7.30 am	BERNEVILLE	
	D.		7.40 am	IZEL	
	E. 196th M.G.Co. Transport	Wagon Lines	10.30 am	ABLAINZEVILLE	BAPAUME - BIHUCOURT - LOGEAST WOOD
Aug. 1st	E.	Road junc. Immediately W. of 1st G in COURCELLES-LE-C.	9. 0 am	SIMENCOURT	AYETTE - ADINFER - RAMSART, Etc.
	F. 206th M.G.Co. Transport	Wagon Lines	9. 0 am	ABLAINZEVILLE	BAPAUME - BIHUCOURT - LOGEAST WOOD
Aug. 2nd	F.	ABLAINZEVILLE	9. 0 am	MANIN	AYESNE - ADINFER - RAMSART, Etc.

No. 2.

MEDICAL ARRANGEMENTS

1. Sick will be collected by horsed ambulance wagon from the 173rd Infantry Brigade Area by the 2/2nd H.C. Field Ambulance at IZEL-LE-HAMEAU.

2. Sick requiring more than three days' treatment will be sent to the Divisional Rest Station administered by the 2/1st H.C. Field Ambulance at AVESNES LE COMTE.

3. Casualty Clearing Stations for the reception of urgent or serious cases are located at AGNEZ-LES-DUISANS and AUBIGNY.

4. Infectious cases to No. 12 Stationary Hospital, ST. POL.

5. Self Inflicted Wounds to No. 6 Stationary Hospital, FREVENT.

6. N.Y.D.,N. Officers to Officers' Hospital, LUCHEUX.
   Other Ranks to No. 3 Canadian Stationary Hospital, DOULLENS.

7. Cases for examination by the Ophthalmic, Ear, Nose and Throat Specialists will be sent to the Divisional Rest Station the evening previous to the day of examination.

8. A Dental Surgeon will attend at the 2/1st H.C. Field Ambulance, Divisional Rest Station, at 9 a.m. on Wednesdays and Fridays. Cases requiring skilled dental treatment will be sent to the Divisional Rest Station by 5 p.m. on Tuesdays and Thursdays.

9. No. 22 Sanitary Section, located at LATTRE ST. QUENTIN.

****

No. 3

NOTES

Brigade Headquarters at MANIN.

Water in MANIN at I.18.d. At IZEL - pumps.

510 H.T.Co., A.S.C. at AVESNES-LE-COMTE.

Refilling Point, 510 H.T.Co. A.S.C. Lines at AVESNES-LE-COMTE

Railhead at AGNEZ

D.A.D.O.S. at WARLUS.

Reinforcement Camp, Depot Bn. - SAVY.

Divisional Disbursing Officer - AGNEZ-LES-DUISANS

French Mission - FOSSEUX.

E.F. Canteen at AVESNES-LE-COMTE.

There is a Town Major in each village, and application should be made to him for all information in connection with billeting certificates, baths, manure dumps, etc.

****

TABLE "A"

TIME TABLE SHEWING MOVE OF UNITS FROM LINE TO STAGING AREA BY LIGHT RAILWAY.

Date	Unit	Place of Entrainment.	Time	Destination
July 30th	2/3rd Lon. Regt.	W.1.c.	7. 0 p.m.	BERTIECOURT
"	2/2nd Lon. Regt.	Q.14.central	9. 0 p.m.	RUYAULCOURT
"	173rd L.T.M.B.	Q.14.central	9. 0 p.m.	NEUVILLE
"	2/4th Lon. Regt.	W.1.c.	9.30 p.m.	NEUVILLE

NOTE :- All Units not mentioned above will proceed by road.

TABLE "B"

TABLE SHEWING MOVES FROM STAGING AREA TO BAPAUME STATION BY LIGHT RY. OR BUS
JULY 31st, 1917.

Unit	Bus	Train	Place of Entraining	Ready to Load	Depart	Destination	Depart
Brigade Headquarters	—	Train	P.22.c.2.5	4.30 a.m.	5. 0 a.m.	BAPAUME	11. 0 a.m.
Signal Section	—	"	P.22.c.2.5	4.30 a.m.	5. 0 a.m.	"	11. 0 a.m.
504 Field Co. R.E.	—	"	P.22.c.2.5	4.30 a.m.	5. 0 a.m.	"	11. 0 a.m.
214th Machine Gun Co.	—	Train	P.22.c.2.5	6.30 a.m.	7. 0 a.m.	BAPAUME	2. 0 p.m.
198th Machine Gun Co.	—	"	P.22.c.2.5	6.30 a.m.	7. 0 a.m.	"	2. 0 p.m.
173rd L.T.M.Battery	—	"	P.22.c.2.5	6.30 a.m.	7. 0 a.m.	"	2. 0 p.m.
2/1st London Regt.) Details of 174th I.B.)	"	Train	P.20.b.2.5	8.30 a.m.	9. 0 a.m.	BAPAUME	4. 0 p.m.
2/3rd London Regt.	"	"	P.20.b.2.5	9.30 a.m.	10. 0 a.m.	"	4. 0 p.m.
2/2nd London Regt.	Bus	—	P.15.b.4.3	—	12. 0 noon	BAPAUME	5. 0 p.m.
2/4th London Regt.	"	—	P.22.d.0.8	—	12. 0 noon	"	5. 0 p.m.

TABLE "C"

The undermentioned Personnel, Transport and Animals will proceed by Omnibus Trains from BAPAUME Stn. to SAULTY at the times stated

Unit	Personnel Off.	Personnel O.Rs.	Horses	G.S. Limbered	Two wheel carts	No. of train	Time of departure BAPAUME	Destination	By Road to
173rd Bde. Headquarters	6	20	9	1	1	No. 1	11.0 a.m	SAULTY	MANIN
Signal Section	1	50	6	1	1	"	"	"	"
2/1st Lon. Regt., Transport									
Lewis Gun Limbers	-	18	8	4	-	"	"	"	IZEL
Cookers	-	12	8	4	-	"	"	"	"
Tool Limber	-	4	4	2	-	"	"	"	"
Maltese Cart	-	2	1	-	1	"	"	"	"
Mess Cart	-	2	1	-	1	"	"	"	"
Water Cart	-	3	2	-	1	"	"	"	"
Riding Horses	-	8	8	-	-	"	"	"	"
Pack Animals	-	7	7	-	-	"	"	"	"
2/3rd Lon. Regt., Transport	5	150	8	1	1	No. 1	11.0 a.m	SAULTY	MANIN
*504 Field Co. R.E.	1	18	20	4	2	No. 1	11.0 a.m	SAULTY	IZEL
198th Machine Gun Co.									BERNEVILLE
TOTAL	15	350	121	27	9				
Transport 2/2nd and 2/4th Bns (as for 2/1st above)			AS ABOVE			No. 2	2.0 p.m.	SAULTY	IZEL
173rd T.M. Battery	2	60	Handcarts and Mortars			No. 2	2.0 p.m.	SAULTY	MANIN
198th Machine Gun Co.	9	130	9	2	-	No. 2	2.0 p.m.	SAULTY	BERNEVILLE
x214th Machine Gun Co.	10	142	12	6	2	No. 2	2.0 p.m.	SAULTY	BERNEVILLE

NOTES:- Senior Officer travelling on Train to be O.C. Train.
* Find Loading Party and Unloading Party of 100 men.
x Find Loading Party and Unloading Party of ~~50 each Company~~ 100 Men.

TABLE "D"

DEPARTURE OF TACTICAL TRAINS FROM BAPAUME - JULY 31st

Train	Unit	Depart BAPAUME.	Detrain

1st Omnibus Train.	173rd Inf. Bde. Headquarters)
	Signal Section)
	*Transport of :-)
	   2/1st London Regt.)
	   2/3rd London Regt.)
	   504 Field Co. R.E.)
	*Part Transport of :-)
	   198 Machine Gun Co.)
		11. 0 a.m.	SAULTY

2nd Omnibus Train.	*Transport of :-)
	   2/2nd London Regt.)
	   2/4th London Regt.)
	   173rd L.T.M.B. (personnel,)
	   Mortars and Handcarts).)
	*Part Transport of :-)
	   198 Machine Gun Co.)
	Personnel - 198 M.G.Co.)
	*Transport and personnel :-)
	   214th Machine Gun Co.)
		2. 0 p.m.	SAULTY

No. 1 Coaching Stock Train.	Personnel of :-)
	   2/1st London Regt.)
	   2/3rd London Regt.)
	   and Lewis Guns)
	Divisional Employment Co.)
		4. 0 p.m.	SAULTY

No. 2 Coaching Stock Train.	Personnel of :-)
	   2/2nd London Regt.)
	   2/4th London Regt.)
	   and Lewis Guns.)
		5. 0 p.m.	SAULTY

* See Table "C".

Defence Scheme

No. 3

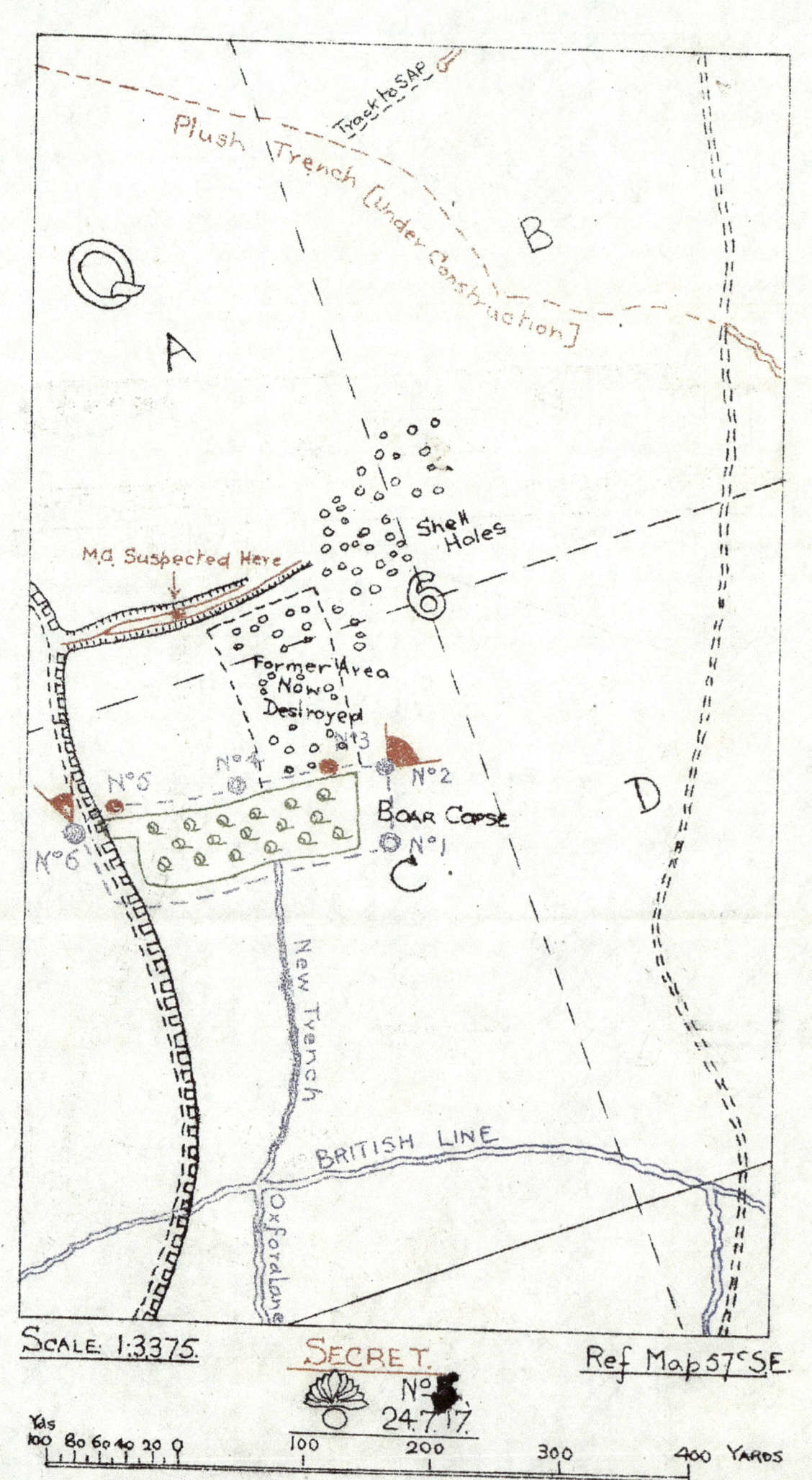

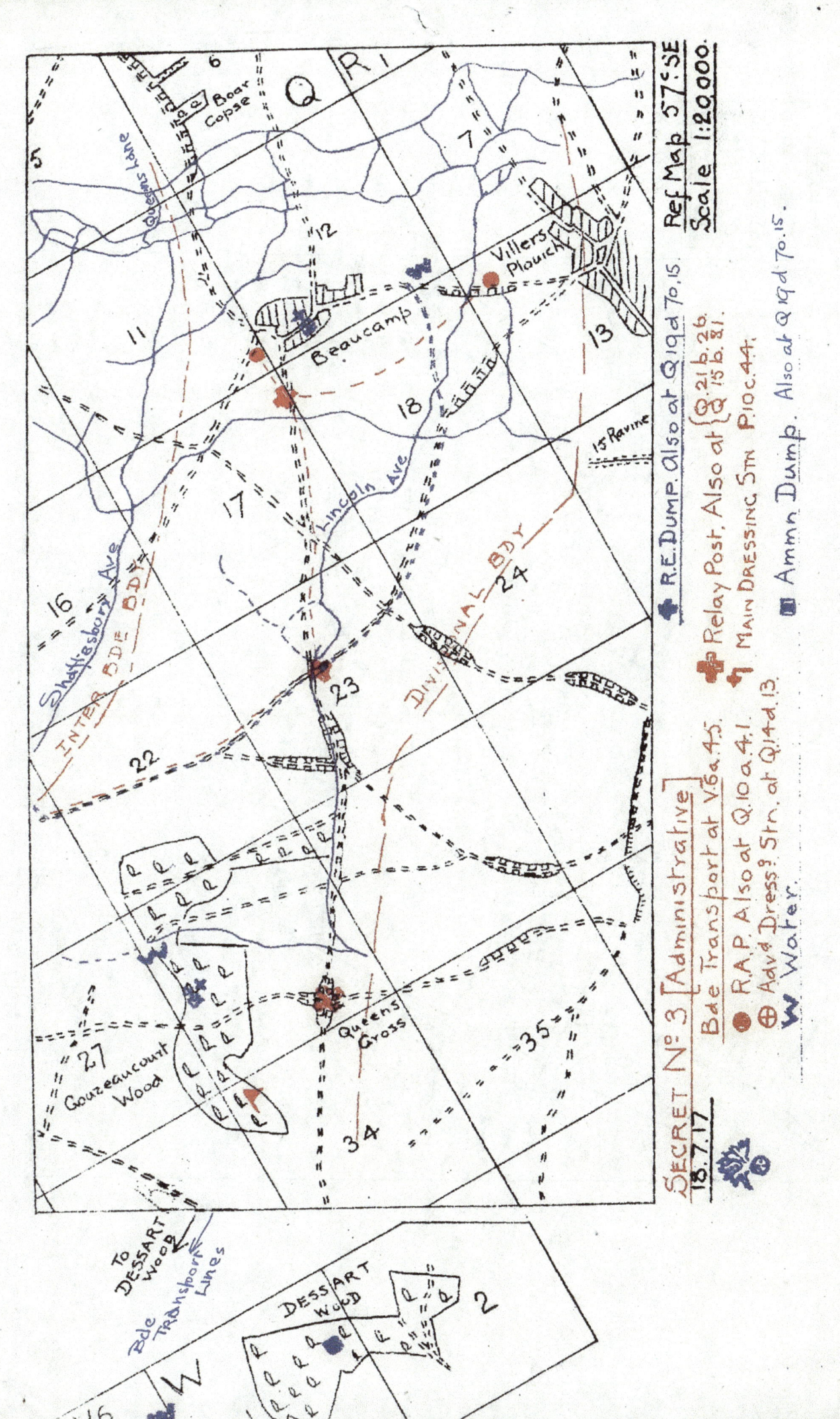

SECRET.
Scale. 1:10,000
Ref Map 57c.
Nº4
22.7.17
Boar Copse
Q
R
Oxford Lane
Brooksby Lane
Grantham Alley
Coalville Lane
Loughbrough Lane
Ashby Alley
Plough Spt.
Plough Res.
Beaucamp Spt.
Oxford Lane
Beaucamp Res
Village Support
Queens Lane
Stafford Sppt
Kings Lane
Leicester Ave
Beaucamp Switch
Stafford Res
Beet Factory
Beaucamp.
SHAFTESBURY AVE
INTER BDE BDY
Villers Plouich
DIVISIONAL BDY
LINCOLN AVENUE
CHARING CROSS.
INTERMEDIATE LINE.
Proposed Work in Green
7
12
13
18
6
H

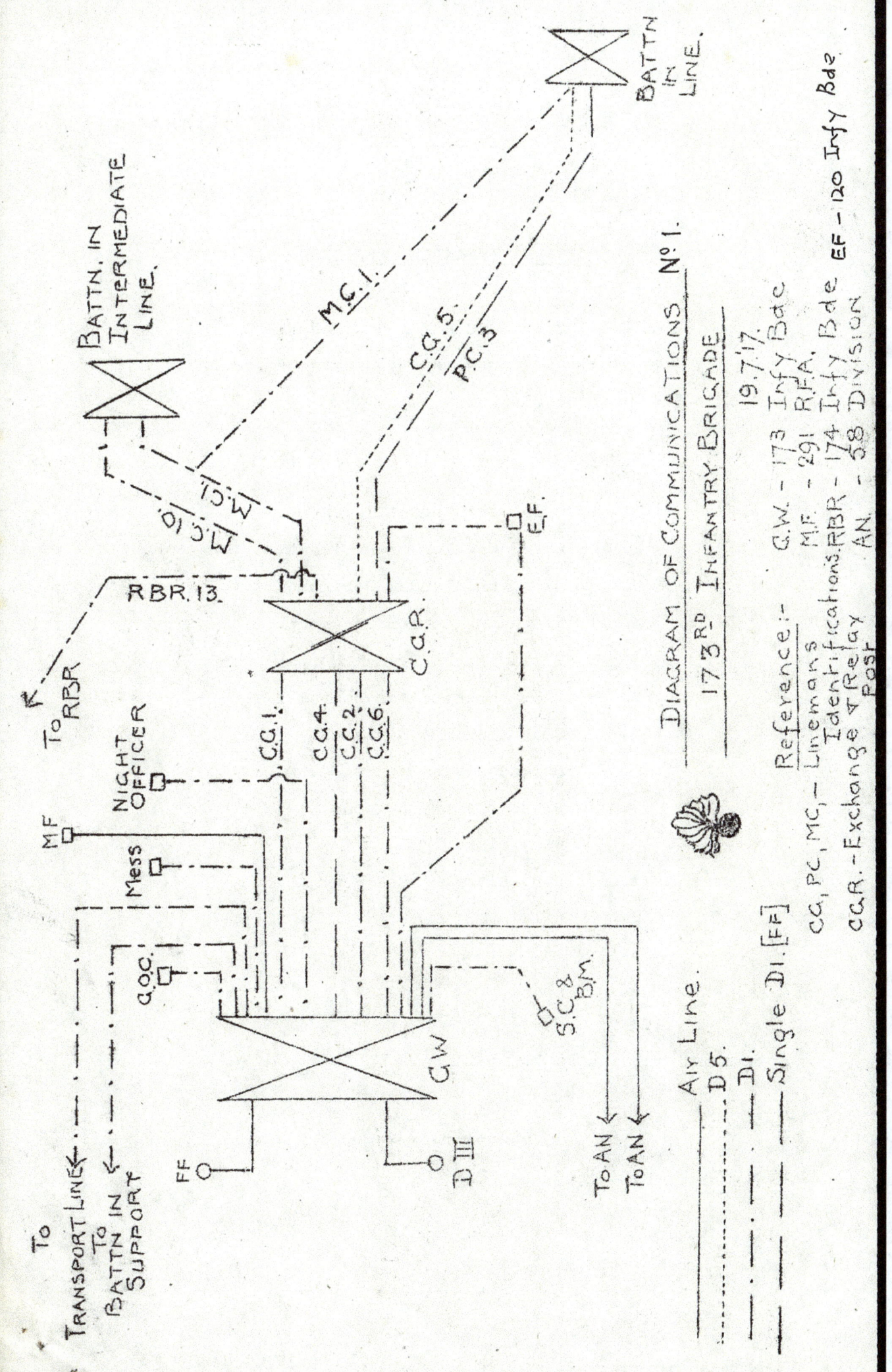

173RD INFANTRY BRIGADE

DEFENCE SCHEME NUMBER 3.

Copy No.

1. 2/1st Bn. London Regiment.
2. 2/2nd Bn. London Regiment.
3. 2/3rd Bn. London Regiment.
4. 2/4th Bn. London Regiment.
5. 173rd. Light Trench Mortar Batty.
6. 206th Machine Gun Company.
7. 58th (London) Division.
8. Brigade Major for G. O. C.
9. 27th Infantry Brigade.
10. War Diary.
11. War Diary.
12. File.
13.)
)
&) Spare.
)
14.)

SECRET.

173RD INFANTRY BRIGADE.

DEFENCE SCHEME.

CONTENTS.

Section A. Defensive System and Communication Trenches.
" B. Disposition of Troops & Allotment of Areas for Work.
" C. Action in Case of Attack.
" D. Disposition of Machine Guns.
" E. Administrative & Medical.

Appendices A. Anti-gas Defences.
B. Establishment of Ammunition.

Maps. 1. Diagram of Communications.
2. Tactical.
3. Administrative.
4. Proposed Work.
5. BOAR COPSE Outpost Scheme.

-*-*-*-*-*-*-*-

25.7.17.

A.G.Shearman
Capt
Bde Major.
173 Infantry Brigade

173RD INF. BDE. DEFENCE SCHEME

(Reference Map Sheet 57C S.E)

SECTION A

1. The Brigade Section of defence is to be known as "The BEAUCAMP Section".

2. **Right Boundary.**

   R.7.b.90.00 - R.7.d.50.80 - R.13.b.35.15 - Q.24.c.60.10 - Q.28.d.80.00.

3. **Left Boundary.**

   Q.5.d.85.10 - Q.11.d.30.65 - Q.17.a.60.65 - Q.21.c.50.50.
   Owing to unequal strength of the Battalions the inter-Battalion Boundary will have to be adjusted on relief.

4. **Defences.** (Fron System).

   (a) Line of outposts (in process of construction) consists of strong posts with Lewis Guns at BOAR COPSE, Q.6.d.40.35, R.7.a.25.90, R.7.a.80.55, and Posts at the junctions of LOUGHBOROUGH LANE and ASHBY ALLEY with our present front line.

   The question of supports for this line I am leaving for the incoming Brigadier.

   (b) Line of Resistance (partially made) will now be our present front trench from QUEEN'S LANE to COALVILLE LANE, down COALVILLE LANE and along PLOUGH SUPPORT.

   (c) Second Line of Resistance (in process of construction). I suggest putting the line BROKEN TRENCH, BEAUCAMP SWITCH, and SUNKEN Road to VILLERS PLOUICH in a state of defence.

   (d) Defended Localities (in process of construction) to be formed at HIGHLAND RIDGE and BEAUCAMP VILLAGE.

   This work is being carried out in the following sequence :-

   (i) Trench to be dug to BOAR COPSE.

   (ii) Double apron of wire to be put out joining BOAR COPSE to front trench at R.7.b.00.65, and across to Q.5.d.80.90.

   (iii) Dig outpost positions at Q.6.d.40.35 and R.7.a.25.90.

   (iv) Wire to be strengthened all along the line of resistance, paying particular attention to that in front of PLOUGH SUPPORT and to the Right of COALVILLE LANE.

   (v) Wire to be put out all round defended localities, and Machine Gun positions constructed to fire to a flank and rear, and dug-out accommodation for one Company and four Machine Guns to be made in defended localities.

   (vi) Second line of resistance to be wired.

Intermediate Line.

This is an old German Trench which requires a great amount of work to be done on it.   Trench runs from R.13.c.05.05 - Q.17.a.65.60.

Second System on Brown Line runs from Q.28.d.95.15 - Q.21.c.60.50.

5. Communication Trenches.

From Forward Support Line the following Communication Trenches exist from Right to Left :-

        ASHBY ALLEY
        LOUGHBOROUGH LANE
        COALVILLE LANE
        GRANTHAM ALLEY.

Main Communication Trenches are LINCOLN AVENUE on the Right, and LEICESTER AVENUE on the Left.

6. Principles of Defence

The following principles will be adopted for holding the line :-

(a) The outpost line will be held by a series of posts connected by C.Ts. to the Front Line, supports to the outposts being in trenches off the C.Ts., situated not less than 100 yards from the outpost line.
Portions of trench which already exist between these posts will be blocked by wire in order to isolate any parties of the enemy which may enter, and they will also be straightened so as to admit of being enfiladed from our posts.

(b) Against local attacks the supports to the outpost line will be employed to reinforce the post in that line, and for the delivery of immediate local counter-attacks. Portions of the reserves may also be employed for this purpose if necessary; this will depend on circumstances and the strength of the hostile attack.
Against a hostile offensive delivered on a large scale, the outposts will act as delaying detachments in front of the main line of resistance, which will be immediately occupied and defended as long as possible, whether flanks are turned or not.

(c) There are three forms of attack that may be anticipated :-

   (i) A raid.

   (ii) An attack on a minor scale to capture some locality, accompanied by a bombardment.

   (iii) A serious attack preceded by a heavy bombardment.

(d) As regards (c) (i). Vigilance - active patrolling, combined with a good system of listening posts and wire, makes the failure of such raids certain.

(e) As regards (c) (ii). Should the enemy succeed in establishing himself in our trenches, he should be counter-attacked immediately from both flanks and from the support trenches, where such are in sufficiently close proximity.

Should these fail, a counter-attack on a larger scale should be launched from the reserve line.

This line must, therefore, be provided with dug-outs, trenches, etc., where troops can be collected.

The extent and intensity of the enemy's bombardment should give an indication of his objective, and enable preparations for counter-attack to be made before his attack develops.

The essential point is to deny the enemy time to consolidate.

Should our counter-attacks fail, the captured portion of our trenches must be isolated by blocking, and all other trenches firmly held until more deliberate preparations can be made. Meanwhile, the artillery must prevent enemy reinforcements from crossing NO MAN'S LAND, and infantry must reconnoitre and locate the exact position held by the enemy so that our artillery may bombard the captured trenches with precision.

In this way a further attack by our reserves will be executed under the most favourable circumstances.

(f) As regards (c) (iii) every effort is to be made to hold the defended areas, HIGHLAND RIDGE and BEAUCAMP, and so prevent the attack penetrating our front system and give time to organise our back areas, and if necessary shift our barrage guns.

(g) The Section is supported by 291st Bde. R.F.A.

       3 Btts. of 18 Pounders.

       1 " of 4.5 Hows.

S.O.S. lines shown on attached (Tactical) Map No. 2.

In addition to these Batteries the Artillery on our left and right can switch in event of our giving the S.O.S. call.

173RD INF. BDE. DEFENCE SCHEME

SECTION B

Disposition of Troops and Allocation of Work

(a) <u>Right Sub-section - No. 1</u>

    See Tactical Map No. 2.

  H.Q., SUNKEN Road at Q.18.b.90.90.

(b) <u>Left Sub-section - No. 2.</u>

    See Tactical Map No. 2.

  H.Q. at CHARING CROSS at Q.17.b.30.70.

(c) <u>Support Sub-section - No. 3</u>

    Intermediate Line - 1 Company.

    GOUZEAUCOURT WOOD - 1 Company.

    DESSART WOOD   - 2 Companies.

    H.Q. at DESSART WOOD, W.1.b.2.7.

(d) <u>Reserve Battalion - No. 4</u>

    In Divisional Reserve at YTRES.

    H.Q. at YTRES.

(e) Brigade H.Q. at Q.27.d.90.60.

    Advanced Brigade H.Q. at Q.23.c.50.40

<u>Allocation of Work.</u>

    The Fron Line Battalions are responsible for construction and wiring and upkeep of the first and second line (except where special work is under construction).

    <u>The Support Battalion</u> under R.E., will work on communications and special work detailed by Brigade H.Q.

    <u>The Reserve Battalion</u> will be used under arrangements with D.H.Q.

173RD INF. BDE. DEFENCE SCHEME

SECTION "C"

ACTION IN CASE OF ATTACK

1. Should any portion of the line be captured, flanking parties will hold on, and by use of Machine Gun, Lewis Gun, and rifle fire, aid an immediate counter-attack to be delivered by the nearest troops.

2. Officer Commanding No. 1 Sub-section may utilise troops of Support Battalion in intermediate trench without reference to Brigade H.Q., but he will immediately report his action to Brigade H.Q. if he finds it necessary to do so.

2a. Officer Commanding No. 2 Sub-section may utilise his men in the intermediate line without further orders, but he will immediately report his action to Brigade H.Q.

3. The Support Battalion (less 1 Company in the intermediate line) will stand to arms in battle order, and be prepared to move to either the line of BEAUCAMP SWITCH, SUNKEN ROAD, or Intermediate Line. The order for this move will come by "Priority" wire from Brigade H.Q. and will be
    (a) Hostile attack aaa Support BEAUCAMP, Move.
    (b) Hostile attack aaa Support Intermediate Line, Move.

4. The reserve Machine Guns will take up previously selected positions in BEAUCAMP defences upon the Priority message.

4a. The L.T.M. personnel not employed in the sector will stand to arms, and be ready to move as required.

5. The R.E. personnel attached to the Brigade will stand to arms in their billets and O.C., R.E. concerned will report to Brigade H.Q. for orders.

6. The 1st Line Transport will stand by to move at shortest possible notice.

7. Brigade H.Q. will remain at Q.27.d.90.60.
   Advanced Brigade H.Q. are only to be used in event of our taking the offensive.

8. General

    (i) Commanders of all units will have plans prepared as to action in event of an enemy attack.
        Schemes to be forwarded to Brigade Headquarters.

    (ii) Commanding Officers will arrange for all routes forward and ground to be attacked over, to be reconnoitred both by day and night by all Officers and by a percentage of N.C.Os.
        All Officers of Support and Reserve Battalions must be acquainted with both sub-sectors of the Brigade front.

    (iii) In the event of an attack parties working on the front line will occupy the positions on which they are working, reporting the whereabouts to the nearest Company Headquarters. Parties from the Support and Reserve Battalions working West of the front line will withdraw to their Battalion areas.

    (iv) The general policy to be adopted is to improve our present trenches, to gain ground to the front, and to harass the enemy by artillery, infantry, and machine gun fire, by active patrolling, and by minor enterprises.

173RD INFANTRY BRIGADE.

DEFENCE SCHEME.

SECTION D.

Machine Guns.

The Brigade Section is supported by the guns of the 206th Machine Gun Company.

Seven of these guns are situated in the front line and are capable of covering our front with bands of fire. Two guns are situated behind, near the Intermediate Line, and will fire indirect fire in event of S.O.S. being given.

One gun is mounted in Sunken Road position near No. 1 Bn. H.Q. for use against aircraft. The remainder of the guns are in reserve and will man BEAUCAMP Defences in event of a hostile attack.

The Divisional Machine Gun Company has its guns in or near the intermediate line.

These guns will be used in defence of this line and will also be used to supplement the S.O.S. barrage, in event of Hostile attack.

For Machine Gun positions (see Tactical Map No. 2.).

173RD INFANTRY BRIGADE.

DEFENCE SCHEME.

SECTION E.

Administrative.

Water and rations can be taken by road in limbers as far as BEAUCAMP and SUNKEN Road at Q.12.d.60.15. by night.

For location of Water Points, S.A.A. and R.E. Dumps and Relay Posts see (Administrative) Map No. 3.

Transport Lines at V.6.a.40.50.

Medical.

For R.A.P's. Relay Stations see Administrative Map No. 3.

Advanced Dressing Station at Q.14.d.1.3.
Main Dressing Station at P.10.c.4.4.

APPENDIX "A"

PRECAUTIONS AGAINST
HOSTILE GAS ATTACKS.

1. When the wind is favourable for a hostile gas attack, the order "WIND DANGEROUS" will be sent out from Divisional Headquarters. This will not be taken off without the authority of the Divisional Commander.

2. The words "GAS ALERT" will not be used.

3. During a period of "WIND DANGEROUS" the precautions laid down in Third Army G.28/151, copies of which have been issued to all concerned, will be rigidly adhered to.

4. P.H. Helmets will be carried by all ranks anywhere in the Corps Area.

5. Box Respirators will be carried by all ranks forward of the line EQUANCOURT - YTRES - BERTINCOURT, and they will always be carried in the alert position forward of the line Q.28.central - Q.14.central - P.6.central.

6. The alarm signal for hostile gas shell bombardment will be the sounding of wooden clappers. (These clappers are now being made and will be issued shortly).

   On no account will Strombos Horns or gongs be used to signify a gas shell bombardment.

===============

APPENDIX "B".

ESTABLISHMENT OF S.A.A. & GRENADES.

	BRIGADE BOMB STORE.	AT BN. H.Q. OF UNITS IN LINE & IN SUPPORT.	IN FRONT LINE SYSTEM OF BATTALIONS.	AT ALL M.G. EMPLACEMENTS (Occupied or not).	T.M. EMPLACEMENT.
MILLS NO. 5.	3000	1000	1000	24	24
" " 23.	500	200	200	--	--
HALES " 20.	500	200	200	--	--
S.A.A.	150000	30000	50000	10000	--
T.M.G.	500	--	--	--	100

1. The above Establishments of S.A.A. and Mills No.5 Grenades will be maintained by using Reg. Reserve of S.A.A. and Mobile Reserve of Grenades. The ammunition thus used will be drawn on indext submitted to Brigade Headquarters. Thus a turn-over of Reserve S.A.A. and Grenades is ensured.

2. Grenades in, and in front of, Brigade Bomb Stores, are to be fused ready for use.

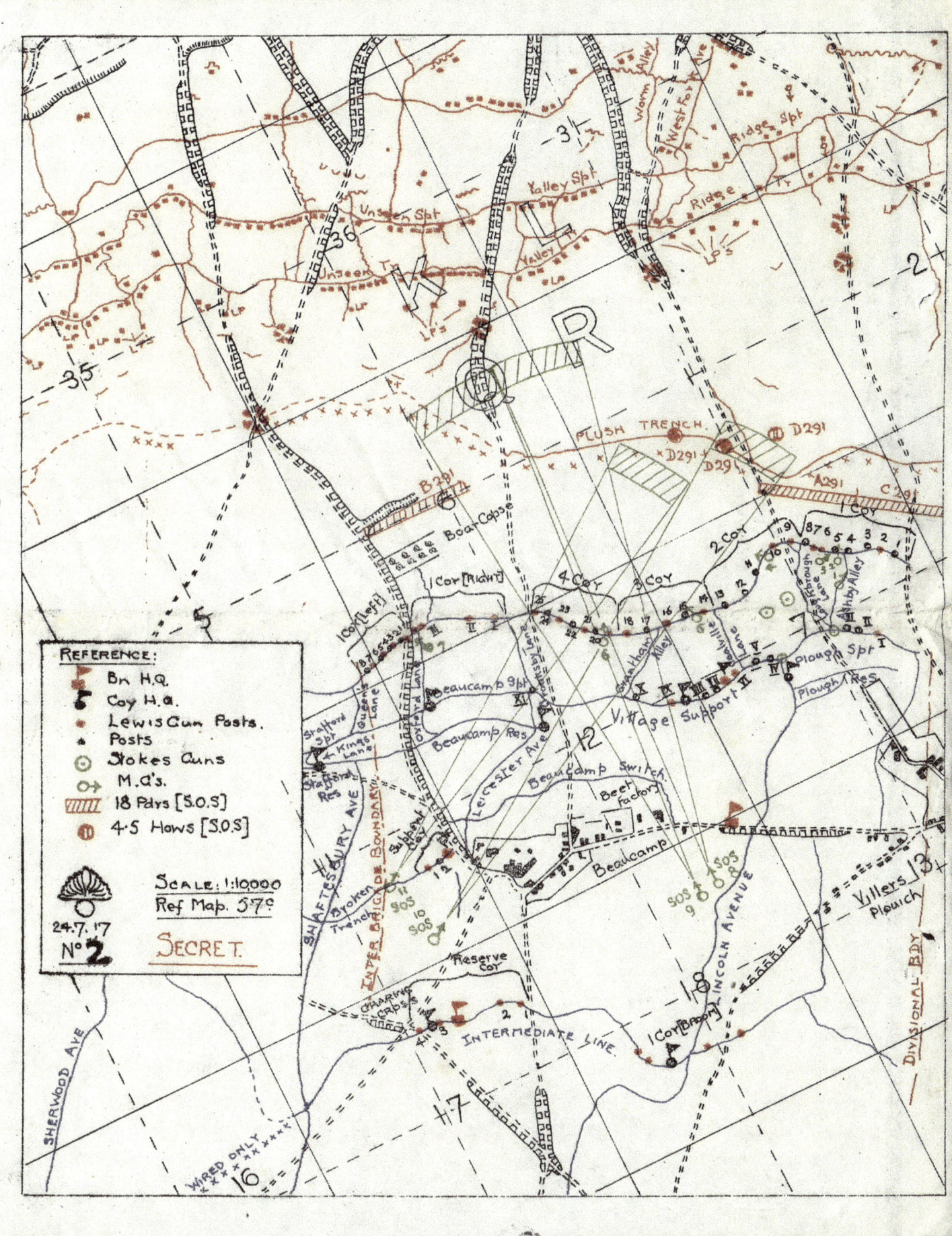

No 10.
War Diary

Army Form C. 2118.

WAR DIARY
~~INTELLIGENCE SUMMARY~~
(Erase heading not required.)

August 1917.

Place	Date	Hour	Summary of Events and Information	Remarks and references to Appendices
MANIN	1		All Units engaged in Interior Economy and Innoculation. Weather wet	C/G
"	2		ditto. Advice in Horsemastership to XVIII Corps inspected Brass simulus of the Bde.	C/G
"	3	3 pm	Interior economy & innoculation. Weather wet. Meeting of Bde. Recreation Committee	C/G
"	4		Wet day, all units engaged in Interior economy & Innoculation.	C/G
"	5		Weather improving. Training. 2nd meeting of Bde. Recreation Committee	C/G
"	6		Training.	C/G
"	7		Training	C/G
"	8		Training. meeting of Bde Sports Committee 7 p.m.	C/G
"	9-17		Training. Weather variable.	C/G
"	18		Brigade Sports. Rain in the afternoon prevented completion of programme	C/G
"	19		Training.	
"	20		Training. Sports programme completed & prizes presented by G.O.C. See Appendix A.	C/G
"	21		Training.	C/G
"	22		G.O.C. & Bde. Major proceeded to V Army area & returned. Training. Lecture by Officer of Third Army Sniping Scouting School.	C/G

WAR DIARY or INTELLIGENCE SUMMARY

Army Form C. 2118.

August 1917

Place	Date	Hour	Summary of Events and Information	Remarks and references to Appendices
MANIN	23		Training. Barrage scheme by L.T.M. Batty carried out. High Wind & rain	GE
	24		178 Bde. transferred to V army. Moved from MANIN to A 30. central Sheet 28, by tactical train from AUBIGNY. See O.O. N° 37. Appendix B	GE
Sheet 28 A 30 central	25		Completion of move by Units of Bde.	GE
"	26		Training.	GE
"	27, 28, 29		Training.	GE
	30		Moved to DAMBRE CAMP & Brigade in Reserve. O.O. N° 38. App. C.	GE
Sheet 28 B 27.3	31st	10:30AM	Conference of O/C Units at Bde. H.Q. Training & situation discussed & Scheme for dealing with same outlined	GE

A.P.Sherman Capt.
Bde. 173 AB

WAR DIARY ~~INTELLIGENCE SUMMARY~~

Army Form C. 2118.

August 1917

Place	Date	Hour	Summary of Events and Information	Remarks and references to Appendices
MANIN	23		Training Barrage scheme by 1 T.M Batty carried out. High Wind & rain	JG
	24		173 Bde. transferred to V army. Moved from MANIN to A 30 central Sheet 28, by tactical train from AUBIGNY. See OO No 37. Appendix B	JG
Sh28 A 30 central	25		Completion of move by Units of Bde	JG
"	26		Training	JG
"	27, 28, 29		Training	JG
"	30		Moved to DAMBRE CAMP ao Brigade in Reserve OO No 35 App C	JG
Sh 28 B 27 d	31st	10.30AM	Conference of O/C Units at Bde H.Q. Training & situation discussed & scheme for dealing with same outlined	JG

Hustman PM 173 Bd.

SECRET. Copy No. 25

173RD INFANTRY BRIGADE ORDER NUMBER 37.

Reference Map Sheet 51c. - 1/40,000.

August 22nd 1917.

---

1. 173rd Infantry Brigade will be transferred from Third Army to Fifth Army on 24th and 25th August 1917.

2. Units will move independently to the entraining point in accordance with ~~attached~~ Administrative Instructions No. 10 attached.

3. During this Move the Brigade Group will be composed as follows:-

2/1st Bn. London Regt.	510th Coy. A.S.C.
2/2nd Bn. London Regt.	504th Fld. Coy. R.E.
2/3rd Bn. London Regt.	2/2nd H. C. Fld. Amb.
2/4th Bn. London Regt.	2/3rd H. C. Fld. Amb.
173rd L. T. M. Batty.	H.Q. Divisional Train.
206th Machine Gun Coy.	58th Mob. Vet. Sect.
No. 2 Signal Sect. &)	Staff of Depot Bn.
Brigade Headquarters)	

4. Exact location of Brigade Headquarters in new area will be notified as soon as possible.

5. ACKNOWLEDGE.

(Sd.) Sherman, Captain,
Brigade Major,
173rd Infantry Bde.

Issued to Signals at........

Copy No.
1. 2/1st Bn. London Regt.
2. 2/2nd Bn. London Regt.
3. 2/3rd Bn. London Regt.
4. 2/4th Bn. London Regt.
5. 173rd L. T. M. Batty.
6. 206th Machine Gun Coy.
7. 510th Coy. A.S.C.
8. 504th Field Coy. R.E.
9. 174th Infantry Brigade.
10. 175th Infantry Brigade.
11. 2/2nd H. C. Field Ambulance.
12. 2/3rd H. C. Field Ambulance.
13. H.Q. Divisional Train.
14. 58th Mob. Vet. Sect.
15. Staff of Depot Battalion.
16. "G" 58th Division.
17. "A" & "Q" 58th Division.
18. S. S. O.
19. Brigade Major for G.O.C.
20. Staff Captain.
21. Brigade Signalling Officer.
22. Brigade Transport Officer.
23. Brigade Intelligence Officer.
24. War Diary.
25. War Diary.
26. File.

173RD INFANTRY BRIGADE

ADMINISTRATIVE INSTRUCTION NO. 10
(issued with Operation Order No. 37)

PART I

ENTRAINING

The attached Table shews the Train Arrangements for the move from AUBIGNY to HOPOUTRE.

ENTRAINING OFFICERS, PARTY ETC.
Captain J.H.Lee, 2/1st London Regt. will act as Brigade Entraining Officer, reporting to R.T.O., AUBIGNY Station at 2.45 a.m., 24th instant.
He will travel by the last train of the Brigade Group at 10 a.m., 25th instant.
Each unit shewn with a serial number on attached table will detail a representative to report to the Entraining Officer one quarter of an hour prior to arrival at the Station of his unit.
O.C., 2/4th London Regt. will detail a Loading Party of 100 men with a proportion of Officers and N.C.Os. They will report to R.T.O., AUBIGNY at 3 a.m., 24th instant. This party will travel by the last train of the Brigade Group at 10 a.m., 25th instant.

ENTRAINING STATES
Entraining States will be handed by Units' representative (see para. 1) to the Entraining Officer IN DUPLICATE immediately on arrival at the Station.
The Entraining Officer will pass one copy to the R.T.O., and forward duplicates to Divisional Headquarters on completion of move.

DETRAINING OFFICER PARTY ETC.
Major J.A.Miller, 2/2nd London Regt., will act as Brigade Detraining Officer. He will travel by the first train, and on arrival at HOPOUTRE will report to R.T.O.
O.C., 203th Machine Gun Co. will detail 100 men with a proper proportion of Officers and N.C.Os. as detraining party. This party will travel with their Company by the first train, and will report on arrival at Detraining Station to Brigade Detraining Officer. They will rejoin their Company on completion of the Detraining of the Brigade Group on the 25th instant.

DETRAINING POLICE
O.C., 2/1st London Regt. will detail six Regimental Police for duty at Detraining Station, HOPOUTRE. They will travel by the first train and remain on duty until the detraining of the Brigade Group is complete, and all troops clear of Station.

The A.P.M. will detail 14 Traffic Control men for duty at Entraining Station. They will report to the Entraining Officer for instructions.

HOUR OF ARRIVAL AT STATION
(a) All transport will arrive at the Entraining Station AUBIGNY three hours prior to the departure of the train.

(b) Marching troops will arrive at the Entraining Station 1½ hours before departure of train.

RENDEZVOUS.	Rendezvous for all troops until required at Station will be at E.7.a.5.6.
WATER	All water-carts will be ontrained full. Water stand-pipes are available at AUBIGNY Station.
	Transport Officers will arrange to take full petrol tins of water in the horse trucks.
	Information as to halts during the journey and where water is available will be given by the R.T.O. and Entraining Officer prior to the departure of the trains.
	Supp
SUPPLY AND BAGGAGE WAGONS	Supply and Baggage wagons will report to units during the afternoon prior to the move and will march and ontrain with the unit to which they are attached.
	Supply wagons will be full.

-----------------oOo----------------

ADMINISTRATIVE INSTRUCTION NO. 10

PART II

SUPPLY ARRANGEMENTS, LORRIES, ETC

LORRIES. Two lorries per Battalion will report at Bn. Headquarters at 10 a.m., 23rd instant.

Two lorries will report to Brigade Headquarters at 8 a.m., 23rd instant.

It is essential that lorries are loaded with the least possible delay. When loaded they will proceed direct to WINNEZEELE.

On arrival the N.C.O. in charge of Stores on each lorry will ascertain from the Area Commandant, WINNEZEELE, where his lorry is to proceed to.

BAGGAGE WAGONS Two Baggage Wagons for each Battalion will report to Bn. Headquarters on the afternoon of the 23rd instant. Two Supply Wagons (full) will accompany the unit to which they are attached.

One Baggage Wagon each for Brigade Headquarters and 206th Machine Gun Coy. The wagon for 206th M.G.Coy. will carry supplies and baggage.

RATIONS All units will be issued with 2 days' rations on the 23rd inst. for consumption on the 24th and 25th. Rations for the 25th will be carried on the Supply Wagons which accompany units.

Those units which entrain on the 25th will draw rations on the 24th for consumption on the 26th.

Rations for consumption on the day following entrainment will be issued by the A.S.C. to units or their Advance Party in the new area.

RAILHEAD Railhead changes from AGNEZ to PROVEN on the 25th inst.

REFILLING POINT On arrival at Detraining Station, Quartermasters, or their representatives, will ascertain from the S.S.O. at the Station, the location of Refilling Point.

H. J. KING, 2/Lieut.
A/Staff Captain,
173rd Infantry Brigade.

22/8/17

MOVE OF 173RD INFANTRY BRIGADE FROM AUBIGNY TO HOPOUTRE

Entraining Station - AUBIGNY   Detraining Station - HOPOUTRE

No. of Train	Serial No.	Unit	Off.	O.Rs.	Horses	Total Axles	Four Wheeled Wagons included under Axles	DEPARTURE Hour	DEPARTURE Date	DETRAINMENT Hour	DETRAINMENT Date
									1917 August		1917 August
1.	1	173rd Bde. Hd.Qtrs.	7	100	29	15	4 G.S.	6.20 a.m.	24th		
	2	1 Coy., 1 Cocker and team, 2/1st Bn. 3 Regtl. police	6	170	3	2	-				
	3	206th Machine Gun Co.	11	173	56	29	1 G.S.	3.20 p.m.	24th	2.30 p.m.	24th
	4	173rd L.T.M.B.	2	60	HANDCARTS - 8						
2.	5	2/1st Bn. Lon.Regt. less Serial No. 2	62	795	60	38	4 G.S.	10. 0 a.m.	24th	6. 0 p.m.	24th
3.	6	2/2nd Bn. Lon.Regt. less Serial No. 9	50	795	60	38	4 G.S.	2.20 p.m.	24th	10.30 p.m.	24th
4.	7	2/3rd Bn. Lon.Regt. less Serial No. 12	55	795	60	38	4 G.S.	6.20 p.m.	24th	2.30 a.m.	25th
5.	8	2/4th Bn. Lon.Regt. less Serial No. 13	28	795	60	38	4 G.S.	10.20 p.m.	24th	6.30 a.m.	25th

MOVE OF 173RD INFANTRY BRIGADE FROM AUBIGNY TO HOPOUTRE (Contd)

Train No.	Serial No.	Unit	Off.	O.Rs.	Horses	Total Axles	4 Wheeled Wagons included under axles	Departure Hour	Departure Date	Detraining Hour	Detraining Date
	9	1 Coy., 1 Cooker and team 2/2nd Bn. Lon. Regt.	6	170	3	2					
	10	510 Coy. A.S.C.	4	54	25	11	4 G.S.				
6.	11	504 Field Coy. R.E.	5	204	76	33	2 G.S. 2 Pontoons 1 Trestle	2.20 a.m.	25th	10.30 a.m.	25th
	20	Staff of Div. Depot Bn.									
	12	1 Coy., 1 Cooker and team 2/3rd Bn. Lon. Regt.	6	170	3	2					
7.	13	1 Coy., 1 Cooker and team 2/4th Bn., less Serial No.19.	2	70	3	2		6.20 a.m.	25th	2.30 p.m.	25th
	14	5 M.M.Ps.		5	6						
	15	2/2nd H.C. Fd. Amb.	8	209	53	32	7 G.S. 3 Ambs.				
	16	H.Q., Div. Train	4	20	25	3	1 G.S.				
	17	2/3rd H.C. Fd. Amb.	10	216	53	32	7 G.S. 3 Ambs.				
8.	18	58th Mob. Vet. Section	1	24	28	6	1 G.S.	10. 0 a.m.	25th	6. 0 p.m.	25th
	19	Loading Party, 2/4th Bn.	4	100							
	21	Traffic Control		14	14						

SECRET.

ADDENDA TO 173RD INFANTRY BRIGADE ORDER No. 37 dated 22/8/17.

Reference Map Sheets 27 and 28 - 1/40,000.

23rd Aug. 1917.

1. On the March to the Entraining Station a distance of 200 yards between Companies will be maintained.

2. All available cover must be used for screening troops from Enemy Aircraft.

3. On the march from the Detraining Station the following distances will be maintained:-

    East of and inclusive of the RENINGHELST - POPERINGHE - PROVEN ROAD - 200 yards between Companies.

    West of the above road - 500 yards between Battalions.

4. Completion of move will be reported to Brigade Headquarters by wire.

5. Brigade Headquarters will close at MANIN midnight, 23/24 August and re-open at BRAKE CAMP (A.30.central), on the 24th instant.

6. The 173rd Infantry Brigade Group will move from HOPOUTRE (Detraining Station) to BRAKE CAMP A.30.central. via:-

    ^ Sheet 28.

    POPERINGHE - ELVERDINGHE ROAD and CHEMIN MILITAIRE.

7. On arrival at the Camp the Wield Coy. R.E. will take over the camp at present occupied by a Field Coy. R.E. of the 23rd Division.

8. ACKNOWLEDGE.

                                                C J Graham
                                                  2/Lieut.,
                                            for Brigade Major,
                                        173rd Infantry Brigade.

To all recipients of Order No.37.

War Diary
Appendix C

SECRET.   Copy No. 20

173RD INFANTRY BRIGADE ORDER NUMBER 58.
Reference Map Sheets
27 & 28 - 1/40,000.   August 28th 1917.

---

1. 58th (London) Division (less Artillery will relieve 48th Division (less Artillery) in the line on night 28/29th August, 1917.

2. Distribution after relief will be:-

   Right Sector.   ...   175th Infantry Bde.
   Left Sector.   ...   174th Infantry Bde.
   Divsl. Reserve ...   173rd Infantry Bde.

3. 173rd Infantry Brigade will move to DAMBRE Camp, B.27.a. on August 30th 1917, in accordance with attached march table.
   + L.T.M SURPLUS
4. Battalion Personnel (vide S.S.155 Page 58) will not move forward from present Camp, but will proceed to join the Divisional Depot Battalion at HOUTKERQUE on August 30th under arrangements to be made by Staff Captain.

5. Brigade Headquarters will close at A.30.central at 8.45 a.m. on August 30th and will open at DAMBRE Camp at the same hour.

6. ACKNOWLEDGE.

                                            Captain,
                                        Brigade Major,
                                    173rd Infantry Brigade.

Issued to Signals at 6.30 a.m.

Copy No.
1. 2/1st Bn. London Regt.
2. 2/2nd Bn. London Regt.
3. 2/3rd Bn. London Regt.
4. 2/4th Bn. London Regt.
5. 173rd L. T. M. Batty.
6. 206th Machine Gun Coy.
7. 510th Coy. A.S.C.
8. 504th Field Coy. R.E.
9. 174th Infantry Bde.
10. 175th Infantry Bde.
11. "G" 58th Division.
12. "A" & "Q" 58th Division.
13. S. S. O.
14. Brigade Major for G.O.C.
15. Staff Captain.
16. Brigade Signalling Officer.
17. Brigade Transport Officer.
18. Brigade Intelligence Officer.
19. War Diary.
20. War Diary.
21. File.

MARCH TABLE ISSUED WITH 173RD INF. BDE. ORDER NO.38.

U N I T.	Pass Starting Point Cross Roads A.30.central.	R O U T E.	D E S T I N A T I O N.
2/1st Bn. Lon. Regt.	8 a.m.	CHEMIN MILITAIRE - VLAMERTINGHE - ELVERDINGHE RD.	DAMBRE CAMP - B.27.a.
2/2nd Bn. Lon. Regt.	8.15 a.m.	ditto. ditto.	ditto.
2/3rd Bn. Lon. Regt.	8.30 a.m.	ditto. ditto.	ditto.
2/4th Bn. Lon. Regt.	8.45 a.m.	ditto. ditto.	ditto.
Brigade Headquarters and 173rd L.T.M. Batty.	9 a.m.	ditto. ditto.	ditto.

An interval of 200 yards will be maintained between Companies and Battalions and between Brigade Headquarters and 173rd Light Trench Mortar Battery.

To all recipients of 173rd Infantry Brigade Order No. 38. dated 28/8/17.

The following are amendments to the above Order and March Table issued with same:-

Order No.38. Para. 5. "to DAMBRE Camp, B.27.a. on August 30th 1917";

now read

"to DAMBRE Camp, B.27.a. and BROWNE Camp, A.23.a.1.9. on August 30th 1917."

March Table:-

The Time to pass starting point, Route and Destination for the 2/3rd and 2/4th Bns. London Regt. will now read as follows:-

UNIT.	Pass Starting Point Cross Roads. A.50.d.7.3.	ROUTE.	DESTINATION.
2/3rd Bn. Lon. Regt.	8.30 a.m.	CHEMIN MILITAIRE.	BROWNE CAMP - A.23.a.1.9.
2/4th Bn. Lon. Regt.	8.45 a.m.	ditto. ditto.	ditto. ditto.

29/8/17.

(signed) Captain,
Brigade Major,
173rd Infantry Brigade.

173RD INFANTRY BRIGADE

PROGRAMME OF SPORTS

To be held at AMBRINES on August, 18th, 1917.

Aug. 15th   5.30 p.m.   <u>PLATOON FOOTBALL - SEMI-FINALS</u>

    (a) 2/1st Bn. London Regt.)
                    V   ) At IZEL
        2/2nd Bn. London Regt.)

    (b) 2/3rd Bn. London Regt.)
                    V   ) Battalions to
        2/4th Bn. London Regt.) toss for Ground

<u>Conditions</u>:- Each Unit to find one Linesman and to provide one ball.
Referees to be appointed by the Brigade Sports Committee. In event of a draw extra time (¼ hour each way) to be played.

Aug. 16th   5.30 p.m.   *<u>PLATOON FOOTBALL - FINAL</u>

<u>Conditions</u>:- Ground to be notified after Semi-Finals.
Ball to be provided by **Brigade** Sports Committee. Each team to bring a reserve ball.
Brigade Sports Committee will appoint Referee and Linesmen.

Aug. 17th   5.30 p.m.   <u>HEATS - BRIGADE 100 YARDS</u>

             6. 0 p.m.   <u>HEATS - BRIGADE 100 YARDS - (OFFICERS)</u>

             6.30 p.m.   <u>PILLOW FIGHTING - PRELIMINARY</u>

Four competitors to be left in.
To take place at AMBRINES RANGES.

Aug. 18th   11. 0 a.m.   *<u>FALLING PLATE COMPETITION - FINAL</u>

<u>Conditions</u>:- Team will consist of 20 men.

<u>Prizes</u> :- 10 Francs to each man of the winning team.

             11.20 a.m.   *<u>ASSAULT COURSE COMPETITION</u>

<u>Conditions</u>:- Team will consist of 10 men.

<u>Prizes</u> :- 10 Francs to each man of the winning team.

             12. 0 noon   <u>TUG-OF-WAR - SEMI-FINALS</u>

<u>Conditions</u>:- Under Olympia Rules.

-: 2 :-

Aug. 18th C 2.15 p.m.   "LIMBER-UP" RACE

              Prizes :-   1st Pair - 20 Francs each.
                          2nd Pair - 10 Francs each.

D 2.35 p.m.   HALF-MILE FLAT RACE - OFFICERS

              Prizes :-   1st
                          2nd
                          3rd

2.50 p.m.   PILLOW FIGHTING - SEMI-FINALS

3. 0 p.m.   BOAT RACE - PRELIMINARY ROUND

              Three teams to be left in.
              Teams will consist of 12 men.

A 3.10 p.m.   RELAY RACE

              Prizes :-   10 Francs for each man of
                            the winning team.

B 3.20 p.m.   REVEILLE RACE

              Prizes :-   1st - 10 Francs.
                          2nd - 5 Francs.

C 3.35 p.m.   QUARTER-MILE - OPEN TO ALL COMERS

              Prizes :-   1st - 50 Francs.
                          2nd - 25 Francs.
                          3rd - 10 Francs.

D 3.50 p.m.   FOUR-LEGGED RACE

              Prizes :-   1st - 10 Francs for each.
                          2nd - 5 Francs for each.

E 4. 0 p.m.   100 YARDS RACE - OFFICERS (a)

              Prizes :-   1st
                          2nd

A 4.10 p.m.   PILLOW FIGHTING - FINAL

              Prizes :-   1st - 10 Francs.
                          2nd - 5 Francs.

B 4.25 p.m.   BRIGADE QUARTER-MILE

              Prizes :-   1st - 30 Francs.
                          2nd - 20 Francs.
                          3rd - 10 Francs.

-: 3 :-

Aug. 19th 4.35 p.m.   BOAT RACE - FINALS

                Conditions :- Team consisting of 12 men.

                Prizes :-   5 Francs for each man of the winning team.

D   4.50 p.m.   MULE RACES

                (a) Professionals

                    Prizes :-   1st - 10 Francs.
                                  2nd - 5 Francs.

                (b) Amateurs

                    Prizes :-   1st - 10 Francs.
                                  2nd - 5 Francs.

                (c) Officers

                    Prizes :-   1st
                                  2nd

E   5.15 p.m.   100 YARDS RACE - OFFICERS (b)

                Prizes :-   1st
                              2nd

B   5.20 p.m.   *TEAM RACE - 3 MILES CROSS COUNTRY

                Conditions :- Team to consist of 20 men.

                Prizes :-   10 Francs to each man of the winning team.

B   6. 0 p.m.   BRIGADE 100 YARDS - FINAL

                Prizes :-   1st - 30 Francs.
                                2nd - 20 Francs.
                                3rd - 10 Francs.

C   6.10 p.m.   *TUG-OF-WAR - FINAL

                Conditions :- Teams will consist of 12 men.

                Prizes :-   10 Francs for each man in the winning team.

--------------oOo--------------

N.B.- Events marked thus * count towards the Brigade Cup

--------------oOo--------------

N O T E S.

1. Entries for all events to reach the Brigade Major by 15th August, 1917.

2. Entries are limited as under:-

    Brigade 100 Yds. (All Ranks). - 1 per 50 or part of 50 (To be reckoned on Total Strength of the Unit).

    Relay Race. - 1 Team per Unit.

    Brigade Quarter Mile - 3 entries per unit.

    Mule Races. - 4 entries per Unit.

    Pillow Fighting. - 4 Entries per Unit.

    Boat Race. - 1 Team per Unit.

    Four Legged Race. - 3 Trios per Unit.

    Limber Up Race. - Two Entries per Unit.

    Platoon Team Events. - 1 Team per Unit for each event.

Entries for all other events are unlimited.

"THE GOODS" - Divisional Concert Party will give performance as under :-

    At IZEL - August 16th) Time to be
    At MANIN - August 17th) notified
    At IZEL - August 18th) later.

THE DIVISIONAL BAND will give performances as follows :-

    August 16th - At the Football Final.
    August 17th - At DENIER.
    August 18th - At ALBRINES

Army Form C. 2118.

HQtrs. 173rd Inf. Bde

WAR DIARY or INTELLIGENCE SUMMARY.

SEPTEMBER 1917.

(Erase heading not required.)

Instructions regarding War Diaries and Intelligence Summaries are contained in F.S. Regs., Part II. and the Staff Manual respectively. Title pages will be prepared in manuscript.

Place	Date	Hour	Summary of Events and Information	Remarks and references to Appendices
28.B27c63				
CAMP DAMBRE	1st to 10th		Training.	
"	11th		Relief of Battns. of 175 & 174 Inf. Bde. by 173 Bde. commenced	O.K.
"	12th		Relief in progress.	see O.O. 39 App A see/sr. App's
SEE Canal Bank C25d 2090	13th		Relief complete & command of Divisional Front passed to C.O.C. 173 Inf Bde) C.J.C. App B 3 C C.J.C	
"	14	3 a.m.	1 Coy. 2/1st Bn unsuccessfully attacked WINIPEG & CEMETERY causing heavy casualties to the enemy but suffering severely themselves.	
"	15th		Holding the line	App D 9%
"	16th		"	App 12 %
"	17th		Attacks on our forward posts repulsed. O.O. No 40 issued App. G.	App 17 %
"	18		Relief of left half of Div. Front by 174 Inf Bde to whom command of Left section passed on night of 18/19. Battalion relief of Right subsection by 2/4 Bn see O.O. No 41 App. H. Operation Instructions for O.O. No 40 issued. Nos 1.2.3.4.	C %
CHIPPR VILLA	19		Preparations for the attack. Brig Genl Freyburg wounded at 4 pm	App I. 9%
"	26th		Attacked at 5.40 AM and gained all objectives BroyField Freybing succeeded by U.A.M. See Operations report App. J	C.J.C App.J.9%

Army Form C. 2118.

WAR DIARY
or
INTELLIGENCE SUMMARY.
(Erase heading not required.)

Instructions regarding War Diaries and Intelligence Summaries are contained in F.S. Regs., Part II. and the Staff Manual respectively. Title pages will be prepared in manuscript.

Place	Date	Hour	Summary of Events and Information	Remarks and references to Appendices
CHEDDAR VILLA	21st		Relieved in the line by 175 Inf Bde and returned to DAMBRE CAMP at 9 p.m.	C/g
DAMBRE CAMP	22nd		The 2/2nd & 2/3rd Battns attached to 175 Inf Bde.	C/g
"	23rd to 2.7th		At DAMBRE CAMP reorganising units & internal economy. Camp bombed almost daily — no casualties or damage.	C/g See App.
BRAKE CAMP	to 30th			C/g O.O. 42
NORDAUSQUES	30th		Move to NORDAUSQUES area with Bde H.Q. at Nordausques. Train bombed on way and one casualty caused to 2/4 Bn.	C/g

A J Thurman Capt.
B.M.
173 I.B.

App. A.

SECRET.   Copy No. 21

173RD INFANTRY BRIGADE ORDER NUMBER 39.

Reference Maps Sheet 28, 1/40,000

and POELCAPPELLE Edition 2.   Sept. 8th 1917.

---

1. 173rd Infantry Brigade will relieve 174th and 175th Infantry Brigades in accordance with attached More Table.

2. On completion of Relief Battalions will be disposed as follows:-

    2/1st Bn. Lon. Regt.   Right Sector.
    2/2nd Bn. Lon. Regt.   Left Sector.
    2/3rd Bn. Lon. Regt.)
    2/4th Bn. Lon. Regt.)   CANAL BANK.

3. All further details of relief will be arranged between C.Os. direct.

4. The following distance must be maintained on the march:-

    500 yards between Battalions.
    200 yards between Companies.

5. Completion of reliefs will be wired to Brigade Headquarters by code word "AXES".

6. Administrative Instructions follow.

7. ACKNOWLEDGE.

                                            Captain,
                                            Brigade Major,
                                            173rd Infantry Bde.

Issued to signals at 10. p.m.

Copy No.
 1. 2/1st Bn. London Regt.
 2. 2/2nd Bn. London Regt.
 3. 2/3rd Bn. London Regt.
 4. 2/4th Bn. London Regt.
 5. 173rd Light Trench Mortar Batty.
 6. 206th Machine Gun Company.
 7. 510th Coy. A.S.C.
 8. 504th Field Coy. R.E.
 9. 174th Infantry Brigade.
10. 175th Infantry Brigade.
11. "Q" 58th Division.
12. "A" & "Q" 58th Division.
13. S.O.O.
14. Brigade Major for G.O.C.
15. Staff Captain.
16. Brigade Signalling Officer.
17. Brigade Transport Officer.
18. Brigade Intelligence.
19. Area Commandant, CANAL BANK.
20. War Diary.
21. War Diary.
22. File.

SERIAL.	SECT.	UNIT.	FROM.	TO.	ROUTE.	RELIEVING.	REMARKS.
A.	11th.	2/1st Bn. Lon. Regt.	DAMBRE CAMP.	CANAL BANK.	BRIELEN.	2/9th Bn. Ln. Rgt.	Not to reach CANAL BANK before 5 p.m.
B.	11th.	2/2nd " "	DAMBRE CAMP.	CANAL BANK.	BRIELEN.	2/8th " " "	Not to reach CANAL BANK before 5 p.m.
C.	11/12.	205th M. G. Coy.	DAMBRE CAMP.	LINE.	BRIELEN.		
D.	12/13.	2/1st Bn. Lon. Regt.	CANAL BANK.	RIGHT SECTOR		2/12th Lon. Regt.	Guides CANAL BANK Bridge 3a. 7.50 pm. 50ˣ between platoons. 100ˣ between Coys.
E.	12/13.	2/2nd Bn. Lon. Regt.	CANAL BANK	LEFT SECTOR.		2/5th Lon. Regt.	Guides CANAL BANK Bridge 5. 7.50 pm. 50ˣ between platoons 100ˣ between Coys.
F.	12/13.	173rd L. T. M. Batty.	DAMBRE CAMP.	LINE.	BRIELEN.		
G.	13th.	2/3rd Bn. Lon. Regt.	BROMFE CAMP.	CANAL BANK.	BRIELEN.	2/12th Lon. Regt.	Not to reach CANAL BANK before 5 p.m.
H.	13th.	2/4th Bn. Lon. Regt.	REIGERSBURG CAMP.	CANAL BANK.	Arr.	2/5th Lon. Regt.	Not to reach CANAL BANK before 5 p.m.

S E C R E T

173RD INFANTRY BRIGADE

ADMINISTRATIVE INSTRUCTION NO. 12

(Issued in connection with 173rd Inf. Bde. Order No.39)

----------oOo----------

9th September, 1917.

ADVANCE PARTIES Each Unit taking over accommodation in the CANAL BANK will send forward a small advance party on the day of their move, to take over billets from the unit whom they are relieving.
    This party should report not later than 2.30 p.m.
    A representative from each unit occupying CANAL BANK should report to Area Commandant, CANAL BANK, and ascertain any local rules.

TRANSPORT & Q.M. STORES Transport & Q.M.Stores of all units will be at DAMBRE CAMP. Attention of Transport Officers is directed to XVIIIth Corps Routine Order No. 450 dated 6/9/17.
    Transport Officers who have not already done so should reconnoitre the Transport and Pack Animal tracks to the Battalions in the Line.

RATIONS Normal system of supply.
    Units going into the line will take two days' rations. 2/1st and 2/2nd Battalions will draw from these Headquarters 8 Hot Food Containers each; the 306th M.G.Coy. will draw 2.

WATER Units going into the line will take two days' water supply. Petrol tins as under will be drawn from these Headquarters :-
        2/1st London Regt. 100
        2/2nd London Regt. 100
        306th M.G.Coy.   40
    These tins will be trench stores in this Brigade.
    Battalion in the line of 175th Inf. Bde. will hand over extra waterbottles. The 2/2nd Battalion will draw from these Headquarters 200 extra waterbottles and carriers - the 306th M.G.Coy. will draw 50. These 250 waterbottles will be trench stores in this Brigade.

    Water Refilling Points: VLAMERTINGHE Cross Roads H.3.c.7.5
                                                    C.27.c.2.9.
    Divisional Water Dump: C.22.b.3.1.
    Attention is directed to this office Sc/0/71 dated 31/8/17.

S.A.A.ETC. DUMPS All units will be in possession of 170 rounds S.A.A. per man to be carried on the man. This will be drawn from the Mobile Reserve, and demands for the exact amount to replace will be sent by units at once to the Staff Captain.

    Divisional Dumps at: I.2.a.2.9 and C.22.d.4.7.

    Brigade Dumps at: C.17.b.9.5, C.16.c.7.7 and C.11.c.9.9.

    All indents for S.A.A. and bombs will be sent direct to N.C.O. in charge of dumps and drawn at once.

R.E. MATERIAL Indents for R.E.Material to reach Staff Captain each morning by 9.30 a.m.
    Dumps are established at C.17.d.3.5 and C.21.b.8.7.

MEDICAL. Regimental Aid Posts under Units' arrangements.

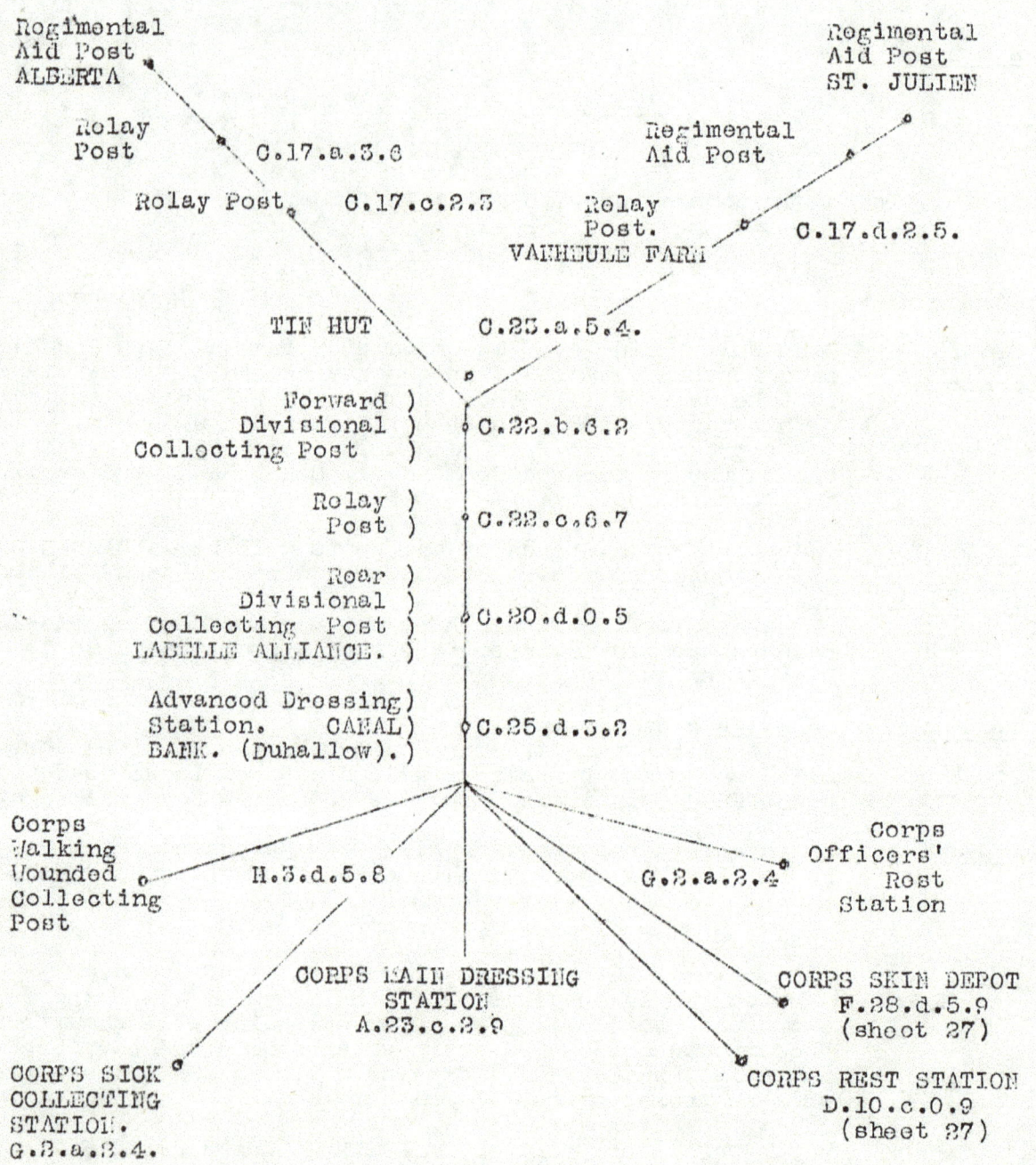

Existing Medical Arrangements for Front Area

WALKING WOUNDED by Flagged Tracks to Advanced Dressing Station at C.25.d.2.3.
Thence to Corps Walking Wounded Collecting Post near VLAMERTINGHE H.3.d.central.
Thence by motor transport to Casualty clearing station.

LYING WOUNDED from Regimental Aid Posts by hand and wheeled stretcher carriage to Forward Divisional Collecting Post at C.22.b.6.2.
Thence by wheeled stretcher or motor ambulance to Rear Divisional Collecting Post at C.20.d.0.5.
Thence by motor ambulance to Advanced Dressing Station at C.25.d.2.3.
From the Advanced Dressing Station Casualties are moved under Corps arrangements to the Corps Main Dressing Station - A.23.c.2.9.

SICK from the Forward Area follow these routes.

H H Garraway
Captain,
Staff Captain,
173rd Infantry Brigade.

WD   App. B.

173RD INFANTRY BRIGADE

Summary of Intelligence – period 24 hours ended 7 a.m. 14/9/17
------oOo------

A. OPERATIONS.

1. <u>Enemy's Attitude & General Activity.</u> Increased activity has generally marked the period; The STEENBECK receiving the most attention from 15 cm and 7.7 cm guns. The enemy, it is noticed, does not now show himself as freely as his predecessors and less movement has been noted.
   On commencement of our barrage last night red lights bursting into two, and Greens in pairs were put up. A barrage was then placed on KEERSELARE - ST.JULIEN Road and MT. HIBOU. The STEENBECK was also shelled. This lasted for 1 hour and 10 minutes, when intermittent shelling took its place. Enemy M.Gs. were also active.
   At 4.5 p.m. the area round C.12.c.1.3 was heavily shelled with 15 cm apparently from the direction of POELCAPELLE. A barrage was placed on area C.12.c., possibly in reply to our bombardment at 5.30 p.m.

2. <u>Our own Activity on same lines, and where it influences enemy action.</u> Has been very active, particularly on tracks, post and support positions. Our aeroplanes also active. At 5.30 pm a light barrage was put over WINNIPEG to the CEMETERY at C.12.b. He then lifted to D.7.a, and b, and continued there.
   At 3 a.m. one Company of the 2/1st Bn. London Regt. advanced under our barrage which began from SPRINGFIELD and continued along the road to cross roads at WINNIPEG. The position is not clear but it is believed they were held up at a MEBUS at C.12.d.80.80. 65.75   65.75
   At 9.30 a.m. MEBUS at C.12.d.80.80 was set on fire. A party of 20 of the enemy were seen to return to the MEBUS about half an hour after flames had died down.

B. INTELLIGENCE.

1. <u>Movement.</u> Noted at MEBUS at C.12.d.8.8, 65.75 enemy being seen in groups of 2. Two men seen at 7.40 a.m. at C.3.d.85.10 going to MEBUS. Periscope seen at C.6.d.80.09 above earthworks. During night men were seen to leave MEBUS at C.3.d.85.20 and go along HUBNER Trench. At 6.10 a.m. 2 men in blue uniform seen to hold their hands up at about C.12.d.75.75.

2. <u>Smoke.</u> Seen issuing from building at about D.1.c.central having been caused by an H.E. Shell about 5.55 p.m.

3. <u>Signals.</u> At 3 a.m. two red lights at beginning of our barrage. At 6.20 p.m. 3 golden rain at about C.3.d.85.18 -no results noted. At 7.30 p.m. signals red and white from lamp at D.1.c.65.45. Signal read S S S, but no results noted.
   Double reds, greens and golden rain used during our bombardment.

4. <u>Aerial Activity.</u> No exceptional activity. 3 E.A. over MT.HIBOU and STEENBECK at 5 p.m.
   An enemy O.Baloon was seen from the BUND in an Easterly direction. It remained up about 5 minutes.

5. <u>General.</u> Enemy snipers active from HUBNER Trench, fired on our shell holes from direction of C.6.a.1.3. Flashes were not seen. Occasional bursts of M.G. from same direction.
   Our snipers fired on MEBUS at C.12.d.8.8 and CEMETERY.
   65.75

C. J. Graham.
2/Lieut.
I.O. for Brigade Major,
173rd Infantry Brigade.

175TH INFANTRY BRIGADE

PATROL REPORTS

Unit	Strength of Patrol	Time and Date	Objective or Task (Fighting or Reconnaissance etc.)	Remarks and Information (Route, Information gained, Action of Enemy etc.)
2/2nd Bn.	1 N.C.O. 2 men	2 a.m., 14/9/17	To ascertain state of ground on far side of road at C.12.b.35.80.	Ground covered with waterlogged shell-holes. No enemy seen. Starting Point C.12.b.1.8, returned to C.12.b.1.8.
2/2nd Bn.	1 N.C.O. 5 men	1.10 a.m. 14/9/17	To reconnoitre ditch from C.3.a. 5.2 to C.3.d.4.4.	Starting Point C.3.d.0.3 returned to C.3.a. No trace of trench or track at C.3.d.1.5. From C.3.d.5.2 two deep ditches of 15 yards each. One runs E. and other N.E. No signs of enemy.

WD   App. C.

173RD INFANTRY BRIGADE

Summary of Intelligence – period 24 hours ended 9 a.m., 15/9/17
----------oOo----------

A. OPERATIONS.

1. **Enemy's Attitude and General Activity.** Enemy's activity has been more marked particularly as regards artillery. At 7.20 p.m. in response to three white lights a barrage was placed on POELCAPELLE - ST.JULIEN Road, and on the STEENBECK. A party which has been variously estimated at from 100 to 300 strong were then seen advancing in the direction of the CEMETERY and towards SPRINGFIELD. In reply to our S.O.S. British artillery at once replied and caused many casualties. The enemy were easily driven off by our posts at SPOT FARM and SPRINGFIELD and suffered many casualties. The enemy's barrages were not so intense as expected, and he appeared to use 10.5 cm and 15 cm weapons.

    Enemy Machine Guns were active during the night, and shooting especially good as regards elevation.

    The enemy's S.O.S. appears to be a red rocket bursting into two early in the morning of the 14th, but on our barrage being placed on him at 7.20 single yellow lights and golden rain were sent up from HUBNER FARM.

    The night of 14/15th was quieter and little activity beyond Machine Gun fire above noted was apparent.

2. **Our own activity on same lines and where it influences enemy action.** Our artillery replied promptly and effectively to S.O.S. signals from our people in the line. As far as can be gathered our positions are now the same as before the attack. It has not been possible to estimate exactly the casualties of the enemy, but all concerned agree that they were heavy.

B. INTELLIGENCE

(1) **M.G. Emplacements located or suspected.** One is suspected at C.6.d.55.30.
    One is suspected at C.12.b.9.3.
    One is located at C.6.d.8.1. (fired long bursts from 7.15 p.m. to U.50 p.m. on to our posts on STEENBECK).

2. **Observation Posts located or suspected.** Is suspected at TIRPITZ FARM.

3. **Movement.** A party of men digging hurriedly reported at C.6.d.80.20 at 12.25
    Digging also seen at C.6.d.65.30 and C.6.d.5.5.
    Men were seen constantly going to and from MEBUS C.12.d.65.75 and CEMETERY.

4. **Work.** Very active at MEBUS C.12.d.65.75.

5. **Smoke.** Following our shelling vast clouds of black smoke seen at D.1.c.20.30 also C.12.d.9.3.

6. **Signals.** Three white lights from C.12.d.65.75 before our barrage and single yellow lights and golden rain from HUBNER FARM.

7. **Aerial Activity.** Our planes patrolled unceasingly flying very low Contact planes also active with KLAXON horns.
    At 2.30 p.m. two E.A. flew over C.6.d. They dropped white lights and 6 rounds 7.7 cm gun followed.

Leonard Selden
2nd Lieut.
I.O., for Brigade Major,
173rd Infantry Brigade.

PATROL REPORT.

173RD INFANTRY BRIGADE.

UNIT.	STRENGTH OF PATROL.	TIME AND DATE	OBJECTIVE OR TASK.	REMARKS AND INFORMATION.
2/2nd Bn. Lon.Regt.	1 N.C.O. 3 men.	10.15 pm. 14/15th.	Reconnaissance.	Patrol proceeded E. from C.6.d.0.3. to ditch running N. from FARM at C.3.d.5.5. Patrol was fired on by M.G. from FARM and rifles from C.6.d.7.4. and returned to C.3.d. at 11.45 pm.
2/1st Bn. Lon. Regt.	2/Lt. P.R. Taylor and 1 O.R.	9.30 pm. 14/15th.		Patrol left our lines at C.12.d.5.5. advanced towards CEMETERY and passed NEBUS at C.12.d.35.75 which is still held by enemy. Ground is very bad particularly at C.12.d.4.8. There appeared to be a trench at far edge of CEMETERY still held by enemy. Patrol returned at 11.0 p.m. to C.12.d.5.5.
2/1st Bn. Lon.Regt.	2/Lt. H.C. Nightingale and 1 O.R.	12 midnight 14/15th.		Patrol left SPRINGFIELD and advanced towards CEMETERY. They were repeatedly fired on by M.G. from CEMETERY and NEBUS at C.12.d.65.75. Ground is very bad and enemy is in his original positions at CEMETERY. Patrol returned to SPRINGFIELD at 2.0 a.m. 14/15.

WD App D

173rd INFANTRY BRIGADE - SUMMARY OF INTELLIGENCE.

For period of 24 hours ending
7 a.m. 16th Sept.

A. OPERATIONS.
1. Enemy's attitude and General Activity. Increased activity has marked the period particularly as regards artillery. Throughout the night he shelled ST JULIEN, STEENBECK border house and ST JULIEN - POELCAPPELLE Road. 15 cm and 10.5 cm guns were chiefly employed. At 2 a.m. direct hits were registered on MON DU HIBOU and other HIBUS in vicinity no damage being done.

M.G. Fire was also specially active more attention being paid to tracks etc. In particular the track from ALBERTA to MON DU HIBOU.

On our Artillery replying to an S.O.S. at 5.30 a.m. the enemy placed a light barrage on the KERRSELARE - ST JULIEN Road.

2. Our Own activity on same lines and where it influences enemy action:- The 2/1st Bn. London Regt. was relieved by the 2/3rd Bn. London Regt. in the right sector, relief being completed by 1.45 a.m.

Our artillery replied promptly and vigorously to hostile fire. Several direct hits were observed at 10.30 a.m. on DIMPLE Trench. In response to an S.O.S. sent by Division or Corps on the left at 5.30 a.m. we quickly replied and maintained a steady fire, chiefly 18 pdrs. until 7.0 a.m. This produced a series of golden rain lights which brought down light enemy barrage noted above.

B. INTELLIGENCE.
(i). M.G.Emplacements (Located or suspected):- M.Gs. very active during night on all roads and tracks. Our Posts in the BUND were intermittently fired on.
(ii). Movement:- 4 men seen to enter emplacement at C.6.d.6.5. at 7.10 p.m.
(iii). Smoke:- White smoke seen issuing from NEW HOUSES.
(iv). Wire:- See patrol report.
(v). Signals:- 7.5 p.m. green lights went up in C.6.d. and enemy put a light barrage on MON DU HIBOU and STEENBECK Valley. Golden rains appeared to be used to obtain increased shelling.
(vi). Aerial Activity:- O.B's more active observing from the POELCAPPELLE group. An E.A. (contact) flew over enemy lines early in this period and dropped coloured lights (1) red, (2) white and pink (3) white but no result was apparent.
(vii)./ Snipers were active
General

Leonard Solole

for

2nd Lieut.
Intelligence Officer
173rd Infantry Brigade.

16/9/17.

173rd Infy Brigade
Patrol Report

Unit	Strength	Time & Date	Objective & Task	Remarks & Information
2/2nd Lon R	1 Officer 2 O.R.	16th Sept 11.45pm	Reconnaissance	Left our lines at C6d.50.70. Patrol reached wire at C6d.75.75. Where gaps of knife rests and staked wire were found. Apparently a double belt between trench but is destroyed, no form no enemies obstacle. No wire was seen. Small party of enemy working on wire at C6d 65.98. Patrol was heard by occupants of trench & advanced posts at C6d 62.96, who sent up many very lights & fired M.G. from direction of C6d 6.90. 7.70

SECRET.   Copy No. 25

173RD INFANTRY BRIGADE ORDER NO.40.

Sept. 17th 1917.

1. **INFORMATION.**   The attack will be made by 4 Companies of the 2/4th Bn. London Regt., with the 2/3rd Bn. London Regt. in reserve.
     Z day and ZERO Hour will be communicated to those concerned.
     16 Officers only, including Bn. Hd. Qrs., will be with each of the two Battalions concerned.
     All unit Commanders will be detailed as soon as possible for the attack so that they may instruct their men in their duties for the attack.
     Understudies will be selected for all Commanders down to Section Commanders, and these will be made to assume command from time to time.
     A camouflage attack will be made (by use of dummy figures) where ground is too wet for troops to advance. This will be carried out by men of the 2/3rd Battalion, position of this attack is marked on attached tracing.
     The 2/3rd Bn. London Regt. will hold the line normally up to - 1 hour when post in SPRINGFIELD and SPOT FARM will withdraw to behind the position of assembly and advance behind the assaulting force to reoccupy their posts.

2. **POSITION OF ASSEMBLY:-** The assaulting troops will assemble on a tape running from 100 yards in rear of SPRINGFIELD to position in rear of JANET FARM, for actual position see attached operation map. Troops will be in assembly position at least two hours before ZERO.
     Great care is to be exercised that touch is established with the 174th Infantry Brigade in assembly.
     Company and Platoon Commanders must adopt their formation to the ground so as to reach their objective in the best formation and condition for the assault.

3. **METHOD OF ATTACK:-** The attack will be carried out under an intensive Creeping Barrage in accordance with attached time table and map.
     On account of the new German System of defensive areas in place of a trench system, success depends upon:-

     (a). Quick location of Strong Points.
     (b). Rushing them before they recover from our Barrage.
     (c). Very careful and methodical Mopping up.
     (d). Consolidation of all our gains.

To accomplish this we are attacking with a wave which advances as close as possible to the barrage to locate Strong Points. Supporting and close to this wave are a number of Sections whose duty it is to immediately attack and mop up all the enemy positions.
     For position of troops in assembly area and after capture of dotted Blue Line see tracing No.1 and 2 and Operation Map.

—: 2 :—

4. **ATTACK OF THE DOTTED BLUE LINE:-** The distance between the assembly position and the dotted Blue Line is about 400 yards.

   1st Phase.
   The first wave will follow the barrage as close as possible to locate any Strong Points, while the troops behind will follow very close behind to mop up enemy positions.
   All known Strong Points will have units told off for their capture and their consolidation, these units may be placed in the wave while the troops they displace follow in rear until after the point is taken.

   2nd Phase.
   Strong Parties will be told off to deal with and consolidate Strong Points at:-

   (1). The CEMETERY.
   (2). The MEBUS at C.12.d.35.80.
   (3). WINNIPEG Cross Roads.

   3rd Phase.
   Each Platoon on the dotted Blue Line will send forward a section to act as covering party during consolidation, these will dig themselves in and act as an outpost line.
   Small parties previously told off will establish Liaison Posts with:-

   (a). 55th Division at D.7.c.4.8.
   (b). 174th Infantry Brigade at D.7.a.00.90.

5. **ADVANCE TO BROWN LINE:-** After capture of the dotted Blue Line there will be a pause in the barrage until + 1 hour 30 minutes, when it will move back by lifts of 50 yards until it rests on the Brown Line. Every effort is to be made to get patrols forward to occupy the ground and strengthen our position on the Ridge.
   If possible small parties previously told off will establish Liaison Posts with 174th Infantry Brigade:-

   at ARBRE
   and Road Junction D.7.b.05.18.

6. **SPECIAL PARTY FOR SCHULER FARM:-** A special party of 1 strong platoon will be detailed to move through the dotted Blue Line under the barrage at + 1 hour 30 minutes to help with the capture of SCHULER FARM by attacking it from the North.
   This party will be working with a Tank, but they are on no account to wait for the Tank in event of it being delayed.

7. **ACTION OF VICKERS GUNS:-** O.C. 203rd Machine Gun Coy. will detail 4 guns to move with the assaulting troops. They will move at +20 minutes to the following points and be used as defensive guns.

   1 gun to shell holes D.7.a.05.50.
   1 gun to shell holes D.7.a.05.10.
   1 gun to MEBUS at C.12.d.35.80.
   1 gun to shell holes near WINNIPEG Cross Roads.

-: 3 :-

8. **VICKERS GUNS:-** 4 guns will be placed in a position to be picked by O.C. 203th Machine Gun Coy. These guns will be used as vigilance guns and will fire at any targets that offer, especially low flying aeroplanes, and German Counter-attacks.
8 guns to be placed in some position near JEW HILL and BORDER HOUSE to be used as indirect barrage and S.O.S. guns.

9. **LIGHT T.M.B.:-** O.C. 173rd L. T. M. Batty. will pick a position for two guns to deal with strong points which may exist in swampy ground to right of JURY FARM and to left of JANET FARM.

10. **THINNING OUT THE LINE:-** On Z night O.C. 2/4th Bn. London Regt. will thin out his line if necessary by moving in four of the barrage M.Gs. into the line and sending back one or two Companies into support.

ACKNOWLEDGE.

Issued to Signals at 11/pm

[signature] Captain,
Brigade Major,
173rd Infantry Brigade.

Copy No.
1. 2/1st Bn. London Regt.
2. 2/2nd Bn. London Regt.
3. 2/3rd Bn. London Regt.
4. 2/4th Bn. London Regt.
5. 173rd L. T. M. Batty.
6. 206th Machine Gun Coy.
7. 174th Infantry Brigade.
8. 175th Infantry Brigade.
9. 166th Infantry Brigade.
10. 153rd Infantry Brigade.
11. "G" 58th Division.
12. "A" "Q" 58th Division.
13. S. S. O.
14. Forward Area Commandant.
15. Right Group.
16. Centre Group.
17. Left Group.
18. Staff Captain.
19. Brigade Major, (for G.O.C.)
20. Brigade Signalling Officer.
21. Brigade Transport Officer.
22. Brigade Intelligence Officer.
23. War Diary.
24. War Diary.
25. File.

SECRET   App H   Copy No. 24

WD

173RD INFANTRY BRIGADE ORDER NO. 41

Ref: Sheet 28 N.W. 1/10,000
     Sheet 28 1/20,000   17th September, 1917.

1. 174th Inf. Bde. will relieve 173rd Inf. Bde. in the Left Sector of the Divisional Front on night 18/19th September.

2. Moves in connection with this relief will be in accordance with attached Relief Table.

3. Previous to relief :-
   (a) 2/2nd Bn. will arrange to inhabit the shelters now ready for occupation at
         HUGEL HALLES
         HUGEL HOLLOW
         C.11.a.85.10
         C.11.a.7.5
so that these may be properly handed over to the relieving unit.

   (b) 2/2nd Bn. will move 2 platoons from GATWICK COT at C.16.b.9.9 to CANADIAN TR. about C.15.d. - and will do everything possible to improve accommodation at the latter locality.

4. Command of Right Forward and Left Forward Sectors will pass to O.C., 2/4th Bn. and O.C., 2/7th Bn. on completion of relief, which will be wired to Bde. H.Q. by code word KAMERADE.

5. All details of relief not provided for by this order will be arranged between C.Os. concerned.

6. Please acknowledge.

                               Captain,
                               Brigade Major,
                          173rd Infantry Brigade.

Copy No.
1. 2/1st London Regt.
2. 2/2nd London Regt.
3. 2/3rd London Regt.
4. 2/4th London Regt.
5. 173rd L.T.M. Battery
6. 205th Machine Gun Coy.
7. 174th Infantry Bde.
8. 175th Infantry Bde.
9. 166th Infantry Bde.
10. 153rd Infantry Bde.
11. 58th Division "G"
12. 58th Division "Q"
13. S.S.O.
14. Forward Area Commandant
15. Right Group
16. Centre Group
17. Left Group
18. Staff Captain
19. Bde. Signal Officer
20. Bde. Transport Officer
21. Bde. Intelligence Officer
22. Brigade Major for G.O.C.
23. WAR DIARY
24. WAR DIARY

Date Sept.	Unit	From	To	Route	Remarks
18/19th	2/2nd Lon. Regt.	Line (Left Div. Sector)	CANAL BANK H.Q. at C.25.b.05.50	—	To be relieved by 2/4th Lon. Regt.
18/19th	2 (support) Cos. 2/3rd Lon. Regt. and H.Q.	Line (Right Div. Sector)	CANAL BANK H.Q. at C.25.d.30.20	—	To be relieved by H.Q., & 2 Cos. 2/4th Lon. Regt.
18/19th	2/1st Lon. Regt.	CANAL BANK	REIGERSBURG CAMP	—	To be relieved by H.Q. and 2 Cos. 2/3rd Lon. Regt.
20th	2/1st Lon. Regt.	REIGERSBURG CAMP	DAMBRE CAMP	QUEENS RD.	To be clear of REIGERSBURG CAMP by 10 a.m.

Orders for the move of the remaining 2 Companies of 2/3rd and 2/4th Battalions will be issued later.

See attached table.

To all recipients of 173rd Infantry Brigade Order No.41 dated 17/9/17.

Ref: Relief Table issued with Brigade Order No.41. Cancel sub-note and substitute:-

DATE.	UNIT.	FROM.	TO.	ROUTE.	REMARKS.
18/19.	2/4th Lon. Regt.	CANAL BANK.	2 Coys to Line. 2 Coys. to CALIFORNIA DRIVE Southern End.		To be replaced at CANAL BANK by 2/2nd Bn. Lon. Regt.
19/20.	1 Coy. 2/3rd Lon. Regt.	Line.	CANAL BANK.		To be relieved in Line by 2/4th Bn. London Regt.

Moves of 2/1st Lon. Regt. should be amended to read as follows:-

| 18/19. | 2/1st Lon Regt. less 1 Coy. | CANAL BANK. | REIGERSBURG CAMP. | | To be relieved by H.Q. & 2 Coys. 2/3rd Bn. Lon. Regt. |
| 20th. | 2/1st Lon. Regt. less 2 Coys. | REIGERSBURG CAMP. | DAMBRE CAMP. | QUEBEC ROAD. | To be clear of REIGERSBURG CAMP by 10 a.m. |

18/9/17.

Captain,
Brigade Major,
173rd Infantry Brigade.

SECRET.   App. I   Copy No. 23

173RD INFANTRY BRIGADE
OPERATION INSTRUCTIONS NO. 4.

TANKS.

1. 3 Tanks of No.13 Company will co-operate with the attack of the 2/4th Bn. London Regt.
2. Objectives, routes and timings for these tanks are shown on attached Tank Action Table.
3. **RALLYING POINTS.**

   When tanks have completed the tasks allotted them and are no longer required to assist the Infantry in consolidation they will return independently to the CANAL Area Tankodrome by the route they came by. There will be no intermediate rallying point.
4. Tanks ditched in the enemy's lines will be held as Strong Points by their own crews. They will not be handed over to the Infantry unless specific orders to do so are issued by the Tank Commander concerned.
5. The following signals will be used between Tanks and Infantry:-

   RED   )
   WHITE) Disc.   Enemy in concrete post.
   RED   )

   GREEN)
   GREEN) Disc.   Enemy clear of concrete post.
   GREEN)

   RED   )
   RED   ) Disc.   Tank broken down.
   RED   )

   Infantry requiring the help of a tank will wave their steel helmets on top of their rifles.
6. Position of tanks on situation maps sent in will be marked as follows:-

          Tank in action.

          Tank out of action.

   The Battalion letter and number of tank should be added.
   The position of all derelict tanks will be reported through Brigade Headquarters.
7. Infantry on no account are to wait the arrival of tanks. On the other hand, if a tank has pushed on ahead of the Infantry and seize an enemy Strong Point, it must be immediately supported by the nearest Infantry.

   This must be impressed on all ranks.

18/9/17.   Captain,
                                         Brigade Major,
                                       173rd Infantry Brigade.

TANK ACTION TABLE

TANK.	OBJECTIVE.	CO-OPERATING WITH	ROUTE.	TIMING.
No.15 Coy.				
"A" Tank.	NEDUS. C.12.d.8.8.	2/4th Bn. Lon. Regt.	BELLEVUE - ST JULIEN - WINNIPEG X ROADS.	Leave BELLEVUE 0 minus 2 hours, passing ST JULIEN 0 minus 30 mins, and WINNIPEG X Roads 0 plus 30 mins.
B & C Tanks.	SCHULER FARM.	2/4th Bn. London Regt.	ditto.	Leave BELLEVUE 0 minus 1 hr. 45 mins, passing ST JULIEN at 0 minus 15 mins, JANET FARM at 0 plus 15 mins, WINNIPEG X ROADS at ZERO plus 50 mins, and Road Junction D.7.c.3.5. at ZERO plus 1 hr. 20 mins.

S E C R E T.

173RD INFANTRY BRIGADE

OPERATION REPORT.

September 19th - 21st 1917.

App. J

In accordance with 173rd Infantry Brigade Order No.40, the Brigade attacked on the right Sector of the Divisional Front.
Four Companies, each 100 strong, of the 2/4th Bn. London Regt. forming the assaulting Force. The 2/3rd Bn. London Regt. was in reserve, and carried out a camouflage attack opposite impassable swampy ground on right of Brigade Front by means of dummy figures.
At 7 p.m. on the 19th instant Advanced Brigade Headquarters opened at CHEDDAR VILLA.
At 8 p.m. Brigadier-General B.C. Freyberg, V.C. D.S.O., was brought to Brigade Headquarters by stretcher bearers, having been severely wounded at 6 p.m., near 2/4th Bn. London Regt. Headquarters at ST. JULIEN. His wounds had been dressed at the R.A.P. and he continued to command his Brigade though wounded in 10 places by an H.E. Shell, which burst almost at his foot.

ASSEMBLY.

Assembly was extremely difficult, owing to state of the ground and the darkness of the night. Rain was falling, the ground was a mass of deep shell holes, full of water, and the men sinking up to their knees in mud. Under those conditions it was found necessary to tie each man of a platoon to those in front and behind him with tape, in order to maintain connection.
Six hours were occupied in assembling the 400 men, though the operation was conducted without a hitch and without being discovered by the enemy who were within 150 yards of the leading platoon.
Assembly was complete by 3 a.m.

THE ASSAULT.

At 5.40 a.m. on the 20th the heavy bombardment of the enemy which had been in progress throughout the afternoon and night of the 19th, was intensified by the fire of the barrage guns which opened punctually at ZERO with perfectly timed bursts, and the troops advanced to the assault.
At 6.15 a.m. O.C. 2/4th Bn. London Regt. reported by Telephone the capture of MEBUS at C.18.d.65.80. At 6.30 a.m. the receipt from "A" Company of report on the captured MEBUS together with a Machine Gun, and that our troops had occupied the DOTTED BLUE LINE was reported by O.C. 2/4th Bn. London Regt. by telephone.
An enemy officer taken prisoner with 15 men at WINNIPEG CROSS ROADS confirmed the report, and at 6.55 a.m. the F.O.O. 79th H.A.G. confirmed the above by wire. At 8.30 a.m. O.C. 2/4th Bn. London Regt. reported no news from left Company, but that he had observed them on DOTTED BLUE LINE.
At 8.10 a.m. a report was received from 174th Infantry Brigade, on our left that their men had reached their two first objectives, and that the advance was progressing satisfactorily.
At 8.15 a.m. 164th Infantry Brigade reported SCHULER GALLERIES taken. At 9.48 a.m. they reported enemy advancing in three waves towards 174th Infantry Brigade Front, and 174th Infantry Brigade were informed.
At 9.30 a.m. AISNE FARM was reported captured.
At 10.5 a.m. the 164th Infantry Brigade reported "58th Division troops in occupation of SCHULER FARM" and a Counter-attack in progress at D.13.b.77.

P.T.O.

At 11 a.m. the A.D.M.S. 58th Division visited General Freyberg whose wounds had again been dressed during the night by a M.O. of the 2/3rd H.C. Field Ambulance, and ordered his evacuation. As our objective had been gained and consolidated General Freyberg who had maintained communication by telephone with O.C. 2/4th Bn. London Regt. throughout the battle and inspired everyone with his own cheerful courage and example, was persuaded to hand over the command to Lieut.-Colonel Dann, D.S.O. commanding 2/4th Bn. London Regt. and Major Thomson M.C. took over the Command of Lieut.-Colonel Dann's battalion.

A smoke barrage was put down by the enemy at about 9 a.m. which had become intense by 10.40 a.m., at which hour the 164th Infantry Brigade reported a counter attack in progress.

At noon another counter attack from direction of NILE FARM was reported.

This had been observed from CHEDDAR VILLA as also on the 174th Brigade Front and the artillery had been informed.

At 12.13 p.m. the 164th Brigade reported an S.O.S. on their front and at 12.53 p.m. the 174th Infantry Brigade reported that a counter attack had been beaten off.

The report that SCHULER FARM had been taken was not contradicted till 3.32 p.m. though doubt had been raised on the point at 1.30 p.m. As it was desirable to clear up the situation at SCHULER FARM and, if it was in our hands, to get into touch with 174th Infantry Brigade at WURST FARM, a battle patrol was ordered at 2 p.m. to carry out the necessary reconnaissance.
This patrol subsequently reported that the operations against SCHULER FARM by a platoon of the 2/4th Bn. London Regt. were not successful owing to:-

(1). The Tank which was to co-operate had been unable to get over the swampy ground and had stuck fast in what had been the road.
(2). A strong point with a Machine Gun was encountered in advance of SCHULER FARM at about D.7.c.75.15. and the platoon commander and all except one sergeant and 6 men were killed by the fire of this gun. The capture of this post and its Machine Gun occupied the survivors for a considerable time and the barrage had passed over the Farm and gone on before this was effected by the small force referred to. The sergeant did not consider the number at his disposal sufficient to attempt the capture of the farm without a barrage and therefore got into touch with 164th Brigade at D.7.c.4.2. and sent in his prisoners of 91st R.I.R. establishing a post with the Bosche Machine Gun at about D.7.c.3.5.

As no touch with 174th Brigade forward of D.7.a.08.90 had been reported, and as owing to casualties not more than 90 to 100 men of the 2/4th Bn. London Regt. remained effective, a platoon of 2/2nd Bn. London Regt. which had been used for the escort of Prisoners, was pushed forward and formed a chain of posts between WINNIPEG Cross Roads and D.7.central and in view of the situation at SCHULER FARM a company of 2/3rd Bn. London Regt. was ordered up to relieve the remainder of the Company of the 2/3rd Battalion which had been holding posts at JANET FARM, SPOT FARM and SPRINGFIELD and which had been reduced by heavy casualties.

One platoon of this Company was detailed for an attack on SCHULER FARM in conjunction with 164th Brigade to take place before dawn on 21st inst.

This order was subsequently cancelled in order to allow a reconnaissance by the officer in charge, and the attack postponed until the night of the 21st.

P.T.O.

Later reports were received from the left flank company whose commanding officer had been wounded and showed that the advance of this company and the right flank of the 174th Brigade had been held up by Machine Gun fire from a strong post at C.12.b.9.9., which caused heavy casualties.   2/Lieut. Walker and 6 men worked around this post and succeeded in capturing the two Machine Guns and 20 men by assault.   The prisoners were sent in under escort of 1 man and the remainder pushed on to their objective getting in touch with 174th Brigade at D.7.a.30.35.

The Machine Guns were left in position and presumably taken over by the 174th Infantry Brigade in consolidation.
Two Machine Guns were also captured at D.7.a.05.45. the gunners being killed by bombs.   The guns were not brought out by this Brigade, the men who captured them becoming casualties later.

At about 3 o'clock the enemy were observed from CHEDDAR VILLA to be advancing in fours along the ADLER FARM - WELLINGTON ROAD at least a battalion strong.   The artillery was immediately informed and opened heavy fire on them.   The enemy deployed and advanced towards the Brigade on our right in lines of platoons in column.   Our fire was very effective, but they came on in excellent order until they extended.   From the moment of extension, the morale which had till then been worthy of the highest praise went to pieces and they disappeared into shell holes with the utmost speed.   Only a few came on and these melted away under the heavy fire.   Subsequently large parties were seen to surrender, one party of about 40 coming in under the white flag.

A quiet night was passed, and there was little enemy activity during the succeeding day.

Our men were observed mopping up and consolidating.

During the night the Officer i/c Platoon detailed to attack SCHULER FARM made a reconnaissance and arrangements were made with 164th Brigade to co-operate in the attack.   This officer again went over the ground with the platoon sergeant in daylight and on reaching D.7.c.4.4. saw the garrison of SCHULER FARM surrender to men of the 164th Infantry Brigade.   Assuming that the situation was then clear he advanced up the road towards SCHULER FARM.   When at D.7.c.5.3. he was wounded by fire from a post at about D.7.c.70.15., where there is a MEBUS.   His report was communicated to 164th Infantry Brigade, who up till 4 p.m. had had no information as to the capture of SCHULER FARM, other than our statement.

At 4 p.m. B.G.C. 164th Brigade confirmed the capture of the farm and the objective of the attack of the Platoon of the 2/3rd Battalion was accordingly changed to the MEBUS from which Lt. Middlemiss had been sniped.

On reaching their objective on night of 21st it was found to be unoccupied by the enemy and a post was established there in touch with 164th Infantry Brigade at SCHULER FARM.

At about 6 p.m. 21st the enemy put down a heavy barrage along the valley of the STEENBEEK and on ST JULIEN.   Shortly afterwards S.O.S. went up on the front of the 164th and 174th Brigades and at 7.55 p.m. a heavy attack on the 164th Infantry Brigade was in progress.   At about 7.30 p.m. the S.O.S. was taken off our front and fire reduced to half rate on that of 174th Brigade.   At 8.5 p.m another S.O.S. was put up on 174th Brigade front and a heavy barrage again put down.

Command of the sector was handed over to B.G.C. 175th Infantry Brigade at 9 p.m. 21st with this Brigade forward of its objective and the line intact at all points.

P.T.O.

During the operations the 206th Machine Gun Company fired over 34,000 rounds from barrage guns in CANOPUS TRENCH in one hour and carried out the duties allotted to them with the utmost energy and success. Owing to the rapid consolidation of positions their casualties were exceptionally light and there were no casualties to guns which were in action throughout the operations. S.O.S. lines of the 214th Machine Gun Company were engaged in addition to their own at the shortest notice owing to an inaccurate report of an officer that no guns of the 214th Machine Gun Coy. on JEW HILL survived a heavy bombardment.

The Signal arrangements worked with perfect smoothness and the Brigade was never out of touch with the Battalion or the Brigade on the left or right. Visual signals by lamp worked well and a signaller of the 2/4th Bn. London Regt. finding he could not use his lamp to advantage in the valley established a visual station on the ridge near CLUSTER HOUSES on his own initiative and unaccompanied.

This station proved very valuable to the artillery officers who got into communication with it from CHEDDAR VILLA.

H.Q. 173rd Inf. Bde.
September 24th 1917.

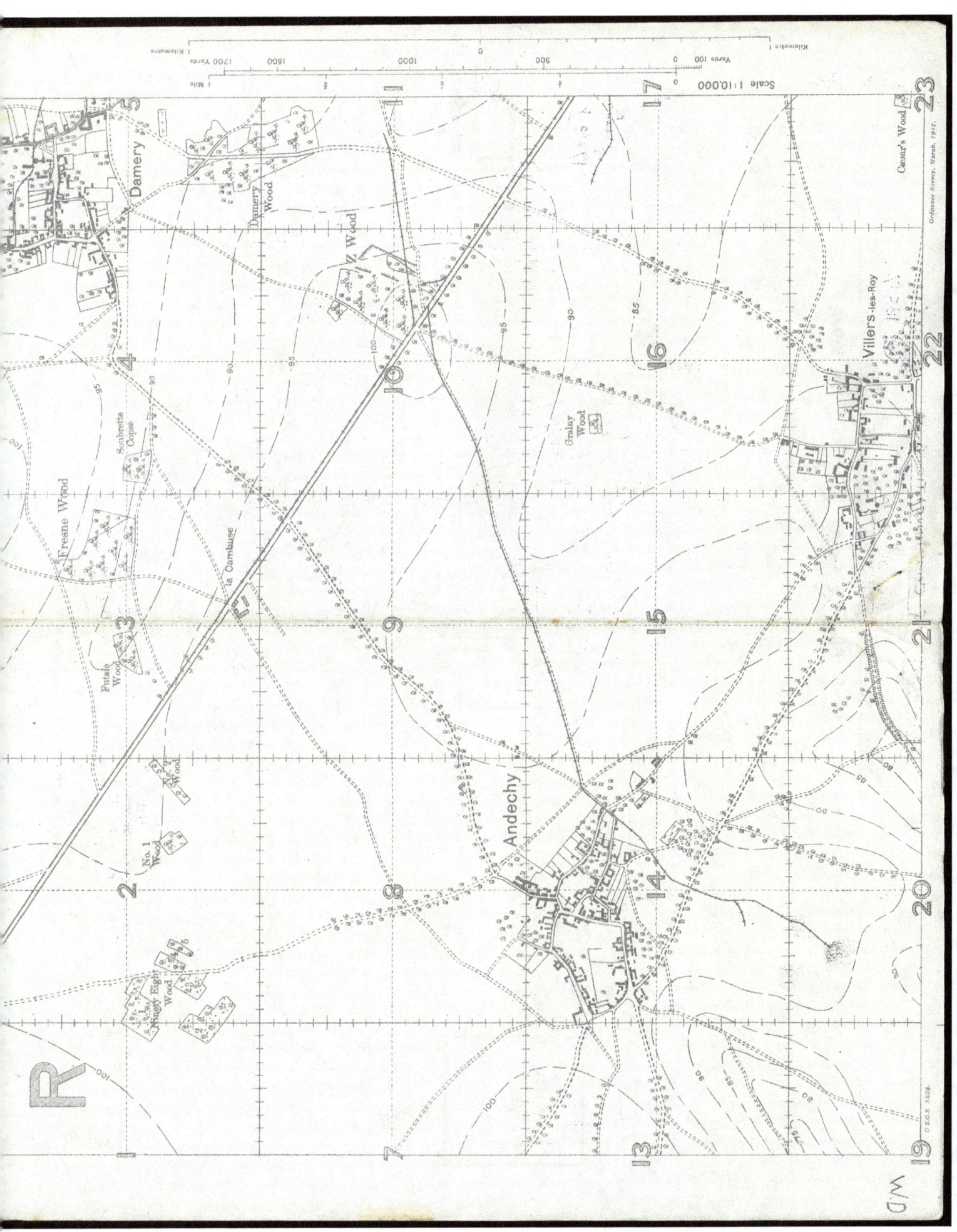

Diagram of Communications

173rd Brigade Area.

18.9.17.

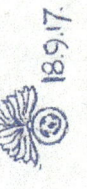

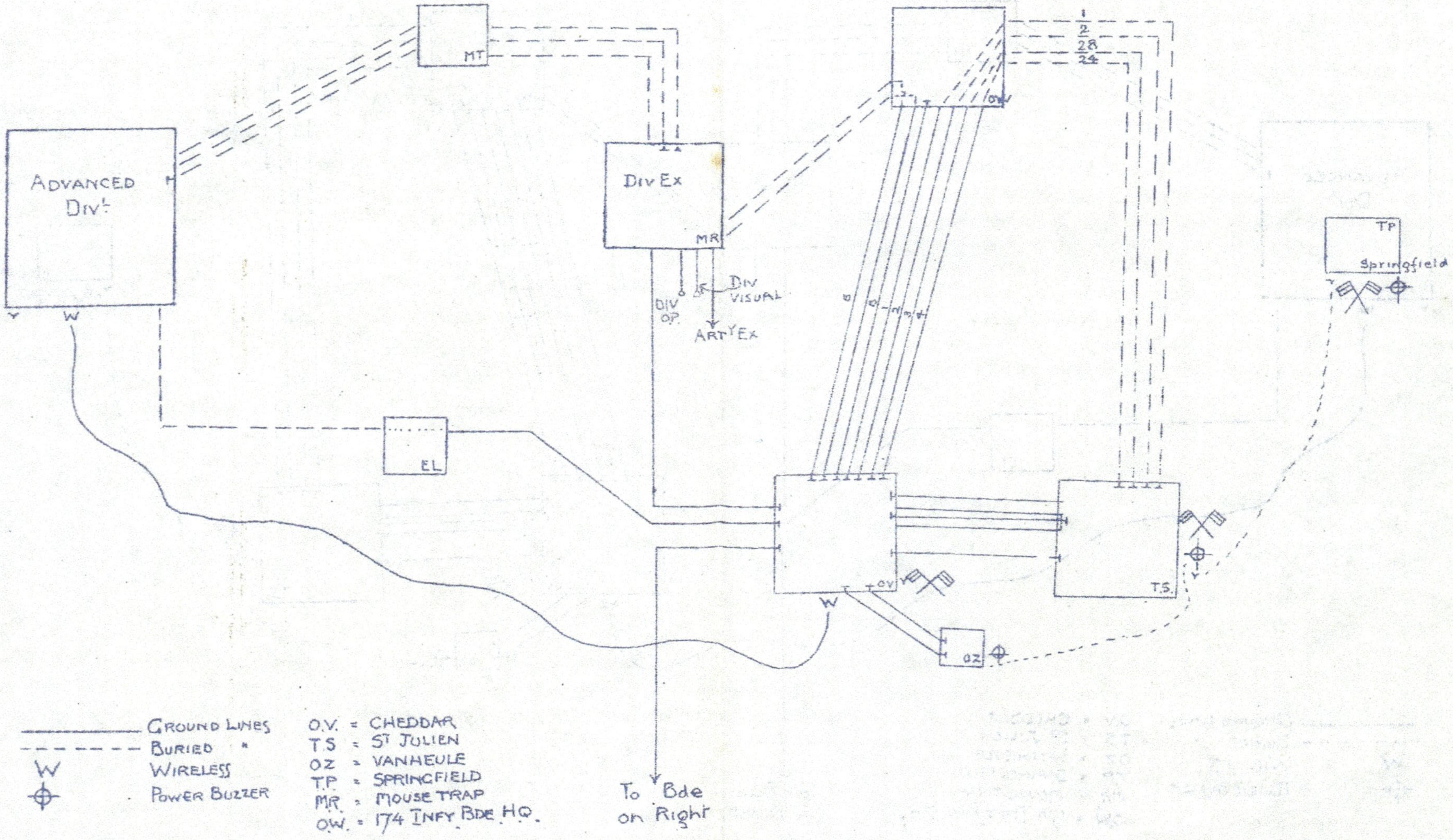

SECRET　　　　　　　　　　　　　　　　　　　　　　　　Copy No. 23

App I

173RD INFANTRY BRIGADE
OPERATION INSTRUCTIONS - NO. 3.
COMMUNICATIONS

ADVANCED BDE. HD. QTRS.	At CHEDDAR VILLA.	18th Sept. 1917.

BURIED CABLE HEAD. At Battalion Headquarters in ST. JULIEN.

TELEGRAPH & TELEPHONES Telegraph by direct Sounder to Division, and by Fullerphone to Battalions and Brigades on Right and Left. Telephone communication as on diagram attached.

RUNNER Relay Posts between CHEDDAR VILLA and ST. JULIEN are at VANHEULE FARM and CORNER COTTAGE.

WIRELESS Installed at CHEDDAR VILLA working back to Corps Directing Station at CANAL BANK.

PIGEONS Five pairs will be sent to Battalion Headquarters in ST. JULIEN daily. When sent forward to Companies they should be given into the charge of a definitely named officer.

VISUAL A lamp Station is established at Battalion Headquarters in ST. JULIEN working back to Brigade Headquarters, also at SPRINGFIELD working back to Battalion Headquarters.
　　2/4th Battalion will take over all lamps at present in use by 2/3rd Battalion, and will also establish a visual station in the O.P. in ST. JULIEN to communicate with Stations at SPOT FARM and WINNIPEG after the latter two Stations are established.
　　Definite parties will be detailed by 2/4th Battalion to accompany the attacking Companies to SPOT FARM and WINNIPEG and establish lamp communication with the O.P. in ST. JULIEN.
　　Before ZERO signalling will be by "D.D." method, but after the attack commences all stations may signal forward and every help should be given by the rear stations to assist the forward stations to align their lamps.

MESSENGER DOGS Will be kept at CHEDDAR VILLA and will be sent to Battalion Headquarters daily or as required. They should not be sent forward of Battalion Headquarters.

POWER BUZZER Two-way working stations will be established before ZERO as follows :-
　　　　　　　　　　　VANHEULE FARM
　　　　　　　　　　　working to and from
　　LION DU HIBOU　　　　　　　ST. JULIEN
　　　　　　　　　　　working to and from
　　　　　　　　　　　SPRINGFIELD

2/4th Battalion will supply two Power Buzzer Operators each to ST. JULIEN and VANHEULE FARM Stations.

MESSAGE ROCKETS 20 rockets will accompany the party taking WINNIPEG. Signallers at ST. JULIEN O.P. will keep a constant watch for them after ZERO.

CONTACT PATROL Aeroplane Signalling Stations will be established at CHEDDAR VILLA and Battalion Headquarters in ST. JULIEN. When a Contact Aeroplane calls for flares either by KLAXON Horn or by firing, a light red flare will be lit by the foremost infantry.

　　　　　　　　　　　　　　　　　　　　　　　Captain,
　　　　　　　　　　　　　　　　　　　Brigade Major,
　　　　　　　　　　　　　　　　　173rd Infantry Brigade

SECRET   173RD INFANTRY BRIGADE   App I

OPERATION INSTRUCTION – NO. 2.
————————oOo————————
G E N E R A L
————————oOo———————— 18th Sept. 1917.

Ref. Sheet 28 N.W. 1/10,000 & Sheet 28 1/20,000.

1. The Battle dispositions of the Brigade at ZERO will be as follows :-

    Advanced Bde. Hd.Qtrs.   - CHEDDAR VILLA C.23.a.8.9. from 6 p.m.
                                                                              19th.
    FORWARD REPORT CENTRE   - ST. JULIEN C.12.c.2.3.
    REAR BDE. HD. QTRS.   - DAMBRE FARM
    2/4th Bn. (attacking)   - H.Q. at ST. JULIEN C.12.c.2.3.
    2/3rd Bn. (reserve)   -(H.Q. & 3 Cos. CANAL BANK C.25.d.
                              (1 Coy. Line
    2/2nd Bn.   - CANAL BANK C.25.a. and b.
    2/1st Bn.(less 2 Cos.) -(REIGERSBURG CAMP – Moving to DAMBRE CMP.
                              (2 Cos. carrying for R.E.)
    206th M.G.Coy.   - Line, H.Q. ST. JULIEN
    173rd L.T.M.B.   - Line, H.Q., C.12.c.4.7.
    Bde. Labour Coy.   - DAMBRE CAMP

2. The following will be the H.Q. of Formations and units on the flanks of the Brigade :-

    <u>ON THE RIGHT.</u>   164th Inf. Bde. H.Q. at WIELTJE.

                       1/8th Liverpool Regt. Left attacking Bn. H.Q.
                          at FORT HILL C.18.d.

    <u>ON THE LEFT.</u>   174th Inf. Bde.
                        Adv. H.Q. at OLD WINDSOR C.17.c.1.8.
                        2/8th Bn. London Regt. attacking up to
                          DOTTED BLUE LINE – H.Q. MON DU HIBOU,C.6.c.2.3
                        2/5th Bn. London Regt. attacking from
                          DOTTED BLUE LINE up to BROWN LINE – H.Q.
                          at MON DU HIBOU moving to D.1.c.1.0 on
                          capture of BROWN LINE.
                        2/6th Bn. London Regt. attacking from BROWN LINE
                          to BLUE LINE – H.Q. at ALBERTA.

3. The Brigade will probably be relieved on the night $Z+1/Z+2$.

4. SYNCHRONISATION. An officer from Bde. Hd.Qtrs. will visit H.Q., 2/4th Bn. London Regt. at 9.30 p.m. Y.day for this purpose.

5. Withdrawal of Posts. All posts in advance of the Assembly Position will be evacuated at 1 hour before ZERO.
   The Post at SPRINGFIELD MEBUS being relieved at the same hour by a Signal party from 174th Inf. Bde.
   On evacuation the garrison of posts will withdraw to a position immediately in rear of 2/4th Bn. London Regt. and will move forward and reoccupy their posts immediately after ZERO.
   Henceforward the Role of these posts will be purely defensive.

6. Liaison.
  (a) 2/1st Bn. London Regt. will detail a senior officer for duty as Brigade liaison with 164th Inf. Bde. Instructions as to when and where this officer is to report will be issued later.
  (b) 2/1st Bn. London Regt. and 2/2nd Bn. London Regt. will each detail a senior officer to report at Divisional Headquarters, CANAL BANK at ZERO + 1 hour for liaison duty. Names (a) and (b) to be forwarded to Bde. Hd.Qtrs. on receipt of this instruction.

                                                     Captain,
                                                 Brigade Major,
                                          173rd Infantry Brigade.

SECRET. COPY NO........

173RD INFANTRY BRIGADE OPERATION INSTRUCTIONS NO.1.

DUMMY FIGURES.

1. Reference para. 1, Brigade Order No.40 - 100 Dummy Figures will be delivered to you to-night under arrangements to be made by the Staff Captain.

2. These should be carried from ST JULIEN to JANET FARM previous to completion of relief. They must be dumped at the latter place.

3. The platoons already detailed to carryout the Dummy Attack will then draw the requisite figures from this dump and place them in the assembly position allotted vide Tracing No.1. Great care will be taken that all figures are prone and camouflaged with a light layer of soil before daylight on "Y" day.

4. On Y/Z Night a thorough examination will be made of all figures to ensure that they are in working order. All figures will remain prone till ZERO Hour when the kneeling figures will be immediately fixed in an upright position and the standing figures worked in accordance with the instructions given by the XVIII Corps Cyclists who have been attached to the Brigade for this purpose.

5. The men of 2/3rd Bn. London Regt. who have been receiving instruction in the use of these figures will return to their platoons to-night.

                                                 Captain,
                                              Brigade Major,
                                        173rd Infantry Brigade.

To Officer Commanding,

    2/3rd Bn. London Regt.

1 Copy to following for information:- 2/4th Bn. London Regt.
                                                 Staff Captain.
                                                58th Division.
                                                166th Infantry Brigade.
                                                174th Infantry Brigade.

173RD INFANTRY BRIGADE SUMMARY OF INTELLIGENCE.

For period of 24 hours ending
7.0 a.m. 17/9/17.

---***---

OPERATIONS.
1. Enemy's attitude and General Activity. Has generally been quieter. His artillery especially has not fired on our positions as frequently as in previous period.

Movement has been observed and he obviously makes great efforts to repair and improve his positions, particularly in the earth-work salient in C.12.b. and at C.6.d.

Shelling on the STEENBECK has been less, but round MON D'HIBOU heavy fire was noted between 7.30 p.m. and 11.30 p.m.

His M.G. are active at night firing on our duck board tracks

Early in the period an E.A. flew over CALIFORNIA DRIVE and signalled with lamp.

At 12.50 a.m. an E.A. again flew over same trench at a height of only 300 feet. No results followed.

2. Our Own Activity on same lines and where it influences enemy action:- Our artillery has carried out harassing fire on enemy emplacements and tracks. Direct hits on HUBNER TR. with our H.E. were observed at 5.20 p.m.

At 4.0 a.m. artillery were notified of a reported German relief and took immediate action. Result so far is not known.

INTELLIGENCE.
1. M.G.Emplacements. A light M.G. is suspected at C.12.b.8.3. and was temporarily silenced by our rifle grenades during the night - it has since been active again.
2. Movement. 7.10 p.m. 3 men seen at STRONG POINT at C.6.d.62.40 and were engaged by our rifle fire.

7.40 p.m. 4 men appeared at C.6.d.55.40. and were similarly engaged. They disappeared and retaliated with M.G. fire.

(3). Work. Has been observed at C.6.d.6.4.
4. Dugout. Seems to be located at C.6.d.65.40.
5. Reliefs. Was suspected about 4 p.m. and artillery were active in consequence. Results not known.
6. Signals. Many red lights bursting into two sent up from enemy lines, opposite our left sector at 3.15 a.m. No result followed.
7. Aerial Activity. Combats frequent over C.12.c. 1 E.A. flew over C.12.c. at 4.55 p.m. and dropped what happened to be leaflets. Unsuccessful search was made for these.

At 4.30 p.m. one of our planes flew low over C.6.d. and fired at enemy with L.G.

At 11.30 a.m. 12 E.A. passed over B.27.a.8.4. and dropped one bomb on UPLIFT QM. Stores - wounding 6 O.R.

2 O.B. seen from O.P. at ST JULIEN to N.E. at 10.30 a.m. (16/9/17).

5 O.B. seen from same spot at 6.30 a.m. (17/9/17) H.N.E. N.E., E.S.E. S.E. respectively.

At 4.35 p.m. two of our planes were brought down and fell in enemy lines.

Leonard Selden
2/Lt. I.O.
for Brigade Major,
173rd Infantry Brigade.

173RD INFANTRY BRIGADE.
SUMMARY OF INTELLIGENCE

Period of 24 hours ending 7 am. 19/9/17.

A. OPERATIONS.
   1. Enemy's attitude and General Activity.
      About 6 a.m. on the 18th the enemy 20 to 30 strong endeavoured to rush our post at C.6.d.25.05. They were supported by a barrage of T.M. but were repulsed with rifle and Lewis Gun fire. Their losses are not known - ours were 1 killed and one wounded.
      Artillery activity on the left was below normal up to 11 pm. The TRIANGLE was rather heavily shelled at intervals, but far fewer rounds were fired on the STEEMBEEK. As a result of the bombardment on the 17th the enemy has shown himself very little during the day. At 7.30 p.m. the enemy, not more than 20 strong, again attempted to rush the post at C.6.d.25.05. but were again repulsed with loss, our artillery putting down a barrage and energetic rifle and L.G. fire meeting the attack.
      At 10.30 p.m. the 2/2nd Bn. Lon. Regt. was relieved by the 2/7th Bn. Lon. Regt. and one company of 2/3rd Bn. Lon. Regt. were relieved in the line on the right by the 2/4th Bn. Lon. Rgt. and command of the Right Forward Sector passed to O.C. 2/4th Bn. Lon. Regt.
      During the relief the right was heavily shelled from direction of PASCHENDAELE Group and neutralising fire was obtained from Corps Heavies with good effect.
      It was reported at 4.20 a.m. that the enemy had apparently discovered the evacuation of SPRINGFIELD and were pushing out a party towards it and that a barrage had accordingly been placed immediately in front of SPRINGFIELD. A daylight patrol subsequently report SPRINGFIELD unoccupied by the enemy.
   2. Our own Activity on same line and where it influences enemy action:- At 10.30 p.m. the 2/2nd Bn. Lon. Regt. was relieved by the 2/7th Bn. Lon. Regt. and one company of the 2/3rd Bn. were relieved in the line on the right by the 2/4th Bn. Lon. Regt. and command of the right forward sector passed to O.C. 2/4th Bn.
      Our artillery has been active as usual, harassing fire being maintained on his tracks and approaches.

   TEST BARRAGE, Left front sub-sector.
      At 5 p.m. a test barrage was put down in front of our posts. the enemy made very little reply save for intermittent shelling of MON DU HIBOU and the STEEMBEEK.
      On the right front of SPRINGFIELD our barrage was excellent, bursts very regular and at the right height.
      On the left the bursts were too high which probably accounted for an apparent gap in the barrage at a point E of N. corner of TRIANGLE.
      On the left the bursts were about 60 yards infront of our posts and over 100 yards in front of our posts on the right.

B. INTELLIGENCE.
   1. Movement. At 7.30 p.m. 14 figures were seen crouching and moving slowly in the PROMENADE (C.12.b.85.95 to C.6.d.80.15.) 10 rounds from a fieldbattery were fired on them with effect. Later a party of 8 were seen walking along PROMENADE and were found to be a burial party with a white flag.
   2. Wire. 6.45 p.m. Four men observed at C.6.d.76.40, mending and examining wire. Dispersed.
      The following is a special observers report from MON DU HIBOU:-

   (1). what wire there has been in front of salient in HUBNER TR. (PROMENADE) appears to have been so shelled as to form no obstacle.
   (2). A belt of wire in front of HUBNER TR. extends from C.6.d.80.30 for about 50 yards and is then lost to view over the ridge. This wire is still standing but has gaps in it.

175RD INFANTRY BRIGADE

PATROL REPORTS

Unit	Strength of Patrol	Time and Date	Objective or Task	Remarks and Information.
2/3rd Lon.Regt.	1 L/c 2 O.Rs.	11 p.m., 17/18th	Reconnaissance	Patrols left our lines at C.12.d.2.7 and examined ground about C.12.d.4.8. Ground is especially bad with water. No enemy seen. Patrol returned at 2 a.m. at C.12.d.2.7.
2/3rd Lon.Regt.	1 N.C.O. 5 O.Rs.	10.20 pm 17/18th	To get in touch with Right post. 2/2nd Bn. Lon.Regt. on left.	Patrol had great difficulty in finding, and so a temporary post was established at C.12.b.3.7. At 2 a.m. 18th inst. touch was established by 2 Officers of 2/2nd Bn. coming in.
2/3rd Lon.Regt.	1 N.C.O. 4 O.R.	11.30 p.m. 17/18th	Reconnaissance	Patrol explored ground 30 yards from Starting Point to JANET FARM. Nothing seen. Patrol left and returned to SPOT FARM.
2/2nd Lon.Regt.	1 Offr. 1 O.R.	9 p.m. 17/18th	Reconnaissance	Patrol left C.12.b.12.98 and reached C.12.b.50.80. No wire was seen and nothing of enemy. Returned 11 pm
2/2nd Lon.Regt.	2 Offrs. 2 O.Rs.	12.30 p.m 17/18th	Reconnaissance	Patrol got into touch with 2/3rd Bn. A sniper fired at C.12.b.63.80. Patrol returned to C.12.b.16.98 at 1.45 a.m., 18th.
2/2nd Lon.Regt.	1 Offr. 10 O.Rs.	11.45 p.m. 17/18th	Reconnaissance	Patrol advanced E. to a point near C.6.d.64.42. No wire or enemy was seen. Returned 12.40 a.m. 17/18th

175RD INFANTRY BRIGADE

Summary of Intelligence - period 24 hours ended 7.30 a.m.,
18/9/17.
--------oOo----------

A. OPERATIONS

1. **Enemy's attitude and General Activity.** No unusual activity during period. Enemy M.Gs. fired intermittently on roads and tracks, but generally speaking M.G.fire has been less. THE TRIANGLE, STEENBECK, BORDER HOUSE, CHEDDAR VILLA were shelled but enemy appeared to concentrate more on counter-battery work. At 2.30 a.m. two rounds were fired into SPOT FARM. Enemy M.G. fire also opened to N. of SPOT FARM. Two red flares were put up but no apparent result. Increased activity was noticed between 4.30 and 4.40 a.m., when 10.5 cm guns fired at the rate of 5 per minute into THE TRIANGLE. Direction apparently from POELCAPELLE Group.
   At 6 a.m. about 30 enemy attacked our posts on the Left Sector covered with T.M.fire. We drove back the enemy with rifle and Lewis Gun fire.

2. **Our own activity on same lines, and where it influences enemy action.** Our artillery has been very busy cutting wire. The enemy posts were also sprayed with shrapnel.
   Our heavies during the day bombarded strong points S. of end of PROMENADE.
   Our 9.2 fired 200 rounds into C.6.d.80.10 and C.12.b.85.95. The second round caused 20 or 30 Germans to run out of the mounds to trenches in rear. Our M.Gs. opened fire from HIBOU causing several casualties. Our field guns also fired on the enemy. At 5.45 a.m. an S.O.S. signal was sent up on our left - no results followed. The opinion is expressed it was a Hun ruse. During the afternoon the 11th R.M.A. bombarded MEBUS at D.1.c.05.00 with 15 inch hows. The 10th round landed directly on the structure, which was seen to rise bodily and was practically destroyed. Our 6" hows. shelled MEBUS at C.6.d.90.45. 50 A.P. were discharged and 3 direct hits observed..

B. INTELLIGENCE.

1. **Machine Gun Emplacements located and suspected.** M.G.activity has been less. Patrol reports M.G. at C.12.b.6.8. M.G. at SPOT FARM is a light one.

2. **Movement.** 2 men in British uniform (Battalion indistinguishable) were seen crawling from shell-hole to shell-hole towards us. They disappeared at C.12.d.7.9 and a search party failed to find them.
   At 12.45 a.m. a stretcher bearer of the 10th Battn. 175 R.I.R. was captured by our post at C.6.c.
   At 4.30 a.m. 20 or 30 men with an officer armed and equipped were seen at C.6.d. They were fired on by our post and disappeared.

3. **Smoke.** At 10.30 a.m. a fire broke out in HUBNER TRENCH and lasted 15 minutes. At 1.30 p.m. a very large fire seen in direction of POELCAPELLE.

4. **Signals.** Golden rain during night produced no apparent results. On the Right two green lights produced increased shelling.

5. **Aerial Activity.** Our planes very active at 4.45 p.m. One crossed enemy lines at height of 200 feet firing his Machine Gun. At 2.20 p.m. 2 E.A. patrolled from HIBOU to HUGEL HOLLOW and were beaten off by our A.A. guns. Enemy aerial activity less marked.

6. **General.** Sniping has been less. Sniper seems to fire from MEBUS at C.12.b.85.97. and also from C.12.d.9.3.

C. J. Graham.
2/Lieut.
I.O., For Brigade Major,
175rd Infantry Brigade.

175RD INFANTRY BRIGADE

PATROL REPORT

Unit	Strength of Patrol	Time & date	Objective or Task (Fighting or reconnaissance etc.)	Remarks and Information (Route, information gained, action of enemy, etc.)
2/5rd Lon.Rgt.	1 Cpl. & 6 O.R.	11 p.m. 16/9/17	Reconnaissance	Patrol was posted at C.12.d.4.6. Ground in front is shell-holes waterlogged. An advance over the locality would present great difficulties. Patrol returned at dawn 17/9/17.
2/3rd Lon.Rgt.	1 N.C.O. & 4 men	12.50 a.m. 17/9/17	Reconnaissance.	Patrol left SPRINGFIELD and proceeded in a N.E. direction to SPRINGFIELD - WINNIPEG Road. They went along road for 100 yards in a S.E. direction and then saw a party of 15 of the enemy attempting to outflank them. Our patrol withdrew to a Vickers Gun post who took action and enemy withdrew. No enemy posts found on S.W. side of road. Patrol returned to SPRINGFIELD at 1.45 a.m. 17th Sept.

SECRET

App. G

173RD INFANTRY BRIGADE

ADDENDUM TO BRIGADE ORDER NO. 40.

———oOo———

18th Sept. 1917.

1. **Contact Patrols**

    (a) A Contact Aeroplane will fly over the Brigade Front at

    Z + 1 hour
    Z + 2 hours & 30 mins.
    Z + 4 hours

    and when ordered by Corps Headquarters.
    Infantry will be ready to light RED flares at these hours, but will not do so unless called for by KLAXON Horn or by the Aeroplane dropping white lights.

    (b) A protective aeroplane will also fly continuously over the front during daylight on Z day from ZERO onwards.
    Its mission will be to detect the approach of enemy counter-attacks.
    Whenever this aeroplane observes hostile parties of 100 men or over moving to counter-attack it will drop WHITE PARACHUTE Lights over that portion of the front to be threatened.
    In this connection attention is drawn to "SMOKE SIGNAL from Counter-attack Aeroplanes" attached. The action of this plane will be carefully explained to all ranks.

2. **Completion of Assembly.**
    This will be wired to Adv. Bde. Hd.Qtrs. by code word "DAN".

3. **Reserve Battalion.**
    3/3rd Bn. London Regt. will be prepared to move forward at half an hour's notice.

4. **Situation Reports.** will be sent to Adv. Bde.Hd.Qtrs. by 2/4th Bn. and 206th L.G.Coy. at Z + 45 minutes and every 2 hours afterwards until further orders.

5. **Artillery.**
    Smoke Barrages will be placed in front of the DOTTED BLUE and BROWN LINES vide instructions already issued.

Reference para. 8 Brigade Order No. 40, line 5, for "TANK" substitute "2 TANKS" - line 6 for "TANK" substitute "TANKS".

Captain,
Brigade Major,
173rd Infantry Brigade.

(3). A very small and thin belt of wire at about C.6.d.50.30. cannot be considered an obstacle.

(4). Groups of badly damaged knife rests extend from C.6.d.75.68 to C.6.d.65.90. Very many gaps in it as a result of the bombardment Sept. 17th.

3. Lebus at D.1.c.0.7. the result of direct hit by 15 in. How. on the 17th inst. as seen from MON DU HIBOU was that the entire structure was shifted bodily and is now leaning on one side showing a huge gap in the centre with heaps of rubble at the side, the enemy who ran from their posts during this bombardment appeared to jump into a trench in rear of the earth works.

4. Spies. The enemy are reported by observers of the 2/3rd Bn. Lon. Regt. and F.O.O. with them to have adopted the ruse of dressing some of their men in BRITISH UNIFORMS, complete in every detail, and these men have been seen endeavouring to penetrate our posts line.

There is no doubt as to the accuracy of the report. One man released a pigeon which flew back over the enemy's lines. These men have been engaged by our snipers whenever they have been seen and attempts have been made to capture them so far without success.

5. General. Visibility has been bad.

C J Graham
2/Lieut.
I.O. for Brigade Major.
173rd Infantry Brigade.

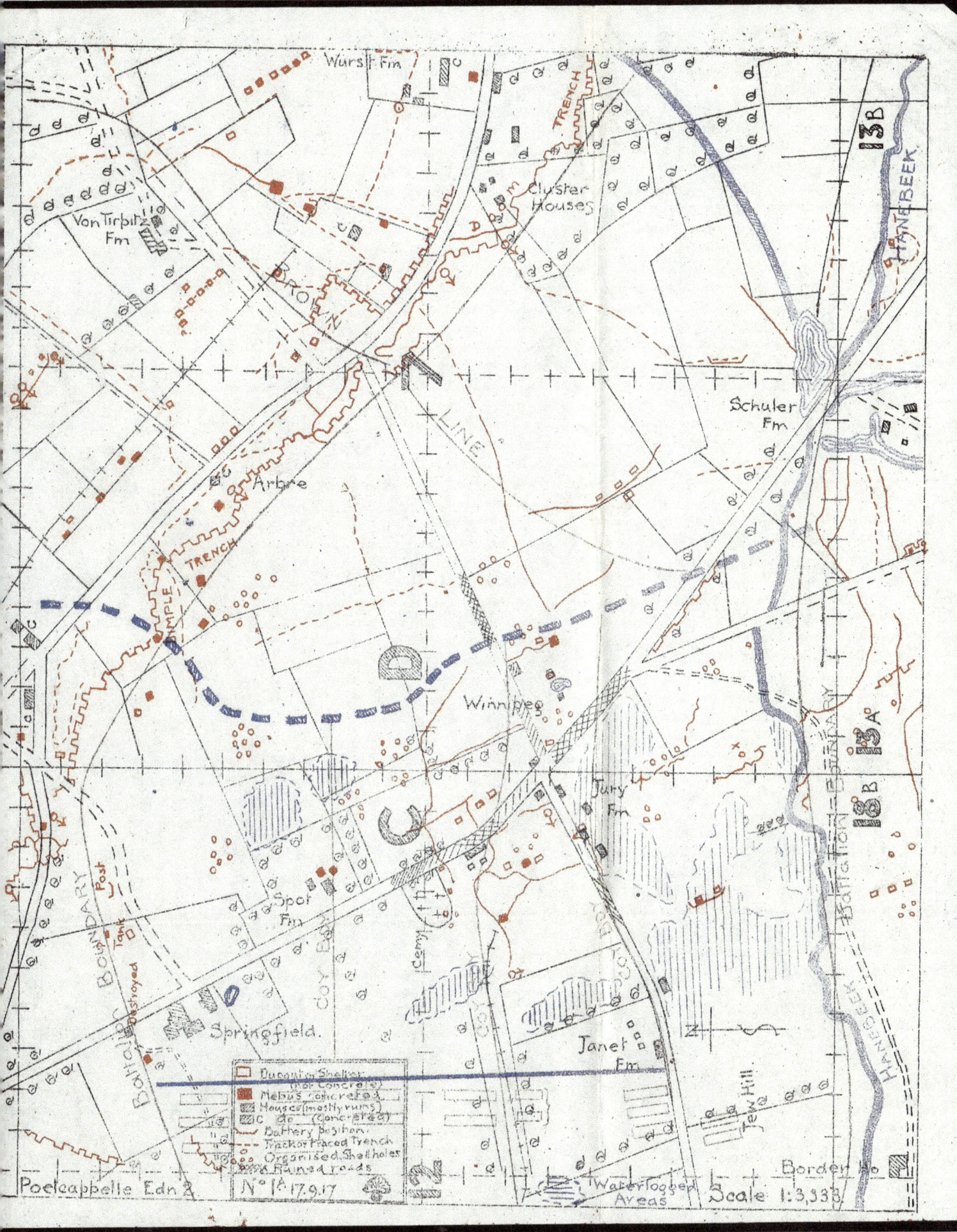

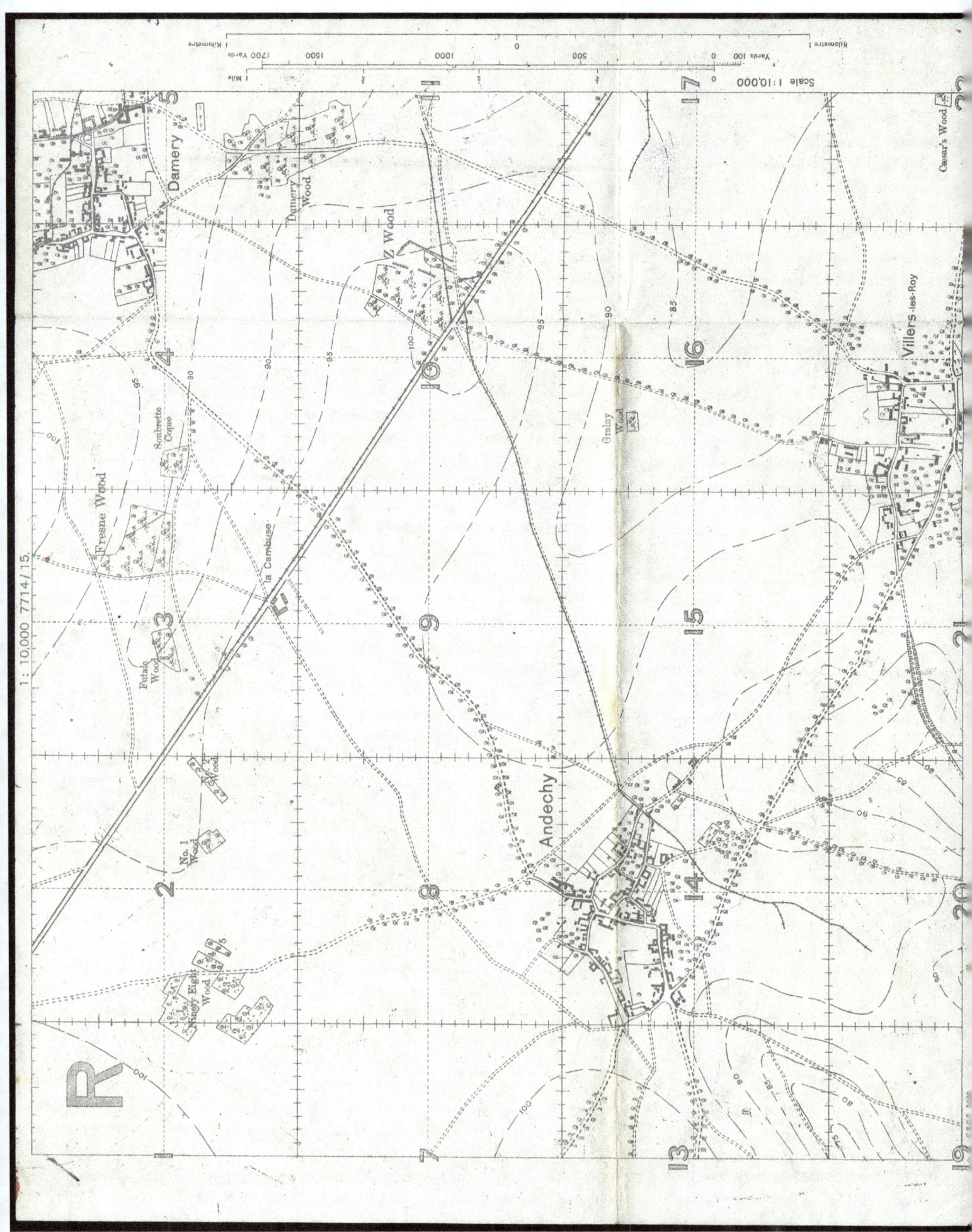

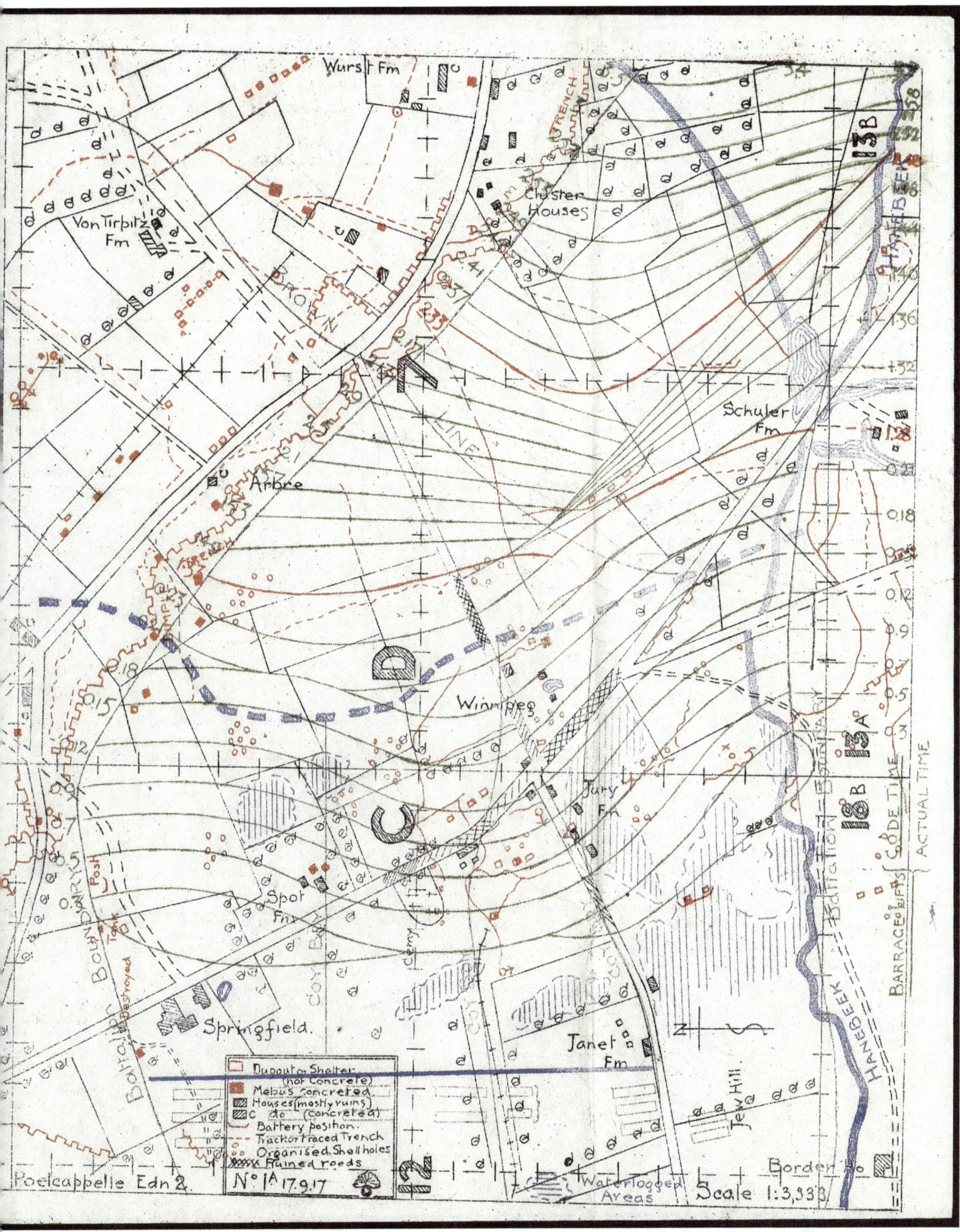

App K

SECRET.   Copy No. 19

173RD INFANTRY BRIGADE ORDER NUMBER 42.

Reference Map Sheets:-
    BELGIUM 28 N.W. - 1/20,000.
    HAZEBROUCK.   - 1/100,000.
    CALAIS.   - 1/10,000.

------oOo------   26th Sept. 1917.

1.   The 58th Division (Less Artillery) is being relieved in the Line by 48th Division (Less Artillery) on night 27/28th September, 1917.

2. (Ref. Map A.2. & A.3.).   On completion of relief the 58th Division will concentrate in the RECQUES Area.
     173rd Infantry Brigade moving in accordance with attached Move Tables "A" and "B".

3.   Captain L.S.E. Page, 2/2nd Bn. London Regt. will be in charge of Brigade Transport.

4.   During the move the Brigade Group will be composed as follows:-

    2/1st Bn. London Regt.
    2/2nd Bn. London Regt.
    2/3rd Bn. London Regt.
    2/4th Bn. London Regt.
    206th Machine Gun Coy.
    173rd L. T. M. Batty.
    504th Field Coy. R.E.

5.   On arrival in RECQUES Area 58th Division will be administered by XIX Corps.

Issued to Signals at 12.30 pm.

                                                     Captain,
                                             Brigade Major,
                                       173rd Infantry Brigade.

Copy No.
1. 2/1st Bn. London Regt.
2. 2/2nd Bn. London Regt.
3. 2/3rd Bn. London Regt.
4. 2/4th Bn. London Regt.
5. 173rd L. T. M. Batty.
6. 206th Machine Gun Coy.
7. 504th Field Coy. R.E.
8. 510th Company A.S.C.
9. 174th Infantry Brigade.
10. 175th Infantry Brigade.
11. "G" 58th Division.
12. "A" & "Q" 58th Division.
13. S. S. O.
14. Brigade Major for G.O.C.
15. Staff Captain.
16. Brigade Signalling Officer.
17. Brigade Transport Officer.
18. Brigade Intelligence.
19. War Diary.
20. War Diary.
21. File.
22. Capt. L.S.E. Page 2/2 Bn London Regt.

MOVE TABLE "A".

SERIAL NO.	DATE.	UNIT.	FROM.	TO.	REMARKS.
1.	27th. Sept.	2/3rd Bn. Lon. Regt.	REIGERSBURG.	BRAKE CAMP.	Move to be completed by 10 a.m.
2.	"	Brigade Headquarters	DAMBRE CAMP.	BRAKE CAMP.	Leave DAMBRE 4 p.m.
		2/1st Bn. Lon. Regt.	DAMBRE CAMP.	BRAKE CAMP.	Leave DAMBRE 4.10 p.m.
		2/4th Bn. Lon. Regt.	DAMBRE CAMP.	BRAKE CAMP.	Leave DAMBRE 4.25 p.m.
		Labour Company.	DAMBRE CAMP.	BRAKE CAMP.	March 200 yards in rear of 2/4th Bn. Lon. Regt.
		175rd L.T.M. Batty.	DAMBRE CAMP.	BRAKE CAMP.	Leave DAMBRE 4.40 p.m.
					INTERVALS:- 200 yards between Companies. All Units march via POTTENHOEK - X ROADS H.3.c.0.4. - CHEMIN MILITAIRE.
	27/28 Sept.	2/2nd Bn. Lon. Regt.	LINE.	REIGERSBURG.	On relief.
	"	206th Machine Gun Co.	LINE.	BRAKE CAMP.	By Bus - not to vacate positions before 8.30 p.m.

2/2nd Bn. Lon. Regt. will move to BRAKE CAMP under orders to be issued later.

MOVE TABLE "B".

SERIAL.	DATE.	UNIT.	FROM.	TO.	REMARKS.
1.	29th. Sept.	Brigade Transport (Less portion moving by train)	DAMBRE FARM.	WORMHOUDT AREA.	By March Route via VLAMERTINGHE SWITCH ROAD - WATOU - HOUTKERQUE To be clear of VLAMERTINGHE by 8.15 a.m.
2.	30th. Sept.	Brigade Group.	BRAKE CAMP.	NORDAUSQUES AREA.	By rail.
3.	30th. Sept.	Serial Number 1.	WORMHOUDT AREA.	NORDAUSQUES AREA.	By March Route via. ZEGGERS -CAPPEL and WATTEN. Start 6 a.m.

NOTE:-

In Serials 1 and 3, Brigade Transport:-

(1). Will be followed by Transport of 175th Infantry Brigade and Divisional Signal Company in that order.

(2). Further details as to time of trains, Billets etc. will be issued by Staff Captain.

S E C R E T.
O.42/2.

AMENDMENTS TO 173RD INFANTRY BRIGADE ORDER NUMBER 42.

Reference Para. 4 of Order No. 42.

    Add following to Brigade Group:-

        2/1st Home Counties Fld Ambulance.
        2/2nd Home Counties Fld. Ambulance.
        510th Company, A. S. C.

Reference Move Table "A" -

    Times in Serial 2, Remarks Column will read as follows:-

        For 4 p.m. read 9.5 a.m.
        For 4.10 p.m. read 9.20 a.m.
        For 4.25 p.m. read 9.35 a.m.
        For 4.40 p.m. read 9.50 a.m.

                                      H. J. Kirk
                                      for Captain,
                                      Brigade Major,
                                  173rd Infantry Brigade.

26/9/17.

To all recipients of OO 42.

S E C R E T

173RD INFANTRY BRIGADE

Administrative Instruction No.14

Issued with reference to 173rd Inf.Bde. Order No. 42

----------oOo----------

26th Sept. 1917.

The Brigade Group, less marching portion, will proceed by train on 30th September in accordance with attached Table "A".

The marching portion will consist of Supply Wagons and transport not detailed in Table "A". They will proceed by march route from present wagon lines on 29th September, under the command of Captain L.S.E.Page, 2/2nd London Regt.

Staging Area for transport - WORMHOUDT.

----------oOo----------

ENTRAINING AND DETRAINING OFFICERS.

The following officers are detailed as Brigade representatives :-

ENTRAINING
   Major G.H.Edwards, 2/3rd London Regt. at BRIELEN
                                        (personnel)
   Lieut. C.M.Roberts, Bde.Transport Offr., at PESELHOEK
                                        (transport).

These officers will report to R.T.O. at stations named
   (a) Personnel Trains- 2 hours before departure of train.
   (b) Transport Trains- 3½ " " " "
and will travel on the last trains.

DETRAINING.
   Major J.A.Miller, 2/2nd Lon.Regt. at AUDRIQUES.
   This officer will travel by the first train proceeding either from BRIELEN or PESELHOEK, and report to the R.T.O. at AUDRIQUES

Each unit entraining will send a representative forward to report to the Brigade representative for instructions, a quarter of an hour before his unit's arrival.. This officer will have in his possession entraining states (in triplicate) which will be handed to Brigade representative, who will pass one copy to R.T.O., forward one to H.Q., 58th Division, on completion of move, and retain the third copy.

Each unit will detail an officer to act as detraining officer, who will travel in the first train in each case.

LOADING PARTIES

As per Table "A".

HOUR OF ARRIVAL AT ENTRAINING STATIONS.

Loading parties, horses, and transport will arrive at Entraining Station 3 hours before the departure of each train. Remainder of troops 1½ hours before departure of each train.
   No horses or vehicles are to travel on Coaching Stock trains.
   Breast ropes will be required for Omnibus trains.
   O.C. train will detail picquets at all stops for each end of the train to prevent troops leaving. Units will arrange for L.G.Limbers to remain near detraining station to await arrival of Lewis Guns, which are being carried on the Coaching Stock trains.
   Water carts will be entrained full.

2.

QUARTERS.	The Brigade will be distributed in the new area as follows:-

        Brigade Headquarters .... NORDAUSQUES
        2/1st London Regt. .... LAPAUNE
        2/2nd London Regt. .... LOUCHES
        2/3rd London Regt. .... NORDAUSQUES
        2/4th London Regt. .... ZOUAFQUES
        173rd L.T.M.Battery .... AUTINQUES
        206th Machine Gun Coy. .... AUTINQUES
        Brigade Labour Coy. .... LAPAUNE
        504 Field Coy. R.E. .... LOUCHES

ADVANCE PARTIES   Advance billeting parties consisting of 2/Lt. C.J.Graham, 2/4th London Regt. as Brigade representative, and one officer and a small party from each battalion, will proceed by lorries on 27th inst. at 7 a.m. from DAMBRE CAMP, reporting to Area Commandant, RECQUES, on arrival.
   L.T.M.B. and 206th M.G.Co. advance parties will travel on Bde. Hd.Qtrs. lorries.
   Sufficient rations should be taken.

LORRIES   Two lorries per battalion and two for Bde. H.Q., L.T.M.B., and 206th M.G.Coy. will report at transport lines at 7 a.m. on 27th inst., and when loaded will proceed direct to the new area.
   Baggage wagons will report to units' wagon lines on the evening of the 28th inst.
   510 H.T.Coy. A.S.C. will travel with marching portion of Brigade.

RATIONS.   Two days' rations will be issued to all units on 28th inst. for consumption on 29th and 30th. Rations will be delivered to units in the new area on the night of arrival for consumption the following day.

RAILHEAD.   WATTEN. First day of drawing, 30th September.

                                                         F.H.Garraway
                                                             Captain,
                                                           Staff Captain,
                                                   173rd Infantry Brigade

Table "A"   The undermentioned Personnel, Transport and animals will proceed by Omnibus Train from PESELHOEK STATION to AUDRIQUES at the times stated.

Date	Unit	Personnel Off.	Personnel O.Rs.	Horses	G.S. Limbered	Two wheeled carts	No. of Train	Time of departure PESELHOEK
30th Sept	173rd Bde. Headquarters	4	20	9	1	-	1	6.20 p.m.
"	Signal Section	-	48	3	1	1	1	"
"	2/1st Lon.Rgt.,Transport	-	-	-	-	-		
	Lewis Gun Limbers	-	18	8	4	-		
	Cookers	-	12	6	4	-		
	Tool Limber	-	4	4	2	-	1	"
	Maltese Cart	1	2	1	-	1		
	Mess Cart	-	2	1	-	1		
	Water Cart	-	5	2	-	1		
	Riding Horses	-	8	8	-	-		
	Pack animals	-	7	7	-	-		
"	2/2nd Lon.Rgt.,Transport	-	-	A S	A B O V E	-	1	"
"	*504th Field Coy. R.E.	5	150	8	1	-	1	"
"	2/1st H.C.Field Ambulance	8	140	6	2	-	1	"
"	173rd L.T.M.Battery	5	65				1	"
	TOTAL	24	535	109	25	7		
				Handcarts and Mortars				
1st Oct.	Transport 2/3rd & 2/4th (as for 2/1st above)						2	12.30 a.m.
"	206th Machine Gun Coy.	10	170	20	7	2	2	"
"	2/2nd H.C.Field Ambulance	8	130	4	-	-	2	"
x	2.14th Machine Gun Coy.	9	150	-	1	1	2	"

NOTES :- *Find unloading party of 100 men to report to Detraining Officer on arrival at AUDRIQUES.
xFind loading party of 100 men to report to Entraining Officer 3½ hours before departure of first train.

Table "A" (Contd)

DEPARTURE OF PERSONNEL TRAINS FROM VLAMERTINGHE

Date	Train	Unit	Depart VLAMERTINGHE
30th Sept	No. 1 Personnel Train	Personnel of :- 2/1st London Regt.) 2/2nd London Regt.) and Lewis Guns) 58th Div. Signal Co. (40 men))	12 noon.
30th Sept	No. 2 Personnel Train	Personnel of :- 2/3rd London Regt.) 2/4th London Regt.) and Lewis Guns) 173rd Bde. Labour Coy.)	4.20 p.m.

WAR DIARY 173 Infantry Brigade. OCTOBER 1917. Army Form C. 2118.

INTELLIGENCE SUMMARY.

Place	Date	Hour	Summary of Events and Information	Remarks and references to Appendices
NORDAUSQUES	1-10-17		Reorganisation and Refitting of Units.	
do	2-10-17		Platoon Training.	
do	3-10-17		Platoon Training. Brigadier General R.B. MORGAN DSO took over command of the Brigade.	
do	4-10-17		} Platoon Training.	
do	5-10-17			
do	6-10-17			
do	7-10-17			
do	8-10-17		} Company Training.	
do	9-10-17			
do	10-10-17			
do	11-10-17			
do	12-10-17			
do	13-10-17			
do	14-10-17			
do	15-10-17		} Battalion Training.	
do	16-10-17			

OCTOBER 1914.   WAR DIARY 173rd Infantry Brigade.   Army Form C. 2118.

INTELLIGENCE SUMMARY.
(Erase heading not required.)

Instructions regarding War Diaries and Intelligence Summaries are contained in F. S. Regs., Part II. and the Staff Manual respectively. Title pages will be prepared in manuscript.

Place	Date	Hour	Summary of Events and Information	Remarks and references to Appendices
NORDAUSQUES	15-10-17		Brigade Services in Attack	—
do	16-10-17		Battalion Training.	—
do	19-10-17			—
do	20-10-17		Brigade Services in Attack	—
do	21-10-17		Brigade Church Parade.	—
do	22-10-17		Brigade Services in Attack. Orders received for Brigade to move into forward area next day (23-10-17)	—
CANAL BANK	23-10-17		Brigade moved into forward area. 2/1st & 2/3rd Bn London Regt Canal Bank. 2/4 v	APPENDIX A
			2/4th Bns to SIEGE CAMP with all Transport.	—
CANAL BANK	24-10-17		206th M.G. Coy. 173rd L.T.M.Coy. arrived CANAL BANK. 1 Officer & 1 NCO from each company	
			accounted for during day. Relief of 5th Inf. Brigade in line. 2/2 Bn Right Subsector Appendix B	
			2/3rd Bn left Subsector.	—
VARNA FARM	25-10-17		Command of Divisional front passed to G.O.C. 173rd Infantry Brigade at 8-30 a.m. Obtained	
			Headquarters VARNA FARM. Rear Headquarters CANAL BANK. Assembly for attack	—
VARNA FM	26-10-17 5:40am		Brigade attacked on Divisional front in conjunction with both flanks. 2/2 2/3 2/4 Bn	APPENDIX C
			London Regt attacked with 2/1st Bn London Regt in support. 2/7 Bn London Regt in	
			reserve.	

WAR DIARY of 173rd Infantry Brigade

Army Form C. 2118.

OCTOBER 1914.

INTELLIGENCE SUMMARY.
(Erase heading not required.)

Instructions regarding War Diaries and Intelligence Summaries are contained in F.S. Regs., Part II. and the Staff Manual respectively. Title pages will be prepared in manuscript.

Place	Date	Hour	Summary of Events and Information	Remarks and references to Appendices
VARNA FM	26-10-17 (cont)		Attacking Battalion relieved by 2/1st Bn London Regt on Left Subsector and 2/4th Bn London Regt on Right Subsector. 2/2nd, 2/3rd & 2/4th Bns to SIEGE CAMP. 2/6 Bn up to relieve at Kempton Park. Lt Col P.W. Beresford comm. 2/3rd Bn died of wounds received in action. Holding Divisional Front with 2/1st & 2/7th Bns London Regt. 2/6 Bn in reserve. 2/4 Bn take over whole front relieving 2/1st Bn, who return to SIEGE CAMP	Sh.
VARNA FM	27-10-17			Sh.
VARNA FM	28-10-17	10 am	Command of Divisional front handed over to O.C. D. w. Fusrs under G.O.C. 173rd Inf Brigade. Line remained same except :- includes Mebus 250 yds East of TRACAS FARM and excludes NOBLE'S FARM. Brigade HQrs moved to SIEGE CAMP.	Sh. Sh.
SIEGE CAMP	29-10-17		Reorganisation and re-fitting of units.	
SIEGE CAMP	30-10-17		2/2nd, 2/3rd, 2/4th Bns, 206 MG Coy, 173rd LTM Coy move to ROAD CAMP. ST JAN TER BIEZEN. Against 206 MG Coy in line assisting 174th Inf Brigade in MG Barrage for attack 2/1st Bn proceeded to KEMPTON PARK to working parties in conjunction with 174th Bde attack. Brigade Headquarters moved to ROAD CAMP. ST JAN TER BIEZEN.	Sh. Sh.
ROAD CAMP	31-10-17		Reorganisation & refitting of units.	Sh.

Shreiner Lt. to Capt.
Brigade Major Infantry Brigade
173rd Infantry Brigade

APPENDIX 'A'

173RD INFANTRY BRIGADE

Administrative Instruction No. 16.
-----------oOo-----------

22nd Oct., 1917.

The Brigade Group, less Marching Portion, will proceed by train on 23rd October, in accordance with Table "A" attached.

Duration of journey - approximately four hours.

ENTRAINING and DETRAINING OFFICERS

The following Officers are detailed as Brigade representatives :-

ENTRAINING.
Major G.H.Edwards, 2/3rd London Regt.
This Officer will report to the R.T.O., AUDRUICQ for instructions 2 hours before departure of 1st personnel train, and will travel on the last personnel train.

DESTRAINING of Omnibus Trains will be superintended by Transport Officers travelling on respective trains.

Each Unit entraining will send a representative forward to report to the Brigade representative for instructions, a quarter of an hour before his unit's arrival. This officer will have in his possession entraining states (in triplicate) which will be handed to Brigade representative, who will pass one copy to R.T.O., forward one to H.Q., 58th Division on completion of move, and retain the third copy.

Each unit will detail an officer to act as detraining officer to personnel trains, and this officer will report to R.T.O., detraining station.

LOADING PARTIES

As per Table "A".

HOUR OF ARRIVAL AT ENTRAINING STATION.

Loading parties, Horses, and Transport will arrive at Entraining Station 3 hours before the departure of each train. Remainder of troops 1½ hours before departure of each train.
No horses or vehicles are to travel on coaching stock trains.
Breast ropes will be required for Omnibus Trains.
O.C. of each train will detail piquets at all stops for ends of train to prevent troops leaving.
Water carts will be entrained full.

BLANKETS

Will be sent by lorry to AUDRUICQ and proceed by XXXXXXXXXXXXX Personnel Train.

ADVANCE PARTIES

A small party from each unit will proceed by lorries mentioned below, and take over Camp.

2.

LORRIES ETC. 3 lorries per Battalion, 1 for 2/1st H.C.Field Ambulance, and 1 for joint use of 206th M.G.Coy. and 173rd L.T.M.Bty., will report at Units' Headquarters at mid-night 22nd/23rd inst. When loaded they will proceed direct to the new area.
    Baggage wagons will report to Units' wagon lines on the evening of the 22nd inst.
    510 H.T.Coy. A.S.C. will proceed with marching portion of Brigade.

RATIONS Each Unit will be issued with 2 days' supply on the 22nd inst. for consumption on the 23rd and 24th Oct. Rations for consumption on 25th inst. will be delivered to units in the new area on night of arrival.

RAILHEAD PROVEN.

ROAD PORTION OF TRANSPORT The marching portion will consist of Baggage, Supply Wagon, and Transport not detailed in Table "A" under the Command of Captain L.S.E.Page, 2/2nd London Regt., and will proceed to the Staging Area, LEDERZEELE as under :-

STARTING POINT - Brigade Headquarters, NORDAUSQUES.

Transport will pass STARTING POINT as under :-
    2/2nd Bn.   at   10. 0 a.m.
    206th M.G.Coy.   at   10. 2 a.m.
    2/1st H.C.Field Amb. at   10. 4 a.m.
    2/4th London Regt.   at   10. 6 a.m.
    2/1st London Regt.   at   10. 8 a.m.
    2/3rd London Regt.   at   10.10 a.m.

O.C., 2/4th Battalion and O.C., 206th M.G.Coy., will detail Transport Officers to accompany marching portion.
    Each unit will send a small advance party forward to take over lines.
    Arrangements for the move to SCHOOL CAMP, West of POPERINGHE will be made by O.C., Column.
    An advance party will be sent to take over lines.

BATTLE PERSONNEL Battle Surplus Personnel proceeding to Divisional Depot Battalion should take sufficient dixies and cooking utensils for their own use.

                                    for Captain,
                                 Staff Captain,
                          173rd Infantry Brigade.

Table "A"   The undermentioned Personnel, Transport and Animals will proceed by Omnibus Train from AUDRUICQ STATION at the times stated.

Date	Unit	Personnel Off.	Personnel O.Rs.	Horses	G.S. Limbered	Two wheeled carts	No. of Train	Depart AUDRUICQ	Arrive at
23rd Oct.	173rd Bde. Headquarters	2	20	9	1	1	No.1 Omnibus	1.0 p.m	HOPOUTRE 4.0 p.m.
"	Signal Section	1	48	6	1	1	"	"	"
"	2/1st Lon. Regt. Transport								
	Lewis Gun Limbers		18	8	4	1			
	Cookers		12	8	4	1			
	Tool Limber		4	4	2	1			
	Maltese Cart		2	1		1			
	Mess Cart		2	1		1			
	Water Cart		3	2		1			
	Riding Horses		8	8					
	Pack Animals		7	7					
"	2/3rd Lon. Regt. Transport				AS ABOVE		"	"	"
"	206th Machine Gun Coy.	1	30	20	7	2	"	"	"
"	173rd L.T.M.Battery	6	60	} 113	29	9	"	"	"
"	TOTAL	11	270		HANDCARTS				
"	Transport 2/2nd and 2/4th Bns. (as for 2/1st Bn. above)	8	140	6	2	1	No.2 Omnibus	12 mid-n't 23rd/24th	HOPOUTRE 5 am 24th
"	2/1st H.C.Field Ambulance						"	"	"

NOTES:- O.sC. 2/1st and 2/3rd Bns. will detail 1 Off. & 50 P.Rs. to act as Loading and Unloading parties for the 1st Omnibus Train.

O.s.C.2/2nd and 2/4th Bns. will detail 1 Off. & 50 P.Rs. to act as Loading and Unloading parties for the 2nd Omnibus Train.

Table "A" (Contd.)

DEPARTURE OF PERSONNEL TRAINS FROM AUDRUICQ

Date	Train	Unit	Depart AUDRUICQ	Arrive
23rd Oct.	No. 1	Personnel of :- 2/2nd London Regt.) 2/4th London Regt.) and Lewis Guns.) Bde. Sniper Section) Bde. Pioneer Coy.)	10. 0 am	BRIELEN 1. 0 pm
23rd Oct.	No. 2	Personnel of :- 2/1st London Regt.) 2/3rd London Regt.) and Lewis Guns) 206th M.G.Coy.) R.E.Sect., attd. 2/3rd Bn.)	12 noon	REIGERSBERG 3.30 p.m.

SECRET.   Copy No..........

173RD INFANTRY BRIGADE ORDER NO. 43.

Ref. Map Sheets - POELCAPPELLE 1/10,000.   AND
                  SPRIET - 1/10,000.

                                                   24th Oct. 1917.

1. The Brigade will relieve 54th Infantry Brigade (18th Div) in the Line and take over Divisional Sector to-night 24/25th October.

2. The Sector will be temporarily held as follows :-

   On Right   -   2/2nd Bn. Lon. Regt. with H.Q.
                    at V.19.a.7.1.

   On Left.   -   2/3rd Bn. London Regt. with
                    H.Q. at V.19.a.7.1.

   In Support -   2/4th Bn. Lon. Rgt.) CANAL
                  2/1st Bn. Lon. Rgt.) BANK.

3. Officers Commanding Battalions will arrange for parties of one Officer and one N.C.O. per Company to reconnoitre the Sector and Duck Board Track. (as far as concernes them) as far forward as possible during daylight to-day.
   A map showing track to PHEASANT FM. (U.30.b.2.3.) to be a good O.P. is attached.   No party larger than 4 should reconnoitre together and consentration at O.Ps must be avoided.
   Party of the 2/2nd and 2/3rd Bns London Regt. will rejoin their units in their line.

4. Times which units should leave their present billets or Camps to proceed to the line, and rendezvous for guides, will be notified later.

5. 206th Machine Gun Coy. will relieve the M. G. Coy. of 54th Infantry Brigade in the line to-night.   O.C. 206th M.G. Coy. will arrange to send immediately at least one Officer forward to reconnoitre position and arrange details of relief.

6. Command will pass to G.O.C. 173rd Inf. Bde. on completion of the relief.

7. Completion of relief will be wired to Advanced Brigade Headquarters at VARNA FM by code word "GRIT".

Issued to Signals... 7.30am.   Captain,
                                                Brigade Major,
                                                173rd Infantry Brigade.

Copy No.   Copy No.
 1. 2/1st Lon. Regt.   12. "G" 58th Division.
 2. 2/2nd Lon. Regt.   13. "A" & "Q" 58th Division.
 3. 2/3rd Lon. Regt.   14. S. S. O.
 4. 2/4th Lon. Regt.   15. Brigade Major for G.O.C.
 5. 173rd L.T.M.Batty.   16. Staff Captain.
 6. 206th M. G. Coy.   17. 188th Inf. Brigade - on Right.
 7. 504th Field Coy. R.E.   18.   Inf. Brigade - on left.
 8. 510 H. T. Coy. A.S.C.   19. 18th Division.
 9. 174th Inf. Bde.   20. Forward Area Commandant.
10. 175th Inf. Bde.   21. Bde. Signalling Officer.
11. War Diary.   22. War Diary.
                                     23. File.

4.

Issued to Signals at ......

Copy No.

1. 2/1st London Regt.
2. 2/2nd London Regt.
3. 2/3rd London Regt.
4. 2/4th London Regt.
5. 173rd L.T.M.Battery
6. 206th M.G.Coy.
7. 504 Field Coy. R.E.
8. 510 H.T.Coy. A.S.C.
9. 174th Inf. Bde.
10. 175th Inf. Bde.
11. 58th Division "G"
12. 58th Division "A" & "Q".
13. Brigade Major for G.O.C.
14. Staff Captain
15. 188th Inf. Bde. - on right
16.   Inf. Bde. - on left.
17.
18. Bde. Signalling Officer
19. Bde. Intelligence Officer
20. Bde. Transport Officer
21. War Diary
22. War Diary
23. File.

N° 15

OPERATION REPORT

OCT 26
1917.

173 INF BDE

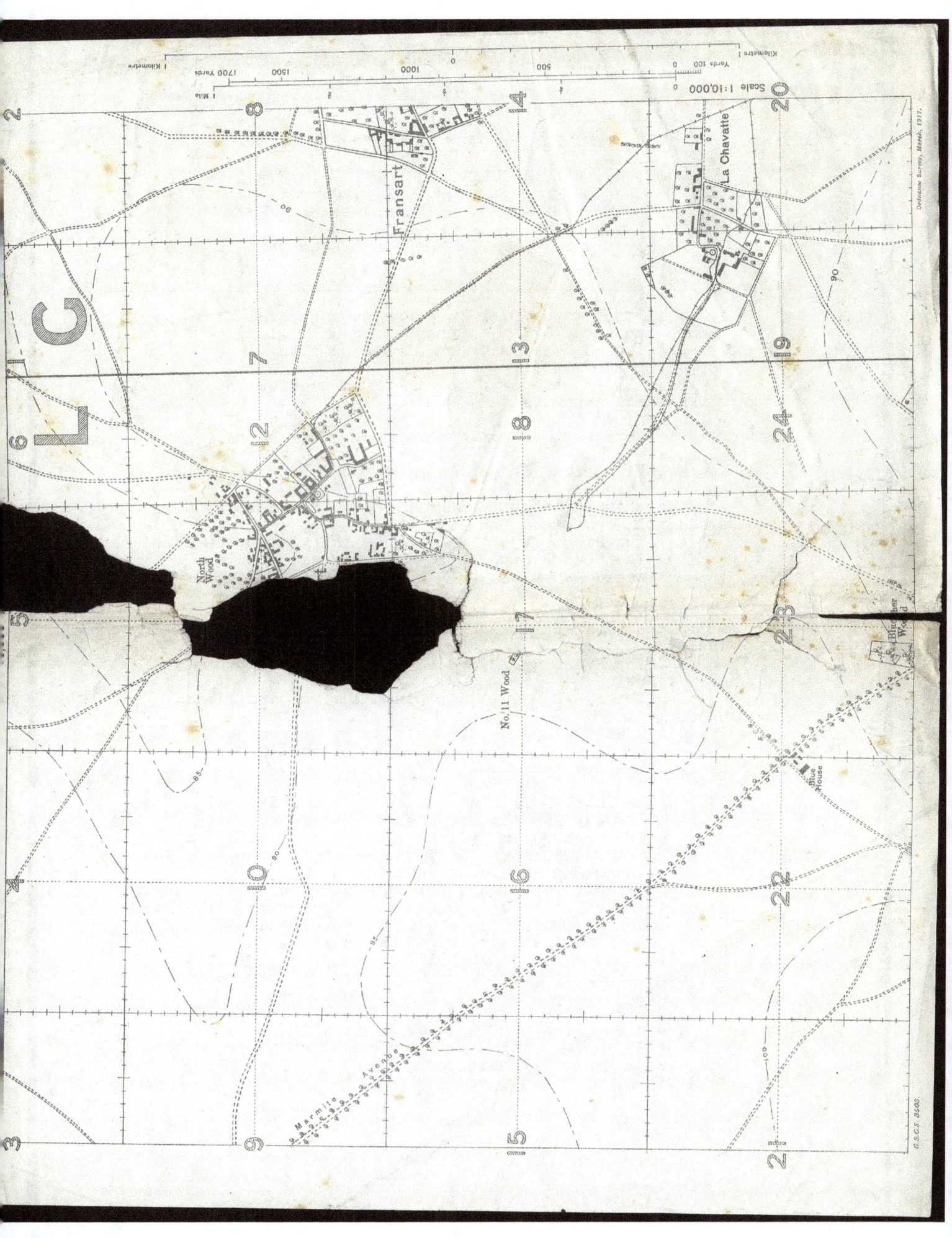

S E C R E T.   Copy No......

173RD INFANTRY BRIGADE ORDER NUMBER 44.

Ref. Map Sheet:-   SPRIET - 1/10,000 .
                   28.N.W. - 1/20,000 .

                                          24th Oct. 1917.
----

1. (a). On a date which has been communicated verbally to those concerned, 173rd Infantry Brigade will renew the attack with 63rd Division on Right and 57th Division (XIV Corps) on the left.
   (b). Instructions as to move etc. previous to ZERO will be found in Appendix "A" attached.

2. ZERO Hour will be notified later.

3. Assembly Areas, Objectives and Boundaries are shown on attached map.
   Maps shewing latest information axxxxxx on 1/5,000 scale will be issued shortly.
   (a). The First Objective will be the DOTTED RED LINE
   (b). The Second and Final Objective will be the solid RED LINE.

4. (a). The Brigade attack will be carried out by 2/2nd, 2/3rd and 2/4th Battalions, with 2/1st Bn. Lon. Regt. in Reserve.
   (b). The 2/2nd and 2/3rd Battalions will capture the 1st Objective.
       The 2/4th Bn. will capture the 2nd and Final Objective.
   (c). 2 Battalions of 174th Infantry Brigade will move up to CANE TR (C.9.) on Z day and come under orders of G.O.C. 173rd Inf. Bde.

5. (a). Definite, distinct, and complete units, will be detailed to capture all known enemy Strong Points.
   (b). The capture and retention of high ground about PAPA FM and WHITECHAPEL is of special importance.
   (c). The 2/2nd and 2/4th Battalions will form a defensive Right Flank as far South as ground will allow, since the 63rd Division are not pushing forward any troops N. of the LEKKERBOTERBEEK and it is essential that all ground N. of this stream should be covered.
   (d). Officers Commanding 2/2nd and 2/4th Bns. will arrange signal communication with 63rd Division across the valey of the LEKKERBOTERBEEK as follows:-
       2/2nd Bn. from vicinity MORAY HOUSE to BANFF HOUSE.
       2/4th Bn. From HINTON FM to V.22.c.8.0.
   (e). 2/3rd Bn. will detail a special party to meet a similar party of 57th Division at SPIDER CROSS Roads V.14.b.9.8.

5. (f). Strong Points will be constructed as follows:-

V.21.c.1.6.	by 2/2nd Lon. Regt.
HORAI HOUSE (V.21.c.90.65.)	by 2/2nd Lon. Regt.
HINTON FM.	by 2/4th Lon. Regt.
PAPA FM.	by 2/4th Lon. Regt.
CAMERON HOUSE.	by 2/2nd Lon. Regt.
WHITECHAPEL.	by 2/4th Lon. Regt.
V.15.a.8.2.	by 2/3rd Lon. Regt.
V.14.d.9.5.	by 2/3rd Lon. Regt.
V.14.b.6.2.	by 2/3rd Lon. Regt.

Each Strong Point will be constructed for all round-defence and to hold a garrison of 1 platoon.

(g). Battalion Commanders will impress on all ranks under their command the great necessity of keeping their rifles as clean as possible and at all times ready and fit for use.

6. (a). The attack will be preceeded by a 48 hours bombardment of all available artillery and will be made under cover of the following barrages:-

(i). A Creeping Barrage.
(ii). A Searching Barrage.
(iii). A back Heavy Artillery Barrage.
(iv). A Machine Gun Barrage.

Details of these and a barrage map will be issued as soon as received.

(b). The creeping barrage will come down at ZERO 150 yards infront of the leading Infantry. It will lift at ZERO plus 8 minutes and will move by lifts of 50 yards at the rate of 100 yards in 8 minutes.
On reaching its protective position about 150 yards beyond the DOTTED RED Line the barrage will pause for 45 minutes, continuing lifts about ZERO plus 113 minutes.

(c). Arrangements are being made for the barrage to dwell on CAMERON HOUSE so as to enable the Infantry to manouevre that place from the South.

(d). Smoke barrages will be put down as follows:-

(i). On Front V.15.c.30.95. - V.15.a.8.2.
    from ZERO plus 25 minutes to ZERO plus 40.min.
(ii). On PAPA FM and NEBUS immediately South of
    it from ZERO plus 32 to ZERO plus 60 minutes.

7. (a). A contact Plane will fly over the objective at:-

ZERO plus 1. hour 30 mins.
ZERO plus 5 Hours.

and when ordered by Corps H.Q.
Each Contact plane will be marked with two BLACK rectangular flags attached to and projecting from the lower plane on each side of the fuselage. Infantry will be ready to light RED flares (in clusters of not less than three) or wave WATSON FANS if no flares are aviable, at the above mentioned hour but will not do so unless called for by KLAXON Horn or by the dropping of WHITE Lights. from the plane. The importance of making their position known to the Contact Planes must be impressed on all ranks.

7. (b) **Counter-attack machine.** An aeroplane will be up continuously during the daylight from ZERO onwards whose mission will be to detect the approach of enemy counter-attacks.

Whenever this patrol observes hostile parties of 100 or over moving to counter-attack, it will drop a smoke bomb over that portion of the front to which the enemy is moving. The smoke bomb will burst about 100 feet below the machine into a white parachute flare which descends slowly leaving a long trail of brown smoke behind it.

8. O.C., 206 Machine Gun Coy. will detail guns as under :-

    2 Guns to support 2/3rd Battalion taking up
        positions V.14.b.30.25) Move to consolidate
                 V.14.d.50.90) at ZERO plus 40.

    2 Guns to support 2/4th Battalion taking up
        positions V.15.c.82.32) Move to consolidate
                 V.15.c.90.20) at ZERO plus 40.

    3 Guns to following positions :-
        1 Gun V.21.a.30.80) Move to consolidate
        2 Guns V.21.c.90.70) at ZERO plus 40.

    3 Guns to following positions :-
        V.21.b.30.20) Move to consol-
        V.21.b.35.12) idate at ZERO
        V.21.d.70.85) plus one hour.

A tracing showing arcs of fire of these ten guns will be issued later.

6 guns to deliver barrage fire from about MEUNIER HOUSE (V.20.b.0.2) on to selected targets in neighbourhood of SPRIET and subsequently to act as offensive guns by taking up the most favourable positions in the captured enemy ground from which they can watch the front and engage any suitable enemy targets that may present themselves.

9. O.C., 173rd L.T.M.Bty. will arrange if possible to place 4 guns in position about TRAGAS FM. (V.20.d.6.5.). These guns will open hurricane fire at ZERO on Mobus V.21.c.00.65, should this prove to be held by the enemy.

10. An Officer from Brigade Headquarters will visit each Battalion Headquarters about 5 p.m. on Y day for the purpose of synchronising watches.

11. Situation reports will be rendered at ZERO plus 2 hours and subsequently every two hours until further orders.

12. Advanced Brigade Headquarters will be at VARNA FM. (C.4.a.5.3). Rear H.Q. at CANAL BANK.

13. The word "RETIRE" will not be used on any account. Anyone heard using this word will be treated as an enemy and shot. This is to be explained to all ranks.

                                                Captain,
                                                Brigade Major,
                                          173rd Infantry Brigade.

SECRET.   Copy No........

173RD INFANTRY BRIGADE ORDER NUMBER 44.

Ref. Map Sheet:-   SPRIET   -   1/10,000.
                   28N.W.   -   1/20,000.

                                                24th October 1917.

1. (a). On a date which has been communicated verbally to those concerned, 173rd Infantry Brigade will renew the attack with 63rd Division on the Right and 57th Division (XIV Corps) on the Left.
   (b). Instructions as to move etc. previous to ZERO will be found in Appendix "A" attached.

2. ZERO Hour will be notified later.

3. Assembly Areas, Objectives and Boundaries are shewn on attached map.
   Maps shewing latest information on 1/5,000 scale will be issued shortly.
   (a). The First Objective will be the DOTTED RED LINE.
   (b). The Second and Final Objective will be the solid RED LINE.

4. (a). The Brigade attack will be carried out by 2/2nd, 2/3rd and 2/4th Battalions, with 2/1st Bn. Lon. Regt. in reserve.
   (b). The 2/2nd and 2/3rd Battalions will capture the 1st Objective.
        The 2/4th Bn. will capture the Second and Final Objective.
   (c). 2 Battalions of 174th Infantry Brigade will move up to CANE TRENCH (C.9.) on Z day and come under orders of G.O.C. 173rd Inf. Bde.

5. (a). Definite, distinct and complete units, will be detailed to capture all known enemy Strong Points.
   (b). The capture and retention of high ground about PAPA FM and WHITECHAPEL is of special importance.
   (c). The 2/2nd and 2/4th Battalions will form a defensive right flank as far south as ground will allow, since the 63rd Div. are not pushing forward any troops N. of the LEKKERBOTERBEEK and it is essential that all ground N. of this Stream should be covered.
   (d). Officers Commanding 2/2nd and 2/4th Bns. will arrange Signal Communication with 63rd Division across the valey of the LEKKERBOTERBEEK as follows:-
      2/2nd Bn. from vicinity MORAY HOUSE to BANFF HOUSE.
      2/4th Bn. from HINTON FM. to V.22.c.8.0.
   (e). 2/3rd Bn. will detail a special party to meet a similar party of 57th Division at SPIDER CROSS Roads V.14.b.9.8.

5. (f). Strong Points will be constructed as follows:-

V.21.c.1.6.	by 2/2nd Lon. Regt.
MORAY HOUSE (V.21.c.90.65.)	by 2/2nd Lon. Regt.
HINTON FM.	by 2/4th Lon. Regt.
PAPA FM.	by 2/4th Lon. Regt.
CAMERON HOUSE.	by 2/2nd Lon. Regt.
WHITECHAPEL.	by 2/4th Lon. Regt.
V.15.a.2.2.	by 2/3rd Lon. Regt.
V.14.d.9.5.	by 2/3rd Lon. Regt.
V.14.b.6.2.	by 2/3rd Lon. Regt.

Each Strong Point will be constructed for all round defence and to hold a garrison of 1 platoon.

(g). Battalion Commanders will impress on all ranks under their command the great necessity of keeping their rifles as clean as possible and at all times ready and fit for use.

6. (a). The attack will be proceeded by a 48 hours bombardment of all available artillery and will be made under cover of the following barrages:-

    (i). A creeping barrage.
    (ii). A searching barrage.
    (iii). A back Heavy Artillery barrage.
    (iv). A Machine Gun Barrage.

Details of these and the barrage map will be issued as soon as received.

(b). the Creeping barrage will come down at ZERO 150 yards in front of the leading Infantry. It will lift at ZERO plus 8 minutes and will move by lifts of 50 yards at the rate 100 yards in 8 minutes.
On reaching its protective position about 150 yards beyond the DOTTED RED LINE the barrage will pause for 45 minutes, continuing lifts about ZERO plus 116 minutes.

(c). Arrangements are being made for a barrage to dwell on CAMERON HO. so as to enable the Infantry to manouevre that plan from the South.

(d). Smoke barrages will be put down as follows:-

    (i). On front V.15.c.30.95. - V.15.a.2.2.
        from ZERO plus 25 minutes to ZERO plus 40 min.
    (ii). On PAPA FM. and MEBUS immediately S of it
        from ZERO plus 32 to ZERO plus 60 minutes.

7. (a). A contact plane will fly over the objective at:-

    ZERO plus 1 hr. 30 mins.
    ZERO plus 5 hours.

and when ordered by Corps H.Q.

Each contact plane will be marked with two BLACK rectangular flags attached to and projecting from the lower plane on each side of the fuselage. Infantry will be ready to light RED Flares (in clusters of not less than three) or Wave WATSON FANS if no flares are available, at the above mentioned hour, but will not do so unless called for by KLAXON Horn or by the dropping of WHITE Lights from the plane. The importance of making their position known to the Contact planes must be impressed on all Ranks.

7. (b). <u>Counter-Attack Machines</u>. An aeroplane will be up continuously during the daylight from ZERO onwards whose mission will be to detect the approach of enemy counter attacks Whenever this patrol observes hostile parties of 100 or over moving to counter attack, it will drop a smoke Bomb over that portion of the front through which the enemy is moving.
The smoke bomb will burst about 100 feet below the machine into a white parachute flare which descends slowly leaving a long trail of brown smoke behind it.

8. O.C. 206th M.G. Company will detail guns as under :-

    2 Guns to support 2/3rd Battalion taking up positions
        V.14.b.30.25.) Move to consolidate
        V.14.d.50.90.) at ZERO plus 40.

    2 Guns to support 2/4th Battalion taking up positions
        V.15.c.82.32.) Move to consolidate
        V.15.c.90.20.) at ZERO plus 40.

    3 Guns to following positions :-
        1 Gun V.21.a.30.80.) Move to consolidate
        2 Guns V.21.c.90.70.) at ZERO plus 40.

    3 Guns to following positions :-
        V.21.b.30.20.) Move to consolidate
        V.21.b.35.12.) at ZERO plus
        V.21.d.70.85.) one hour.

A tracing showing arcs of fire of these 10 guns will be issued later.
    6 Guns to deliver barrage fire from about MEUNIER HOUSE (V.20.b.0.2.) on to selected targets in neighbourhood of SPRIET and subsequently to act as offensive guns by taking up the most favourable positions in the captured enemy ground from which they can watch the front and engage any suitable enemy targets that present themselves.

9. O.C. 173rd L.T.M. Battery will arrange if possible to place four guns in position about TRAGAS FM (V.20.d.6.5.). These guns will open hurricane fire at ZERO on MEBUS V.21.c.00.65. should this prove to be held by the enemy.

10. An Officer from Brigade Headquarters will visit each Bn Headquarters about 5.pm. on Y day for the purpose of synchronising watches.

11. Situation reports will be rendered at ZERO plus 2 hours and subsequently every 2 hours until further orders.

12. Advanced Brigade Headquarters will be at VARNA FM (C.4.a.53). Rear H.Q. at CANAL BANK.

13. The word "RETIRE" will not be used on any account. Anyone heard using this word will be treated as an enemy and shot. This is to be explained to all ranks.

                              (Sgd) C.E.G. Shearman.
                                          Captn.
                                        Brigade Major.
                                   173rd Infantry Brigade.

SECRET

24th Oct., 1917

APPENDIX "A"
=================================

(Issued with 173rd Bde. Order No. 44.)

---

1. **ASSEMBLY.** Officers Commanding 2/2nd, 2/3rd and 2/4th Bns. London Regt. will arrange for the reconnaissance of their assembly positions to be carried out during the early morning of Y day.
     The actual assembly lines will be taped under battalion arrangements immediately after dusk on Y evening.
     Those for 2/3rd and 2/2nd Bns. will be as far as possible along our present front line.
     2/4th Bn. will assemble in V.20.a. and c.
     Assembly will be completed by 1 a.m. on Z day and completion will be wired to Advanced Bde. Headquarters by Code Word "GOODELF".
     Previous to assembly 2/4th Bn. will move up to positions of readiness about V.19.c.

2. Moves in connection with assembly will take place in accordance with attached Move Table.

3. The Brigadier wishes to draw Unit Commanders' attention to the following points :-

    (a) To again impress all ranks that they MUST get round strong points.

    (b) There must be as little movement as possible in the trenches to-morrow, special care being taken when aeroplanes are overhead.

    (c) Steel helmets to be rubbed over with mud.

    (d) The most valuable information in recent operations has come back by pigeons; full use must be made of this excellent means of communication, and birds must not be hoarded.

(Sd) C.E.G.SHEARMAN, Captain,
Brigade Major,
173rd Infantry Brigade.

Move Table Attached, APPENDIX "A"

Date	Unit	From	To	Route	Remarks
Oct. 25th	2/1st Bn.	CANAL BANK	ROSE TR. Area - U.24.d.	Duckboard track from 5 CHEMINS	Break journey at CANE TR (C.9.a.). Leave CANAL BANK 11 a.m. Assembly in ROSE TR to be complete by 1 a.m., 26th.
"	2/2nd Bn.	Right Front Sector	Assembly position V.20.d.3.0 - TRACAS FM - V.20.b.3.3 - V.20.b.5.8	------	Assembly to be complete by 1 a.m. 26th.
"	2/3rd Bn.	Left Front Sector	Assembly position V.20.b.5.8 V.14.d.1.8 V.14.c.7.9	------	Assembly to be complete by 1 a.m. 26th.
"	2/4th Bn.	CANAL BANK	Assembly Area V.20.a. and c.	Duckboard track from 5 CHEMINS	Break journey at CANE TR (C.9.a.). Leave CANAL BANK 11 a.m. Assembly to be complete by 1 a.m. 26th.

2.

MEDICAL

Regimental Aid Posts at :-
    V.19.a.6.1
    V.20.c.4.2

Relay Posts at :-
    U.30.b.1.6
    U.30.d.6.9
    U.29.d.8.3
    C.5.b.2.8
    C.5.c.0.5

Advanced Dressing Stations at :-
    C.3.d.3.3
    C.10.c.3.6

CASUALTIES

The following instructions with regard to reporting casualties during the operations are issued :-
 The ordinary detailed casualty return will be rendered, and in addition an estimated casualty return will be forwarded twice daily to reach Rear Brigade Headquarters at 12 noon and 7 p.m.
 (Estimated casualties, however, exceeding 10 per cent. of any unit will be reported at once).
 The following information will be given in reporting casualties :-
  (a) Total estimated loss of officers since the commencement of operations.
  (b) Total estimated loss of O.Rs. since the commencement of operations.
All wires will commence "Total estimated aaa" and the total will be accumulative.
 At the termination of the operations, or as soon as a unit is withdrawn from the line, an accurate return of the casualties sustained during the preceding period will be rendered.
 This return must give the dates covered, ranks, initials and names of officers, and total numbers of O.Rs. killed, wounded or missing.
 Accuracy is essential in this return.

DRYING ROOMS

A drying shed is established at GOURNIER FARM under the charge of Forward Area Commandant.
 A Drying Hut and Incinerator combined is about to be erected East of the CANAL BANK at C.25.a.9.7.
 A drying installation has been fixed up in the Divisional Surplus Kit Dump at 7, Rue Tete d'Or, POPERINGHE.

CEMETERIES

Cemeteries, East of CANAL BANK, are looked after by Divisional Burial Officer. The main ones now used are situated at :-
  MINTY FARM   C.10.c.2.5
  PHEASANT TRENCH U.30.a.8.3
         U.30.a.3.8
         U.30.d.2.7

FIELD POST OFFICE

At Brigade Wagon Lines, SIEGE CAMP.

D.A.D.O.S.

The address of D.A.D.O.S. is :-
  33, Rue de DUNKIRK   )
     or   ) POPERINGHE
  "C" Mess, 76, Rue d'Ypres)

          (Sd) F.H.GARRAWAY, Captain,
               Staff Captain,
             173rd Infantry Brigade.

APPENDIX "B"

(Issued in connection with 173rd Inf.Bde. Order No. 44)

COMMUNICATIONS

ADVANCED BRIGADE HEADQUARTERS — VARNA FARM.

BRIGADE FORWARD REPORT CENTRE — PHEASANT FARM.

BURIED CABLE HEAD — PHEASANT FARM.

TELEPHONE & TELEGRAPH — Direct sounder to Division. Telephone forward of Brigade Headquarters to Battalion Report Posts at 28, V.19.a.7.1 and GLOSTER FARM.

WIRELESS — Working between Bde. Headquarters and PHEASANT FM.

POWER BUZZERS & AMPLIFIERS — Are installed at PHEASANT FARM, GLOSTER FARM, and Battalion Headquarters at V.19.a.7.1.

PIGEONS — A supply of 8 per Battalion will be delivered on 25th inst.

ROCKETS — Rocket Receiving Station will be at PHEASANT FARM. Four men trained as rocketeers will be distributed as follows :-
- 1 to 2/3rd Bn. at V.19.a.7.1
- 1 to 2/2nd Bn. at GLOSTER FARM
- 1 to 2/4th Bn. at GLOSTER FARM
- 1 to report to 2/2nd Bn. for despatch to MEUNIER HOUSE.

Extreme range of the rockets are given as being 2,250 yards, and the following ranges are given as being useful for rockets :-
- PHEASANT FARM to V.19.a.6.2 .... 1,100 yds.
- PHEASANT FARM to GLOSTER FARM ..... 1,700 yds.
- PHEASANT FARM to BREWERY .... 2,100 yds.
- PHEASANT FARM to MEUNIER HOUSE .... 2,150 yds.
- PHEASANT FARM to TRACAS FARM ...... 2,300 yds

CONTACT AEROPLANE — Flares will be lit by foremost Infantry or Watson Fans used when the aviator calls for signals by means of a Klaxon Horn or drops a white light.

RUNNERS — Relay Posts are established at SNIPE HOUSE and PHEASANT FARM.
Battalions will arrange to establish Relay Posts for Runners - positions of which should be fixed approximately prior to ZERO.

VISUAL — A Lamp Station is already established at MEUNIER FARM working to PHEASANT FARM and this will be taken over by 2/2nd and 2/4th Bns. jointly.
Every endeavour should be made to pick up the Brigade Visual Station at PHEASANT FARM.

(Sd) C.E.G. SHEARMAN, Captain,
Brigade Major,
173rd Infantry Brigade.

25/10/17

APPENDIX "C"

(Issued in connection with 173rd Inf. Bde. Order No. 44)

SITUATION AT ZERO

ADVANCED BRIGADE HEADQUARTERS	VARNA FARM.
REAR BRIGADE HEADQUARTERS.	CANAL BANK (W).
2/1st Bn. London Regt.	ROSE TRENCH AREA
	Headquarters - V.19.a.7.1
2/2nd Bn. London Regt.	RIGHT ASSEMBLY
	Headquarters - GLOSTER FM,
2/3rd Bn. London Regt.	LEFT ASSEMBLY.
	Headquarters - V.19.a.7.1
2/4th Bn. London Regt.	ASSEMBLY.
	Headquarters - GLOSTER FM.
206th Machine Gun Coy.	ASSEMBLY
	Headquarters - GLOSTER FM.
173rd Light T.M.Battery	Between GLOSTER FM. and TRACAS FM.

2/5th L.N.Lancs. Regt.
    (Right attacking Bn.)
    170th Inf. Bde.
    57th Division.   Headquarters - FIRDAN HOUSE

1st Royal Marines) Left attacking Headquarters - BURNS HOUSE
)   Bns.
) 188th Inf.Bde
2nd Royal Marines) 63rd Division Headquarters - WINCHESTER FM.
    (Move to BERKS HOUSES on objective being taken).

170th Infantry Brigade	Advd. Headquarters - STRAY FARM
188th Infantry Brigade	Advd. Headquarters - HUBNER FARM
Prisoners of War Cage	GOURNIER FARM (C.9.d.).

                                      (Sd) C.E.G.SHEARMAN, Captain,
                                              Brigade Major,
                                        173rd Infantry Brigade.

173RD INFANTRY BRIGADE

Administrative Instruction No. 17.

(Issued in connection with 173rd Inf. Bde. Order No. 44)
---------------oOo---------------

24th Oct., 1917.

TRANSPORT & Q.M. STORES	FANTASIA FARM, Nr. SIEGE CAMP. Q.M. Stores will be prepared to move on Z plus 1 day. Brigade Transport Officer will arrange for the Brigade Pack Animal Company to be ready to move at short notice. 2 sections of the Company will be at 10 minutes notice.
BATTLE STORES	All extra battle stores, including rations, will be delivered to Units under arrangements made by this office.
SUPPLY OF RATIONS & WATER.	Rations and water are carried to troops in the line by either of two methods :- (a) By pack via REGINA CROSS, TRIANGLE FARM, and KEERSELARE. (b) By limbered wagon via ST. JULIEN and POELCAPPELLE Road as far as TRIANGLE FARM. (c) By limber to MINTY FARM and thence by tram to Tram Terminus, where carrying parties meet them.
DUMPS	See Table "A".
REPLACEMENT OF ORDNANCE STORES	The quick replacement of Lewis Guns is important. Units will report to Rear Brigade Headquarters directly any deficiencies occur.
STRAGGLER POSTS	Brigade Straggler Posts will be established at U.30.d.5.5 U.29.b.9.9 U.24.b.0.2 O.C., 2/1st Bn. will find personnel for these posts in accordance with detailed instructions sent him direct. Divisional Straggler Posts are established at C.9.d.6.3 C.9.d.2.7 C.10.c.2.6 Main Collecting Station at C.9.b.2.7

PRISONERS OF WAR	A temporary Collecting Station for Prisoners of War will be established at U.30.d.5.5.
	  O.C., 2/1st Bn. will detail 1 N.C.O. and 6 men for duty at the post.
	  Battalions will be responsible for escorting prisoners back to this post where the escort will be given a receipt. The N.C.O. i/c of the post will, when he has collected 12 or more prisoners, forward them to the Divisional Collecting Station at C.10.c.3.6 near GRUNE FARM, obtaining a receipt.
	  Officer prisoners will be kept separate from the men.

TABLE "A".

D U M P S.

R.E.

        RAILWAY COTTAGE   B.30.b.2.2.
        MORTELDJE   C.15.c.7.2.
                                       C.9.d.0.3.   (Shovels).

S.A.A. Bombs, Very Lights, etc.

        Divisional Dump.   POND COTTAGES. (C.19.c.8.2.)

        Brigade Dumps.   SNIPE HOUSE.
                                     BULOW FARM.
                                     DELTA HOUSE.

RATIONS.

        PHEASANT TRENCH   2160   Rations.
        C.19.d.3.1.   1870   "
        SNIPE HOUSE.   400   "

WATER.

        PHEASANT TRENCH.   210 Tins.
        C.19.d.3.1.   930 Tins.
        BULOW FARM.   50 Tins. (This Dump is
                                                    being increased).

-----------oOo-----------

26th Oct. 1917.

SUMMARY OF MESSAGES.
SENT AFTER ZERO.

(1). 7.40 a.m. UMPIRE - NAIL - FRUIT. Assembly of UPLIFT, UPPER and UPSHOT reported complete no report from UPSTART AAA No reports received about progress of attack.

(2). 8.40 a.m. UPLIFT UPSTART UPPER UPSHOT 188th Inf. Bde. report capture of BANFF HO. V.27.b. AAA Information required from our front urgently required none received as yet.

(3). 9.35 a.m. UPPER Wounded Officer at MEUNIER HOUSE reports our men at SPIDER CROSS ROADS

(4). 9.35 a.m. NAIL FRUIT Situation Report AAA Contact aeroplane reports our men seen at V.26.b.6.8. White Very Light seen at CAMERON HOUSE AAA Pigeon message from Right Battalion reports MORAY HOUSE taken about 25 prisoners sent down AAA Wounded Officer reports our men at SPIDER CROSS ROADS.

(5). 10.15 a.m. UPLIFT UNCORK UMPIRE UPSHOT reports his Companies have heavy casualties AAA CAMERON HOUSES were captured after stiff fighting 6.30 a.m. MORAY HOUSE also captured AAA UPSHOT also reports some of our men reported to be withdrawing past TRACAS FM believed owing to counter attack AAA UPLIFT will immediately send three companies to occupy line NOBLES FM. MEUNIER HOUSE TRACAS FM. and hold line at all costs AAA UNCORK will move to vicinity ROSE TRENCH AAA Bn. H.Q. at V.19.a.7.1. AAA O.C. UNCORK will call at Advanced UPHILL, VARNA FM. on his way forward.

(6). 10.35 a.m. ARTILLERY LIAISON OFFICER (VERBAL) Instructed to place barrage on front V.15.d.4.4. to V.20.c.4.6.

(7). 11 a.m. HEAVY ARTILLERY Ordered to fire along WHITECHAPEL - SPRIET ROAD V.15.d.5.4. - V.15.c.25.55. AAA along Road from WINDMILL WEST of SPRIET to LIND COT and along track V.16.c.6.6. to V.22.a.95.10.

(8). 11.50 a.m. UMPIRE NAIL FRUIT Situation Report AAA Enemy have re-captured CAMERON HOUSE we hold MEBUS U.21.c.0.6. and possibly MORAY HOUSE AAA Three Companies UPLIFT have been ordered to hold line NOBLES FM. MEUNIER HOUSE TRACAS FM at all costs AAA UNCORK have been ordered move forward to ROSE TRENCH V.25.a. AAA Casualties reported heavy AAA Ground waterlogged and in many places impassible.

(9). 11.45 a.m. UPLIFT UMPIRE NAIL FRUIT Contact plane reports our men in CAMERON HOUSE and V.21.c.1.4. AAA Flares and Fans very clearly seen AAA send out Officers patrol to reconnoitre CAMERON HOUSE AAA

(10). 12.15 p.m. UPSHOT NAIL UPLIFT UMPIRE Send out patrol to ascertain whether we still hold MORAY HO. and do utmost to establish communications with Bn. on your Right who are reported to be on line N.W. and S.E. through BANFF HOUSE.

(11). 12.20 p.m. UPPER No reports have yet been received from you AAA Urgently required AAA Contact aeroplane reports enemy definitely at SPIDER CROSS ROADS.

(12) 2.52 pm. UPLIFT UPSTART UPPER UPSHOT UNCORK UNBOLT UNCLE UMPIRE UMBALA O.C. Detachment UPSET STAFF CAPTAIN. Previous orders re relief are cancelled AAA UPLIFT will forthwith take over line from WESTROOSEBEKE ROAD inclusive and UNCORK will forthwith take over line SOUTH of WESTROOSEBEKE ROAD to Right Divisional Boundary relieving all troops of UPSTART UPPER and UPSHOT in these Areas AAA On relief these Battalions will concentrate on CANAL BANK by DIVISIONAL HEADQUARTERS where busses or trains will take them to SIEGE CAMP under arrangements of STAFF CAPTAIN AAA Bn. Hd. Qtrs. will be established as follows UPLIFT V.19.a.7.1. UNCORK GLOSTER FM AAA Further details of relief will be arranged between C.Os. concerned AAA Completion of relief will be notified to Brigade Headquarters by quickest possible method AAA Command of Divisional Sector remains with G.O.C. UPHILL at same location AAA M.G. defence of Sector will be arranged by Lieut. DAVIS O.C. Detachment UPSET at V.19.d.5.8. direct with O.C. UNCORK and UPLIFT AAA Detachment UPSET will relieve UMBALA the latter reporting to STAFF CAPTAIN on CANAL BANK on completion AAA UNBOLT is moving to KEMPTON PARK C.15.b.4.5. and will form Brigade Reserve under G.O.C. UPHILL.

(13) 4.35 pm. UPSTART UPSHOT UPPER Ref. my Bm.108 (12) AAA Busses will wait at ESSEX FM where you should concentrate AAA ESSEX FM is C.25.a.2.9. just West of the CANAL.

(14) 4.50 pm. UMPIRE NAIL FRUIT Situation report AAA Situation still obscure AAA Right Bn. reports posts held as follows BEEK HOUSES V.21.a.10.65. one Vickers and 100 men MEUNIER HOUSE 2 Vickers and 100 men TRAGAS FM AAA Several enemy attacks beaten off AAA many enemy wounded East of MEUNIER HOUSE AAA Left Bn. approximate position along line V.15.c.21.5, V.14.b.6.3. with three Coys. UPLIFT consolidating line from V.20.b.8.8. to V.14.c.7.9. Strong Point at V.14.c.9.5. possibly with Vickers guns AAA Bde. on left reported back on original line.

(15) 5.0 pm. UPLIFT UNCORK UMPIRE Barrage line is as follows AAA V.21.c.0.2. - V.21.c.5.6. just W. of CAMERON HOUSE MEBUS - 150 yds. W of SPIDER CROSS ROADS AAA every possible effort will be made to push out patrols to-night to endeavour to get into touch with any parties of UPPER UPSTART & UPSHOT that may be holding out W of above barrage line AAA Such posts if found will be taken over and consolidated and our line pushed forward to confirm AAA

(16) 5.45 pm. UPLIFT aeroplanes report our men at V.14.b.2.2. AAA Enemy posts at V.14.b.85.60. and V.15.a.5.7. at 3.25 p.m. AAA You will relieve our post and form defensive flank to meet Battalion on your left.

(17) 6 p.m. UNCORK Bn. on your right reports they hold BANFF HOUSE with supports in BERKS HOUSES AAA pocket of enemy holding out in V.27.a.9.3.

(18) 6.20 pm. UMPIRE NAIL FRUIT Situation report AAA 4.38 p.m. Left Bn. reports post half company at V.14.d.5.1. no other posts known Rifles and Lewis Guns unusable owing to mud AAA on relief UNCORK are going to occupy line V.20.b.50.75. to V.21.c.02.63. Two Companies front line and two in support Headquarters at GLOSTER FM. AAA Patrol reports CAMERON HOUSE occupied by enemy.

(19) 6.45 pm UNCORK UPLIFT UNCLE UMPIRE Contact lane observing from 1500 to 500 feet between 7 a.m. and 8 a.m. to-day reports our men at MORAY HOUSE and V.20.b.97.56. AAA enemy at CAMERON HO. and HINTON FM and at concrete structure V.15.c.40.96. AAA S.O.S. line is accordingly been altered to run as follows V.21.d.45.65. - V.21.central. - V.21.a.16. - V.15.c.3.3. - V.14.b.8.5. AAA UNCORK will do utmost to get into touch with Posts at MORAY HO. and V.20.b.97.56. AAA Former post will be relieved and line established MORAY HO - MEBUS V.21.c.0.6. AAA Post at V.20.b.97.56 will be withdrawn if found AAA These operations will be undertaken at dusk.

SUMMARY OF MESSAGES.

RECEIVED AFTER ZERO 26th.
OCTOBER 1917.
-----------o0o-----------

(1). 7.20 a.m. From UPSHOT. Timed 5.50 a.m. Bosch signal for attack was twin red rocket AAA Some white ones also sent up AAA Bosch barrage came down three minutes after ZERO about midway between GLOSTER FM and TRACAS FM. on a line roughly N. and S. but was not very heavy AAA It consisted mostly of 4.2 H.E. with a few 5.9 H.E. AAA Neighbourhood of GLOSTER FM also receievd some shells AAA This Battalion moved forward at ZERO.

(2). 8.15 a.m. From UMPIRE by telephone. Contact aeroplane saw our men only at V.20.b. 6.8. One white very light went up from CAMREON HOUSE Machine was heavily fired on from line WHITECHAPEL - BANFF HOUSE.

(3). 8.45 a.m. From UMPIRE by telephone - Wounded Officer reports our men at SPIDER CROSS ROADS.

(4). 8.50 a.m. From UMPIRE by telephone. From Capt. Sinnatt, UPSTART, to UPSTART by Pigeon. MORAY HOUSE taken about 30 Germans left MEBUS many of them were killed about 25 Prisoners sent down.

(5). 9.47 a.m. From UPLIFT Timed 8.20 a.m. Our Artillery active from 10 a.m. to 2 p.m. intermittantly AAA Enemy Artillery fairly active between 10.20 p.m. to 11 p.m. and about 1.30 a.m. AAA Our Barrage came down at 5.40 a.m. AAA Hostile barrage came down about 5.50 am AAA One prisoner of 467 I.R. captured by UPPER passed on to Brigade at 10.30 p.m. AAA Aeroplane reported seen to fall out of control about 8 a.m. within our lines whether our own or hostile not known.

(6). 10.15 a.m. From UPSHOT timed 9.30 a.m. CAMERON HOUSE appears now to be in enemy hands AAA we hold TRACAS FM and MEBUS in front of it AAA Am putting MEUNIER HOUSE into a state of defence AAA Our (UPSTART and UPSHOT) casualties appear to have been very heavy and I do not know what force of ours I have AAA Bosche does not seem to be attacking in any force AAA would like two companies to counter attack CAMERON HOUSE AAA No news from N. of Main Road.

(7). 10.25 a.m. From D. UPSHOT. timed 9.45 a.m. Advance held up ground impassible and waterlogged AAA Company on left in line with me AAA My position remains in front of MEBUS behind TRACAS FM 21.c.01.61.

(8). 10.20 a.m. From UPLIFT Timed 9.55 a.m. Have sent one Company to UPPER and am collecting two more Companies here AAA Have sent Pigeon message informing Corps of this.

(9). 10.28 a.m. From UPSHOT Timed 9.57 a.m. Retiring on Right Enemy counter attacking near main SPRIET road AAA Situation not clear help needed.

10.	10.32 a.m.	From UMPIRE timed 10.19 a.m. 174th Bde. may be moved to ROSE TRENCH not to be employed further forward without ref to these H.Qrs aaa Original line must be held at all costs.
11.	10.40 a.m.	From UMPIRE by telephone. Contact aeroplane seen flares and fans plainly at U.21.c.1.4 and CAMERON HOUSE. Enemy at WHITECHAPEL.
12.	10.46 a.m.	From UPLIFT timed 10.35 a.m. A second Company has just left here to support UPPER and a third will be going shortly aaa A flag signal message has just been received here from UPPER asking for us aaa Third Company leaving now.
13.	10.50 a.m.	From UMPIRE by telephone. 14th Corps Contact Aeroplane reports SPIDER CROSS ROADS in enemy hands aaa NAIL report cannot get in touch with UPHILL
14.	10.55 a.m.	From UMPIRE by telephone. Pigeon message addressed Capt. PULLAR. Boche counter-attack on TRACAS FARM. Lt. PITHOUSE holding out with 4 guns and 30 infantry.
15.	11. 0 a.m.	From UPLIFT timed 9.30 a.m. I have received a message (8.45 a.m.) from UPPER that we are losing ground cannot verify aaa I replied (9.15 a.m.) asking if they wanted assistance and have a Company standing to aaa 3 stragglers UPPER have just come in, they say they reached their objective SPIDER CROSS ROADS with D Company but were driven back, they dont know where their officers are aaa I dont consider them very reliable aaa A fair number of wounded 57 have passed near here aaa Have seen parties of prisoners evidently from 2/2nd and 2/4th
16.		From UMBALA (untimed) There are 5 Machine Guns in action at V.21.c.10.60 aaa Our infantry on right are again attacking aaa At earliest moment these guns will move further forward aaa I have ordered 1 gun and team from the battery to MEUNIER HOUSE for defence aaa My section officer reports CAMERON HOUSE not in our hands.
17.	11.35 a.m.	From UMPIRE (telephone) Contact aeroplane 10.40 a.m. Our men seen CAMERON HOUSE and V.21.c.1.4. Flares and fans very plain. Barrage to be altered clear of CAMERON HOUSE to include WHITECHAPEL.
18.	12.55 p.m.	From UMBALA. Machine Gun at TRACAS FARM HEBUS V.21.a.10.60 reports counter-attack made against this position at 9 a.m. aaa This was repulsed by 2 Machine Guns aaa 4 guns are now in action at this point mounted ready for counter-attack aaa I am sending up ammunition to this position drawing from BULOW Dump.
19.	1. 0 p.m.	From UPHILL timed 11.20 a.m. 3 Companies have already gone to support UPPER aaa My messages regarding this apparently crossed yours aaa I shall do nothing further until I hear from you, I have only 1 weak Company left, having found Straggler Posts from that Company.
20.	1.35 p.m.	From UMBALA timed 12.5 p.m. Report from section officer attached to 2/3rd Bn. went over top to previously selected positions at ZERO plus 40 and dug in at about ZERO plus 100 aaa Infantry retired beyond previously held positions aaa Held out in forward positions to ZERO plus 115 and then retired by 4 bounds on to original position at intervals of 15 minutes aaa Have managed to gather half platoon of infantry and have formed a small strong point at V.14.c.9.5. All rations lost aaa No news of sub-section under Mr OWENS

21.	2.15 p.m.	From UPLIFT timed 12.45 p.m. I have just heard from Capt GAIN who is with my 3 Companies that have gone up aaa He is consolidating on original line from V.14.c.7.9 to V.20.b.5.8 aaa A wounded man just in reports that enemy are just to their front firing rifle grenades aaa Adjutant UPPER states that his approximate position is along line V.14.b.6.3 to V.15.c.2.1 aaa Assistant Adjutant of Battalion on our left has just been in and says their right Company is back on original line.
22.	2.24 p.m.	From UMPIRE timed 2.10 p.m. Following moves will take place to-night aaa UPLIFT and UNCORK will hold the front line aaa UPSTART UPPER and UPSHOT return to CANAL BANK whence they will move by bus or train to SIEGE CAMP under arrangements of Q aaa UNBOLT will move from CANAL BANK to KEMPTON PARK C.15.b.4.5 clearing CANAL BANK by 4 p.m. UNDER and UNBIND will move by march route from SIEGE CAMP to CANAL BANK not to reach CANAL BANK before 4 p.m.
23.	2.30 p.m.	From UNCORK timed 1.10 p.m. In position 1.5 p.m.
24.	2.37 p.m.	From UMPIRE timed 2.25 p.m. Following from F.O.O. 75th Siege Bty timed 11 a.m. begins aaa Have since ascertained CAMERON HOUSE had to be given up owing to retirement on left and parties retired into MEUNIER which they are holding with about 100 men and 1 Vickers aaa Another party of same unit R.F. 2/2nd Londons are holding TRACAS with 100 men and 2 vickers but shortage of ammunitionaaa Much enemy sniping of MEUNIER also shelling 7.7 and 4.2 aaa Many wounded enemy about 30 yards due East MEUNIER.
25.	2.40 p.m.	From UPLIFT timed 1.10 p.m. Following received from Capt GAIN aaa Companies have moved to their positions shewn on map previously sent you aaa shelling considerable and going very bad so they will take some time to get there aaa This refers to line mentioned in my AP747 and not the line in your Bm/102 aaa It would be a very difficult matter to extend the line.
26.	4.7 p.m.	From UPSHOT timed 2.30 p.m. Enemy establishing a line of posts 300 yards E of MEBUS which is 200 yards E of TRACAS and S of TRACAS FARM and S of CAMERON HOUSES aaa We hold the original line with MEBUS E of TRACAS in addition with about 150 men which is all remaining of 2/2nd and 2/4th Bns signallers and runners being used to assist in garrisoning posts aaa Please arrange S.O.S. line accordingly aaa A former message to this effect has been sent you and 83rd Brigade R.F.A aaa Ammunition and about 30 stretchers with bearers are urgently required aaa Have had 3 boxes from BULOW FARM but no further carrying party available.
27.	4.20 p.m.	From UPLIFT timed 2.50 p.m. Following received from Lieut PREEDY commanding Company on left aaa The 2/3rd have not been heard of since they went over this morning aaa I have seen a Sergeant of L.N.Lancs who says that his battalion did not advance this morning aaa I have seen some of them about V.14.a.5.5 and going over myself to get touch with them aaa Machine Gun can be heard on right flank aaa No sign of Boche aaa Several casualties aaa I would suggest that the Sergt said this to cover the fact that he is back on original line aaa Following received from Adjutant UPPER aaa I am afraid position is rather bad on the left aaa our men seem to have been practically wiped out on the left and the line there appears to be back on the assembly position aaaIf shelling permits could you

possibly get the Colonel back to your H.Q. there is absolutely no room here even to dress him properly aaa Our M.O. says he must get to hospital very soon if we hope to save him aaa Unfortunately at present there is still a barrage down on this place aaa I have sent four men to do this aaa A stretcher bearer of UPSHOT has just come in aaa Has a party of 40 or 50 wounded collected about an hour's walk from here aaa UNCORK and I are sending a mixed party with 5 stretchers aaa Its as much as we can spare aaa Lieut PREEDY is just in wounded not badly aaa We have got touch with UPSHOT on right but not with unit on left aaa He cant find any of UPPER except their H.Q. aaa He states that Boche is sniping POELCAPPELLE.

28. 4.35 p.m. From UPLIFT timed 3.5 p.m. Have just received a message from Capt GAIN(my right Company) aaa The message arrived very muddy and is in parts undecipherable but I gather that he has pushed posts to MEUNIER HOUSE where he is in touch with UPSHOT aaa The line now being held and consolidated is slightly in rear of assembly line.

29. 5.35 p.m. D.R. PHEASANT FM S.O.S.

30. 6.5 p.m. From UPLIFT timed 4.35 p.m. Following received from UPPER aaa We have as far as I can find out about half a Company at V.14.d.5.1 aaa There does not seem to be any more of the battalion left aaa Rifles and Lewis Guns are unusable owing to mud aaa Could you get instruction for me from Brigade as it would be impossible for me to hold up an attack aaa Reference Bm/102 I have received suggested dispositions from UPSHOT which I have passed on to UNCORK who is going to take up line from my right to TRACAS with 2 Companies in front and 2 in support and H.Q. at GLOSTER FARM aaa No relief orders received aaa This has been arranged with UNCORK in anticipation aaa Patrol just returned from CAMERON HOUSES aaa They are in possession of the enemy.

31. 6.45 p.m. From UPPER timed 3.15 p.m. Enclosed map shews position as far as could be ascertained after attack aaa Battalion on left apparently lost direction also battalion on right 2/4th did not come up aaa Now holding original assembly position with 3 Companies of 2/1st aaa Unable at present to find out if we still have any post in front of assembly line aaa 2/4th position shewn by red and blue line aaa they are coming up to Black line on our right aaa Casualties very severe including Colonel who is I'm afraid mortally wounded
    (Note:Dotted Blue Line V.14.b.3.2 to V.15.a.8.1)
        Blue and Red Line V.20.b.1.8 to MEUNIER HO.)

32. Untimed. From UPSHOT Battalion on our left withdrew leaving flank of CAMERON HOUSE exposed aaa Men then withdrew to positions as shewn on map aaa Please fix a new barrage line aaa Boche are about 200 yards in front of posts at MEUNIER HOUSE and TRACAS FARM aaa We have beaten off several attacks aaa Ammunition urgently required aaa Have so few men dont like to lessen garrison very much aaa Can get no information from 2/3rd on left flank.
    (Note on map dispositions, 100 men round TRACAS FARM
        and 100 men round MEUNIER HOUSE. Post at
        BEEK HOUSES and V.21.c.0.6).

33. 11. 5 p.m.   From UNCORK. Relief complete 11. 5 p.m. aaa
                   Companies at MEUNIER TRACAS BEER and V.20.a.4.0.

October 27th, 1917

34. 9.33 a.m.   From UMPIRE aaa Aeroplane reports we hold MORAY
                   HOUSE and V.20.b.97.56 aaa Nobody seen in SAUCE
                   TRENCH BANFF and BRAY HOUSES aaa Enemy hold CAMERON
                   HOUSE HINTON FARM Concrete structure V.15.c.40.96
                   aaa Every effort should be made to obtain touch with
                   our men at MORAY HOUSE to-day.

35. 2.15 p.m.   From UPHILL. Right Company from V.20.b.55.80 to
                   V.14.d.3.3 (just in front of NOBLES FARM) Left
                   Company from thence to V.14.c.90.80 aaa Right
                   Company H.Q. V.14.c.25.20 aaa Right post of battal-
                   ion on left REQUETE FARM aaa Right Company in
                   consolidated shell holes aaa Left Company has post
                   with 2 Vickers Guns at V.14.c.90.80 and 2 weak pla-
                   toons in support near Coy H.Q. aaa Right Company
                   of battalion on left has orders to advance his post
                   in line with ours and will then move his Coy H.Q.
                   from FERDAN HO (V.19.a.70.55) to REQUETE FARM aaa
                   This I presume will not take place until dark.

36. 10.25 p.m.   From UNCORK. MORAY not ours aaa Report follows aaa
                   Other question not yet solved.

37. 11.45 p.m.   From UNCORK. Platoon sent to reconnoitre MORAY
                   HOUSE reports aaa begins aaa Advanced to within
                   50 yards of MORAY HOUSE when we were met by rifle
                   fire aaa decided to withdraw being satisfied no
                   British holding out there aaa When the rifle fire
                   broke out an M.G. from left flank also opened
                   traversing fire.

---------------oOo---------------

SECRET.   24th Oct. 1917.

APPENDIX "A".

(issued with 173rd Bde. Order No.44.)

---

1. **ASSEMBLY:-** Officers Commanding 2/2nd; 2/3rd and 2/4th Bns. London Regt. will arrange for the reconnaissance of their assembly positions to be carried out during the early morning of Y Day.
   The actual assembly lines will be taped under Battalion arrangements immediately after dusk on Y evening.
   Those for 2/3rd and 2/2nd Battalions will be as far as possible along our present front line.
   2/4th Battalion will assemble in V.20.a. and c.
   Assembly will be completed by 1 a.m. on Z day, and completion will be wired to Advanced Brigade Headquarters by Code Word "GOODELF".
   Previous to assembly 2/4th Bn. will move up to positions of readiness about V.19.c.

2. ...es in connection with assembly will take place in accordance with attached Move Table.

3. The Brigadier wishes to draw Unit Commanders' attention to the following points :-

    (a) To again impress all ranks that they MUST get round Strong Points.

    (b) There must be as little movement as possible in the trenches to-morrow, special care being taken when aeroplanes are overhead.

    (c) Steel Helmets to be rubbed over with mud.

    (d) The most valuable information in recent operations has come back by pigeons: full use must be made of this excellent means of communication, and birds must not be hoarded.

                                                         Captain,
                                                       Brigade Major,
                                                 173rd Infantry Brigade.

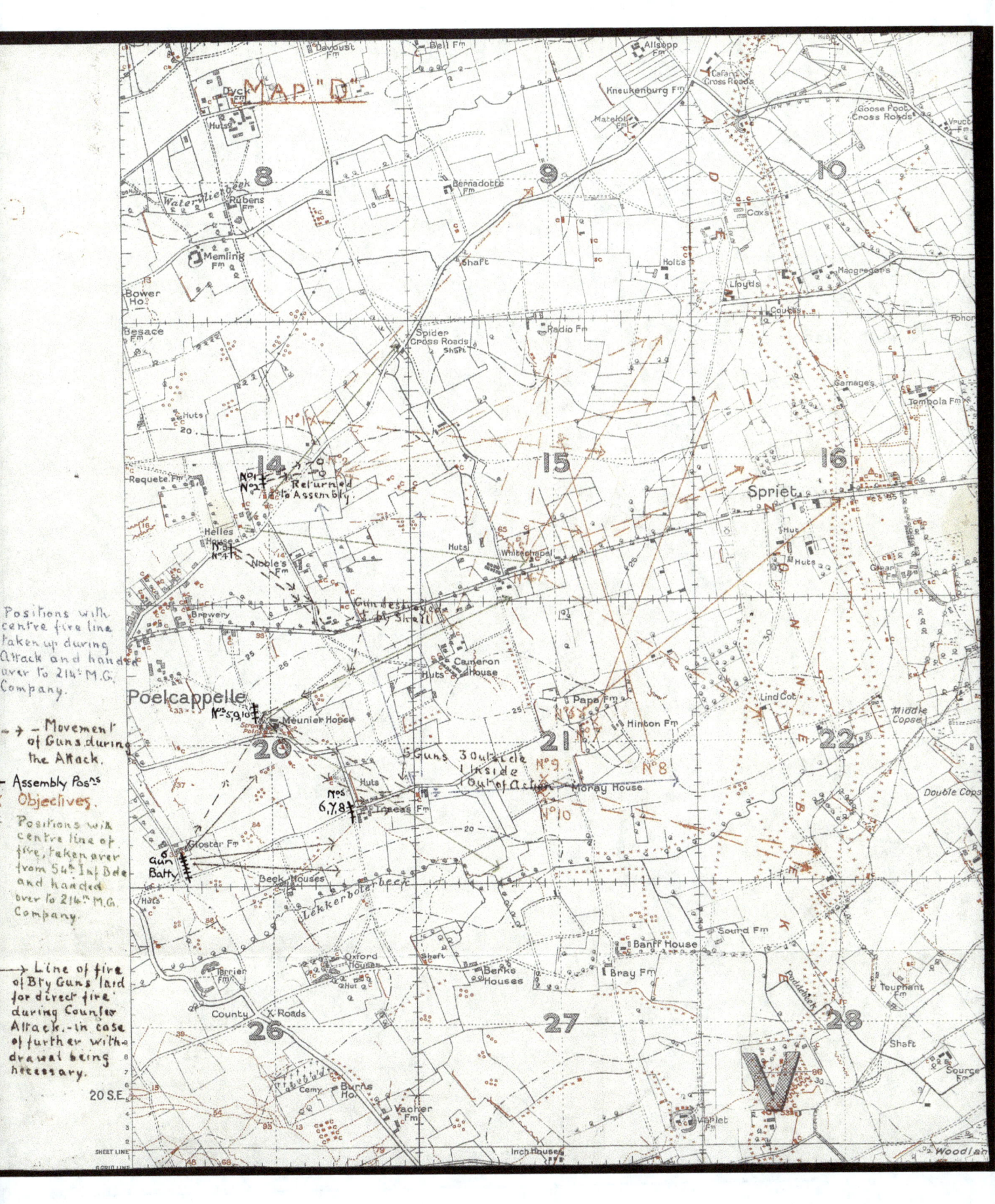

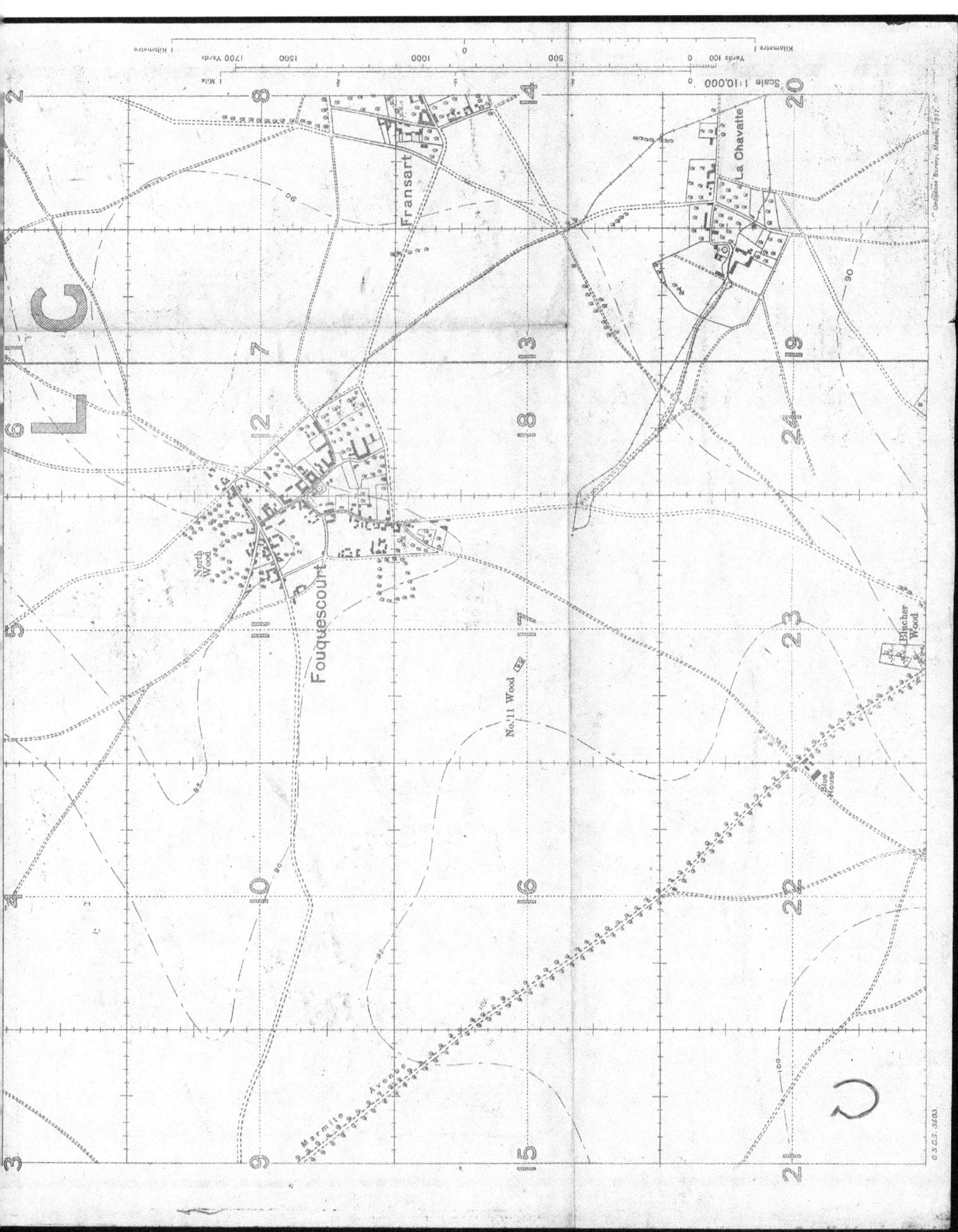

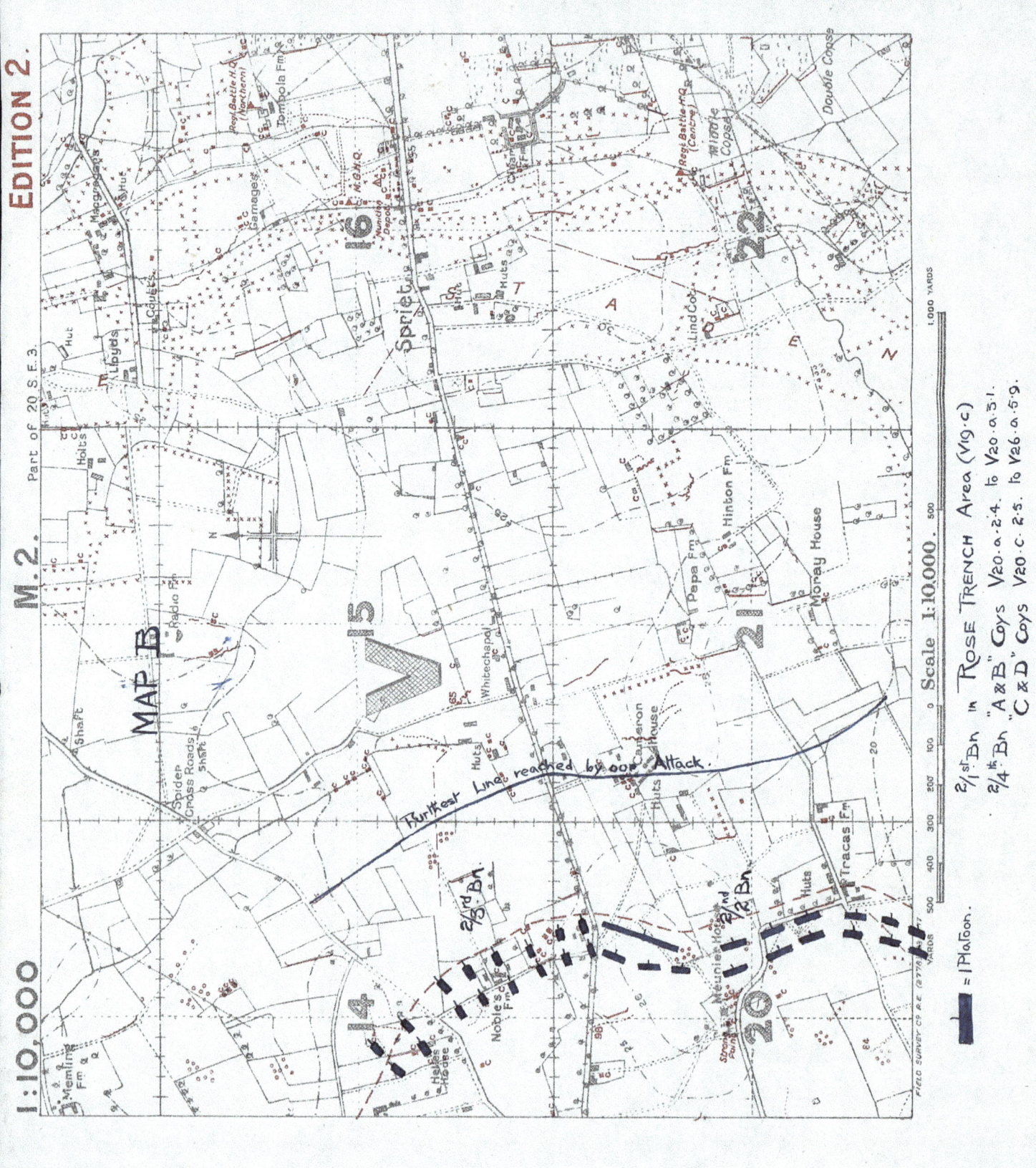

Message Form.

..................Division.

Map reference or mark own position on Map at back.

1. I am at..

2. I am at..and am consolidating.

3. I am at..and have consolidated.

4. Am held up at...by M.G. at..................

5. I need :—Ammunition.
    Bombs.
    Rifle Grenades.
    Water.
    Very lights.
    Stokes shells.

6. Enemy forming up for counter-attack at..

7. Enemy withdrawing at...

8. I am in touch with..........................on Right/Left at..............................

9. I am not in touch on Right./Left.

10. I estimate my present strength at..rifles.

11. Hostile { Battery / Machine Gun / Trench Mortar } active at..............................

Time..................a.m. (p.m.)   Name..................................

Date..................................   Platoon.............. Company............

                                    Battalion...................................

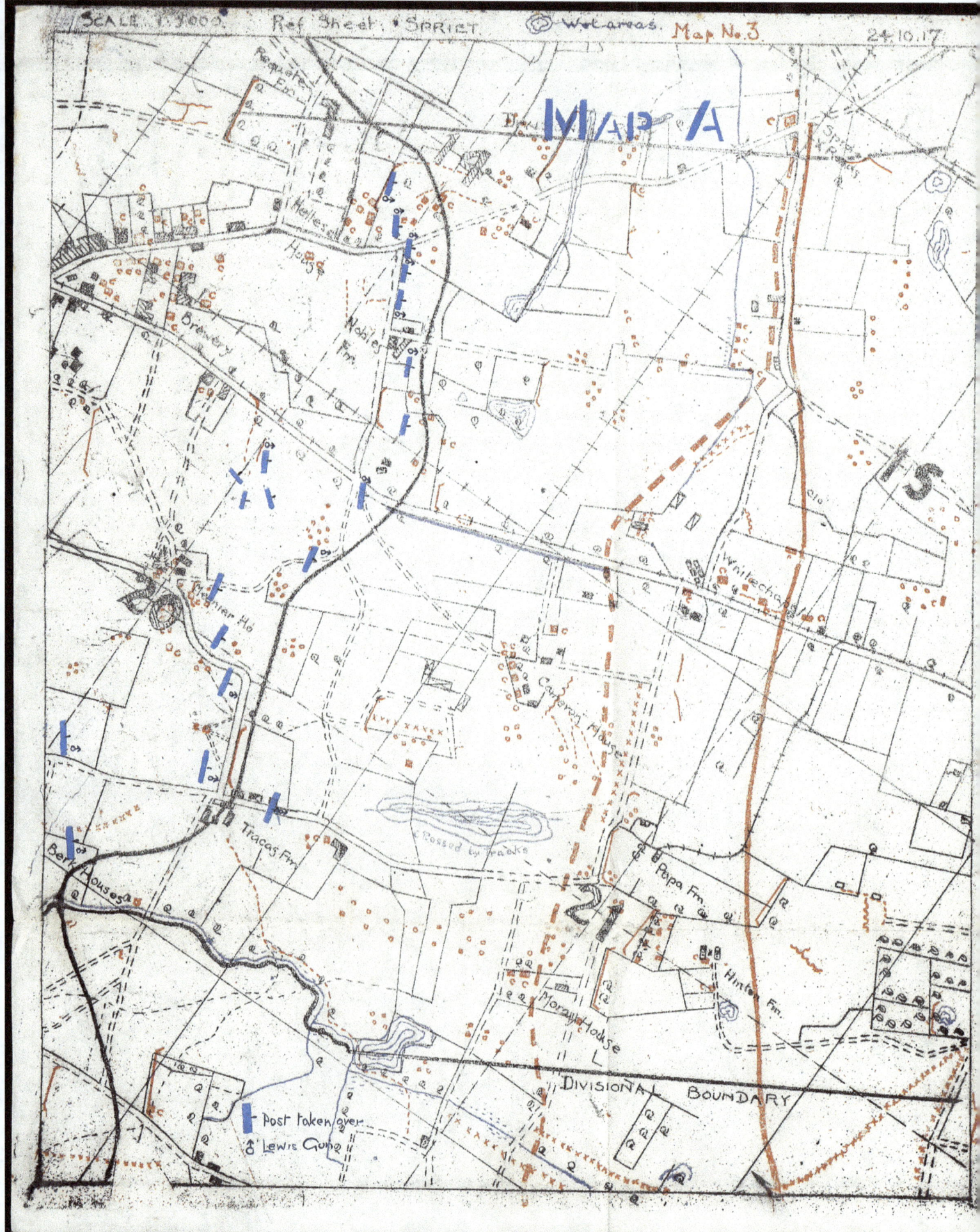

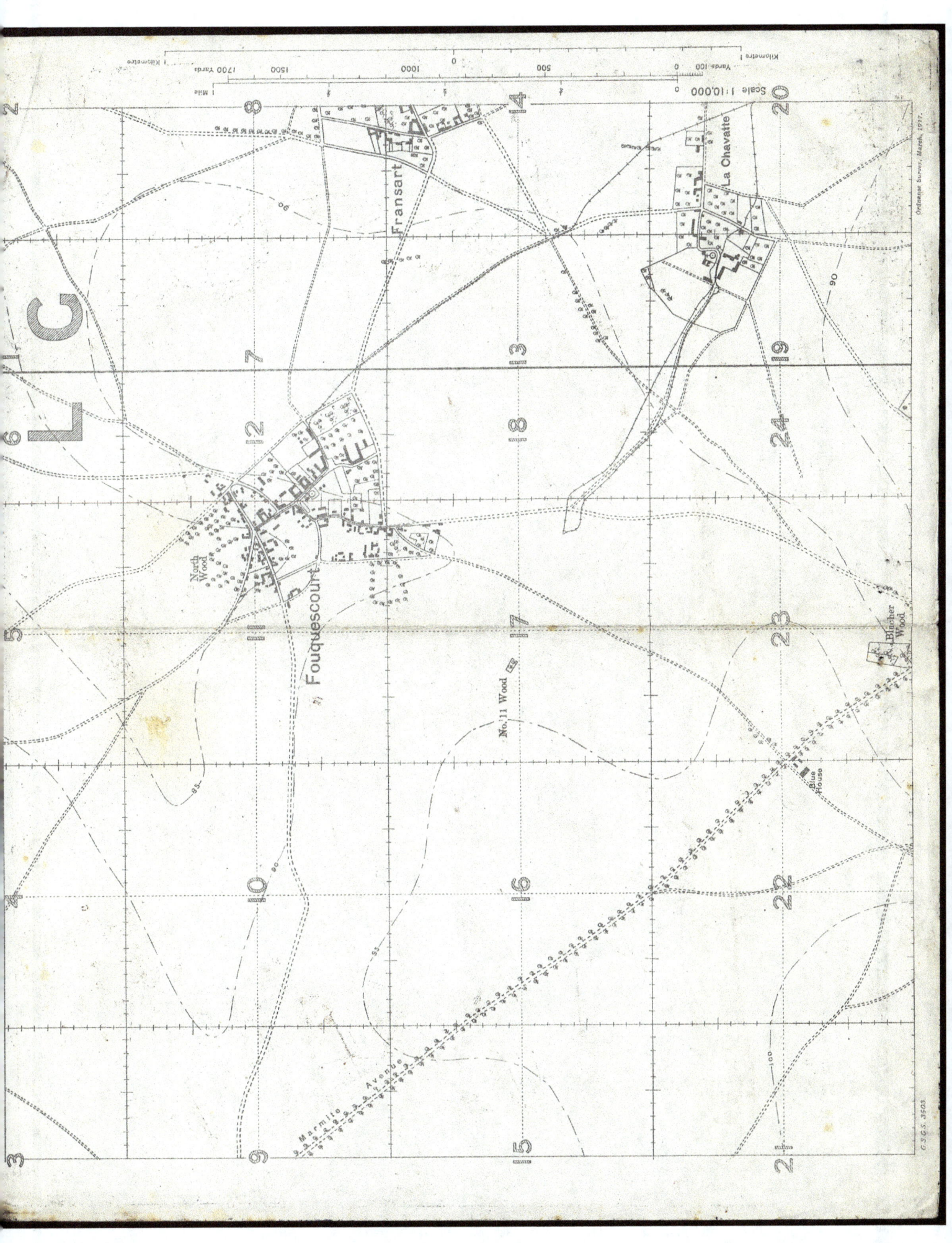

APPENDIX "B". Copy

Communications

Issued in connection with 173rd Inf Bde Order no 44

Advanced Brigade Headquarters — VARNA FARM.

Brigade Forward Report Centre — PHEASANT FARM.

Buried Cable Head — PHEASANT FARM.

Telephone & Telegraph — Buzzer sounder to DIVISION. Telephone forward of Bde Hqrs. to Battalion report posts at 28 V 19 a 71 and GLOSTER FARM.

Wireless — Working between Bde Hqrs & PHEASANT FARM.

Power Buzzers & Amplifiers are installed at PHEASANT FARM, GLOSTER FARM and Bn Hqrs at V 19 a 71.

Pigeons — A supply of 8 per Bn will be delivered on 25th inst.

Rockets — Rocket receiving station will be at PHEASANT FARM. Four men trained as Rocketeers will be distributed as follows.

 1 to 2/3rd Bn at V 19 a 62.
 1 to 2/2nd Bn at GLOSTER FARM.
 1 to 2/4th Bn at ——— do ———
 1 to report to 2/2nd Bn for dispatch to MEUNIER HOUSE.

Extreme range of the rockets are given as being 2250 yds & the following ranges are given as being useful for rockets.

PHEASANT FARM	to V 19 a 62	1100 yds
	to GLOSTER FM	1400 "
	to BREWERY	2100 "
	to MEUNIER HO	2150 "
	to TRACAS FM	2300 "

Contact Aeroplane — Flares will be lit by foremost infantry or Watson fans used when the Aviator calls for signals by means of a Klaxon Horn or dropping a white light.

<u>Runners</u>   Relay posts are established at SNIPE HOUSE and PHEASANT FARM.
Battalions will arrange to establish relay posts for Runners – positions of which should be fixed approximately prior to ZERO.

<u>Visual</u>   A Lamp station is already established at MEUNIER FARM working to PHEASANT FARM and this will be taken over by 2/2 & 2/4 Bns jointly.
Every endeavour should be made to pick up the Bde Visual Station at PHEASANT FARM.

                          [signature] Capt
                              Brigade Major
                              173rd Inf. Brigade.

Move Table Attached, APPENDIX "A"

Date	Unit	From	To	Route	Remarks
Oct. 25th	2/1st Bn.	CANAL BANK	ROSE Tr. Area - U.24.d.	Duck board track from 5 CHEMINS	Break journey at CANE TR (C.9.a.). Leave CANAL BANK 11 a.m. Assembly in ROSE TR to be complete by 1 a.m., 26th.
"	2/2nd Bn.	Right Front Sector	Assembly position V.20.d.5.0 FRAGAS MI V.20.b.5.5 V.20.b.5.8	---	Assembly to be complete by 1 a.m., 26th.
"	2/3rd Bn.	Left Front Sector	Assembly position V.20.b.5.8 V.14.d.1.8 V.14.c.7.9	---	Assembly to be complete by 1 a.m. 26th
"	2/4th Bn.	CANAL BANK	Assembly Area ....d. and c.	Duckboard track from 5 CHEMINS	Break journey at CANE TR (C.9.a.). Leave CANAL BANK 11 a.m. Assembly to be complete by 1 a.m., 26th.

173RD INFANTRY BRIGADE

Administrative Instruction No. 17

(Issued in connection with 173rd Inf. Bde. Order No. 44)

---oOo---

24th October, 1917

TRANSPORT & Q.M. STORES.	FANTASIA FARM, Nr. SIEGE CAMP.

Q.M. Stores will be prepared to move on Z plus 1 day. Bde. Transport Officer will arrange for the Brigade Pack Animal Company to be ready to move at short notice. Two sections of the Company will be at 10 minutes notice.

BATTLE STORES

All extra battle stores, including rations, will be delivered to units under arrangements made by this office.

SUPPLY OF RATIONS & WATER.

Rations and Water are carried to troops in the line by either of two methods :-

(a) By pack via REGINA CROSS, TRIANGLE FARM and KEERSELARE.

(b) By limbered wagon via ST. JULIEN and POELCAPELLE Road, as far as TRIANGLE FARM.

(c) By limber to MINTY FARM and thence by Tram to Tram Terminus where carrying parties meet them.

DUMPS

See Table "A".

REPLACEMENT OF ORDNANCE STORES.

The quick replacement of Lewis Guns is important. Units will report to rear Bde. Headquarters directly any deficiencies occur.

STRAGGLER POSTS

Brigade Straggler Posts will be established at

      U.30.d.5.5
      U.29.b.9.9
      U.24.b.0.2

O.C., 2/1st Battalion will find personnel for these posts in accordance with detailed instructions sent him direct.

Divisional Straggler Posts are established at

      O.9.d.6.3
      O.9.d.2.7
      O.10.c.2.6

Main Collecting Station at

      O.9.b.2.7.

PRISONERS OF WAR

A temporary Collecting Station for prisoners of war will be established at U.30.d.5.5.

O.C., 2/1st Bn. will detail 1 N.C.O. and 6 men for duty at the post.

Battalions will be responsible for escorting prisoners back to this post where the escort will be given a receipt. The N.C.O. i/c of the post will, when he has collected 12 or more prisoners, forward them to the Divisional Collecting Station at O.10.c.3.6 near GRUNE FARM, obtaining a receipt.

Officer prisoners will be kept separate from the men.

2.

MEDICAL. — Regimental Aid Posts at :-
        V.19.a.6.1
        V.20.c.4.2

Relay Posts at :-
        U.30.b.1.6
        U.30.d.6.9
        U.29.d.8.3
        C.5.b.2.8
        C.5.c.0.5

Advanced Dressing Stations at :-
        C.3.d.3.3
        C.10.c.3.6

CASUALTIES. The following instructions with regard to reporting casualties during the operations are issued :-
    The ordinary detailed casualty return will be rendered, and in addition an estimated casualty return will be forwarded twice daily to reach Rear Brigade Headquarters at 12 noon and 7 p.m.
    (Estimated casualties, however, exceeding 10 per cent. of any unit will be reported at once).
    The following information will be given in reporting casualties :-
        (a) Total estimated loss of Officers since the commencement of operations.
        (b) Total estimated loss of O.Rs. since the commencement of operations.
    All wires will commence "Total estimated aaa" and the total will be accumulative
    At the termination of the operations, or as soon as a unit is withdrawn from the line, an accurate return of the casualties sustained during the proceeding period will be rendered.
    This return must give the dates covered, ranks, initials and names of officers, and total numbers of O.Rs. killed, wounded or missing.
    Accuracy is essential in this return.

DRYING ROOMS A Drying Shed is established at GOURNIER FARM under the charge of Forward Area Commandant.
    A Drying Hut and Incinerator combined is about to be erected East of the CANAL BANK at C.25.a.9.7.
    A drying installation has been fixed up in the Divisional Surplus Kit Dump at 7, Rue Tete d'Or, POPERINGHE.

CEMETERIES Cemeteries, East of CANAL BANK, are looked after by Divisional Burial Officer. The main ones now used are situated at :-
        MINTY FARM   C.10.c.2.5
        PHEASANT TRENCH U.30.a.8.3
                          U.30.a.3.8
                          U.30.d.2.7

FIELD POST OFFICE At Brigade Wagon Lines, SIEGE CAMP.

D.A.D.O.S. The address of D.A.D.O.S. is :-
        33, Rue de DUNKIRK   )
                or   ) POPERINGHE.
        "C" Mess, 76, Rue d'Ypren)

                                              H.H.Garraway
                                                Captain,
                                            Staff Captain,
                                      173rd Infantry Brigade.

TABLE "A"

D U M P S

R.E.

        RAILWAY COTTAGE   B.30.b.2.2
        MORTELDJE   C.15.c.7.2
                               C.9.d.0.3 (Shovels)

S.A.A., Bombs, Very Lights, Etc.

        Divisional Dump   POND COTTAGES (C.19.c.8.2

        Brigade Dumps   SNIPE HOUSE
                               BULOW FARM
                               DELTA HOUSE

RATIONS

        PHEASANT TRENCH   2160 Rations
        C.19.d.3.1   1870   "
        SNIPE HOUSE   400   "

WATER

        PHEASANT TRENCH   210 Tins
        C.19.d.3.1   930 "
        BULOW FARM   50 " (This dump is being
                                                        increased)

---------------oOo---------------

S E C R E T.   25th October, 1917.

APPENDIX "C".

Issued in connection with 173rd Infantry Brigade Order No.44.

SITUATION AT ZERO.

Adv. Brigade Headquarters.   - VARNA FARM.

Rear Brigade Headquarters.   - CANAL BANK. W.

2/1st Bn. London Regiment.   - ROSE TR. Area - H.Q. V.19.a.7.1

2/2nd Bn. London Regiment.   - RIGHT ASSEMBLY - H.Q. GLOSTER FM.

2/3rd Bn. London Regiment.   - LEFT ASSEMBLY - H.Q. V.19.a.7.1

2/4th Bn. London Regiment.   - ASSEMBLY.   - H.Q. GLOSTER FM.

206th Machine Gun Company.   - ASSEMBLY.   - H.Q. GLOSTER FM.

173rd Light T. M. Battery.   - Between GLOSTER FM and TRAGAS FM.

2/S L.N.Lancs. Regiment.
(Right attacking Bn., 170th   - H.Q. JORDAN HOUSE.
Infantry Brigade, 57th Div.)

1st Royal Marines.)Left attacking   - H.Q. BURNS HO.
)Bns., 188th Bde.
2nd Royal Marines.)63rd Division.   - H.Q. WINCHESTER FM.
     (Move to BERKS HOUSES on Objective being taken).

170th Infantry Brigade (Adv.).   -   STRAY FARM.

188th Infantry Brigade (Adv.).   -   MUSKER FM.

Prisoner of War Cage - GOURNIER FM. (C.9.d.).

[signature]
Captain,
Brigade Major,
173rd Infantry Brigade.

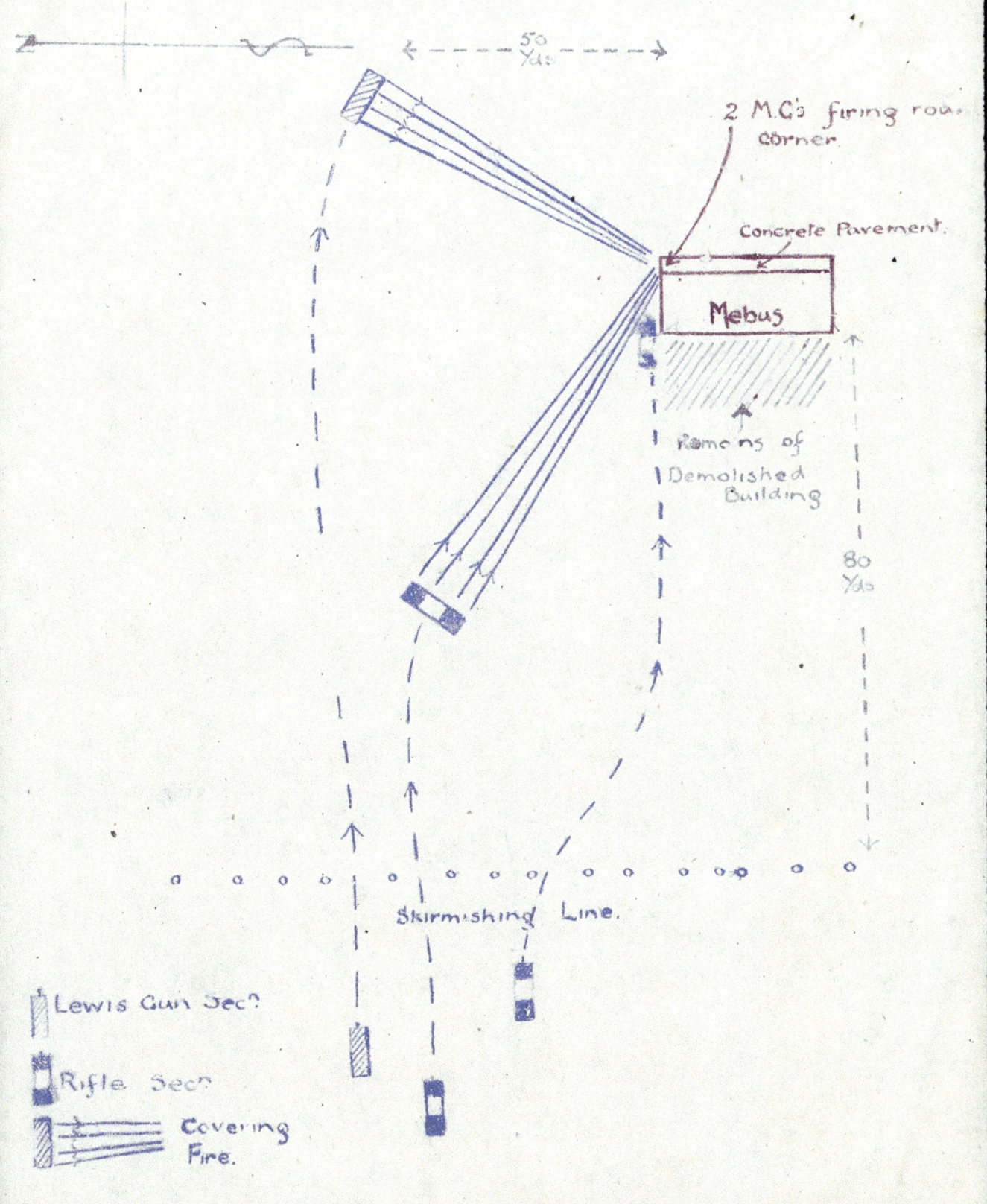

Sketch Map referred to in NOTES Para 4. Attack on Mebus at V.21c.0.6., under 2/Lt J. HOWIE, 2/2nd Bn. Lond. Regt.

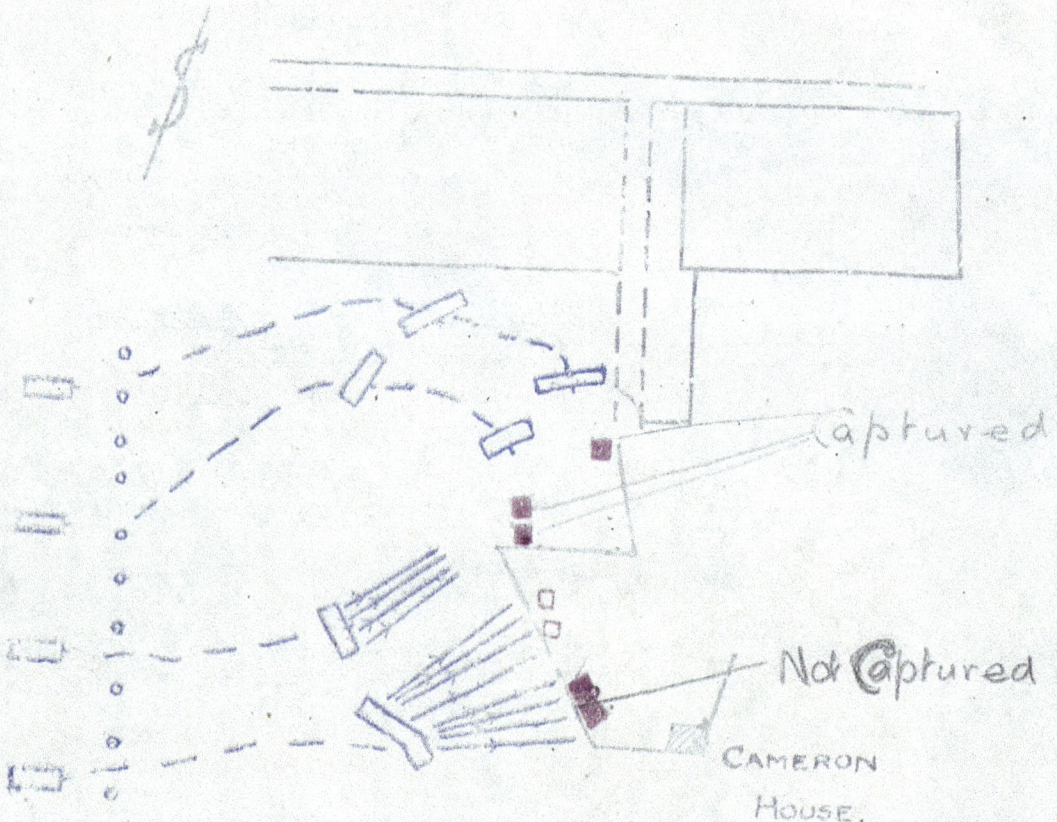

173RD INFANTRY BRIGADE

OPERATION REPORT
---oOo---

Period - 25th - 27th October,
1917
****

NARRATIVE

The report covers the period from completion of relief of 54th Infantry Brigade, 18th Division, at 8 a.m., 25th Oct., to completion of relief of the attacking troops by 2/1st and 2/7th Battalions London Regt., at 4.50 a.m., 27th October, 1917.

On taking over the Line the Brigade was disposed as shewn on Map "A". At 10 a.m. and 11 a.m. respectively the 2/1st and 2/4th Battalions moved forward from CANAL BANK to CANE TRENCH and KEMPTON PARK. At 3 p.m. these Battalions again moved forward. The 2/1st Bn. to ROSE TRENCH - 2/4th Bn. to Assembly Area in V.20.a. and c.

The time taken in assembling varied from 3 hours in the case of the 2/3rd Bn. to 9 hours in the case of the 2/2nd Bn. The assembly was complete by 2 a.m., 26th October, and dispositions at this period are shewn on Map "B".

Up to about 3 a.m., the weather was excellent, and the crater lips of shell holes were reported to be drying fast. At this hour, however, the weather broke, and a driving rain set in which did not cease until the night of 26th/27th, making all movement a matter of extraordinary difficulty.

At ZERO (5.35 a.m.) the attack was launched in accordance with Brigade Order No. 44 (copy attached).

The 2/2nd Bn. attacked on the Right with 2/3rd Bn. on their Left, each Battalion being on a four Company front, as shewn on map "B".

The 2/4th Bn., who were also on a four Company front, and had assembled in V.20.a. and c. moved forward at ZERO in readiness to leapfrog through the other two battalions on capture of the first objective.

In spite of the appalling state of the ground and weather, the attack started well, although the barrage, which was too fast, was speedily lost. The 2/2nd Bn. captured Hebus at V.21.c.0.6 and three out of four of the HEBUS at CAMERON HOUSES. The 2/3rd Bn. captured HEBUS about V.14.d.4.2 and their left Company advanced (unsupported on their Left) to what was thought at the time to be SPIDER X ROADS, but was probably the junction of roads at V.14.b.6.3. It is certain, however, that this battalion reached the general line V.14.b.6.3 - V.15.c.2.1. This line on our Left, and a line CAMERON HOUSES (inclusive) - V.20.d.9.9 - V.21.c.5.4, was the limit of our advance, our men being held up either by the ground or by enemy M.G. fire, which was universally reported as very heavy - our total prisoners up to this time amounted to 1 Officer and 63 Other Ranks.

At this juncture (about 7.10 a.m.) the enemy counter-attacked in great strength, both on our left flank, which owing to the Brigade on our left being held up, was unprotected, and also against CAMERON HOUSES. His counter-attack was unfortunately successful, mainly owing to our weak strength at the time (due to casualties), the exhaustion of the men, and the muddy condition of all rifles and Lewis Guns, hardly any of which could be used at all.

As a result of these counter-attacks, our troops were forced back to the line shewn on Map "C", where the attacking enemy were held up by the surviving troops of 2/2nd and 2/4th Bns. on the Right assisted by guns of 206th Machine Gun Coy., and 2/3rd and 2/1st Bns. on the Left.

3 Companies of this latter Battalion were sent up to assist 2/3rd Bn. in response to an urgent message for help from that battalion, when the enemy counter-attack first developed. No further advance was made, and the line remained as on Map "C" up to the end of the period under review.

At 2.52 p.m. an order was sent out from Brigade for the immediate relief of the 2/2nd, 2/3rd and 2/4th Bns. by 2/7th and 2/1st Bns. - 2/7th Bn. were to take over the line South of main POELCAPPELLE - WESTROOSEBEKE Road, and 2/1st Bn. the line to the North of this road.

The Machine Gun defence of this sector was to be taken over from the 206th Machine Gun Coy. by 214th Machine Gun Coy.

The relief was completed by 4.50 a.m., 27th October.

---oOo---

NOTES

1. **ASSEMBLY.** In the absence of tape, which was late in arriving, one Battalion used leaves from Field Message Pads, and these which were attached to pieces of wood and stuck into the ground, proved an excellent guide.

    The assembly position on the Left was fair (until rain fell) the lips of the craters having dried considerably - on the Right towards the LEKKER-BOTTERBEKE the ground was very bad - and the Right Companies of the 2/2nd and 2/4th Bns. were in great difficulties both during assembly and advance.

    The times of commencement and completion of assembly were as follows :-

	Commenced	Completed
2/2nd Bn. London Regt.	5 p.m., 25th	2 a.m., 26th
2/3rd Bn. London Regt.	9 p.m., 25th	12 midnight 25/26th
2/4th Bn. London Regt.	6.15 p.m., 25th	10.15 p.m., 25th
206th Machine Gun Coy.	--	6.45 a.m., 25th.

2. **OUR BARRAGE.** Universally reported as thin and too fast. 100 yards in 12 minutes is suggested for conditions such as prevailed on the 26th.

    In many cases our men never even closed up to the barrage which opened 150 yards from our foremost troops.

3. **ENEMY BARRAGE.** Descended at ZERO plus 5 minutes on a line running N. and S. through MEUNIER HOUSE and all three attacking battalions report that this barrage followed our advance. It may have been, however, that the enemy had set apart a certain number of guns for the shelling of his own defensive positions as soon as they were evacuated. In any case this latter barrage was light and casualties suffered from it were not excessive.

4. **THE ATTACK.**
    (a) **Skirmishers** :- Owing to the bad state of the ground these were neither able to keep any sort of line, nor to keep close to the barrage.

    (b) **Assaulting Parties** :- Both the party detailed to take CAMERON HO and the party detailed to take MEBUS V.21.c.0.6, employed the enveloping tactics taught in training - in each case the enemy evacuated their position as soon as our men in any way threatened their rear. In the case of the MEBUS at V.21.c.0.6, advantage was taken of the fact that the enemy's Machine Guns defending this place took up a position on the N. side of the MEBUS, from which it was impossible for fire to be delivered on our troops manoeuvring to the S. 2/Lieut. HOWIE, 2/2nd Bn. commanding the platoon detailed to capture this MEBUS, promptly took advantage of this fact, and detailing a portion of his platoon to engage the enemy with covering fire from

N. and W., he himself with the remainder of his men worked round to the S. and entered the MEBUS from the rear, capturing 1 Machine Gun and 25 O.Rs. - the total strength of 2/Lieut. Howie's party on capturing the MEBUS was 18, 10 of whom gave covering fire only.

The MEBUS by CAMERON HO were taken from the N. under Capt. HARPER, 2/2nd London Regt., who advanced under covering fire from just W. of the enemy position.

Sketch Maps showing dispositions for the attack on these two strongholds made by 2nd Lieut. Howie and Capt. Harper are attached.

5. ACTION OF OUR M.G'S. Guns were numbered from Left to Right 1 to 16. Following were dispositions of guns in assembly :-
    Nos. 1 to 4   In vicinity of V.14.c.90.50.
    Nos. 5,9 & 10. MEUNIER HOUSE V.20.b.
    Nos. 6,7 & 8   TRACAS FARM Post. V.20.d.
    Nos. 11 - 16   Barrage guns firing from prepared positions near GLOSTER FARM V.20.c.

No casualties were suffered in assembly, which was completed on night 24/25th, with this exception - an Officer and N.C.O. in advancing to assembly position near TRACAS FARM decided to reconnoitre forward, and encountered about 30 of the enemy in consolidated shell holes 50 to 100 yards in front of MEBUS V.31.c.01.65. The N.C.O. was captured and Brigade notified of the man's reliability and that he did not know date or time of operations. He subsequently escaped with a fractured skull, and has been evacuated to C.C.S.

At ZERO the barrage guns opened fire and continued until ZERO plus 2.32, when half the guns were dismounted for cleaning and cooling, and remainder continued to fire at intervals in bursts. Two tripods were destroyed and three casualties suffered during barrage.

On information being received that the whole line was falling back owing to success of counter-attack, the barrage battery was ordered to abandon S.O.S. Lines and lay for direct protection in event of further withdrawal. One gun in front of MEUNIER HOUSE was isolated by withdrawal, and withdrew to MEUNIER HOUSE, and one gun from battery was sent forward to assist in forming a strong point at MEUNIER.

Lines of fire were laid to protect the position in conjunction with three remaining guns of the battery.

The original front line was now practically secure. These guns did not have occasion to fire as the counter-attack on the Right was successfully broken up and repulsed by the Infantry, and the three guns at TRACAS FARM.

As soon as possible the three guns which were detailed to consolidate objective on the Right were ordered to remain at TRACAS FARM MEBUS with the three guns detailed to hold it, and thus form a very strong point. One gun outside TRACAS FARM was damaged by shell splinter. One was inside in reserve, and four guns in action at TRACAS FARM after the counter-attack. These guns under 2nd Lieut. J.R.WALKER and 2/Lieut. W.PITHOUSE repulsed the counter-attack, fired at several attempts to form a line, and dispersed an attempt to form up for another counter-attack. Attempts to communicate with No. 5 gun were unsuccessful.

On the Left sector the Infantry were reported well in rear of the M.Gs. at ZERO plus 100. The latter hung out in forward positions for a further 15 minutes, and then withdrew in four bounds to original positions collecting about half a platoon of Infantry.

Subsequently a party of three horsemen appeared in direction of CAMERON HOUSE about 300 to 400 yards from TRACAS FARM. The Machine Guns at TRACAS FARM immediately opened fire and the horses and riders were apparently killed.

6. **ENEMY COUNTER-ATTACKS.** The first and main counter-attack was launched at 7.20 a.m. all along our front and on our Left flank which, owing to the Right of the Brigade on our Left being held up, was unprotected.
The main points on which this counter-attack developed appeared to be :-
    (a) MEBUS about V.15.a.2.0
    (b) The line of the road from PAPA FARM to WHITECHAPEL through V.21.a.

The enemy covered his advance by first throwing out a line of skirmishers who rapidly developed a hot covering fire, and from the excellence of their shooting it seems probable that these were selected sharpshooters. These sharpshooters did not advance, but as soon as they had opened fire, waves of men extended to about six paces advanced through them. The sharpshooters continued their fire throughout the attack, firing through the advancing waves.

A second counter-attack was launched against our position at V.21.c.0.6 between 4 and 5 p.m., but was repulsed by rifle and M.G. fire.

As a result of these counter-attacks our line was back to positions shown in map "C". Here the enemy advance was checked, on the Right by mixed posts of 2/2nd and 2/4th Bns. and 206th Machine Gun Coy; on the Left by 2/1st and 2/3rd Bns.

7. **INTELLIGENCE.**
  (a) *Enemy M.Gs.* These were definitely located at
      V.15.c.0.8
      V.14.d.9.8
      V.14.d.2.9
      SPIDER X ROADS
      RADIO FARM
      CAMERON HO.
      MORAY HO.

Enemy M.Gs. also developed long distance and barrage fire from position about SPRIET - this fire was exceedingly vigorous and effective, and caused many casualties.

(b) *Wire.* None was encountered, and the wire reported to run along W. side of PAPA FARM - WHITECHAPEL Road could not be observed.

(c) *Entrances to MEBUS.* These were all on the enemy side.

(d) *Passable ground.*
    (i) SPRIET Road and the ground about 150 yards to the E. of it.
    (ii) Road leading N.W. from about V.14.d.3.4
    (iii) Ground between road leading to SPIDER X ROADS and Left Divisional Boundary.

(e) *Concealed enemy works.* There appears to be a camouflaged trench running along the PAPA FARM - WHITECHAPEL Road. Many of the enemy who retired on our advance laboured heavily until they reached the line of this road. They were then seen to jump into a trench and RUN along it. Also when the enemy counter-attacked large numbers of the enemy debouched from this trench, and were all in a comparatively clean condition.

(f) *Trench Mortars.* From the trench mentioned in (e) or its immediate vicinity, a fairly heavy barrage of Light T.M. shells of the pineapple type was fired on the TRAGAS FARM Area during the attack.

8. EQUIPMENT.

(a) For consolidation the large entrenching tools, (i.e.- shovels) were found invaluable. They should not however be carried up by attacking troops but by special parties following them up.

(b) Every man should be given two water-bottles, one of which should be filled with cold tea: this can be warmed up by Tommy's Cookers, whereas if tea is to be made on the spot, it is necessary to <u>boil</u> the water - a difficult task under present conditions.

(c) All rifles and Lewis Guns must be completely covered during an advance. For the rifle the long cover is the most suitable. The Lewis Guns can be wrapped round with sacking. Covering should not be removed until absolutely necessary.

(d) It is suggested that the practice of carrying the P.H. helmet should be discontinued - these speedily became quite useless being sodden with mud and water, and only added unnecessary weight to the already overladen soldier.

9. GENERAL NOTES AND SUGGESTIONS.

(a) Under existing conditions it is considered that 300 to 400 yards is the limit of advance that can be made by the same troops on the same day - and even this should be carried out under an intense barrage and by troops carrying just the bare necessities for fighting, i.e.- water, rifle, bayonet, grenades and ammunition.

It is further considered essential that assaulting troops should advance close under our barrage, and not rely on manoeuvre under their own covering fire as in dry weather.

(b) Attacking troops should be bussed or railed up to the furthest possible point - in the recent operations the long walk from CANAL BANK to the line was a great disadvantage, the majority of the troops being practically exhausted long before ZERO.

(c) It is considered by Units and especially by the Machine Gun Coy. that in the present condition of the ground, a double duckboard track from forward positions to the nearest road or solid ground is essential. One of these tracks should be reserved for incoming and one for outgoing troops. The tracks should not be laid side by side, but at such a distance apart as to ensure their use as one way tracks only.

(d) Casualties in relieving.

2/1st Bn.	2/2nd Bn.	2/3rd Bn.	2/4th Bn.	M.G.Co.	Total
-	15	4	20	-	39

Casualties in assembly up to ZERO.

2/1st Bn.	2/2nd Bn.	2/3rd Bn.	2/4th Bn.	M.G.Co.	Total
-	62	10	30	-	102

Casualties from ZERO to completion of relief

2/1st Bn.	2/2nd Bn.	2/3rd Bn.	2/4th Bn.	M.G.Co.	Total
103	326	378	348	53	1208

Total number of casualties 1349

10. **COMMUNICATIONS.**

(a) <u>Headquarters</u>. The long distance at which VARNA FARM is situated from the Line made forward communications very difficult. The maintenance of long lengths of cable over ground was almost an impossibility, and in consequence heavy work was thrown on runners.

(b) <u>Buried Cable</u>. The Buried Cable System which should have been a great help to communications in front of Brigade Headquarters proved quite the contrary. A direct hit caused a serious breakdown in nearly all communications of the Brigade area, and the alternative ditched cables suffered severely from shell fire. Owing to the hurried take-over on the part of the Division, linesmen had no opportunity of becoming properly acquainted with the lines and test boxes with the result that when the "bury" became dis, confusion reigned for some considerable time.

(c) <u>Visual</u>. Good facilities for visual signalling existed and better results might have been obtained had there been time before the attack to thoroughly reconnoitre the positions and get lamps properly aligned.

(d) <u>Power Buzzer</u> was installed at Battalion Headquarters at V.19.a.7.2 and GLOSTER FARM. The former one was working nearly continuously although the earth wires were cut frequently, but these might have been buried had there been time. The latter one failed to work owing to accommodation for the personnel, GLOSTER FARM being the H.Q. of 2 battalions and Machine Gun Coy., being insufficient.

(e) <u>Pigeons</u>. Pigeons again proved a valuable means of communication, but more are required - each Company should have five - one for each platoon commander and one for Company Commander.

(f) <u>Wireless</u> was not much used, and it was found that runners were a much quicker means of transmission between Brigade and PHEASANT FARM (the places where the two sets were installed), owing to VARNA FARM Station having to work through Corps Directing Station.

(g) <u>Runners</u>. A vast amount of work was thrown on the men owing to the great difficulty of keeping forward lines through. A much larger number was actually required under the existing conditions.

C. J. Graham
2nd Lieut,
A/Brigade Major,
173rd Infantry Brigade.

3/11/17

WAR DIARY

173rd Infantry Brigade November 1917

Army Form C. 2118.

WO/173 July 1917

INTELLIGENCE SUMMARY

(Erase heading not required.)

Place	Date	Hour	Summary of Events and Information	Remarks and references to Appendices
	Nov. 1917			
ST. JANS TER	1st to 4th		ROAD CAMP. Reorganisation, Refitting and Training. 21st Bn London Regt.	
BIEZEN			On working parties in forward areas.	
—	5th		"OPERATION REPORT - OCTOBER 26th 1917" issued.	Appendix A.
—	6th		The Brigade less 21st Bn London Regiment moved to forward area. Brigade Headquarters at BRAKE CAMP. 21st Bn London Regiment moved to SIEGE CAMP and came under orders of 174th Infantry Brigade for duty in LINE.	Appendix B.
BRAKE CAMP	7th		Training.	
—	8th		500 O.R from all Battalions moved to KEMPTON PARK for duty as working parties.	
—	10th		21st Bn London Regiment moved from SIEGE CAMP to CANAL BANK	
—	12th		21st Bn London Regiment moved from CANAL BANK to KEMPTON PARK in KEMPTON PARK	
—			Move to 174th Infantry Brigade	
—	14th		21st Bn London Regiment moved from CANAL BANK to LINE under 174th Infantry Brigade.	
—	15th		Working parties from KEMPTON PARK reformed their units. Brigade less 21st Bn London Regiment relieved by 185th Infantry Brigade and	Appendix C.

Army Form C. 2118.

WAR DIARY
or
INTELLIGENCE SUMMARY.
(Erase heading not required.)

Instructions regarding War Diaries and Intelligence Summaries are contained in F.S. Regs., Part II. and the Staff Manual respectively. Title pages will be prepared in manuscript.

2.

Place	Date	Hour	Summary of Events and Information	Remarks and references to Appendices
	Nov. 1917.			
			moved into P.L. Area PROVEN, Brigade Headquarters at PENGE CAMP.	(In.
PENGE CAMP	16.		Reorganisation & Training. 4/4th Bn London Regiment relieved from the LINE and moved into SIEGE CAMP.	(In.
—	17.		Training. 2/1st Bn London Regiment moved into P.L. Area PROVEN and came under command of 173rd Infantry Brigade.	(In.
—	18/24		Training. Reorganisation.	(In.
—	25.		Brigade transferred to XVIII Corps and moved by train to LUMBRES Area A. Brigade Headquarters at SAMETTE. Transport moved by march route.	Appendix D (In.
LUMBRES A.	26.		Brigade moved to LUMBRES Area C. by road. Brigade Headquarters opened at CHATEAU ALINCTHUN at 10 a.m.	(In.
ALINCTHUN	27/30		Training (Platoon & Company)	(In.

SECRET.　　　　　　　　　　　　　　　　　　　　　　Copy No...... 19.

173RD INFANTRY BRIGADE ORDER NUMBER 45.

Ref. Maps:- Sheets 27 N.E. and 28 N.W.
　　　　　　　Both 1/20,000.

29/10/17.

1. The Brigade less 2/1st Bn. London Regt. and 1 Section, 208th Machine Gun Coy., will move to ROAD CAMP to-morrow, 30th inst.

2. Personnel will proceed by Rail and Transport by Road under arrangements to be made by Staff Captain.

3. 2/1st Bn. London Regt. will proceed by March Route to-morrow, 30th inst., to KEMPTON PARK completing move by 5 p.m. On arrival there they will be employed on Working Parties details of which have been already issued.

　　　　　　　　　　　　　　　　　　　　for Captain,
　　　　　　　　　　　　　　　　　　　　Brigade Major,
　　　　　　　　　　　　　　　　　　　173rd Infantry Brigade.

Issued to Signals at .. 7.30 p.

Copy. No.

1. 2/1st Bn. London Regt.
2. 2/2nd Bn. London Regt.
3. 2/3rd Bn. London Regt.
4. 2/4th Bn. London Regt.
5. 173rd L. T. M. Batty.
6. 208th Machine Gun Coy.
7. 510th H.T. Co. A.S.C.
8. 504th Field Coy. R.E.
9. 174th Infantry Brigade.
10. 175th Infantry Brigade.
11. "G" 58th Division.
12. "A" & "Q" 58th Division.
13. S. S. O.
14. Brigade Major for G.O.C.
15. Staff Captain.
16. Brigade Signalling Officer.
17. Brigade Intelligence Officer.
18. Brigade Transport Officer.
19. War Diary.
20. War Diary.
21. File.
22. Camp Commandant.

SECRET.   Copy No. 20.

173RD INFANTRY BRIGADE ORDER NUMBER 46.

Reference Maps:- Sheet 27 and Sheet 28.

November 5th 1917.

---

1. The Brigade less 2/1st London Regt. will move to Camps in A.16.(Sheet 28) on 6th November, 1917.

2. Units will move by road in the following order and by the following Route.
    Intervals of 500 yards between Battalions and 200 yards between Companies will be maintained. East of BRAKE CAMP units will march in file.   First Line Transport will move independently under orders of Battalion Commanders concerned.
    ROUTE:-
        NORTH SWITCH RD - A.26.b. - MILITARY RD.

    ORDER OF MARCH:-

    Bde. Hd. Qtrs. pass Starting Point (Bde.Hd.Qtrs.) 8.45 am.

    2/3rd Lon. Regt.   "   "   "   "   "   "   9.0 am.

    2/2nd Lon. Regt.   "   "   "   "   "   "   9.10 am.

    2/4th Lon. Regt.   "   "   "   "   "   "   9.20 am.

    206th M.G.Co.)
    173rd L.T.M.B.)   "   "   "   "   "   "   9.30 am.

3. Brigade Headquarters will close at ROAD CAMP at 8.45 a.m. and will reopen at the same hour at BRAKE CAMP.

ADMINISTRATIVE   INSTRUCTIONS.

DISTRIBUTION. The Brigade will be distributed in the new area as follows:-

    Brigade Headquarters.   BRAKE CAMP.
    2/1st Bn. London Regt.   SIEGE CAMP (under orders
                                        of 174th Inf. Bde.)
    2/2nd Bn. London Regt.   FX CAMP.
    2/3rd Bn. London Regt.   BRAKE CAMP.
    2/4th Bn. London Regt.   P CAMP.
    206th Machine Gun Coy.)
    173rd L. T. M. Batty.)   S CAMP.

ADVANCE PARTIES. O.C. Units will detail a small advance party to report to Camp Commandants at the various camps to take over camps and Transport Lines.

LORRIES ETC.   Two Lorries per Battalion, one for Machine Gun Coy. and one for Light T. M. Batty. will report at Brigade Headquarters at 7 a.m. to-morrow.   Units will have guides at Brigade Headquarters at this hour to take same over.
    The usual Baggage Wagons will report on the evening of the 5th inst.

RATIONS.   Rations for consumption on the 7th inst, WILL BE delivered in the new area.

REAR PARTY.   Each Unit will detail a small rear party to clean up Camp, a certificate will be obtained from Camp Adjutant (Near Brigade Headquarters) that camps have been left in a clean and sanitary condition and forwarded in duplicate to Brigade Headquarters.

C.J. Graham
2/Lieut.,
A/Brigade Major,
173rd Infantry Brigade.

Issued to Signals at ......

Copy No.
1. 2/1st Bn. London Regt.
2. 2/2nd Bn. London Regt.
3. 2/3rd Bn. London Regt.
4. 2/4th Bn. London Regt.
5. 173rd L. T. M. Batty.
6. 206th Machine Gun Coy.
7. 510th H.T. Co. A.S.C.
8. 504th Field Coy. R.E.
9. 174th Infantry Brigade.
10. 175th Infantry Brigade.
11. "Q" 58th Division.
12. "A" & "Q" 58th Division.
13. S. S. O. 58th Division.
14. Brigade Major for G.O.C.
15. Staff Captain.
16. Brigade Signalling Officer.
17. Brigade Transport Officer.
18. Brigade Intelligence Officer.
19. War Diary.
20. War Diary.
21. File.
22. Camp Commandant, Road Camp.

173RD INFANTRY BRIGADE ORDER NO. 47

No 23

SECRET

13th November, 1917

1. The Brigade is to be relieved by the 105th Infantry Brigade and their Machine Gun Coy., relief taking place on the 14th and 15th instant.

2. On relief the Brigade Group will be composed as follows :-
   - 2/2nd Bn. London Regt.
   - 2/3rd   Do.
   - 2/4th   Do.
   - 2/6th   Do.
   - 206th M.G.Coy. (less 1 Section)
   - 214th M.G.Coy.

3. The Brigade will move on the 15th inst. to the PROVEN Area by road.

4. The 2/1st Bn. London Regt. will move under the orders of the 174th Inf. Bde., and the 173rd L.T.M.Battery will move with the 504 Field Coy. R.E., and will not rejoin the Brigade until after the arrival of the Field Coy. in the Back Area.

5. Times of moves, route, and order of march, will be announced later.

C. J. Graham
2/Lieut.
A/Brigade Major,
173rd Infantry Brigade.

ADMINISTRATIVE INSTRUCTIONS

DISTRIBUTION — Distribution in new area will be announced later.

ADVANCE PARTIES — Os.C., Units will be prepared to send Advance Parties on the morning of the 15th to take over Camps, location of which will be notified later.

LORRIES ETC. — 10 Lorries will report at Bde. H.Q., BRAKE CAMP, at 7 a.m., 15th inst., and are allotted as follows :-
- Bde. H.Q. .... One
- 2/2nd Bn. .... Two
- 2/3rd Bn. .... Two
- 2/4th Bn. .... Two
- 2/6th Bn. .... Two
- 206th M.G.Coy.)
- 173rd L.T.M.B.) ..... One (to be shared)

Os.C. Units will arrange for guides to be at Bde.H.Q. at 7 a.m. to take over lorries.
The usual Baggage Wagons will report to units on the afternoon of the 14th inst.

RATIONS — Rations for consumption on the 16th inst. will be delivered in the new area.

REAR — Each unit will detail a small rear party to clean up Camp; a certificate will be obtained from Camp Adjutant that Camps have been left in a clean and sanitary condition, and forwarded to Bde. H.Q.

J.H. Ganaway
Captain,
Staff Captain,
173rd Infantry Brigade.

Copy No.
1. 2/1st London Regt.
2. 2/2nd London Regt.
3. 2/3rd London Regt.
4. 2/4th London Regt.
5. 173rd L.T.M. Battery
6. 206th M.G.Coy.
7. 2/6th London Regt.
8. 510 H.T.Coy. A.S.C.
9. 504 Field Coy. R.E.
10. 174th Inf. Bde.
11. 175th Inf. Bde.
12. 58th Division "G"
13. 58th Division "A" & "Q"
14. 214th M.G.Coy.
15. S.S.O.
16. Camp Commandant, BRAKE CAMP
17. Brigade Major for G.O.C.
18. Staff Captain
19. Bde. Signalling Officer
20. Bde. Transport Officer
21. Bde. Intelligence Officer
22. 105th Inf. Bde.
23. War Diary
24. War Diary
25. File

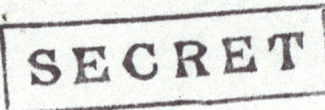

Reference 173rd Infantry Brigade Order No. 47.
Administrative Instructions - 13/11/17.

DISTRIBUTION will be as follows:-

AREA. P2. (PROVEN).

Brigade Headquarters.	-	PENGE CAMP.
2/2nd Bn. London Regt.	-	PADDINGTON CAMP.
2/3rd Bn. London Regt.	-	PUTNEY CAMP.
2/4th Bn. London Regt.	-	PICCADILY CAMP.
2/6th Bn. London Regt.	-	PEGWORTH CAMP.
206th Machine Gun Coy.	-	PLAISTOW CAMP.
214rh Machine Gun Coy.	-	PARTRIDGE CAMP.
173rd L. T. M. Batty.	-	PRAED CAMP.

Map attached.

Advance Parties should be sent off early to take over from units now occupying above Camps.

14/11/17.

J.H. Garraway,
Captain,
Staff Captain,
173rd Infantry Brigade.

Copy to all recipients of 173rd Inf. Bde. Order No.47.

SECRET

173RD INFANTRY BRIGADE

MARCH TABLE ISSUED WITH ORDER NO. 47.

14/11/17.

Ref. Map Sheets 27 & 28, and attached Map.

Serial No.	Unit.	From.	To.	Time passing Starting Point	Route.	Remarks.
1.	Bde. H.Q.	BRAKE CAMP.	PERGE CAMP.	9.30 a.m.	MILITARY ROAD to INTERNATIONAL CORNER (A.9.a.2.4)	STARTING POINT – Junction of MILITARY ROAD and PESELHOEK – WORSTEN Road in A.16.a. Transport will move with units 200 yards in rear of each column. 500 yards distance will be maintained between Battalions and 100 yards between Coys. Particular attention will be paid to March Discipline as ordered in this office No. Bm.17/525/1 dated 10/10/17. The Brigade Labour Coy. will move with and be accommodated by 2/4th Bn. Lon. Regt. and Bde. Sniping Section will move with and be accommodated by the 2/3rd Bn. London Regt.
2.	2/4th Bn.	P. CAMP.	PICCADILLY CAMP	9.35 a.m.		
3.	2/3rd Bn.	BRAKE CAMP.	PUTNEY CAMP	9.47 a.m.	MILITARY ROAD to F.21. sheet 27. to No.2. Area PROVEN as shown on the attached Map.	
4.	2/2nd Bn.	FX. CAMP.	PADDINGTON CAMP.	9.59 a.m.		
5.	2/6th Bn.	BRAKE CAMP.	PEGWORTH.	10.11 a.m.		
6.	214th M.G. Coy.	S. CAMP.	PARTRIDGE CAMP.	10.20 a.m.		
7.	206th M.G. Co.	S. CAMP	PLAISTOW CAMP	10.27 a.m.		

PERGE CAMP   Sheet 19.– X.27.a.4.6.
PICCADILLY CAMP.   Sheet 19.– X.20.d.5.3.
PUTNEY CAMP.   Sheet 19.– X.27.a.2.1.
PADDINGTON CAMP.   Sheet 27.– F.3.a.05.15.
PEGWORTH.   Sheet 19.– X.25.d.3.5.
PARTRIDGE CAMP   Sheet 19.– X.26.c.05.30.
PLAISTOW CAMP.   Sheet 27.– F.9.a.15.90.

ACKNOWLEDGE.-

Issued to all recipients of 173rd Inf. Bde. Order No. 47.

C. J. Graham
2/Lieut.
A/Brigade Major,
173rd Infantry Brigade.

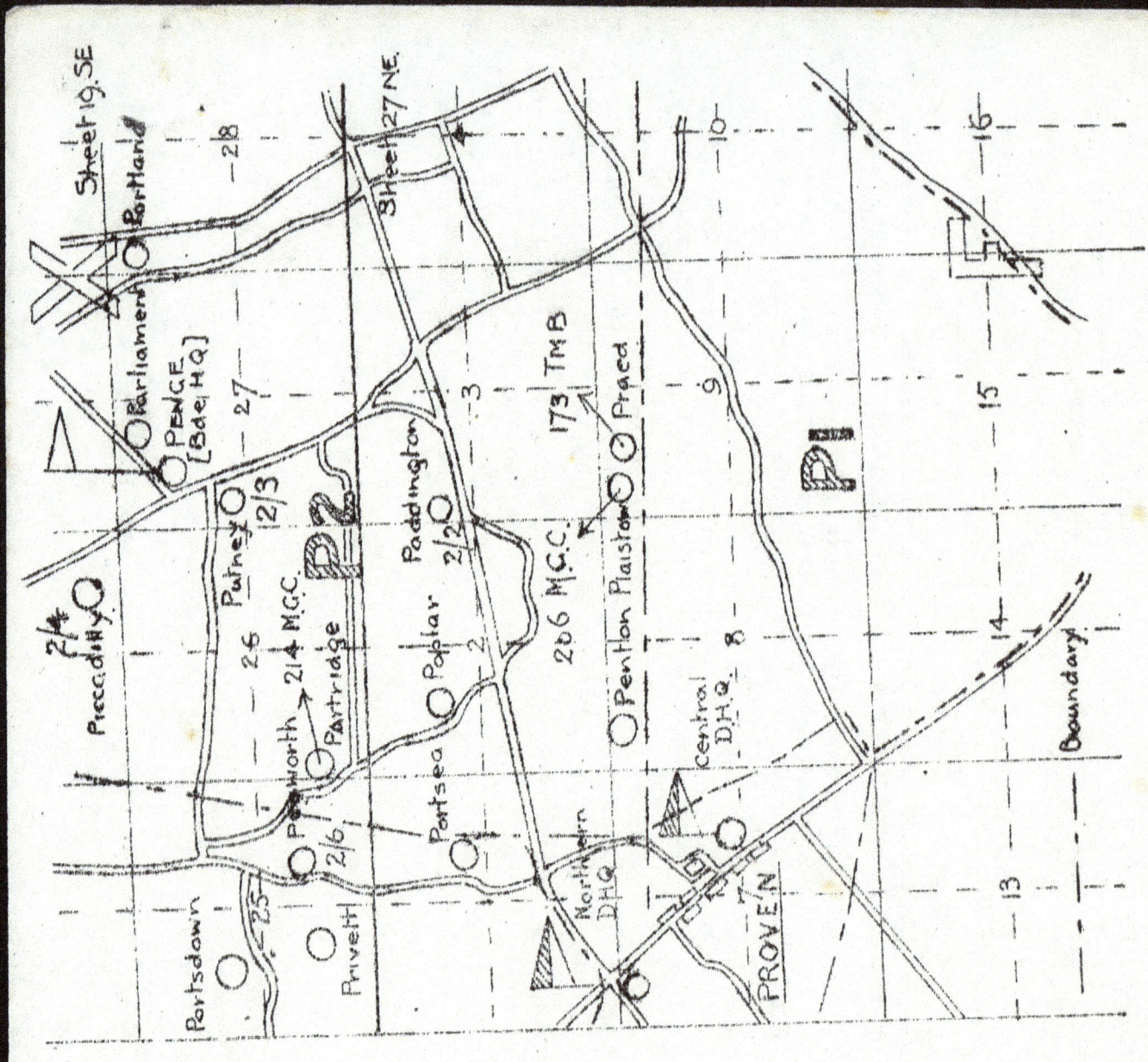

S E C R E T.   Copy No. 20

173RD INFANTRY BRIGADE ORDER NUMBER 48.

Reference Maps - HAZEBROUCK AND CALAIS.

November 24th 1917.

---

1. The Brigade will be transferred from the XIX Corps to the XVIII Corps (LUMBRES AREA) in accordance with Administrative Instructions and attached Tables.
2. For the purpose of this Move the Brigade Group will be composed as follows:-

Brigade Headquarters.	206th Machine Gun Coy.
2/1st London Regt.	173rd L. T. M. Batty.
2/2nd London Regt. & .	2/1st H.C. Field Amblce.
2/3rd London Regt.	504th Field Coy. R. E.
2/4th London Regt.	510th H.T. Co. A.S.C.

3. The Brigade Transport will move by road throughout as detailed by Staff Captain.
4. Personnel will move on the 25th inst. by Train to WIZERNES, thence to LUMBRES Area "A", where they will find their Transport and be Billetted for Night 25/26 November. On the 26th inst. Personnel and Transport will move to Area "C".
5. The Brigade Snipers Company will move under the orders of and be rationed till further notice by the 2/3rd Bn. Lon. Rgt.
6. Brigade Headquarters will close at PENGE CAMP at 11.0 AM and re-open at SAMETTE at Noon on 25th inst. closing at 10.AM on 26th and re-opening at CHATEAU D'ALINCTHUN at Same hour,
7. ACKNOWLEDGE.

                                        C.J. Graham
                                          2/Lieut.,
                                        A/Brigade Major,
                                      173rd Infantry Brigade.

Issued to Signals at ....

Copy No.
1.	2/1st Bn. Lon. Regt.	13.	S.S.O. 58th Division.
2.	2/2nd Bn. Lon. Regt.	14.	Camp Commandant.
3.	2/3rd Bn. Lon. Regt.	15.	Brigade Major for G.O.C.
4.	2/4th Bn. Lon. Regt.	16.	Staff Captain.
5.	173rd L. T. M. Batty.	17.	Bde. Signalling Officer.
6.	206th Machine Gun Coy.	18.	Bde. Transport Officer.
7.	510 Coy. A.S.C.	19.	Bde. Intelligence Offr.
8.	504 Field Coy. R.E.	20.	War Diary.
9.	174th Infantry Bde.	21.	War Diary.
10.	175th Infantry Bde.	22.	File.
11.	58th Division "G".	23.	2/1st Home Counties Field Ambulance.
12.	58th Division "A" and "Q".		

MOVE TABLE ISSUED WITH 173RD INFANTRY BRIGADE ORDER NO. 48.

SERIAL NO.	DATE.	UNIT.	FROM.	TO.	METHOD.	ROUTE.	REMARKS.	DETAIL OF BILLETS FROM.
1.	24th. Nov.	Brigade Transport.	PROVEN.	ST MOMELIN	March.	HOUTKERQUE - WORMHOUDT - ZEGGERS CAPPEL - LEDERZEELE.	To reach WORMHOUDT at 12 noon.	Town Major, ST MOMELIN.
2.	25th.	Serial 1.	ST MOMELIN	LUMBRES AREA "A"	March.	ST OMER - TATTINGHEM.	To reach ST OMER 11 a.m. - In LUMBRES Sub-area "A" Transport will rejoin its own units and move with them on 26th inst.	From Advance Parties of units in area.
3.	25th.	173rd Bde. Hd. Qtrs.	PROVEN.	SAMETTE.	Rail & March.	SERQUES - LUMBRES.	Detraining Station WIZERNES. Transport will rejoin its unit in their Billeting Area and proceed with them on the 26th to their Billets in Sub-Area "C".	Advance Party.
4.	25th.	2/4th Bn. Ln. Regt.	PROVEN.	GOULOMBY	Rail & March.	SERQUES - LUMBRES - BAYENGHEM - SENINGHEM.	Same as Serial 3.	Advance Party.
5.	25th.	2/1st Bn. Ln. Regt.	PROVEN.	SENINGHEM	Rail & March.	SERQUES - LUMBRES - BAYENGHEM.	Same as Serial 3.	Advance Party.
6.	25th.	2/2nd Bn. Ln. Regt.	PROVEN.	SENINGHEM & AFFRINGUES	Rail & March.	SERQUES - LUMBRES - BAYENGHEM.	Same as Serial 3.	Advance Party.

PAGE 2 of MOVE TABLE ISSUED WITH BRIGADE
ORDER NO. 48.

SERIAL NO.	DATE. NOV.	UNIT.	FROM.	TO.	METHOD.	ROUTE.	REMARKS.	DETAIL OF BILLETS FROM.
7.	25th.	2/3rd Bn. Ln. Regt.	PROVEN.	BAYENGHEM	Rail & March.	SERGUES – LUMBRES.	Same as for Serial 3.	Advance Party.
8.	25th.	206th M. Gun Coy. and 173rd L. T.M.Bty.	PROVEN.	AFFRINGUES	Rail & March.	SERGUES – LUMBRES – BAYENGHEM.	Same as for Serial 3.	Advance Party.
9.	25th.	2/1st H. C. Field Ambce.	PROVEN.	LART.	Rail & March.	SERGUES – LUMBRES – BAYENGHEM – AFFRINGUES.	Same as for Serial 3.	Advance Party.
10.	25th.	504 Field Coy. R.E.	PROVEN.	LUMBRES Sub Area "A".	Rail & March.	Any.	Same as for Serial 3.	Area Commandant, LUMBRES.

Note:- Move Table for move from Sub-Area "A" to Sub-Area "C" will be issued later.

TABLE "B" ISSUED WITH 173rd INFANTRY BRIGADE
ORDER NUMBER 46.

SERIAL NO.	UNIT.	Date Nov.	FROM.	TO.	Leave camp.	ROUTE.	REMARKS.
5.	173rd Bde. Hd. Qrs.	26th.	SAMETTE.	Gateau D'ALINCERUE.	10.10 a.m.	Direct.	O.C. Battalions will be notified later which Bn. is "A" – "B" – "C" and "D" etc. and time of departure from Camp.
4.	"A" Battn. 2/4 BN.	26th.	"A" Area.	(GREHARAST BELLEERUE	10 am	Direct.	
5.							
6.	"B" Battn. 2/4 BN.	26th.	"A" Area.	HENEEVEUX.	10 am	Direct.	
7.	"C" Battn. 2/3 BN.	26th.	"A" Area.	(ALINCTHUN. (LE WAST.	10.20 am	Direct.	Transport will in all cases accompany their respective units.
	"D" Battn. 2/2 BN.	26th.	"A" Area.	BOURNONVILLE (SURQUES. (ESCOEUILLES.	10.15 am	Direct.	
8.	173rd L. T.M.Bty.	26th.	AFFRINGUES	NABRINGHEM.	10 a.m.	Direct.	
8a.	206th M. Gun Coy.	26th.	AFFRINGUES	BRUNEMBERT.	10.5 a.m.	Direct.	
9.	2/1st H. G.Fld.Amb.	26th.	LART.	BRUNEMBERT.	10 a.m.	Direct.	
10.	504 Fld.Co. R.E.	26th.	SAMETTE.	COLEMBER.	10.12 a.m.	Direct.	
11.	510 H.T. Co.A.S.C.	26th.	SAMETTE	LONGUEVILLE ALINCTHUN.	under own arrangements.		

Note:- Serial Numbers are same as those in Other Move Table issued.

173RD INFANTRY BRIGADE

ADMINISTRATIVE INSTRUCTION NO. 19

(Issued in connection with 173rd Inf. Bde. Order No. 48)

---oOo---

24th November, 1917.

The attached table shews the train arrangements for the move from PROVEN to WIZERNES.

Transport of all units will proceed by road.

ENTRAINING OFFICER Capt. B.J. BARTON, 2/2nd London Regt. will act as Entraining Officer, reporting to the R.T.O., PROVEN, at 10 a.m., 25th inst. for instructions. He will travel on the last train. He will wear a white brassard 5" wide on the right arm.

UNIT REPRESENTATIVES Each unit entraining will send a representative to report to the Entraining Officer for instructions half an hour before the arrival of the unit at the Station.

ENTRAINING STATES Entraining States in duplicate will be handed by the Unit's representative to the Entraining Officer, who will pass one to the R.T.O., and forward duplicate to these Headquarters on completion of move.

TIME OF ARRIVAL AT ENTRAINING STATION Troops will arrive at PROVEN Station 1 hour before departure of train.

DETRAINING OFFICER Lieut. S.G. ASKHAM, 2/4th London Regt. will act as Bde. Detraining Officer. He will proceed by the first train, and on arrival at the Detraining Stn. (WIZERNES) will report to R.T.O. for instructions. This officer will also wear a white brassard on right arm.

FIELD COOKERS & WATER CARTS Field Cookers and Water Carts still remaining with units will proceed by road under orders of Brigade Transport Officer.
They will pass the entrance to PENTON CAMP (Sheet 27 F.2.c.3.8) at 8.30 a.m., with the exception of those from 2/1st Bn. which will join the column at Road Junction S. of 19th milestone PROVEN – POPERINGHE Road (Sheet HAZEBROUCK) at 8.50 a.m.

BLANKETS One blanket per man will be carried on the man to WIZERNES, from whence they will be conveyed to "A" Area by lorry.
The second blanket will be conveyed by lorry direct to Area "C".

LORRIES Lorries are allotted as under :-
```
           2/1st Bn. ............. 2
           2/2nd Bn. ............. 2
           2/3rd Bn. ............. 2
           2/4th Bn. ............. 2
           504 Fd. Coy. R.E. .... 1
           206th M.G.Coy.)
           173rd L.T.M.B.)....... 1 for joint use
```

Lorries will report to these Headquarters at 6 a.m. 25th inst. Units concerned will send a guide to meet them

2.

LORRIES
(Contd)
The lorries will first be loaded with such stores as are required to proceed by the train from PROVEN STN.
On completion of this journey they will return and be loaded with blankets and stores detailed to proceed direct to new Area "C".
One officer and one N.C.O. of each Unit proceeding on the lorry to Area "C" will ascertain from Area Commandant, LUMBRES, the location of their unit in Area "C" as arranged by Staff Captain.
2 lorries only will meet each train at WIZERNES STN. and convey stores and blankets to Area "A".

STORES
Stores which cannot be carried on the lorries proceeding direct to Area "C" will be carried by train.

CAMPS
Certificates that the Camps have been left in a clean and sanitary condition will be forwarded to this office.

MARCH DISCIPLINE
Os.C. Units will forward to Bde. Headquarters on arrival at Area "C" a statement shewing numbers of men who fall out on the march for each day.

H. J. King
Lieut.
for Staff Captain,
173rd Infantry Brigade.

3.

TIME TABLE OF TRAINS

Train No.	Unit	Depart PROVEN	Detrain WIZERNES
1 " " "	Bde. H.Q.) 2/1st Bn.) 2/4th Bn.) 504 Fd.Coy. R.E.)	12 noon 25th inst.	About 3. 0 p.m. 25th inst.
2 " " " " "	2/2nd Bn.) 2/3rd Bn.) 206th M.G.Coy.) 173rd L.T.M.B.) 2/1st H.C.Fd.Amb.) Bde. Sniper Sec.)	1. 0 p.m. 25th inst.	About 4. 0 p.m. 25th inst.

****

DISTRIBUTION

The Distribution of the Brigade Group in the new area will be as follows :-

Area "A" - 25th inst.		Area "C" - 26th inst.	
Bde. H.Q.	SAMETTE	Bde. H.Q.	CHATEAU D'ALINCTHUN
2/1st Bn.	SENINGHEM	2/1st Bn.	To be notified later
2/2nd Bn.	SENINGHEM & AFFRINGUES	2/2nd Bn.	Do. do.
2/3rd Bn.	BAYENGHEM	2/3rd Bn.	Do. do.
2/4th Bn.	COULEMBY	2/4th Bn.	Do. do.
206th M.G.Coy. ..	AFFRINGUES	206th M.G.Coy.	BRUNEMBERT
173rd L.T.M.B. ..	AFFRINGUES	173rd L.T.M.B.	NABRINGHEM
2/1st H.C.Fd.Amb.	LART	2/1st H.C.Fd.Amb	BRUNEMBERT
504 Fd.Coy. R.E.)	To be notified	504 Fd.Coy.R.E.	To be notified later
510 Coy. A.S.C.)	later	510 Coy. A.S.C.	LONGUEVILLE

RAILHEAD from 27th instant   -   LUMBRES

****

On His Majesty's Service.

D. A. G.

Army Form C. 2118.

173rd Inf. BDE. WAR DIARY December 1917

Instructions regarding War Diaries and Intelligence Summaries are contained in F.S. Regs., Part II. and the Staff Manual respectively. Title pages will be prepared in manuscript.

INTELLIGENCE SUMMARY.
(Erase heading not required.)

Place	Date	Hour	Summary of Events and Information	Remarks and references to Appendices
ALLOUGNE	1/12 to 5/12		Training (musketry on ranges + recreational training).	
to	7/12/17		173rd Bde. Group Training – Roulyhan move from Area C to LUMBRES area H	
	8th		Brigade H.Q. closes 10.30 am at ALINCTHUN Chateau + opens SAMETTE + near Remonville. 6 Bns. ilk men from Area C to Area H.	
SAMETTE				
WHITE MILL CAMP	9th		Bde H.Q. closes + opens + SAMETTE + opens 4 pm at WHITE MILL Camp. Brigade garrisons WIZERNES + obtain EVERDINGE 1/1st Bn to White Mill Camp. 2/2nd Bn to Bridge Camp No 1. 2/3rd Bn to Bridge Camp No 2. 1/4th Bn to Scott Camp. 2/6 Holding to the REAR Camp. 173 A.T.M.B. to Belleau Camp.	
	10th to 15th		Training. Divisional Scheme of the time.	

Army Form C. 2118.

Instructions regarding War Diaries and Intelligence Summaries are contained in F. S. Regs., Part II. and the Staff Manual respectively. Title pages will be prepared in manuscript.

WAR DIARY
or
INTELLIGENCE SUMMARY.
(Erase heading not required.)

Place	Date	Hour	Summary of Events and Information	Remarks and references to Appendices
LINE	16th		Brigade relieve 75th Inf. Bde in the line on the night of 16/17.	A
	17th		Bde H.Q. etc while Mell Camps topping at VARNA Fm.	A
			2/1st Bn. Right out sector.	A
			2/2nd Bn. Right centre (KEMPTON). 2/4th Bn. left support (Cond.)	A
			2/3rd Bn. left out sector.	A
	18th		73rd Bn captured 2 prisoners of 7th H.B. NURTENBURGER Regt.	A
	19th		E.A drawn down 1000 x N.E PERONCHEUS.	
	20th		During night 20th/21st enter Battalion relief.	
	21st		2/2nd Bn. relieved by 2/1st Bn. 2/4th Bn relieved 2/3rd Bn. MEUNIER Fm	B
			Hostile artillery on the increase, especially normal counter-battery work effectively	
	22nd		Our guns engaged enemy in counter battery V10 6 - 7.4.	C
			5 enemy O.P's located in	
	23rd		Enemy put down barrage at 4.10 pm. No infantry action followed.	
			On our front except mean GRAVEL Fm and on left Div. front.	
			Our barrage came down promptly on the S.O.S being sent up at 4.18 pm.	
			No enemy succeeded in reaching our left posts.	

Army Form C. 2118.

WAR DIARY
or
INTELLIGENCE SUMMARY.
(Erase heading not required.)

Place	Date	Hour	Summary of Events and Information	Remarks and references to Appendices
Line	24		Enemy artillery quieter. Usual night patrolling	MGA
	24th to 25th		The Brigade was relieved on the night of 24/25th by	UCK
			175th Inf Bde.	
	25th		Command of Dis[t]rict passes to G.O.C 175th Bde 11.0 am	RFA
	26th to 31st		Refitting, cleaning. Training	

Instructions regarding War Diaries and Intelligence Summaries are contained in F.S. Regs., Part II. and the Staff Manual respectively. Title pages will be prepared in manuscript.

SECRET.   Copy No...21...

173rd INFANTRY BRIGADE ORDER NUMBER 49.

Ref. Maps:—   CALAIS — 1/100,000 and
               HAZEBROUCK — 1/100,000.

December 5th 1917.

1. The 58th Division less Artillery is to relieve the 35th Division less Artillery in the left Sector II Corps Front.

2. The Front to be occupied by the 58th Division extends from V.28.a.6.6. on the right to the BROEMBEEK in V.7.b. exclusive on the left.
    The Right Boundary will be notified later.
    The Left Boundary will run from the BROEMBEEK in V.7.b. — U.17.d.7.9. thence along STADEN — YPRES Railway inclusive to 58th Division.
    The 32nd Division, II Corps, is holding the Sector on the right and the 18th Division, XIX Corps the Sector on the left of the 58th Division.

3. The 173rd Infantry Brigade will on completion of relief be in Divisional Reserve with Headquarters at SIEGE CAMP.

4. The 173rd Infantry Brigade will move to SIEGE CAMP in accordance with Administrative Instructions attached and the attached move table.

5. On the March the following intervals will be maintained:—

	(Battalions.	500 yards.
	(Companies.)	
Between	(Unit & its Transport.)	100 yards.
	((Transport of each)	
	((unit when Brigaded.)	

East of VLAMERTINGHE — ELVERDINGHE ROAD all movements will be in file.

6. Transport less portion detailed in Administrative Instructions will be Brigaded and Move by road under Command of Captain Pago, 2/2nd Bn. London Regt. on the 7th inst.

7. 173rd Bde. Hd. Qtrs. will close at CHATEAU D'ALINGTHUN at 10.30 a.m. on 8th opening at SANETTE at noon same day, closing at 9 a.m. on the 9th and opening at SIEGE CAMP at 4 p.m. on the same day.

8. ACKNOWLEDGE.

                                         C J Graham 2/L
                                         Captain,
Issued to Signals at ......p.m.   Brigade Major,
                                         173rd Infantry Brigade.

Copy No.   Copy No.
 1. 2/1st Bn. London Regt.   14. S.S.O. 58th Division.
 2. 2/2nd Bn. London Regt.   15. Area Commandant.
 3. 2/3rd Bn. London Regt.   16. Brigade Major for G.O.C.
 4. 2/4th Bn. London Regt.   17. Staff Captain.
 5. 173rd L.T.M. Batty.   18. Bde. Sig. Officer.
 6. 206th Machine Gun Coy.   19. Bde. Transport Officer.
 7. 504th Field Coy. R.E.   20. Bde. Intelligence Officer.
 8. 2/1st H.C. Field Amb.   21. War Diary.
 9. 510th Coy. A.S.C.   22. War Diary.
10. 174th Inf. Bde.   23. File.
11. 175th Inf. Bde.   24. Div. Graves Officer.
12. 58th Division. "G".   25. Div. Salvage Coy.
13. 58th Division "A" & "Q".   26. 209th Employment Coy.

P.T.O

MOVE TABLE ISSUED WITH 173RD INFANTRY BDE. ORDER NO. 49.

SERIAL NO.	DATE. DEC	FORMATION.	FROM.	TO.	ROUTE.	REMARKS.
1.	7th.	510 Co. A.S.C. & 173rd Bde. Group Transport - Road Portion.	Area "C"	LUMBRES	ESCOEUILLES HARLETTES.	Billets from Area Commandant LUMBRES. Order of March, Starting Point etc. See Administrative Instructions.
2.	8th.	2/1st H.C.F.A.	BRUNEMBERT	LART	Via BOULOGNE - ST OMER Road.	Move off from BRUNEMBER 10 a.m.
3.	8th.	206th M.G. Co.	BRUNEMBERT	AFFRINGUES	As for Serial 2.	Move off from BRUNEMBERT 10.10 a.m.
4.	8th.	173rd L.T.M.Bty.	NABRINGHEM	AFFRINGUES	As for Serial 2.	Move off from NABRINGHEM 9.35 a.m.
5.	8th.	504 F.Co. R.E.	COLOMBERT.	SAMETTE	As for Serial 2.	Move off from COLOMBERT 9.30 a.m.
6.	8th.	2/3rd Lon. Rgt.	LE WAST.	BAYINGHEM.	As for Serial 2.	Move off from LE WAST 9.10 a.m.
7.	8th.	2/1st Lon. Rgt.	HENNEVEUX.	SENINGHEM.	As for Serial 2.	Move off from HENNEVEUX. 10.30 a.m.
8.	8th.	2/2nd Lon. Rgt.	BOURNONVILLE	AFFRINGUES & SENINGHEM.	Via - QUESQUES.	Move off from BOURNONVILLE 10 a.m.
9.	8th.	2/4th Lon. Rgt.	BELLEBRUNE & CREMAREST.	COULOMBY.	Via - QUESQUES.	Move off from CREMAREST 10 a.m.

Page 2 of Move Table issued with 173rd Bde. Order No. 49.

SERIAL NO.	DATE DEC	FORMATION	FROM.	TO.	ROUTE.	REMARKS.
10.	9th.	Serial No.1.	LUMBRES	ST. MOMELIN.	TATTINGHEM - ST OMER.	Billets from Area Commandant ST MOMELIN.
11.	9th.	Serial No.1.	ST. MOMELIN	ST JANTER BIEZEN "B" AREA.	LEDERREELE - ZEGGERS CAPPEL - WORMHOUDT.	Billots from "B" Area Commandant.
12.	9th.	2/3rd Bn. with Train Portion Transport.	BAYENGHEM	SIEGE CAMP	Road to WIZERNES Rail to ELVERDINGHE Personnel Train No.1. Transport Train No.3.	Pass Junction with Main Road at 2.45 a.m.
13.	9th.	504th Fld. Co. R.E. with Train Portion of Transport.	SAMETTE.	As ordered by C. R. E.	As for Serial 12.	Pass Cross Roads East of S. in LUMBRES at 3.30 a.m.
14.	9th.	2/2nd Bn with Train portion of Transport.	AFFRINGUES & SENNINGHEM	SIEGE CAMP.	As for Serial 12.	Pass Road Junction south of M in BAYENGHEM at 2.50 a.m.
15.	9th.	206th M.G. Coy.with Train Portion of Transport.	AFFRINGUES	SIEGE CAMP	As for Serial 12.	Pass AFFRINGUES CHURCH 2.50 a.m.
16.	9th.	173rd L. T. M. Bty. with handcarts and guns.	AFFRINGUES	SIEGE CAMP	Road to WIZERNES Train No.3. to VLAMERTINGHE.	Pass AFFRINGUES CHURCH 3.40 a.m.
17.	9th.	Train Transport of 2/1st H.C.F.A.	LART.	As ordered by A.D.M.S.	As for Serial 16.	Join NIELLES - SAMETTE Rd. at 3.25 a.m.

P.T.O.

Page 3 of Move Table issued with 173rd Bde. Order No.49.

SERIAL NO.	DATE. DEC	FORMATION	FROM.	TO.	ROUTE.	REMARKS.
18.	9th.	Train Transport of 2/1st Lon. Rgt.	SENNINGHEM	SIEGE CAMP	As for Serial 16.	Pass SENNINGHEM CHURCH at 3.40 a.m.
19.	9th.	Train Transport of 2/4th Lon. Regt.	COULOMBY.	SIEGE CAMP	As for Serial 16.	Pass COULOMBY CHURCH at 3.20 a.m.
20.	9th.	2/1st R.C.F. Amb.	LART	As ordered by A.D.M.S	Road to IVZERNES. Train to ELVERDINGHE Train No. 2.	Join NIELLES - SAMETTE ROAD at 5.55 a.m.
21.	9th.	2/1st Bn. Lon. Rgt.	SENNINGHEM	SIEGE CAMP	As Serial No. 20.	Pass SENNINGHEM CHURCH at 6.10 a.m.
22.	9th.	2/4th Bn. Lon. Rgt.	COULOMBY.	SIEGE CAMP	As Serial No. 20.	Pass COULOMBY CHURCH at 5.55 a.m.
23.	9th.	Div.Employment Coy. Div. Salvage Coy. and Burials Party.	NIELLES LES BLEQUIN.	?	As Serial No. 20.	Move off 5.30 a.m.
24.	9th.	173rd Bde. H. Q.	SAMETTE.	SIEGE CAMP.	As Serial No. 20.	Move off 7.45 a.m.
25.	10th.	Serial Number 1.	ST JANTER BIEZEN - "B" AREA.	SIEGE CAMP.	POPERINGHE - North SWITCH ROAD - G.3.c.1.9. - A.23.a.3.1. - MILITARY ROAD.	To be clear of G.3.c.1.9. by 12 noon.

DETAILS OF TRAINS for move.

	DEP. WIZERNES.	ARR. ELVERDINGHE.
No. 1. Train Personnel.	7.30 a.m.	11 a.m.
No. 2. Train Personnel.	11.30 a.m.	3 p.m.
		ARR. VLAMERTINGHE.
No. 3. Omnibus Train.	10.30 a.m.	1.25 p.m.

Completion of each moves to be notified to this Office by the quickest possible method.

SECRET.   Copy No...2.1..

173rd INFANTRY BRIGADE WARNING ORDER NO. 1.

3rd December 1917.

1. The 58th Division (less Artillery) is to relieve the 35th
   Division, II Corps, in the line on the 8/9th inst.
   The 35th Division, on relief, moves to the area now occupied by
   this Division.
2. The Front to be occupied is to be from the LEKKERBOTERBEEK at
   approximately point V.21.c.1.1. to the BROEMBEEK, Square V.7.b.
   The relief by the 175th Inf. Bde. of the Brigade 35th Division
   in occupation of the line is to be completed by 6 a.m. on 9th
   inst.
   The front is held by two Battalions.
   Brigades will each in turn be probably in the line for a tour of
   four days at a time.
   The 63rd (R.N.) Division, II Corps, is holding the Divisional
   Sector on the Right of the Sector to be occupied by this
   Division; the 17th Division, XIX Corps is holding the Divisional
   Sector on the Left of the Sector to be occupied by this Division.
3. Detailed Orders for the move will be issued later.
4. For the purpose of this move the 504th Field Coy. R.E. and
   2/1st H. C. Field Ambulance will be ibcluded in the 173rd Inf.
   Bde. Groupd.
5. 173rd Infantry Brigade Group will move from the present area to
   Area "A" on the 8th December 1917.
   The Group will then move from Area "A" to SIEGE CAMP on the 9th
   Dec. 1917. For this second move VIZERNES will be the Entraining
   Station.

                                                C. J. Graham.
                                                     2/Lieut.,
                                                 A/Brigade Major,
                                              173rd Infantry Brigade.

Copy No.

1. 2/1st Bn. London Regt.
2. 2/2nd Bn. London Regt.
3. 2/3rd Bn. London Regt.
4. 2/4th Bn. London Regt.
5. 173rd L. T. M. Batty.
6. 206th Machine Gun Coy.
7. 504th Field Coy. R. E.
8. 2/1st H. C. Field Amb.
9. 510th H.T. Co. A.S.C.
10. 174th Infantry Brigade.
11. 175th Infantry Brigade.
12. 58th Division "G".
13. 58th Division "A" & "Q".
14. S.S.O. 58th Division.
15. Area Commandant.
16. Brigade Major for G.O.C.
17. Staff Capt in.
18. Bde. Signalling Officer.
19. Bde. Transport Officer.
20. Bde. Intelligence Officer.
21. War Diary.
22. War Diary.
23. File.
24. D.S.O.
25. D.S.C.
26. D.E.O.

AMENDMENT to 173rd Inf. Bde. O.O. No.49.

SERIAL No. 11.   - cancel route stated and substitute

    WINNAERS CAPPEL - WINNEZEELE head of
    column to cross WORMHOUDT - CASSEL ROAD
    at 1 p.m.

SERIAL No. 25.   - Remarks Column - substitute

    To be clear of A.18.d.2.8. by 12 noon
    - BELGIUM Sheet 28.N.W.

                                     C J Graham.
                                          2/Lieut.

Copy to all recipients   for Brigade Major,
of O.O. 49 - 7./12/17.   173rd Infantry Brigade.

173RD INFANTRY BRIGADE

ADMINISTRATIVE INSTRUCTION NO. 20

5th December, 1917

PART I

The personnel of the Brigade Group, with Cookers and transport detailed in this office Sc/0/106 dated 4/12/17, will move by train on the 9th instant in accordance with attached Time Table.

Entraining Station. - WIZERNES.

Detraining Station - ELVERDINGHE (for personnel)
VLAMERTINGHE (for transport)

ENTRAINING OFFICERS
Lieut. J.CAIRNS, 2/4th London Regt., will act as Transport Entraining Officer, and will report to R.T.O., WIZERNES STATION 3 hours before the departure of the Omnibus train. He will travel on the train and will also be responsible for the detraining of transport.

Lieut. E.GIBSON, 2/1st London Regt. will act as Personnel Entraining Officer, and will report to R.T.O., WIZERNES STATION 2 hours before departure of 1st train. He will travel on the 2nd Personnel Train.

DETRAINING OFFICER
Lieut. L.W.BINDON, 2/2nd London Regt., will act as Detraining Officer. He will travel on the 1st Personnel Train, and report to R.T.O., ELVERDINGHE for instructions.

Entraining and Detraining Officers will wear a white Brassard on Right arm.

ENTRAINING STATES
All Units entraining will send a representative to report to Entraining Officer half an hour before the arrival of his Unit. He will be in possession of duplicate Entraining States, which will be handed to the Entraining Officer, who will hand one to the R.T.O., and forward the duplicate to these Headquarters on completion of move.

TIME OF ARRIVAL AT STATION
Marching troops will arrive at the Entraining Station 1½ hours before departure of the train.
Transport will arrive 3 hours before departure of Omnibus Train.
Loading Parties will arrive 3 hours before departure of Omnibus Train.

ADVANCE PARTIES
Each Battalion will send a small advance party of 1 Offr. and 4 O.Rs.
    206th M.G.Coy. will send 1 Off. & 2 O.Rs.
    173rd L.T.M.B. will send 1 Off. & 1 O.R.
    504 Fd.Coy.R.E. will send 1 Off. & 2 O.R.
    2/1st H.C.Fd.Amb.will send 1 Off. & 1 O.R.
to take over accommodation at SIEGE CAMP. These parties will proceed by train from WIZERNES Station on the 8th inst. and will move with the 174th Inf.Bde. - time of departure of train will be wired as soon as known. The above parties will proceed from present area to WIZERNES Station by cycle.

ADVANCE PARTIES (Contd) — Each Unit will send a small advance party to take over billets in "A" Area.
The distribution of the Brigade Group in "A" Area will be as under :-

```
Bde. H.Q. .................. SAMETTE
2/1st London Regt. ......... SENINGHEM
2/2nd London Regt. ......... SENINGHEM & AFFRINGUES
2/3rd London Regt. ......... BAYENGHEM
2/4th London Regt. ......... COULEMBY
206th M.G.Coy. ............. AFFRINGUES
173rd L.T.M.B. ............. AFFRINGUES
504 Fd. Coy. R.E. .......... SAMETTE
2/1st H.C.Fd. Amb. ......... LART
```

RATIONS — All units will move with one day's rations in addition to the unexpended portion of the day's rations.
Rations for consumption on 7th and 8th Dec. will be delivered on the 6th inst.
Rations for consumption on the 9th and 10th Dec. will be delivered on the morning of the 8th inst. at Area "A" to Units' Advance Parties.
Rations for transport marching portion will be delivered on the 6th for consumption on the 7th and 8th inst.
Transport Officers will send their Supply Wagon to the Brigade Supply Officer, SAMETTE at 7 a.m. on 8th inst. to draw rations for consumption on the 9th and 10th inst.

BAGGAGE & SUPPLY WAGONS — 2 Baggage wagons per Battalion and 1 Baggage wagon for Bde. H.Q. will report to Units' Headquarters at noon on 6th inst.

LORRIES — Arrangements for moving stores, and lorry programme will be issued later.

BILLETS — All Units will render to the Area Commandant a certificate to the effect that their billets are left in a clean and sanitary condition.

TRAINING MATERIAL — Attention is drawn to the Standing Orders for 2nd Army Training Areas issued from this office on 26/11/17.
All Training Material will be left at Units' Q.M. Stores ready to be taken over by incoming Unit.
Duplicate lists will be rendered: one to Area Commandant, HENNEVEUX and one to Bde. H.Q.

DAMAGE TO BILLETS — Certificates re damage to billets will be obtained for each billet occupied, and forwarded to this office on arrival in new area

MARCH DISCIPLINE — A certificate will be rendered to this office on completion of move shewing the number of men who fell out during the march for each day.

AREA MAPS ETC. — All maps and billeting papers the property of Area Commandant will be returned to him without delay.

RAILHEAD — ELVERDINGHE.

PART II

Marching Portion of Transport

Captain L.S.E.PAGE, 2/2nd London Regt. will be in charge of the Marching Portion of the Transport of Brigade Group.
All Transport Officers will move with their own columns.
Transport will move to LUMBRES on the 7th inst.
The Transport Officer of each unit will detail a cyclist to proceed on the 6th inst. to the Area Commandant's Office, LUMBRES, reporting to M. LAMTSHMERE, Belgian Interpreter, at 3 p.m., who will allot lines.

STARTING POINT. Cross roads S. of the first E in ESCOEUILLES.

Units will pass the Starting Point in the following order :-

206th M.G.Coy.
2/1st H.C.Fd. Amb.
2/2nd London Regt.
2/1st London Regt.
2/3rd London Regt.
2/4th London Regt.
Bde. H.Q.
504 Fd. Coy. R.E.

206th M.G.Coy. will pass the Starting Point at 10.30 a.m., 7th inst. An interval of 100 yards between each unit will be maintained.

4 M.M.P. will report to Captain PAGE at the Starting Point, and will move under his orders.

BAGGAGE & SUPPLY WAGONS — Will move with the unit to which they are attached, and will carry forage and rations.
Supply wagons will report to their Company Lines as soon as possible on the day previous to the last day's march.

MOVE FROM LUMBRES TO ST.MOMELIN, ST.JAN TER BIEZEN AND SIEGE CAMP

Orders for the move from LUMBRES to ST.MOMELIN, ST.MOMELIN to ST.JAN TER BIEZEN, and ST.JAN TER BIEZEN to SIEGE CAMP, will be issued by Captain PAGE.

ROUTE from LUMBRES will be as indicated in 173rd Inf. Bde. Order No. 49 dated 5/12/17.

H. J. King
Lieut.
A/Staff Captain,
173rd Infantry Brigade.

TRAIN TIME TABLE

(Issued with 173rd Bde. Administrative Instruction No. 20)

TRAIN	UNIT	DEPART VIZERNES	ARRIVE ELVERDINGHE
No.1 Personnel	2/2nd Lon. Regt. with Lewis Guns 2/3rd Lon. Regt. with Lewis Guns 206th M.G.Coy. 504 Fd. Coy. R.E.	7.30 a.m. 9th Dec.	11. 0 a.m. 9th Dec.
No.2 Personnel	2/1st Lon. Regt. with Lewis Guns 2/4th Lon. Regt. with Lewis Guns 2/1st H.C.Fd.Amb. Div. Employment Coy. Div. Salvage Coy. Div. Burials Party	11.30 a.m. 9th Dec.	3. 0 p.m. 9th Dec.
Omnibus Train	Cookers, blankets and stores of all Units. 173rd L.T.M.B., Handcarts & Guns	10.30 a.m. 9th Dec.	Arrive VLAMERTINGHE 1.25 p.m. 9th Dec.

The 173rd L.T.M.Battery and 5 O.Rs. per Battn. will act as loading and unloading party.

To all recipients of 173rd Inf. Bde. Warning Order No. 2.

Amendment No. 1 to W. O. No.2.

1. Brigade Warning Order No.2 of to-day is cancelled.

2. The Brigade will probably relieve 175th Infantry Brigade in the line on the night 16/17th December.

3. Orders regarding Future Policy, reconnaissance of the line, etc., will be issued later.

10/12/17.

C. J. Graham 2/Lt.
for Captain,
Brigade Major,
173rd Infantry Brigade.

S E C R E T.   Copy No...20...

173rd Infantry Brigade Warning Order No.2.

1. The 173rd Infantry Brigade will relieve the 175th Inf. Bde. in the line, Command passing to G.O.C., 173rd Infantry Brigade on the morning of the 13th inst.

2. Disposition of Battalions on completion of relief at 6 a.m. on the 13th inst. will be:-

    2/1st London Regt.   - Right Sub-Sector.
    2/3rd London Regt.   - Left Sub-Sector.

    2/2nd London Regt.   - Support on the Right.
                               H.Q. KEMPTON PARK.
    2/4th London Regt.   - Support on the Left.
                               H.Q. DOUBLE COTT.

3. 206th Machine Gun Coy. will relieve the Machine Gun Coy. in the line on the night 13/14th December under arrangements of the D.M.G.O.

4. Battalion Reliefs will take place during the night 12/13th December. The 2/1st and 2/3rd Battalions will probably travel part of the way by train. The 2/2nd and 2/4th Battalions will travel by march route.

5. Officers of 2/1st and 2/3rd Battalions will reconnoitre to-morrow, 11th inst.
    They will be at Brigade Headquarters at 9 a.m. and will be conveyed by bus.

6. ACKNOWLEDGE.

10th Dec. 1917.

                                                    C.J. Graham 2/Lt
                                                        Captain,
                                                      Brigade Major,
                                                  173rd Infantry Bde.

Copy No.

1. 2/1st Bn. London Regt.
2. 2/2nd Bn. London Regt.
3. 2/3rd Bn. London Regt.
4. 2/4th Bn. London Regt.
5. 173rd Light T. M. Bty.
6. 206th Machine Gun Coy.
7. 504th Field Coy. R.E.
8. 510th Coy. A. S. C.
9. 174th Infantry Brigade.
10. 175th Infantry Brigade.
11. 58th Division "G".
12. 58th Division "A" & "Q".
13. S.S.O. 58th Division.
14. Brigade Major for G.O.C.
15. Staff Captain.
16. Bde. Signalling Officer.
17. Bde. Transport Officer.
18. Bde. Intelligence Officer.
19. War Diary.
20. War Diary.
21. File.

SECRET.   Copy No. 21

173rd INFANTRY BRIGADE ORDER NUMBER 50.

Ref. Sheet 28, 1/100,000.
    BIXSCHOOTE - S.4.   )
    ST JULIEN. 28 N.W. 2.   ) 1/1,000.
    WESTROOSEBEKE 20 S.E. 3.)

-o-o-o-o-o-o-o-o-o-o-o-o-o-o-o-o-o-o-o-o-

December 15th 1917.

1. The Brigade will relieve 175th Infantry Brigade in The Line on 16th and 17th Dec., taking over the whole of the Divisional Sector as defined in the Brigade Provisional Defence Scheme.

2. Movements in connection with the relief will take place in accordance with attached Move Table. Train arrangements will be notified to units by Staff Captain.

3. Brigade Headquarters will close at WHITE MILL CAMP at 10 a.m. on 17th inst. opening at VARNA FARM at the same hour - at which time Command of Sector passes to G.O.C. 173rd Infantry Brigade.

4. Relief of Machine Gun Companies has taken place under orders of D.M.G.O.

5. 175th Infantry Brigade have been asked to leave following personnel behind for 24 hours after completion of relief in Left Front Sector only.

    1 Runner at Bn. H. Q.
    1 Runner at each Coy. H. Q.
    1 Observer at each O.P.

6. All Trench Stores - Maps, plans, etc., will be taken over on relief and a duplicate list will be rendered to Brigade Hd. Qtrs. on 17th December. Special care will be taken in the case of Tracer Ammunition for Anti-aircraft Work. 175th Infantry Brigade are arranging to hand over 3 drums (already prepared in proportion of 1 Tracer bullet to 3 ordinary) per Lewis Gun and any reserve of their ammunition available.

Tracer ammunition will be kept separate and handed over in turn on every ensuing relief. This ammunition is very scarce.

7. Relief will be completed by 6 a.m. 17th Dec. (with the exception of 173rd L.T.M.Bty) and completion will be wired to Bde. Hd. Qtrs. by code word "CRUMPS".

8. All further details of relief will be arranged between Commanding Officers concerned.

9. Units will acknowledge.

                                                         Captain,
                                                   Brigade Major,
Issued to Signals at ... 1 pm   173rd Infantry Brigade.

Copy No.		Copy No.	
1.	2/1st London Regt.	14.	S.S.O. 58th Div.
2.	2/2nd London Regt.	15.	Area Commandant.
3.	2/3rd London Regt.	16.	Brigade Major for G.O.C.
4.	2/4th London Regt.	17.	Staff Captain.
5.	173rd L. T. M. Batty.	18.	Bde. Signalling Officer.
6.	206th Machine Gun Coy.	19.	Bde. Transport Officer.
7.	504th Field Co. R.E.	20.	Bde. Intelligence Officer.
8.	2/1st H. C. Field Amb.	21.	War Diary.
9.	510th H. T. Co. A.S.C.	22.	War Diary.
10.	174th Infantry Brigade.	23.	File.
11.	175th Infantry Brigade.	24.	Brigade on Left.
12.	58th Division "G".	25.	Brigade on Right.
13.	58th Division "A" & "Q".		

P.T.O.

MOVE TABLE TO ACCOMPANY 173RD INF. BDE.
ORDER NUMBER 50, 16/12/17.

Date.	Unit.	From.	To.	Route.	Remarks.
Dec. 16th.	2/1st Bn.	WHITE MILL CAMP	Right Sub-sector H.Q. NORFOLK HOUSES	Train to RUDOLF FM thence via GROUSE & GLOSTER Avenues.	
16th.	2/2nd Bn.	BRIDGE CAMP No.1.	Right Support - KEMPTON PARK.	Train Direct.	Coy. detailed to relieve Coy. of 175th Inf. Bde. in PHEASANT TRENCH to complete relief as early as train will allow - remainder to complete by 2 p.m.
16th.	2/3rd Bn.	BRIDGE CAMP NO.2.	Left Sub-sector H.Q. LOUIS FM.	Train to RUDOLF FM thence via Track "A".	
16th.	2/4th Bn.	CANAL BANK.	Left Support - H.Q. CANDLE TR.	March via ZOUAVE ROAD.	Relief to be complete by 2 p.m.
17th.	173rd L.T.M. Batty.	MORTAR CAMP.	KEMPTON PARK.	Train Direct.	Relief to be complete by 10 a.m. 17th Dec.

Following intervals will be maintained on the March:-

Between Companies 100 yards.
Between Battalions 500 yards.

All movements of Infantry on roads E. of the ELVERDINGHE - VLAMERTINGHE Road will be in FILE.

P.T.O.

S E C R E T

173RD INFANTRY BRIGADE

Administrative Instruction No.21

---oOo---

(Issued in connection with 173rd Inf.Bde. Order No.50)

==

Transport and Q.M.Stores of all units will remain in their present camps.

RATIONS.   Normal system of supply.
    Units going into the line will take two days' rations.
    Tommy Cookers will be issued on demand from Bde. Q.M. Stores to units going into the line.

WATER.   Extra water-bottles will not be used.
    Petrol tins as under will be drawn from these H.Q.

        2/1st Bn. 150
        2/3rd Bn. 150
        208th M.G.Coy. ... 50

    Every effort will be made to send as many empty tins as possible back to wagon lines.
    Drinking water can be drawn by water-carts at Water Point between KEMPTON PARK and HINTY FARM.

COOKERS   Cookers may be taken to KEMPTON PARK. There is a Cookhouse in CANDLE TRENCH.

CARE OF FEET   The Brigadier-General directs that every man shall take off his boots and socks, and massage his feet at least twice a day.
    Powder as described in this office No. Sc/O/74 dated 15/12/17 will be available on application to these Headquarters. A small supply will be taken in the line by each man.
    Whale oil is available on indent from Brigade Supply Officer.

SOCKS   Clean socks will be issued to Q.Ms. in exchange for dirty ones, from Bde. Q.M.Stores.

S.A.A., BOMBS, ETC   All units will be in possession of 120 rounds of S.A.A. per man.
    1 rifle grenade per man will be issued to 2/1st and 2/3rd Bns.: these to be handed over on relief.
    S.A.A. and grenades will be taken over in the line, and maintained in accordance with a scale to be issued later.
    Indents for S.A.A. and R.E.Material to reach Staff Captain each morning by 9.30 a.m.

DUMPS   TRAMWAY TERMINUS DUMP (U.30.b.75.05.
        S.A.A. .... 260,000 rounds
        No. 5 Grenades   1,200
        S.T.M. Shells   150

    EAGLE DUMP (U.24.c.30.90)
        S.A.A. .... 236,000 rounds
        Very Lights 1" White ..   8 boxes
        No. 5 Grenades   1,080

    YORK DUMP (U.23.a.5.8)
        S.A.A. .... 189,000 rounds
        S.T.M.Shells 3"   279
        No. 5 Grenades   1,584
        No.23 Grenades   720

P.T.O

PRISONERS OF WAR — Divisional Prisoners of War Cage is at HAMMOND'S CORNER. Escorts should be given clear instructions as to their destination, and obtain a receipt from the Provost's representative at the Cage.
When possible this office should be notified that prisoners are being sent down.

MEDICAL — Regimental Aid Posts under Units' arrangements.

RELAY POSTS

Left Sector
EAGLE TRENCH U.23.b.6.3
PIG & WHISTLE ... U.28.b.3.2
CEMENT HOUSE U.28.c.2.2

Right Sector
PHEASANT PARK ... U.30.b.2.6
PHEASANT TRENCH . U.30.d.4.6
WAANIXBEEK FARM . C.5.b.1.7

Routes for walking wounded:- To Advanced Dressing Station, CEMENT HOUSE (U.28.c.2.2), and MINTY FARM (C.10.c.2.6), thence by Decauville Railway to Corps Main Dressing Station, DUHALLOW.

Sick from all units will be evacuated along the same route as walking wounded.

H. S. King
Lieut.
A/Staff Captain,
173rd Infantry Brigade.

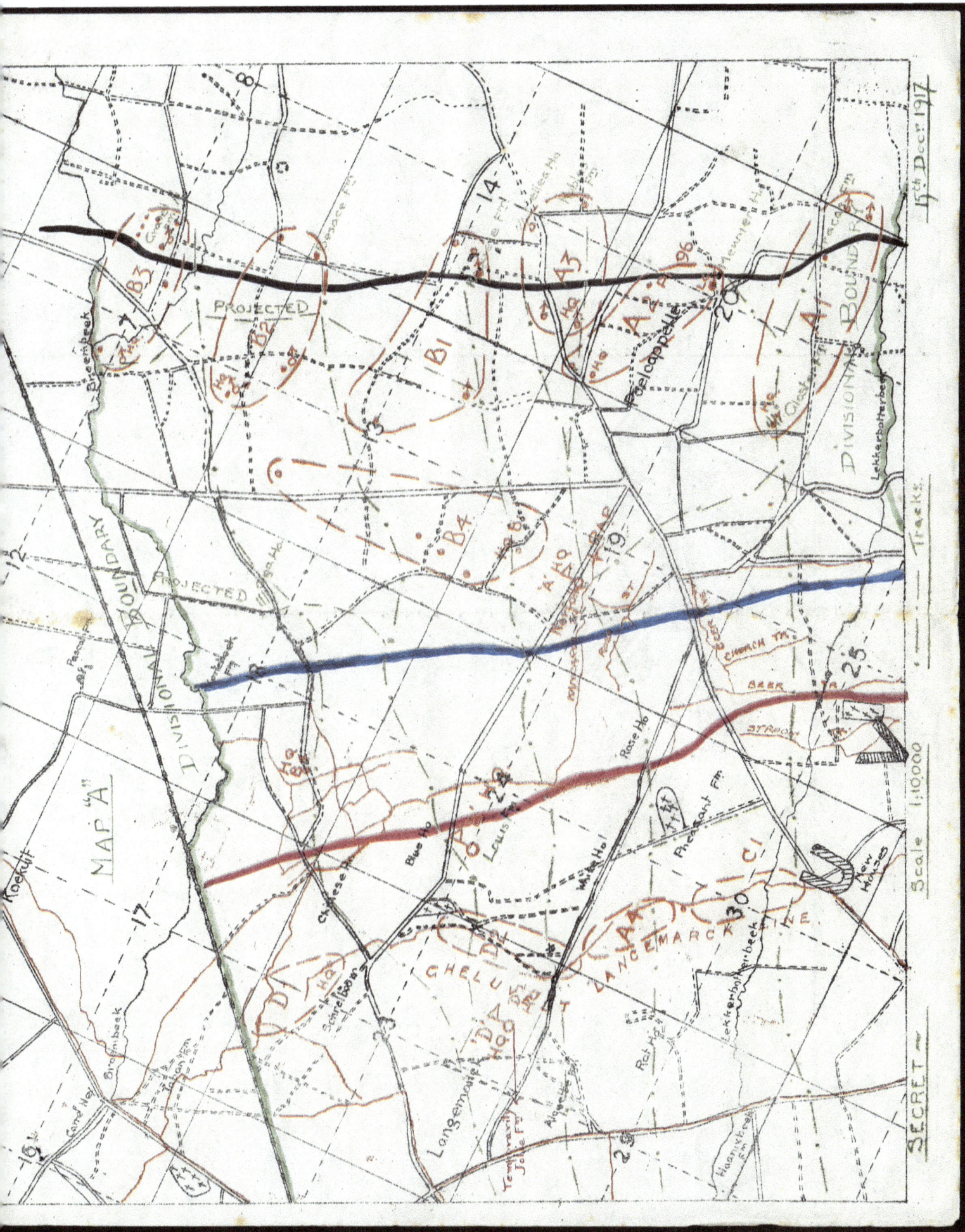

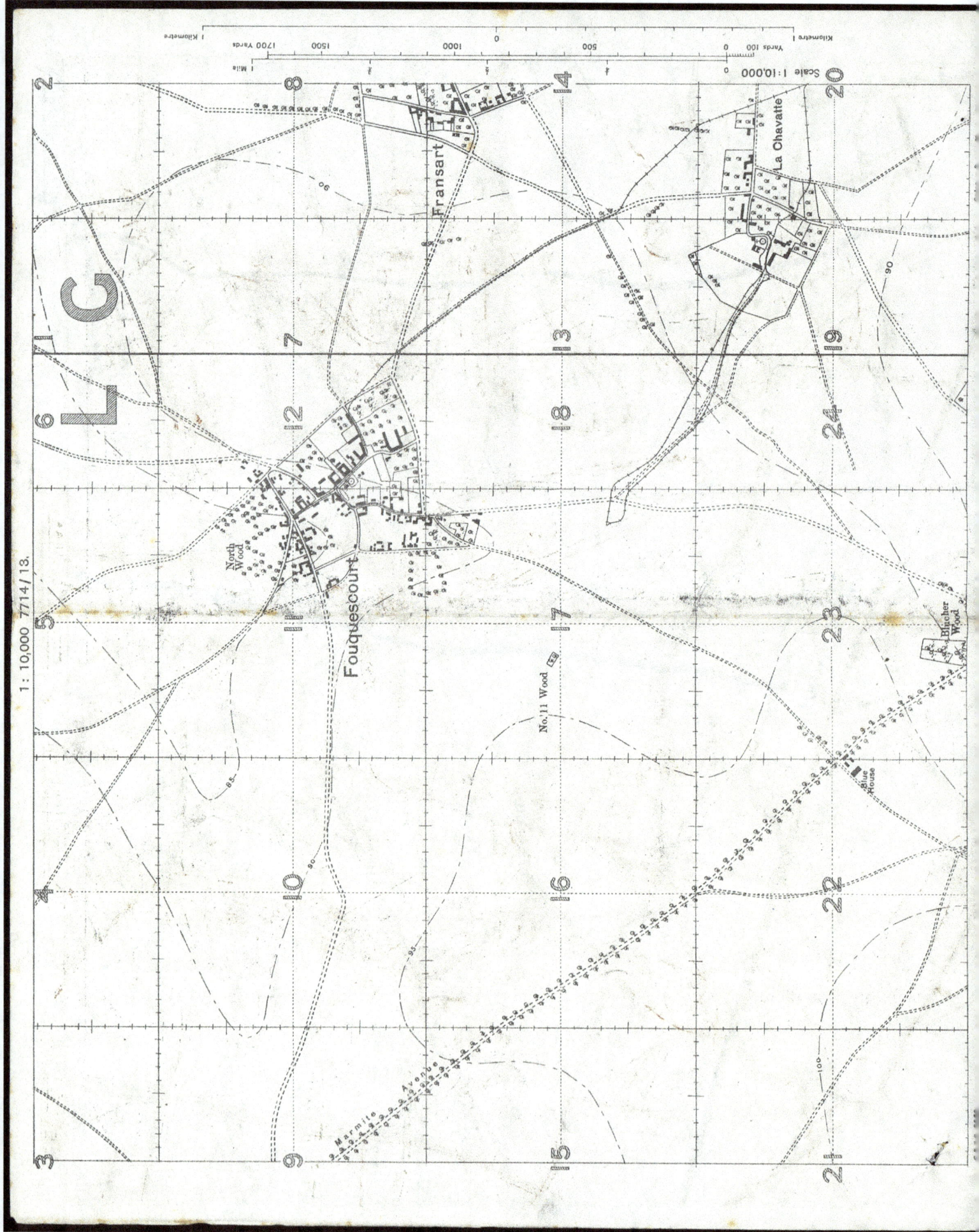

173RD INFANTRY BRIGADE.

PROVISIONAL DEFENCE SCHEME.

Copy No.

1. 2/1st Bn. London Regiment.
2. 2/2nd Bn. London Regiment.
3. 2/3rd Bn. London Regiment.
4. 2/4th Bn. London Regiment.
5. 173rd Light T. M. Battery.
6. 206th Machine Gun Company.
7. Brigade Major.
8. G. O. C.
9. 58th Division "G".
10. 96th Infantry Brigade (Right).
11. 55th Infantry Brigade (Left).
12. 174th Infantry Brigade.
13. 175th Infantry Brigade.
14. War Diary.
15. War Diary.
16. File.

15th December 1917.

S E C R E T.   Copy No. 15

173RD INFANTRY BRIGADE DEFENCE SCHEME.
(Reference Map "A" 1/10,000 attached)

December 15th 1917.

---

1. The Brigade Sector extends from the LEKKERBOTTERBEEK on the Right (V.20.d.8.1.) to the BROEMBEEK on the left (V.7.b.6.6.). Boundaries coincide with those of Division and are as follows:-

    RIGHT BOUNDARY. - The LEKKERBOTTERBEEK to V.26.a.00.25. - V.25.d.00.15. - D.1.a.00.00. - Cross Roads at C.6.c.70.10.

    LEFT BOUNDARY. - The BROEMBEEK to U.17.d.33.70. thence along the YPRES - STADEN Railway (exclusive).

    INTER BATTALION BOUNDARY. - V.14.central - V.13.d.65.00. - V.19.c.00.80 - U.24.c.00.

2. DEFENCE OF SECTOR.
    The Defence of the Sector is organised in three distinct zones.

    (a). Outpost System - East of and including the BLACK LINE shewn on Map "A" attached.
    (b). Main Defensive System - All ground between the BLUE AND BLACK LINES.
    (c). Corps System - The RED LINE.

3. HOLDING OF THE SECTOR.
    The Sector will be held as follows:-

    Outpost System)   "A" and "B" Battalions
    &   )   plus One Company of "C"
    Main Defensive)   and 2 Companies of "D"
    System.   )   Battalions - 16 M. Gs.

    Corps System   -   8 M. Gs.

    2 Battalions in Brigade Support less 3 Companies.

    Actual Dispositions are shewn on Map "A".

4. ACTION IN CASE OF ATTACK.
    All posts will be held and there will be no retirement. Three forms of attack may be expected:-

    (i). A General Attack along the whole front of the Brigade.

    (ii). A Local Attack designed to gain and occupy a particular Strong Point or locality in our line.

    (iii). A raid on one of Our Posts with the object of securing Prisoners and information.

    In the event of (i) - proving successful action will be as follows:-
    (a). Supporting Platoons in Main Defensive system will not counter attack but will immediately take up and hold defensive positions allotted to them.

(b). Battalion Commanders holding Front Sub-sectors will immediately counter attack with their counter attack companies. The object of the counter attack on Right Sub-sector will be the retention of POELCAPPELLE and on the Left Sub-sector of the High Ground - 19 METRE HILL - TRAGIQUE FM.

(c). An organised counter attack will be delivered by the troops in Brigade Support and reserve under orders of Brigade or Divisional Headquarters. This attack however cannot be expected to materialize under six hours from the alarm being received at Brigade Hd. Qtrs.

In the event of (i) proving only partialy successful the Battalion Commander concerned will immediately endeavour to restore the situation by means of all forces at his disposal i.e. - supporting platoons and counter attack companies, reporting progress to Bde. Hd. Qtrs., who will if necessary order a further attack as in (c) above.

In the event of (ii) proving successful an immddiate counter attack will be launched by the Company Commander concerned with his counter attack platoons - further attacks as in (b) and (c) above being delivered if necessary.

In the event of (iii) - This will probably take place by night - and prompt offensive action on the part of the Company Commander concerned will be essential - counter attack platoons will immediately move forward to reinforce the post threatened and if it is found that enemy are in possession will forthwith attack them.

5. ACTION IN CASE OF ALARM.

(a). All Garrisons of Posts and Defended Localities throughout the three systems of defence will "stand to" in their allotted positions.

(b). Surplus M.G. gun personnel will stand by ready to take up spare boxes of ammunition to their respective gun positions as soon as an attack developes or appears certain.

(c). Brigade Headquarters will be immediately imformed as to cause of alarm and where attack is expected.

(d). Battalions in Brigade Support will immediately move forward and join their forward Companies in EAGLE and PHEASANT TRENCHES, ready to Counter-attack on orders to this effect being given by Brigade Headquarters.

(e). All working and carrying parties will immediately proceed to the localities assigned to them or where no locality is assigned to the nearest Company or Battalion Headquarters in the direction of the enemy.

6. WORK. The following tasks have been allotted to the Brigade holding the line Outpost System:-

Wiring, Drainage and flooring of all posts, also provision of splinter and weather proof cover for the same. To be carried out by Garrisons under R.E. arrangements and supervision.

Note:- The R.E. can only supervise a certain number of posts at a time, but the garrison of all other posts must carry on with wiring and drainage unassisted.

Improvement of accommodation and communications in EAGLE and PHEASANT TRENCHES:- This will be carried out by the 2 Companies of the Left Support Battalion each finding 120 and 60 men respectively daily for this work

Working Hours for these Companies will be -

> 10 a.m. to 1 p.m.
> 2 p.m. to 3 p.m.

on days of relief there will be no work after 1 p.m.

It is to be taken as a Standing Order that all N.C.Os. and men of Platoons, Companies and Battalions in Support do 4 hours work <u>daily</u> on allotted tasks whenever tactical considerations allow. In clear weather care must be taken to subdue movement in large numbers as such movement invariably leads to enemy shelling.

7. <u>ARTILLERY.</u> The Sector is covered by the following:-

> 290th Bde. R.F.A.
> 291st Bde. R.F.A.
> 34th. (Army Bde.)

with

> 23rd (Army Bde.) in Reserve.

The S.O.S. line runs 150 yards East of a line joining our front posts.

S.O.S. SIGNAL is:-

> PARACHUTE RIFLE GRENADE BURSTING INTO THREE
> COLOURED LIGHTS GREEN OVER RED OVER ORANGE.
> at 12 noon

and changes on 19th December/to:-

> RIFLE GRENADE SIGNAL BREAKING INTO 2 RED
> 2 WHITE STARS SIMULTANEOUSLY.

8. <u>ANTI-AIRCRAFT.</u>

Machine Guns and Lewis Guns for Anti-aircraft work are at following places:-

> BREWERY - MEUNIER - GLOSTER - PHEASANT - U.30.a.9.1.
> - U.30.d.3.7. - U.18.central - FERDAN - SENEGAL -
> TAUBE - CANDLE, C.9.a.5.4. - CANDLE, C.9.a.60.75. -
> EAGLE, V.29.b.97.97. - EAGLE, V.17.c.85.15. -
> V.19.b.95.60. - V.20.a.3.9. - ~~V.20.a.3.9.~~ - V.20.c.3.5.
> -U.30.b.1.6.

Captain,
Brigade Major,
173rd Infantry Brigade.

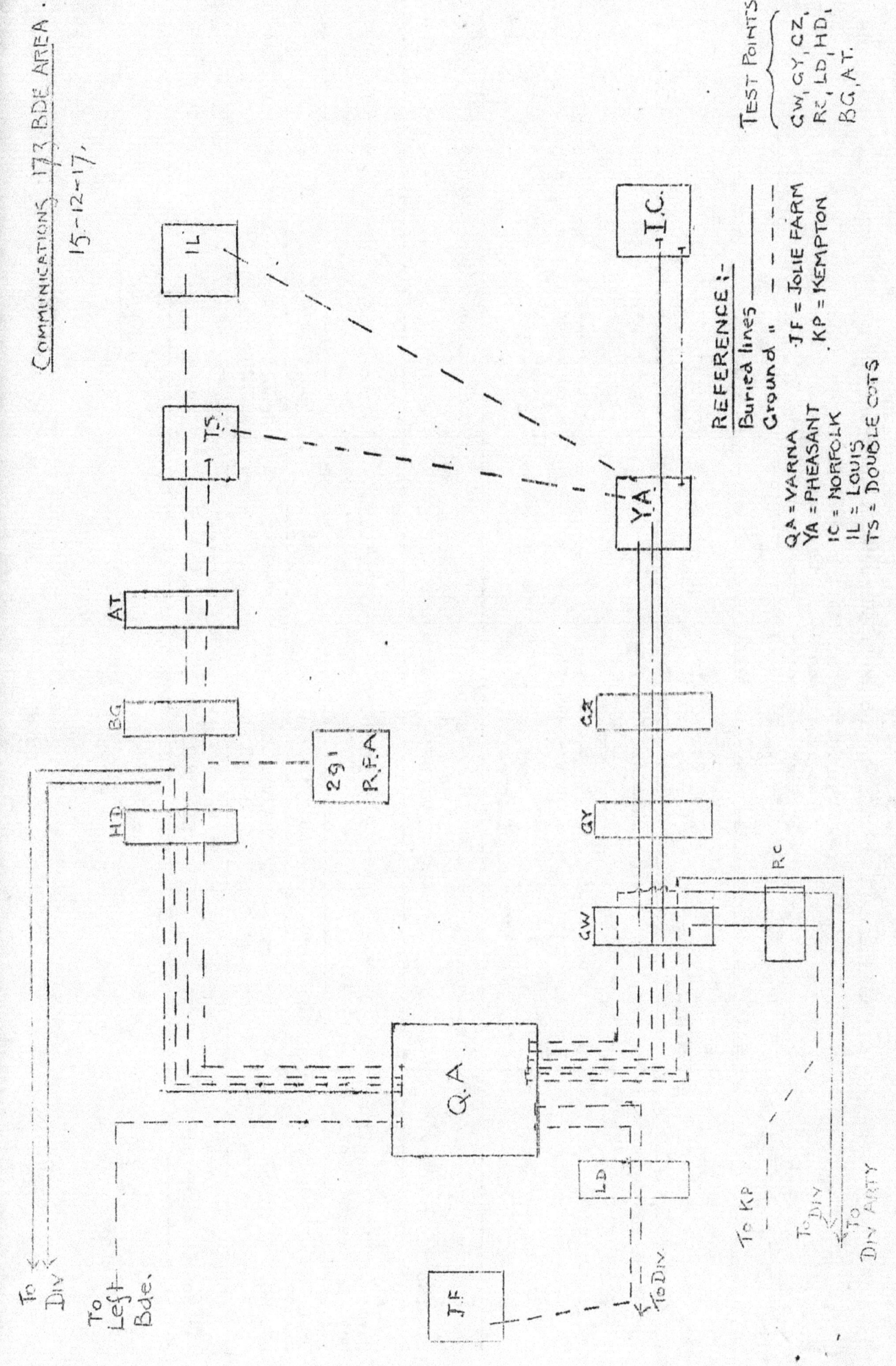

APPENDIX "A" to 173RD INF. BDE. PROVISIONAL DEFENCE SCHEME.

Moves on "S.O.S." or on "Attack Move" being received from Bde. Hd. Qtrs.

U N I T.	FROM.	T O.	VIA.	REMARKS.
A.4.	Shelters in PHEASANT TR. or Working Areas.	Alarm Post:- near JUNCTION TRACKS at U.30.b.1.7.	Nearest Route.	On arrival at Alarm Post to await orders of O.C. "A" Bn. or Higher Authority.
Personnel 255th Tunnelling Co. R.E. & attached Infantry.	Working on PHEASANT TR.	Man PHEASANT TR. between LEKKERBOTERBEEK & GROUSE AVENUE.	—	Replacing A.4. in defence of PHEASANT TR.
C.1.	Shelters in PHEASANT TR. or Working areas.	Alarm Post:- Astride POELCAPPELLE - ST. JULIEN ROAD about U.30.central.	Nearest Route.	Occupy and Defend Alarm Post pending orders from O.C. "C" Bn. or Higher Authority.
WHITE MILL Working Party of 183 Tunnelling Coy. & attached Infantry.	Working Area.	WHITE TR between GROUSE AV. and WHITE MILL.	Nearest Route.	Come under Orders of O.C. "D".?.
ALOUETTE FM Working Party of 253 Tunnelling Coy. & attached Inf.	Working Area.	Ditto. Ditto.	Ditto.	Ditto. Ditto.
BEAR TR Working Party.	Working Area.	EAGLE TRENCH.	Ditto.	Report to O.C. "D.1."
DOG RG Working Party.	Working Area.	PHEASANT TRENCH	Ditto.	Report to Senior Officer in PHEASANT TRENCH.
Party Working immediately West of 19 METRE HILL.	Working Area.	Post in vicinity 19 METRE HILL .	Ditto.	

P. T. O.

Page 2 of Appendix "A".

UNIT.	FROM.	TO.	VIA.	REMARKS.
Miscellaneous Parties working under orders of C.R.A. and C.R.E.	Working Area.	Nearest Bn. or Coy. H.Q. in direction of the enemy.	Nearest Route.	Report on arrival to Bn. or Coy. Commander and act under his orders. Positions of those H.Q. must be made clear to all ranks previous to work commencing.
(F) C.2 - C.3 - C.4. and H.Q. C. Bn.	KEMPTON PARK.	PHEASANT TRENCH - Bn. H.Q. to RAT HO. D.04	GLOSTER AVENUE.	Portion of PHEASANT TR between NEW HOUSES & FLORA COTT. must be occupied as well as portion N. of NEW HOUSES & WHITE MILL (exclusive)
(F) D.3. - D.4. and H.Q. "D"	CAMBLE TRENCH	SCHREIBOOM Bn. H.Q. to DOUBLE COTT.	Tracks "A" & "S"	D. Bn. will be responsible for holding EAGLE and WHITE TRENCHES fr. WHITE MILL to BROEMBEEK
(F) 4 Reserve Vickers Machine Guns.	KEMPTON PARK	RAT HO. D.04	GROUSE AVENUE	
(F) 4 Reserve Vickers Machine Guns.	GOURRIER FM	DOUBLE COTTS.	GROUSE AVENUE -VARNA FM. - TRACK "E"	

Numbered Letters i.e:- D.3. - C.2. etc. refer to Companies occupying positions as shewn on Provisional Defence Scheme Map "A".

Movements marked (F) will take place on the receipt of a message from Bde. H.Q. ordering Frost Precautions.

15/12/17.

Captain,
Brigade Major,
173rd Infantry Brigade.

SECRET.   Copy No..........
            173rd INFANTRY BRIGADE ORDER NUMBER 51.
            Ref. Sheet 28, 1/100,000.
                  BIXSCHOOTE - S.W.4.   )
                  ST JULIEN. 28. N.W. 2.) 1/1,000
                  WESTROOSEBEEK 20. S.E. 3.)

                                            December 22nd 1917.

1. 173rd Infantry Brigade will be relieved in the line by 175th Infantry Brigade on 24/25th December.
2. On completion of relief the Brigade will be disposed as under:-
      2/1st London Regt. - White Mill Camp.
      2/2nd London Regt. - Canal Bank.
      2/3rd London Regt. - Bridge Camp No.2.
      2/4th London Regt. - Bridge Camp No.1.
      173rd L. T. M. Bty - Redan Camp.
3. Battalions will be relieved as follows:-

      2/2nd Bn. by 2/12th Bn. in Right Front.
      2/4th Bn. by 2/10th Bn. in Left Front.
      2/1st Bn. by 2/9th Bn. in Right Support.
      2/3rd Bn. by 2/11th Bn. in Left Support.

4. Relief in EAGLE, WHITE and PHEASANT TRENCHES will be carried out by day, but no troops are to pass this line before 4.30 p.m.
5. All Maps, Aeroplane Photos, sketches and intelligence will be handed over and special efforts will be made to ensure that information with regard to R.E. Dumps and schemes of work generally is complete and accurate when handed over.
6. Trench Stores etc., will be handed over on relief and duplicate list forwarded to Brigade Headquarters in due course.
7. Relief will be complete by 6 a.m. 25th December and completion will be wired to Brigade Headquarters by Code Word MISTLETOE.
8. Intervals laid down in Fourth Army "Distances to be observed on the March" will be strictly adhered to.
9. Instructions as to Light Railways will be issued by the Staff Captain.
10. Command passes to G.O.C., 175th Infantry Brigade at 10 a.m. 25th December, at which hour Bde. Hd. Qtrs. will close at VARNA and re-open at WHITE MILL CAMP.
11. All further details of relief will be arranged between Commanding Officers concerned.
12. Units will ACKNOWLEDGE.

                                            Captain,
                                            Brigade Major,
                                            173rd Infantry Brigade.

Copy No.   Copy No.
 1. 2/1st Bn. Lon. Regt.   15. Area Commandant, Canal Bank
 2. 2/2nd Bn. Lon. Regt.   16. Brigade Major for G.O.C.
 3. 2/3rd Bn. Lon. Regt.   17. Staff Captain.
 4. 2/4th Bn. Lon. Regt.   18. Bde. Signalling Officer.
 5. 173rd L. T. M. Batty.   19. Bde. Transport Officer.
 6. 206th Machine Gun Coy.   20. Bde. Intelligence Officer.
 7. 504th Field Coy. R.E.   21. War Diary.
 8. 2/1st H. C. Field Amb.   22. War Diary.
 9. 510th H. T. Co. A.S.C.   23. File.
10. 174th Infantry Brigade.   24. Brigade on Left.
11. 175th Infantry Brigade.   25. Brigade on Right.
12. 58th Division "G".   26. Area Commandant, K.P.
13. 58th Division "A" & "Q".   27. Area Commandant WHITE MILL.
14. S.S.O. 58th Division.

S E C R E T.

173RD INFANTRY BRIGADE.

Administrative Instruction No.23.

(Issued in connection with 173rd Inf. Bde. Order No.51)

==

1. **TRAIN ARRANGEMENTS.**   Units will move to WHITE MILL CAMP by Trains as under:-

Date. Dec.	Unit.	Entrain.	Time of Departure	Detrain.	
24th.	2/1st Bn.	BATTLE.	12 noon.	READING	for WHITE MILL
"	2/3rd Bn.	do.	do.	do.	" BRIDGE CAMP
"	2/2nd Bn.	do.	8 p.m.	CANAL BANK.	" CANAL BANK
"	2/4th Bn.	do.	8 p.m.	READING	" BRIDGE CAMP
25th.	(Bde.H.Q.	VARNA			WHITE MILL
	(173rd L.		9 a.m.	READING	" &
	(T.M.Bty.	FARM.			REDAN.

    173rd L.T.M.Bty. will act as carrying and loading party at VARNA FARM, reporting at 8 a.m. 25th inst.

2. **PETROL TINS.**   As many full tins as possible will be handed over to relieving unit.
    Every effort should be made to carry all empty tins back to Wagon Lines.

3. **S. O. S.**   All S.O.S. Rifle Grenades will be handed over on relief and a receipt obtained.

4. **TRACER AMMUNITION.**   Special care will be taken in handing over the DRUMS containing TRACER Ammunition and any Reserve of this Ammunition.
    175th Infantry Brigade will hand over 500 rounds at WHITE MILL CAMP. This will be issued to units on demand on 25th inst.

5. **SOUP KITCHENS.**   The following Soup Kitchens will be prepared to supply hot soup:-
    CEMENT HOUSE (U.28.c.2.2.) on TRACK "A".
    RUDOLF FARM on GROUSE AVENUE.
    Lr. MARSOUIN FARM, near TRACK "B" 50 yds. East of Main Road.

6. **BATHS.**   Baths will be allotted on arrival in Camp. Arrangements are being made for the issue of Clean Clothing.

7. **FOOT TREATMENT.**   Foot Treatment should be carried out under units arrangements in Camp. Soap and Powder will be issued on demand by 2/2nd H.C.F.A., ESSEX FARM, and 2/3rd H.C.F.A., CANADA FARM.

December 22nd 1917.

                                                Captain,
                                                Staff Captain,
                                           173rd Infantry Brigade.

173rd Infantry Brigade

Further to 173rd Inf. Bde. Intelligence Summary for Period 24 hours ended 8 a.m., 17/12/17 :-
UPPER reports the following Patrols :-

Constitution of Patrol.	Time & Point of departure.	Report	Time & Point of Return.
1 N.C.O. & 2 O.R.	Every hour during night from REQUETE FM.	To get in touch with Bn. on Right at HELLES HO. Liaison was obtained and all reported correct.	To REQUETE FM.
1 N.C.O. & 3 O.R.	9.30 p.m., BESACE	To obtain liaison between posts at BESACE & BOWER HO. Accomplished.	10.30 p.m. BESACE.
1 N.C.O. & 2 O.R.	10 p.m., V.7.b.	To find out if GRAVEL FM. was occupied. Post found occupied by enemy. Very Lights sent up.	10.45 p.m.
1 N.C.O. & 3 O.R.	Left Coy.	To obtain liaison with Bn. on Left. Accomplished.	-----

17/12/17

2nd Lieut., I.O.,
for Brigade Major,
173rd Infantry Brigade.

173RD INFANTRY BRIGADE

Summary of Intelligence - Period 24 hours ending 8 a.m. 17/12/17.

---oOo---

ARTILLERY

Hostile Artillery was generally quiet. POELCAPPELLE was shelled at intervals (medium calibre.) The vicinity of PHEASANT FARM was intermittently shelled by salvos of 5 or 6.

M.G's

"A.2" reports slight activity during relief of one of the posts, otherwise generally quiet.

MOVEMENT

None observed.

PATROLS

At 8.30 a.m. 16/12/17 a lateral patrol of the Northumberland Fusiliers visited our forward post at TRAGAS, and at 8 p.m. a patrol of "A.1" Company got into touch with "A.2" Company at MEUNIER HOUSE.

2/Lieut., I.O.
for Brigade Major,
173rd Infantry Brigade.

173rd Infantry Brigade Summary of Intelligence.
Period 8 a.m. 17th December to 8 a.m. 18th December 1917.

A. OPERATIONS.

1. Enemy's attitude and General Activity. Generally Quiet. Usual intermittent shelling on LANGEMARK - POELCAPPELLE Rd. PHEASANT TRENCH, with 5.9's between 10 a.m. and Noon, also 3 p.m. and 5 p.m. 17/12/17. Duck Board Tracks received attention NORFOLK HO. and forward was shelled at intervals with 5.9's up till 4.30 p.m. The Line MEUNIER HO. - TRACAS FM was shelled at 8.45 a.m. 17/12/17.

Left Battalion report hostile activity chiefly between 12 noon and 5 p.m. 17/12/17 -

at 8 a.m. 6 H.E. (10.5 cm.) were fired at V.13.b.5.4.
9 a.m. 8 H.E. (5.9.) " " " TAUBE HOSPITAL.
8.45 am 6 H.E. (10.5 cm) " " round V.24.d.
10.25 a.m. 50 HE.)
& Gas.) were fired round WATER HO and SENEGAL FM.
9.15 - 10 a.m. HE and Shrapnel on "B" Track behind EAGLE TR.
10.45 a.m. 3 HE. (10.5) behind REQUETTE FM.
12 - 1.30 p.m. H.E. and Shrapnel around U.30.b. and Valley of LEKKERBOTTERBEEK.

POELCAPPELLE - ST JULIEN Rd. from U.30.d.3.4. to C.6.b.1.5. was subjected to harrasing fire from about 3.45 p.m. to 4.30 p.m. Vicinity of BREWERY received 50 H.E. between 11 a.m. and noon. and 100 H.E. between 10 p.m. and 11.30 p.m. 17/12/17.

GAS SHELLING.

6.30 p.m. 50 2.4's MUSTARD GAS 100^x left of NORFOLK HO. Shells came roughly from Pt. 500 yards N. of VALUATION HOUSES. Gas was quickly dispersed.
10.25 a.m. 50 H.E. and Gas round WATER HO. and SENEGAL.

2. Our Own Activity on same lines and where it influences enemy action:- At about 7 p.m. when our 18 pdrs. were firing two flares were observed from enemy lines, apparently a small dump was hit.
Left Battalion captured two prisoners of 413 WURTENBURGER REGT. opposite post at BESACE FM. at 1.30 a.m. They were unarmed and supposed to have lost their way. Prisoners state that their Coy. is in post 350^x away from our own lines. They state their regiment came from CAMBRAI on Nov. 11th. They further state that they only know a very little of our positions.

B. INTELLIGENCE.
a. M.G. Emplacements (Located and Suspected). Enemy M.G. at V.15.a.4.2. (approx), came into action after dark. Enemy M.G. fires from MEMLING FM towards SENEGAL FM. M.G. located near V.14.d.80.60.
b. Movement. Enemy. Clouds of smoke observed in direction of WESTROOSEBEEK believed to be railways. At dawn three men approached TRACAS NEBUS from East, were challenged and did not answer were at once fired on, and went off N.E.
Extreme Right Posts (Right Sector) was visited by Officer of K.O.Y.L.I.
c. SIGNALS. 4.30 p.m. enemy sent up 3 Orange Lights, after which a 5 minute Shrapnel Barrage fell between WATER HO. COMPROMIS FM.

Page 2.

d. **Aerial Activity.** 3.20 p.m. three of our planes were driven back over our line by enemy AA. Our planes were very active yesterday afternoon. About 6.5 p.m. one of our machines was heard making for enemy lines. The enemy sent up following lights - 2 White bursting into a group of seven white small stars each -One white bursting into a group of 5 stars.
Numerous Very Lights sent up same colour. Following these signals enemy A.A. and M.Gs. opened fire. Three Search Lights were opened on bearing of 83 degrees from NORFOLK HO.
At 6.15 this activity ceased until the plane was heard returning from enemy lines, when it opened up again. The plane passed back over NORFOLK HO.
At 2.30 p.m. 9 E.A. were counted along our front, mostly over POELCAPPELLE.
At 2.40 p.m. 2 of our planes were seen flying towards some of them, who turned back and made for home.
At 1.30 p.m. 7 E.A. crossed our lines on our left, but were driven back by A.A. fire.
At 2.30 p.m. 4 E.A. were over our lines and engaged by our machines. One E.A. was seen to be brought down, the other 3 returned to their own lines.
Our planes were active over enemy lines from 12 noon to 3.30 p.m.
At about 10 a.m., 17th a plane came down in flames outside POELCAPPELLE. It has not yet been ascertained whether it was an E.A. or one of our own.

L.F.C.Hinold
2nd Lieut., I.O.,
for Brigade Major,
173rd Infantry Brigade.

PATROL REPORTS. 18/2/17.

Time & Pt of Departure	Report	Time of Return
11.20 pm 17th TAUBE H°	1 NCO. and 2 O.R. of 2/3rd Inf. Regt. left to ascertain if GRAVEL F.P. was occupied and position of enemy's forward posts. Patrol proceeded along road from BERTHIER H° to GRAVEL F.P. Patrol took up a position at 1.96.91.05. drawing GRAVEL F.P. Patrol took up a position at 1.96.91.05. drawing GRAVEL F.P. Very light was fired nor CRAVEL F.P. was seen to be a large fut, large enough to hold 10-20 men and an enemy post was noticed 30-50 yds in advance of Mehrs at 1.96.91.05. At 12.5 am two men were seen to jump up at this post and fire at patrol which had fired Very light. Another patrol of 1 NCO and 10 R. took same route and took up position in rear of 1st patrol. At 12 m. they fired Very light. T then advanced to reconnoitre Mehrs but was immediately fired on as stated above. If our half of 1 patrol took were seen across road in front of GRAVEL at about M.10 93.	1 am. TAUBE HOUSE
do -	The patrol was sent out to reconnoitre. Patrol proceeded 400-500 yds due East in direction of MORAY H° where enemy M.G. heard. Fire of M.G. was almost impassable but almost impassable for any footed. The ground is frozen hard between the numerous large shell holes which are filled with water.	1.10 am TAUBE HOUSE
1 Off + 2 OR 9.30 pm TRACAS MEEKS		10.15 pm TRACAS MEEKS
1 NCO + 2 O.R. 7 pm HELLES H°.	The patrol found two MEBUSES about 200* in front of HELLES H°. to be unoccupied and smashed in. It was very difficult to keep direction owing to the bad condition of ground.	

7B 1/14 a.m. PATROL REPORTS.   13/11/17

Time & Pt. of Departure	Report	Time of Return
11.20 pm 12/11/17 TAUBE H⁰	1 N.C.O. and 2 O.R. of 2/13 Lond Regt left to ascertain if GRAVEL F⁰ was occupied and position of enemy's forward posts. Patrol proceeded along road from BERTHIER H⁰ to GRAVEL F⁰. Patrol took up a position at V.9b.8².05, observing GRAVEL F⁰. At 12 midnight a Very light was fired over GRAVEL F⁰ appeared to be a large pill box, large enough to hold 50-60 men. GRAVEL F⁰ appeared to be a large pill box, large enough to hold 50-60 men. and an enemy patrol was noticed 30-50 yds in advance of Mebus at V.9b.9.05. At 12.5 am two Germans were seen to jump up at the post and fire at patrol which had just fired Very light.	1 am TAUBE HOUSE
Do.	Another patrol of 1 N.C.O. and 1 O.R. took came work and took up position in rear of 1st patrol. At 12 mn they fired Very lights & then advanced to reconnoitre Mebus but were immediately fired on as stated above. Left of patrol were more across road in front of GRAVEL at about V.9d.8.03.	1.10 am TAUBE HOUSE
1 Off & 3 oR. 9.35 pm from TRACAS MEBUS	Off. & patrol was sent out to reconnoitre Patrol proceeded 400-500 yds due East in direction of MORAY H⁰ where enemy was heard to open fire M.G. The ground was unsuitable for the movement of small parties, but almost impracticable for large bodies. The ground is frozen hard between the numerous large shell holes which are filled with water.	10.15 pm TRACAS MEBUS
1 NCO + 2 OR from HELLES H⁰	The patrol found two MEBUSES about 200× in front of HELLES H⁰ to be unoccupied and smashed in. It was very difficult to keep direction owing to the bad condition of ground.	

War Diary

173rd INFANTRY BRIGADE SUMMARY OF INTELLIGENCE.

Period:- 8 a.m. 18th Dec. to 8 a.m. 19th Dec. '17.

A. OPERATIONS.

1. <u>Enemy Artillery.</u>

Time.	Number.	Calibre.	Target.
9 am - 10 a.m.		H.E.	Front Line near REQUETE FM
10.45-11.45 am	20.	10.5 H.E.	U.29.b.
12 noon	6.	Shrapnel.	U.23.b.
2 pm - 4 pm.		5.9's.	C.4.a.
9 am - 1 pm.	40.	5.9's.	Near MEUNIER HOUSE.
4 am.-	2.	Medium.	NOBLES FARM.
9 am - 12.30 pm		Medium.	NOBLES FARM.
7.15 - 8.30 pm.)			TRACAS - GLOSTER FM
9 p.m.)		Medium.	Sector.

During Period under review hostile artillery has not been so active as during previous 24 hours.
POELCAPPELLE has been intermittently, but lightly shelled, day and night. Other Targets have been U.24.a., U.23.d., U.24.d., and round BLUE HOUSE, MILLERS HOUSE and TRAGIQUE. VARNA FARM was shelled during the night at intervals of one hour by 5.9's commencing at 11 p.m.
POELCAPPELLE - LANGEMARCK Road received attention during the night.

2. <u>Our Own Artillery.</u> Has been steadily and intermittently harrasing enemy positions during day and night.

B. INTELLIGENCE.

(a). <u>M.G. Emplacements.</u> M.G. at V.15.a.4.2. active after 5.30 p.m.
(b). <u>Movement.</u> Small parties of the enemy were seen on the ridge in front of V.20. during the morning. In the evening enemy transport heard approximately at V.21.a. Later our Artillery shelled in this direction.
   Two men were observed to come out of NEBUS at GRAVEL FM.
   7 a.m. Smoke seen in rear of HOULTHURST FOREST - presumably from an engine.
(c). <u>Aerial Activity.</u>
   1. <u>Our Own.</u> - 4 p.m. One of our planes flew low over enemy post and engaged it with L.G. Fire: it was fired on by A.A. and M.G.
   2. <u>Enemy.</u> - E.A. were reported in the morning as directing enemy artillery fire whilst flying over about V.13. and 19.
   At 3 p.m. 5 E.As. were driven from our lines by A.A. Guns.
(d). <u>General.</u> - Very few Very Lights were sent up by the enemy during the night, practically all those used were in the direction of TRACAS FARM.
   At 4 a.m. as connection was being obtained between posts at V.7.b.70.15. and V.7.b.70.05., a German Patrol was seen approaching our lines on the road from GRAVEL FM. On observing our men enemy retired quickly.

J.C.Hruntal.
2/Lieut.
I.O.
for Brigade Major,
173rd Infantry Brigade.

173rd Infantry Brigade — Patrol Report

Strength of Patrol	Unit	Time & Date	Remarks and Information	Time & Date of Return
2 Offrs 1 N.C.O. & 5 O.R.	2/4 L.R.	10.15 p.m. from V.g.d.30.95	Patrol went out to reconnoitre front & to try & locate enemy posts. Connection was obtained with post at Bower Hs. No enemy were seen. Liaison was obtained between all posts in Left Sub. Sector	11.5 p.m. to V.g.d.30.95
2nd 2/4 Lt M.C.O. & 2 O.R.	2/4 L.R.	7.10 p.m. from Hollis Ho	Patrol was sent out to reconnoitre Enemy posts on road & Borden Cross Roads. The road was found to be cut up & difficult to follow. Patrol proceeded 400 x in N.E. direction when Very lights were sent up from an enemy post about 200 yds N.E. of road. Occasional rifle fire came from this post.	9.5 p.m. to Hollis Ho.
1 Offr & 3 O.R.		9.15 p.m. from Jirwar Mebus	Ground in front found to be very hard & unsuitable for patrol work. Enemy working party was heard in direction of Cameron Ho. Otherwise very quiet	10.45 p.m. to Jirwar Mebus

173rd INFANTRY BRIGADE SUMMARY OF INTELLIGENCE.

Period:- 8 a.m. 19/12/17. to
8 a.m. 20/12/17.

A. OPERATIONS.
1. Enemy Artillery.

Right Sub-sector.

Time.	Number.	Calibre.	Target.
10.10 a.m.	10	Medium.	TRACAS F. - TEUFIER HO
12.5 p.m.	few.	5.9's.	NORFOLK HO.
1.20 p.m.	few.	5.9's.	MEUNIER HO - GLOSTER FM

A.2. and A.3. report intermittent shelling of POELCAPPELLE.
POELCAPPELLE, LANGEMARK RDS., and PHEASANT TRENCH received usual attention.
Shelling of forward parts has decreased.
Tracks shelled about 8 p.m. - 8.15 p.m.

Left Sub-Sector.

Time.	Number.	Calibre.	Target.
3.35 - 3.45 am	10. Shrapnel		over U.24.c.
8.10 a.m.	4.	Gas.	on U.24.b.20.25.
9.30-10.30 am.	at intervals H.E.		on U.23.d.05.90.;
At intervals -	Several direct hits on Track were obtained		U.29.a. & b. and B. Track between U.29.a. & FERDAN.
5 p.m.	7.	5.9's.	Directed on Battery position in U.30.c.

VARNA FARM was shelled with about 100 Mustard and Phosgene Gas shells at 9.15 p.m.

2. Our Artillery.
Intermittent shelling of enemy positions and approaches.

B. INTELLIGENCE.
(a). <u>Snipers</u>. A Sniper in front of NOBLES FM. fired occasional shots at NOBLES between dusk and dawn.
(b). <u>Movement</u>. In front of A.1. Sector an enemy O.B. was put up at 8.40 a.m. (19th) and taken down at 9 a.m. on account of mist.
The usual White Very Lights were sent up last night.
Enemy patrol of 3 men were seen from B.3. Sector, were fired on and withdrew.
A Pigeon (Carrier) flew over in direction of POELCAPPELLE at 3 p.m. (19th).
(c). <u>Signals</u>. No enemy signals are reported, save a few white lights.
(d). <u>Aerial Activity</u>. Ours. 7 am. - 1 pm. our aircraft was very active. During period under review a considerable amount of patrolling is reported.
Enemy. Active over MILLERS HO. from 12 - 1 p.m.
6 p.m. - 8 p.m. 4 bombs dropped V.13.a.6.3.
1 p.m. E.A. over A.1. Sector was fired upon by our M.Gs. and A.A.
12.40 p.m. (19th) Our planes engaged E.A. and drove them off.
11.30 a.m. (19th). One E.A. reported driven down about 1,000 yards N.E. TRACAS MEBUS.
During period under review E.A. has been very active, but mostly flying at hight altitudes. Nearly all E.A. were engaged by our planes who were successful in most cases in driving them off.

2/Lieut.
I.O. for
Brigade Major, 173rd I. Bde.

1st/3rd Infantry Brigade

Patrol Report.

Unit	Strength	Time & Point of Departure	Report	Time & Place of Returning
2nd /1st C.R.	2nd Lt. Gibson + 7 O.R.	6 p.m. Noble's Farm	Patrol reports wooden shelters as in Sprict map. Eastern B post held by the enemy. Shelters are all to dig encircled in Enemy post located on Sprict Rd. at 10.40 p.m. from shelter at V.14.d.5.1. also at V.20.a.8.9	8.40 p.m. Noble's Farm
2nd /3rd C.R.	1 N.C.O. + 3 O.R.	7.30 p.m. Water etc.	To get touch with A Company on the right. Object was achieving all reported correct.	8.30 p.m. Water etc.
1st /3rd C.R.	1 N.C.O. + 3 O.R.	10 p.m. Noble's Farm	To patrol company frontage in front of our posts. Object was achieved. All reported correct.	12 Midnight Noble the
			Patrol was dispatched between posts on our front & all reported correct	

20.10.17

173RD INFANTRY BRIGADE SUMMARY OF INTELLIGENCE.

Period 8 a.m. 20th Dec. to 8 a.m. 21st Dec.1917

A. OPERATIONS.
Enemy Artillery.
Right Sub-Sector.

Time.	Number.	Size.	Direction of Battery	Target.
9.30 pm.(20th) to 5.30 a.m(21st)	150.	5.9 and 4.2.	WESTROOSEBEEK.	BREWERY.
10 am. (20th) to 4.15 pm (20th)	One every 5 mins.	5.9.	ditto.	U.30.a.
12 noon to 3 pm 20th.	One every 20 mins.	5.9.	ditto.	U.30.c.9.9.
6 p.m. to 6.30 p.m.	continuously.	5.9.	ditto.	POELCAPPELLE
1.30 a.m. to 5 a.m. 21st.	ditto.	5.9.	ditto.	ditto.

Enemy artillery activity has steadily increased on right sub-sector during the last 24 hours. Majority of shelling 4.2 H.E. from WESTROOSEBEEK and 5.9 H.E. from WESTROOSEBEEK and PASCHENDALE. Chief Targets MEUNIER HO. and POELCAPPELLE more especially in neighbourhood of BREWERY and duck board tracks from NORFOLK HO. to to TRACAS via GLOSTER HO., and from NORFOLK HO. to NOBLES.

Left Sub-Sector.

Time.	Number.	Size.	Direction of Battery.	Target.
7 - 8 p.m.	30 H.E.	4.2.	WESTROOSEBEEK.	REQUETTE FM.
9 - 10 p.m.	50 H.E.	4.2.	ditto	ditto
11 - 1 a.m.	50 H.E.	4.2.	ditto	ditto
1.30 - 4.30 am	60 H.E.	4.2.	ditto.	ditto
7 p.m-4 a.m.	160 H.E.	5.9.	ditto.	STRING HOUSES
6 p.m.-5.40am	120 HE.) 30 H.V.)	5.9 & 4.2 Small	HOUTHOLST FOREST.	COMPROMIS FM

"A" Track has been badly shelled and broken about V.13.a.9.2. EAGLE DUMP received attention during the night, gas and H.E. shells falling in that neighbourhood at irregular intervals. About 5 p.m. was the period of greatest activity.

Our Own Artillery.
During the early hours of last night close liaison was maintained between the Artillery and ourselves. Our heavies engaged the enemy guns in counter battery work and was successful in practically neutralising batteries which were firing on our right sub-sector. Our 18 pdrs. fired salvoes on our S.O.S. line in front of MEUNIER.

B. INTELLIGENCE.
(a). Machine Guns. Enemy M.G. fired short burst of about 6 rounds every half hour from about V.14. central. An M.G. is suspected at V.20.b.50.85.
(b). Patrols. Patrol reports are attached. Owing to the fog patrolling is difficult as it is very hard to keep direction. Touch is kept between posts throughout night.
(c). Movement. None observed owing to fog. Very few lights were sent up by enemy during night.

F. Arnold
2/Lieut.
I.O. for Bde. Major
173rd Infantry Brigade.

173rd Infantry Brigade.

Patrol Report.

UNIT.	Strength of patrol	Time and Date	Objective or task.	Remarks and information.
2/2nd Bn. Lon.Rgt.	2/Lt.Bennett & 3 O.R.	Left 11.30 p.m. 20th. Returned 1.15 a.m. 21st Dec.	Reconnaissance of ground 200 yards in front of post at TRACAS FARM.	Route. EAST from TRACAS mebus, which was visible on sky-line for about 150 yards. About 200 yds. from mebus patrol turned SOUTH until trees along LEKKERBOTERBEEK appeared. Patrol returned obliquely to TRACAS mebus. Succession of intersecting shell holes 25 to 30 feet by 10 feet, filled nearly to the top and frozen hard. Ground. Quiet progress difficult. Enemy. No hostile post or fire encountered.
2/2nd Bn. Lon.Rgt.	Lt.Andrews & 3 O.R.	1.15 a.m.	Reconnaissance of ground 200 yards in front of post at NOBLES FARM.	Left NOBLES FM. direction N.E. Patrol reached V.14.d.50.45. Where shouting was heard ahead - on searching nothing was discovered. Turned S. to about 0.50.25. No hostile post discovered. Ground frozen hard and passable. Returned at 5.15 a.m.
2/4th Bn. Lon.Rgt.	2/Lt.Peryer & 2 O.R.	8 p.m.	To get in touch with Battalion on the Left.	Patrol left TAUBE FM. H.Q. of right Coy. of the Bn. on the Left were found to be at U.6.d.85.30. Dispositions of this Company were then ascertained and patrol returned at 11.30 p.m.
2/4th Bn. Lon.Rgt.	3 O.R.	7.30 & 11.30 p.m. 20th. 3.30 a.m. 21st Dec.	" "	Patrols left VATER HOUSE at those times to keep touch with Company at COMPROMISE FM.
2/4th Bn. Lon.Rgt.	3 O.R.	7 p.m. 20th Dec.	" "	Patrol left SENEGAL Post to get in touch with Company at TAUBE. Returned 9 p.m.

173rd Infantry Brigade Intelligence Summary.
Period 24 hours ending 8 am.
22nd December 1917.

A. OPERATIONS.

1. Enemy Artillery.

Left Sub-sector. Active throughout the day especially on following points:-

Area.	No. of Rounds.	Time.	Calibre & Kind.	Battery.
V.19.c.	200.	During day.	4.2. Hows. 77 mm.	Unknown.
Track "B" in V.19.a. and c.	60.	6.15 pm and 8 p.m.	5.9.	2 Guns - 77½° True from V.13.b.4.8.
V.13.c.4.1.	30.	9 - 10 p.m.	H.E.	HOUTHOLST FOREST.
Vicinity of EAGLE DUMP.	irregular few intervals		Gas.	?
Right Sub-Sector.				
NORFOLK HO.	2 per Min.	9 a.m. to 5 p.m.	4.2 & 5.9.	WESTROOSEBEEK
GLOSTER FM & across to V.19.b.9.3.	200	10 a.m. to 4 p.m.	4.2. & 5.9.	?
BREWERY & POELCAPPELLE.	140	8 am. to midday.	4.2. & 5.9.	WESTROOSEBEEK.
BREWERY.	Very heavily shelled	7 - 7.15 p.m.	4.2. & 5.9.	HOUTHOLST.
Tracks GLOSTER- MEUNIER- TRACAS.	Heavily shelled.	5 pm. to 6.30 pm.	4.2.	-

2. Our Own Artillery.
Succeeded in considerably lessening enemy shelling on right sub-sector.

B. INTELLIGENCE.

(a). **Enemy M.Gs.** Patrol going from NOBLES to HELLES HO. were fired on by M.G. from approx. V.14.d.7.8. (confirmed). From 300 yards east of TRACAS MENUS occasional short bursts were fired.

A M.G. from about V.14.d.5.9. fired bursts on "B" Track near REQUETE FM.

(b). **Observation Posts.** Five enemy O.Ps. located in trees at V.10.b.7.4. Observation is very good to-day.

(c) **Work and Movement.** One German in grey uniform seen at V.14.d.9.9. approx. at 10 a.m. 21st. He disappeared when fired on Work, probably wiring was heard at about V.7.b.8.5. Transport was heard at 12 mid-night seemingly from direction of V.1.d.9.7.

(d). **Patrols.** Our left Bn. sent out patrols at intervals throughout the night from front line posts to get in touch with neighbouring posts. They encountered no hostile patrol and observed no movement.

P.T.O.

(e). **Aerial Activity.** One low flying aeroplane dropped two bombs near FERDAN HO. at 7.45 a.m. (22nd). It then flew up and down our lines at a very low altitude until fired on by M.Gs. from one of our left posts, when it returned to its own lines. When there it dropped a White Light. It then started over our lines again but 4 of our planes had arrived by this time and drove it off. Our 4 planes fired bursts on enemy positions. Enemy A.A. Guns were very active against these planes.

(f). **Signals and Lights.** On Right od Divisional Sector at 8.30 p.m. a Golden rain rocket was sent up followed by barrage lasting 30 minutes. Very lights were plentifully used by enemy on our extreme left (B.3.) last night. About 7 a.m. this morning Golden Rain was also observed along enemy line starting from the right and continuing along to the left.

(g). **General.** GRAVEL FM. was occupied during last night - voices and coughing could be heard.

I F C Hewitt

2/Lieut. I.O.
for Brigade Major,
173rd Infantry Brigade.

173RD INFANTRY BRIGADE.

PATROL REPORT.

UNIT.	Strength of Patrol	Objective or Task.	Remarks and information.	Time & Date.
2/2nd Bn. Lon.Regt.	2/Lt.GEDGE & 2 O. Rs.	Reconnaissance to discover locality of enemy posts on or near SPRIET ROAD.	Patrol left V.20.a.9.8. and proceeded along road towards SPRIET for 300 yards. Here saw enemy post 50 yards to left of road (V.20.b.57.90) Patrol proceeded along road for another 100 yards from where enemy M.G. was heard to right of road (location uncertain) This M.G. was firing occasional bursts at our left Coy. Posts. Patrol returned to V.20.a.9.8. Going Very Difficult. Tree stumps clearly marked road.	5.30 pm. 21st. Returned 9.30 pm.

173rd Infantry Brigade Intelligence Summary.
Period 24 hours ending 8 am.
22nd December 1917.

A. OPERATIONS.

1. Enemy Artillery.

Left Sub-sector. Active throughout the day especially on following points:-

Area.	No. of Rounds.	Time.	Calibre & Kind.	Battery.
V.19.c.	200.	During day.	4.2. Hows. 77 mm.	Unknown.
Track "B" in V.19.a. and c.	60.	6.45 pm and 8 p.m.	5.9.	2 Guns - 77½° True from V.13.b.4.8.
V.13.c.4.1.	30.	9 – 10 p.m.	H.E.	HOUTHOLST FOREST.
Vicinity of EAGLE DUMP.	few	irregular intervals	Gas.	?

Right Sub-Sector.

Area.	No. of Rounds.	Time.	Calibre & Kind.	Battery.
NORFOLK HO.	2 per Min.	9 a.m. to 5 p.m.	4.2 & 5.9.	WESTROOSEBEEK
GLOSTER FM & across to V.19.b.9.3.	200	10 a.m. to 4 p.m.	4.2. & 5.9.	?
BREWERY & POELCAPPELLE.	140	8 am. to midday.	4.2. & 5.9.	WESTROOSEBEEK.
BREWERY.	Very heavily shelled	7 – 7.15 p. m.	4.2. & 5.9.	HOUTHOLST.
Tracks GLOSTER- MEUNIER- TRACAS.	Heavily shelled.	5 pm. to 6.30 pm.	4.2.	—

2. Our Own Artillery.
Succeeded in considerably lessening enemy shelling on right sub-sector.

B. INTELLIGENCE.

(a). **Enemy M.Gs.** Patrol going from NOBLES to HELLES HO. were fired on by M.G. from approx. V.14.d.7.8. (confirmed). From 300 yards east of TRACAS MEBUS occasional short bursts were fired.

A M.G. from about V.14.d.5.9. fired bursts on "B" Track near REQUETE FM.

(b). **Observation Posts.** Five enemy O.Ps. located in trees at V.10.b.7.4. Observation is very good to-day.

(c) **Work and Movement.** One German in grey uniform seen at V.14.d.9.9. approx. at 10 a.m. 21st. *He disappeared when fired on.* Work, probably wiring was heard at about V.7.b.8.5. Transport was heard at 12 mid-night seemingly from direction of V.1.d.9.7.

(d). **Patrols.** Our left Bn. sent out patrols at intervals throughout the night from front line posts to get in touch with neighbouring posts. They encountered no hostile patrol and observed no movement.

P.T.O.

(e). <u>Aerial Activity.</u> One low flying aeroplane dropped two bombs near FERDAN HO. at 7.45 a.m. (22nd). It then flew up and down our lines at a very low altitude until fired on by M.Gs. from one of our left posts, when it returned to its own lines. When there it dropped a White Light. It then started over our lines again but 4 of our planes had arrived by this time and drove it off. Our 4 planes fired bursts on enemy positions. Enemy A.A. Guns were very active against these planes.

(f). <u>Signals and Lights.</u> On Right od Divisional Sector at 8.30 p.m. a Golden rain rocket was sent up followed by barrage lasting 30 minutes. Very lights were plentifully used by enemy on our extreme left (B.3.) last night.
About 7 a.m. this morning Golden Rain was also observed along enemy line starting from the right and continuing along to the left.

(g). <u>General.</u> GRAVEL FM. was occupied during last night - voices and coughing could be heard.

L F Hewitt

2/Lieut. I.O.
for Brigade Major,
173rd Infantry Brigade.

173RD INFANTRY BRIGADE.

PATROL REPORT.

UNIT.	Strength of Patrol	Objective or Task.	Remarks and information.	Time & Date.
2/2nd Bn. Lon.Regt.	2/Lt.GEDGE & 2 O. Rs.	Reconnaissance to discover locality of enemy posts on or near SPRIET ROAD.	Patrol left V.20.a.9.8. and proceeded along road towards SPRIET for 300 yards. Here saw enemy post 50 yards to left of road (V.20.b.57.90) Patrol proceeded along road for another 100 yards from where enemy M.G. was heard to right of road (location uncertain) This M.G. was firing occasional bursts at our left Coy. Posts. Patrol returned to V.20.a.9.8. Going Very Difficult. Tree stumps clearly marked road.	5.30 pm. 21st. Returned 9.30 pm.

173rd INFANTRY BRIGADE INTELLIGENCE SUMMARY.
Period 24 hours ending 8 a.m. Dec. 23rd 1917

A. OPERATIONS.

Enemy Artillery.

Enemy Activity. Hostile Artillery activity was normal during the day until 4.10 p.m. when a heavy hostile barrage was put down just in rear of our front posts along B. Sub-sector and extending for some distance on both flanks, more especially on our left. At 4.18 p.m. S.O.S. Signals were sent up by Battalion on our left. Bosche were seen advancing by our left Company from direction of GRAVEL FM. The S.O.S. was sent up by this Company (B.3.) and also by B.2. Our barrage came down at 4.21 p.m. and drove the enemy back at this point before he came in touch with our posts. The bosche barrage slackened off about 4.40 p.m. and at 4.50 p.m. it had practically ceased. There was comparative quiet along our line until 4.45 a.m. (23rd) when another bombardment of our left Coy. (B.3.) posts re-opened and continued until ? a.m. No infantry attack developed. An S.O.S. is reported to have been put up this morning and our artillery responded. This S.O.S. was not observed at VARNA FARM, where we had posted a look-out, but two white lights were seen. It seems highly probable that this was one of the respective Bosche lights the two reds only being observed from a few places of which VARNA FM was not one.

B. INTELLIGENCE.

(A). Aerial. E.A. very active during the period under review. At 6 p.m. 22nd, E.A. were observed dropping White, Red, Green and Orange Lights some distance behind their lines. At midnight 4 E.A. dropped Bombs on and around V.13.b.4.2. At 9.40 a.m. 22nd, a British plane attacked an enemy O.B. The observer was seen to descend by his parachute. 10 Enemy O.Bs. were counted from U.24.c.48.95.

(b). Enemy Signals. Many Red, Green, and Golden Rain Lights were sent up by the enemy during the barrage yesterday afternoon, but their significance could not be determined. It seems highly probable that the Bosche has a similar signal to our own S.O.S. but it differs in that instead of the two reds bursting out simultaneously with the two whites the two white lights first appear followed by two reds which do not burst appear until the rocket is well on its downward journey.

Note. No intelligence summary has turned up from our right battalion yet. Anything further of importance will be wired as sokn as this summary is received.

2/Lieut.,
I.O. for,
Brigade Major, 173rd Inf. Bde.

173rd Infantry Brigade.

Patrol Report.

U N I T.	STRENGTH OF PATROL.	TIME AND DATE	OBJECTIVE OR TASK.	REMARKS AND INFORMATION.
2/2nd Battn. London Regt.	2/Lieut.GLADSTONE and 1 O.R.	12 midnight 22/23rd.	Reconnaissance of No Mans Land.	Left NOBLES FM at 12 midnight 22/23rd and proceeded 200 yds. on bearing 158 Mag. Discovered that two MEBUS at V.14.d.30.15. are demolished. MEBUS at V.14.d.42.09. is badly knocked about. It is unoccupied. returned by same route reaching NOBLES FM 2 a.m. Just at this time cries were heard from about 750 yards East of NOBLES FM. following a short burst by our artillery at this time. No enemy was seen.
2/2nd Battn. London Regt.	2/Lt. V.GILLINGS and 3 O. R..	11.5 pm. 22nd. to 2.45 am. 23rd.	To locate enemy M.G. suspected about V.21.c.5.0.	Patrol proceeded due East for about 300 yds. from TRACAS MEBUS, when it halted for some time to listen for movement of enemy. Nothing heard. One short burst was fired from enemy M.G. about MORAY HO. Patrol returned to TRACAS MEBUS about 2.45 a.m.

To all recipients of 173rd Inf. Bde. Intelligence Summary
of 23rd Dec. 1917.

Following Intelligence received from "A" Battalion:-

ARTILLERY.   Report of "B" Battalion on enemy artillery
confirmed.   POELCAPPELLE and BREWERY received particular attention.

AIRCRAFT.   Several E.A. flew along our line between 9 a.m.
and 11 a.m. (22nd). Also one crossed our line at 7 p.m. and
another at 9.15 p.m. Bombs were dropped near MEUNIER HO. at
about 4.45 a.m. (23rd).
        Our own aircraft was active over our own and enemy's
lines during yesterday.

MACHINE GUNS.   (a). Emplacement suspected at V.21.c.65.65.
               (b). 4 Enemy seen with a M.G. moving about
V.20.b.9.1. at 4.10 p.m.

O. P's.   5 Enemy O.Ps. located at V.10.b.7.4. in trees.

MOVEMENT.   About 5 p.m. 6 enemy were seen running from
V.15.c.3.4. They disappeared at approximately V.15.central.

SIGNALS.   One Green Light sent up at 5.15 p.m. by enemy.
His barrage lessened considerably.
During our barrage about 5 p.m. lights were sent up along the line
by the enemy which burst into a string of 5 White Lights.

TRANSPORT.   Much heard apparently moving along SCHAAP-BALIE -
VIJEWEGEN Road.

Note:- The S.O.S. signal which was sent up this morning was ours
and not an enemy signal as at first thought. It was sent up from
MEUNIER.

                                                2/Lieut.,
                                                I.O. for,
                                           Brigade Major,
                                     173rd Infantry Brigade.

To all recipients of 173rd Inf. Bde. Intelligence Summary
of 23rd Dec. 1917.

Following intelligence received from "A" Battalion:-

ARTILLERY. Report of "B" Battalion on enemy artillery
confirmed. POELCAPPELLE and BREWERY received particular attention.

AIRCRAFT. Several E.A. flew along our line between 9 a.m.
and 11 a.m. (22nd). Also one crossed our line at 7 p.m. and
another at 9.15 p.m. Bombs were dropped near MEUNIER HO. at
about 4.45 a.m. (23rd).
  Our own aircraft was active over our own and enemy's
lines during yesterday.

MACHINE GUNS. (a). Emplacement suspected at V.21.c.65.65.
  (b). 4 Enemy seen with a M.G. moving about
V.20.b.9.1. at 4.10 p.m.

O. P's. 5 Enemy O.Ps. located at V.10.b.7.4. in trees.

MOVEMENT. About 5 p.m. 6 enemy were seen running from
V.15.c.3.4. They disappeared at approximately V.15.central.

SIGNALS. One Green Light sent up at 5.15 p.m. by enemy.
His barrage lessened considerably.
During our barrage about 5 p.m. lights were sent up along the line
by the enemy which burst into a string of 5 White Lights.

TRANSPORT. Much heard apparently moving along SCHAAP-BALIE -
VIJEWEGEN Road.

Note:- The S.O.S. signal which was sent up this morning was ours
and not an enemy signal as at first thought. It was sent up from
MEUNIER.

  [signature]
  2/Lieut.,
  I.O. for,
  Brigade Major,
  173rd Infantry Brigade.

173rd Infantry Brigade.

Patrol Report.

UNIT.	STRENGTH OF PATROL.	TIME AND DATE	OBJECTIVE OR TASK.	REMARKS AND INFORMATION.
2/2nd Battn. London Rgt.	2/Lieut. GLADSTONE and 1 O.R.	12 midnight 22/23rd.	Reconnaissance of No-Mans Land.	Left NOBLES FM at 12 midnight 22/23rd and proceeded 200 yds. on bearing 158° Mag. Discovered that two MEBUS at V.14.d.30.15. are demolished. MEBUS at V.14.d.42.09. is badly knocked about. It is unoccupied. returned by same route reaching NOBLES FM 2 a.m. Just at this time cries were heard from about 750 yards East of NOBLES FM following a short burst by our artillery at this time. No enemy was seen.
2/2nd Battn. London Regt.	2/Lt. V. GILLINGS and 3 O.R.	11.5 pm. 22nd. to 2.45 am. 23rd.	To locate enemy M.G. suspected about V.21.c.5.0.	Patrol proceeded due East for about 300 yds. from TRACAS MEBUS, when it halted for some time to listen for movement of enemy. Nothing heard. One short burst was fired from enemy M.G. about MORAY HO. Patrol returned to TRACAS MEBUS about 2.45 a.m.

173rd INFANTRY BRIGADE INTELLIGENCE SUMMARY.
Period 24 hours ending 8 a.m. 24th Dec.1917.

A. OPERATIONS.

1. **Artillery Activity.** Enemy Artillery was much quieter - following places received attention EAGLE DUMP & LOUIS FM at irregular intervals, TAUBE HO was fairly heavily shelled with shells up to 5.9 calibre from 6. a.m. - 9.30 a.m. 23rd inst. SENEGAL FM was shelled lightly between 4.30 and 5.30 p.m. Also Duckboards in vicinity. A few gas shells fell near KANGAROO Huts. V.15.a.9.3. was also lightly shelled. NORFOLK HO, V.19.b. and V.1x.d. were shelled intermittently with 4.2; 5.9 and gas this morning between 4.50. a.m.-5.35 a.m.

2. **Our Own Artillery** - at 6.30 a.m. and 7 a.m. this morning 24th concentrated shoots took place for 5 minutes on enemy positions. Otherwise normal.

B. INTELLIGENCE.

1. **Patrols.** B. Battalion sent out Patrols at intervals throughout the night to get in touch with neighbouring posts of Bns. on Left and Right. Patrol report of A. Battalion is attached. No enemy patrols were encountered. Last night no Mans Land was reported as being quite passable, the ice in shell holes being strong enough to bear weight of a man.

2. **Machine Guns.** An enemy M.G. fired at intervals at the BREWERY from approximately V.15.c.5.3. (Note:- It is interesting to notice that a dug-out was reported approximately at this point on 10.12.17 by 175th Inf. Bde.). An M.G. fired short bursts during night from V.20.b.75.80. (Note:- An earth work was reported at this point on 10.12.17 by patrol of the 175th Inf. Bde.).

3. **Lights etc.** 10 a.m. (23rd) - Very Light bursting into 2 reds was followed by light shrapnel barrage which ceased when 2 Golden Rain Rockets were fired.

4. **Aerial Activity.** At 5.20 p.m. 7 bombs were dropped by 2 E.A. which were flying over SPRIET - POELCAPPELLE Road. They were fired on by L.G. No low flying E.A. have been reported. 8.40 p.m. 2 E.A. passed over VARLA FM.

5. **Work.** Probably consolidation of Posts or shell holes was seen in ground captured by the enemy on our left yesterday.

[signature]
2/1Ieut. I.O.
for Brigade Major,
173rd Infantry Brigade.

173rd Infantry Brigade.　　　　2/2nd London Regiment.　　　　Patrol Report.

Strength of Patrol.	Time and Date.	Object or Task.	Remarks and Information.
2/Lt.BAINES and 2 O.R.	23rd.Dec. 6.50 pm	Reconnaissance of No-Mans-Land.	Patrol left post on SPRIET RD. (96) and proceeded along South of ROAD 180 yards. They waited there ½ hour listening and watching. Nothing was seen, but short burst of enemy M.G. fire from approx. V.14.d.6.4. were heard. M.G. was firing across our front between MEUNIER and TRACAS. Patrol moved 200 yards South and again halted. Nothing further was heard. Owing to slight ground mist observation was difficult. Patrol returned to SPRIET RD post by shortest route arriving at 8.50 p.m. Ground Hard. Shell holes frozen sufficiently hard to bear the weight of men.
2/Lt.GLADSTONE and 2 O.R.	23rd.Dec. 8 p.m.	Reconnaissance of area in vicinity of TRACK from HELLES to SPIDER CROSS RDS.	Patrol proceeded from HELLES to a point about V.14.d.30.95. on the track to SPIDERS Cross Roads where it was fired on from the direction of the Cross Roads. Patrol advanced a further 50 yards and was again fired on, after remaining in the neighbourhood until 10.50 p.m. patrol returned by same route. Ground hard.

S E C R E T.   Copy No. 16

173RD INFANTRY BRIGADE ORDER NUMBER 51.

19/12/17.

1. Following reliefs will be carried out during 20th/21st Dec.

2/2nd Bn. will relieve 2/1st Bn. in Right Sub-Sector.
2/4th Bn. will relieve 2/3rd Bn. in Left Sub-Sector.

On Relief:- (a). 2/1st London Regt. will return to
KEMPTON PARK (Right Support) less
Two Companies which will remain in
PHEASANT TRENCH.
(b). 2/3rd London Regt. Hd. Qtrs. and
3 Companies will move to EAGLE and
WHITE TRENCHES (Left Support) and
1 Company to CANDLE TRENCH.

2. Should "Frost Precautions" be taken off by Brigade Headquarters - Normal Dispositions will be resumed by Right and Left Support Battalions.

3. No relieving Troops will move forward of PHEASANT TRENCH - EAGLE TRENCH Line prior to 4.30 p.m.

4. All further details of relief will be arranged between Commanding Officers direct.

5. Units will ACKNOWLEDGE.

Captain,
Brigade Major,
173rd Infantry Brigade.

Copy No.
1. 8/1st Bn. London Regt.
2. 8/2nd Bn. London Regt.
3. 8/3rd Bn. London Regt.
4. 8/4th Bn. London Regt.
5. 173rd L. T. M. Batty.
6. 205th Machine Gun Coy.
7. 56th Division "G".
8. 97th Infantry Brigade.

Copy No.
9. 171st Infantry Bde.
10. Staff Captain.
11. Transport Officer.
12. Intelligence Officer.
13. Signalling Officer.
14. 198th Machine Gun Coy.
15. War Diary.
16. War Diary.
17. File.

INSTRUCTIONS AS TO USE OF LIGHT-RAILWAY FOR DELIVERY OF STORES & RATIONS.

1. **RATIONS.**
   (a). The Corps Light-Railway will be used to carry Stores and Rations from READING JUNCTION to BATTLE JUNCTION.
   (b). One Truck is allotted to 173rd Infantry Brigade on the Train leaving READING daily at 11 a.m.
   (c). On arrival at BATTLE the stores and rations will be off loaded and conveyed to Forward Area by Limbers.
   (d). Units will arrange for one representative to accompany the Stores on the train.

2. **TRANSPORT.** The following Transport and Personnel will be maintained at the Standing and Nissen Huts on Boundary Road (C.21.a)

	N.C.Os.	G.S.Limbers.	Animals.	Drivers.	Cook.
Right Forward Battalion.	1	4	10	4	1
Left Forward Battalion.	1	4	8	4	-
206th Machine Gun Coy.	1	4	8	4	-

   These details will be Brigaded, Transport Officer of Left Bn. will be the Officer i/c and will allot vehicles for such duties as are required, preference being given to delivery of rations.
   He will be accommodated by the Area Commandant KEMPTON PARK.
   On completion of the Units tour of duty in the Front Line the above Transport & Personnel will be relieved by the relieving units.
   O.C., 206th M.G.Coy. will arrange reliefs of Horses and Personnel of his Coy. after 4 days.

3. **ROUTES.** Transport for Right Battalion and Nos. 1 and 2 Coys., "C" Bn. will proceed as far as PHEASANT TRENCH by the POELCAPPELLE-ST.JULIEN Road.
   Transport for Left Battalion will proceed via. LANGEMARCK-POELCAPPELLE Road to point where Duck Board Track joins road at U.24.a.50.15.
   Transport for "D" Bn. will use same route to a point where "A" Track cuts the road (U.23.b.70.20.)
   Brigade Headquarters by limber to VARNA FARM.
   Transport personnel from each unit will be provided with 2 Camp Kettles.

   O.C., Units will arrange their own carrying parties.
   The Garrisons of PHEASANT and EAGLE TRENCHES, earmarked for special purposes, will, as far as possible, be untouched.
   Any unit unable to provide its own carrying party will notify this office.

   Captain,
   Staff Captain,
   173rd Infantry Brigade.

29/12/17.

SECRET.   Order Copy No......

173RD INFANTRY BRIGADE ORDER NUMBER 53.
Ref. Sheet 28, 1/100,000.
    BIXSCHOOTE S.7.4.   )1/1,000.
    ST JULIEN 28 N.V.2.   )
    WESTROOSEBEEK 20 S.E.3.)

December 29th 1917.

1. The Brigade will relieve 175th Infantry Brigade in the line on 1/2nd January, 1918, taking over the whole Divisional Sector as defined in Brigade Provisional Defence Scheme.
2. Movements in connection with the relief will take place in accordance with attached Move Table. Train arrangements will be notified to units by the Staff Captain.
3. All Trench Stores (including Tracer Ammunition), Maps, Plans, and schemes of work, will be taken over on relief and a duplicate list of these will be rendered to Brigade Headquarters on 3rd January. Especial care must be taken to ensure continuity of work.
4. Brigade Headquarters will close at WHITE MILL CAMP at 10 a.m. 2nd January, re-opening at the same hour at VARNA FARM.
5. Relief will be complete by 5.30 a.m. 2nd January, completion being wired to Brigade Headquarters by Code Word "YULE".
6. Commanding Officers will visit the units which they are to relieve to-morrow, 30th December, in order to arrange outstanding details of relief not provided for by this order.
7. Units will ACKNOWLEDGE.

                                                  Captain,
                                                Brigade Major,
                                            173rd Infantry Brigade.

Copy No.
1. 2/1st Bn. Lon. Regt.
2. 2/2nd Bn. Lon. Regt.
3. 2/3rd Bn. Lon. Regt.
4. 2/4th Bn. Lon. Regt.
5. 173rd L.T.M. Baty.
6. 206th Machine Gun Co.
7. 504th Field Coy. R.E.
8. 2/1st H.C. Field Amb.
9. 510th H.T. Coy, A.S.C.
10. 174th Infantry Brigade.
11. 175th Infantry Brigade.
12. 58th Division "G".
13. 58th Division "A" & "Q".

Copy No.
14. S.S.O. 58th Div.
15. Area Commandant, W.M.C.
16. Brigade Major for G.O.C.
17. Staff Captain.
18. Bde. Signalling Officer.
19. Bde. Transport Officer.
20. Bde. Intelligence Officer.
21. War Diary.
22. War Diary.
23. File.
24. Brigade on Left.
25. Brigade on Right.
26. Area Commandant, K.P.
27. Area Commandant, CANAL BANK.

MOVE TABLE.
(Issued with 173rd Bde. Order No.50.)

Date. Jan.	Unit.	From.	To.	Relieving.	Route.	Remarks.
1st.	2/1st Bn. Lon.Regt.	WHITE MILL CAMP.	Right Sub-Sector. H.Q.NORFOLK HOUSE.	2/9th Lon. Regt.	Train.	
1st.	2/2nd Bn. Lon.Regt.	CANAL BANK	Right Support - H.Q. & 2 Coys. KEMPTON PK 2 Coys. PHEASANT TRE	2/12th Lon. Regt.	March via BOUNDARY ROAD.	
1st.	2/3rd Bn. Lon.Regt.	BRIDGE CAMP No.2	Left Sub-Sector. H.Q. SOUVENIR HO.	2/11th Lon. Regt.	Train.	
1st.	2/4th Bn.	BRIDGE CAMP No.1	Left Support - H.Q. PIG & WHISTLE - 3 Coys. EAGLE AND WHITE TRENCHES. 1 Coy. CANDLE TRENCH	2/10th Lon. Regt.	Train.	
1st.	173rd Light T.M.Bty.	REDAN CAMP.	4 Guns POELCAPPELLE 4 Guns KEMPTON PARK.	175th L.T.M.Bty.	Train.	
1st.	Bde. Sniping Company		CANDLE TRENCH		Train.	Take over O.Ps. etc under arrangements of Capt. HETLEY, Bde. Hd. Qtrs.

Intervals as in 4th Army Order "Distances to be maintained on the March".
No troops to pass line:- EAGLE - PHEASANT TRENCH before 4.30 p.m.

TO ALL RECIPIENTS OF ADMINISTRATIVE INSTRUCTIONS No.24
(Issued with 173rd Inf. Bde. Order No. 53.)

AMENDMENT to Administrative Instructions No.24, page 2,

line 5,

For PIG & WHISTLE (U.28.b.3.2.)

read TRAFALGAR SQUARE (U.23.c.0.0.)

H.H. Garraway

Captain,
Staff Captain,
173rd Infantry Brigade.

30/12/17.

173RD INFANTRY BRIGADE.

ADMINISTRATIVE INSTRUCTION NO. 24.

(Issued with 173rd Inf. Bde. Order No. 53.

TRANSPORT & Q.M. STORES:- Will remain as at present, except for Transport as detailed in "INSTRUCTIONS AS TO USE OF LIGHT RAILWAY", attached.

RATIONS:- Normal system of supply. Units going into the line will be issued with two days' rations.
Tommy Cookers will be issued on demand from Brigade Headquarters Stores to Units going into the line.

WATER:- Water Point between KEMPTON PARK and HINTY FARM.
Units of 175th Infantry Brigade will hand over Petrol Tins.

COOKERS:- Cookers may be taken to KEMPTON PARK.
There is a Cook House in CANDLE TRENCH.
Hot Soup will be available at the following Soup Kitchens:-

    CEMENT HOUSE (U.28.c.2.2.) on Track "A".
    RUDOLF FARM on GROUSE AVENUE.
    Near MARSOUIN FM., near Track "B" 50 yds.
    East of Main Road.

CARE OF FEET:- The Brigade Commander directs that every man shall take off his boots and socks, and massage at least twice a day.
Powder as described in this Office No.Sc/0/74 dated 15/12/17 will be available on application to 2/2nd or 2/3rd Home Counties Field Ambulance. A small supply will be taken in the line by each man.
Whale Oil is available on indent from Brigade Supply Officer.
The Foot Baths as under, are available for use:-

    KEMPTON PARK.
    MARSOUIN FARM.
    RUDOLF FARM.

SOCKS:- 300 pair of Clean Socks will be issued to the two units going into the line on demand from these Headquarters. Dirty Socks can subsequently be exchanged for clean ones from Brigade Headquarters Stores.

DUMPS ETC:- As laid down in Administrative Instruction No.21 issued with Brigade Order No. 50.
Demands for S.A.A. etc. to reach Staff Captain, VARNA FM each morning by 9.30 a.m.

PRISONERS OF WAR:- Divisional Prisoners of War Cage is at HAMMOND'S CORNER.
Escorts should be given clear instructions as to their destination, and obtain a receipt from PROVOST'S Representative at the Cage.
When possible this Office should be notified that Prisoners are being sent down.

P.T.O.

MEDICAL:- Regimental Aid Posts under Unit arrangements.

RELAY POSTS.

Left Sector.
EAGLE TRENCH .... U.25.b.6.3.
PIG & WHISTLE.... U.28.b.3.2.
CEMENT HOUSE .... U.28.c.2.2.

Right Sector.
PHEASANT PARK.... U.30.b.8.8.
PHEASANT TRENCH.. U.30.d.4.8.
HAANIXBEEK FARM... C.5.b.1.7.

Routes for Walking Wounded:- To Advance Dressing Station, CEMENT HOUSE (U.28.c.2.2.) and MINTY FARM (C.10.d.2.8.), thence by DECAUVILLE Railway to Corps Main Dressing Station, DUNALLOW.

Sick from all units will be evacuated along the same route as Walking Wounded.

TRAINS:- Times of Trains will be notified later.

SALVAGE:- The Brigade Commander wishes every effort to be made to collect and clean S.A.A. and Bombs in the Forward Area in order to reduce demands for fresh supplies.

29/18/17.

Anaway
Captain,
Staff Captain,
173rd Infantry Brigade.

MQ173 Supp't
Vol 12

b

www.ingramcontent.com/pod-product-compliance
Lightning Source LLC
Chambersburg PA
CBHW080818010526
44111CB00015B/2573